PROBLEMS OF CONTEMPORARY MILITARISM

Problems of Contemporary Militarism

Edited by

ASBJØRN EIDE and MAREK THEE

ST. MARTIN'S PRESS NEW YORK

 For information write:
St. Martin's Press, Inc., 175 Fifth Avenue, New York, N.Y. 10010
Printed in Great Britain
First published in the United States of America in 1980
Library of Congress Card Catalog Number 79-3379

Library of Congress Cataloging in Publication Data

Main entry under title:

Problems of contemporary militarism.

Bibliography: p. 396
Includes index.
1. Militarism – Addresses, essays, lectures.
2. Munitions – Addresses, essays, lectures.
I. Eide, Asbjørn. II. Thee, Marek.
U21.2.P657 355'.0213 79-3379
ISBN 0-312-64744-1

CONTENTS

PART I

INTRODUCTION

INTRODUCTION

Asbjørn Eide and Marek Thee

Militarisation is one of the most conspicuous aspects of contemporary global development. Militarisation manifests itself in the increase in armaments, advances in the destructive capacity of weapons, growing number of people under arms, and dramatic increases in military expenditure. Militaristic attitudes accompany this process of militarisation. The inclination to rely on military means of coercion for the handling of conflicts, which is the most pervasive feature of militaristic attitudes, seems to be gaining ground everywhere.

In 1941, when the world was in turmoil due to aggression unleashed by some highly militarised states, President Roosevelt outlined the values that were to be promoted when the war was over. One of them was the following:

> The fourth is freedom from fear – which, translated into world terms, means a world-wide reduction of armaments to such a point and in such a fashion that no nation will be in a position to commit an act of physical aggression against any neighbour anywhere in the world.

Alas, this was not to be. Starting with the very participation in World War II itself, by way of the growth of military production and other military preparations, a qualitative leap into a dynamic process of militarisation had been inaugurated. It was to be quickly accelerated under the impact of the Cold War.

The dramatic increase in the influence of the military was highlighted by President Eisenhower who, in his memorable farewell address, warned 'against the acquisition of unwarranted influence in the councils of government and state' by what he terms 'the military-industrial complex'. As subsequently revealed in many studies, this influence has today a very large socio-political base. It relies on a competitive alliance of vested interests which include not only the military and the military industry, but also the state political bureaucracy interested in using military power as an instrument of diplomacy and politics. Included also is a strong establishment of physical and engineering scientists working for military research and development and planning armaments for years ahead. It is therefore more appropriate to speak now of the military-industrial-technological-bureaucratic complex which favours and stimulates armaments, and serves to enhance the position of the military in national and international life.

The impact of this complex is most strongly felt within the superpowers, East and West. But through military alliances, it also has serious consequences for medium powers and small nations. The military alliances give rise to a bureaucracy of security specialists, and simultaneously there is an increasing integration of armament production. The net effect of this is the formation, on the level of the alliance itself, of an *international* military-industrial-bureaucratic network, much more concerned with the maintenance of the alliance than with the protection of the national security of the individual member of the alliance.

Furthermore, the process of decolonisation, on the one hand, and of neo-colonial aspirations of the industrialised countries on the other, brought about the creation and strengthening of the position of armed forces of many of the new states. These have been actively encouraged to intervene in domestic politics, to replace civilian governments and to carry out rigid, coercive policies. The effects of contemporary militarisation in Third World countries are, therefore, most detrimental. Many of these live under military regimes, some of which are extremely cruel. The burden these countries have had to pay in the economic, political, social and cultural field is staggering. Development priorities have been distorted, political expression has been suffocated, and human rights have been extensively violated. Thus, militarisation has today a global reach. Given the constant increase and sophistication of the tools of war, conventional and nuclear, tactical and strategic, a dynamic has been set in motion which corrupts society, wastes precious human and material resources, undermines democracy and increases the probability of armed conflict and war. The armament dynamic seems to have gone beyond social and political control.

It is important that we become conscious of the dangers of contemporary militarisation and militarism. At stake is the fate of the human being and the survival of humanity.

This book is intended as a modest contribution by the International Peace Research Institute in Oslo, and by the wider community of peace researchers, to the study of the problems of contemporary militarism. Its aim is to spread awareness of the dangers inherent in the growth of armaments and militarism. The social, economic, political and other processes which are forced by militarisation need to be made more transparent. Better knowledge should help to increase awareness and activate public opinion in the struggle to halt the arms race and to counteract militarism and militarisation.

The nature and the strength of the forces behind the arms race have been extensively studied by peace researchers over the last years, and they have also demonstrated convincingly the lack of serious commitment to disarmament. Their work is one of the stimuli for this study. Another impulse came from the programme of the World Council of Churches on Militarism and the Arms Race, and we are also inspired by the stand against armaments by the concerned international scientific community as represented by the Pugwash Conferences on Science and World Affairs.

Some of the papers in this book were presented, in preliminary versions, at the Pugwash Symposium on Militarism and National Security held in Oslo in 1977, and at the Consultation on Militarism held by the World Council of Churches at Glion in 1977. Other papers have been produced by members of the Study Group on Militarization Versus Development and Human Rights of the International Peace Research Association.

We are grateful to all those who have made this book possible. In particular, we are indebted to those who have contributed their papers for this collection, but also we are grateful to those who have joined the discussions in the peace research community during the last years, and whose knowledge and insights are reflected in the present collection.

PART II

THE GLOBAL DIMENSION

1 MILITARISM AND MILITARISATION IN CONTEMPORARY INTERNATIONAL RELATIONS*

Marek Thee

1 Introduction: the Problem Defined

Ours is a sick society. One symptom of the sickness is the spread of militarism and militarisation around the globe. Yet, except in peace research circles, this phenomenon has not attracted sufficient attention in scholarly literature. Militarism is discussed rather as a local or regional issue, while its overall international aspects, its structure, dynamics, mushrooming growth and implications are seldom analysed. Scholars seem alarmed – and rightly so – at the spread of military regimes to Third World countries. Yet the roots and interrelations that this development has with the current international political, social and economic structure are rarely examined.

In the following, under the term 'militarism' I subsume such symptoms as a rush to armaments, the growing role of the military (understood as the military establishment) in national and international affairs, the use of force as an instrument of supremacy and political power, and the increasing influence of the military in civilian affairs. Seen from this angle, militarism has indeed become a global phenomenon. I understand 'militarisation' as being an extension of military influence to civilian spheres, including economic and socio-political life. The impact of militarism and militarisation, in a disguised or open form, is deeply felt in international relations, and increasingly in the internal life of many nations as well.

We need more research and a more informed discussion on problems of militarism and militarisation. The very terms 'militarism' and 'militarisation' need more elucidation, and need to be given a meaningful contemporary currency. These terms are often used with different connotations in East and West, North and South, and are too often applied in the political debate without precise definition. Generally,

* Paper presented at the Pugwash Symposium on Militarism and National Security, Oslo, 21-5 November 1977, and at the 7th General Conference of the International Peace Research Association, Oaxtepec, Mexico, 11-16 December 1977. First version published in *Bulletin of Peace Proposals*, vol. 8, no. 4 (1977). References and reading list are amalgamated into the bibliography at the end of the book.

'militarism' is used to convey developments paralleling such well known historical phenomena as Bonapartism, the rise of the German imperial strength, the ascendancy of Japan as a world power, or some Fascist variants of expansionist regimes. However, these models are inadequate for a deeper understanding and analysis of contemporary militarism, both in the Third World and in the developed countries, capitalist and socialist. And such case studies as exist on the new role of the military in Asia, Africa or Latin America usually lack the global perspective necessary for understanding the internal dynamics.

The aim of this chapter is to outline and take up for initial discussion the role of the military and the impact of military ascendancy in contemporary international relations. Starting from the historical context, I point to the socio-political dynamics, present a set of indicators and arrive at a typology and classification of contemporary militarism. Guided by the thinking developed in the peace research community, the paper then discusses some aspects of the world military order, its structure and hierarchy, the militarism and armaments dynamics and the spread of military regimes to Third World countries. The intention is to take account of existing findings and attempt to define a coherent global perspective. Finally, some remarks are made on possible action, in research and socio-political life, to confront the danger of militarism.

2 The Phenomenon of Militarism

2.1 The Historical Context

Historically, militarism developed as a corollary to rule and privilege. The military habitually served the interests of the ruling classes, and in the process tended to acquire autonomous strength and a privileged socio-political position in society. It also produced its own doctrine of state and government marked by a cult of power and national aggrandisement. A product of existing conflicts by the use of force, contributing at times to revolutionary change but most often sustaining conservative rule. In relations between states, militarism tended to channel into expansionism. War became a simple extension of politics with other means.

In modern times militarism has become associated mainly with great-power politics, imperialism, territorial conquest and war. It is militarism which has generated the arms races and sought a controlling influence of the military in politics, the economy and national life. The material basis for the rise of militarism in modern times was created by the imposition of universal military conscription by Napoleon and the parallel emergence of large national armies with a well organised professional officer class. The officer clan, usually allied to the ruling classes, became the driving force behind militarism.

The term 'militarism' enjoyed high currency, especially before World War I, in connection with German expansionism, the birth of imperialism and of a labour movement actively opposed to war. Between the wars, militarism was associated mainly with the dictatorships and rapacious policies of Germany, Italy and Japan. After World War II the focus was still initially on the dangers of a revival of German and Japanese militarism. But soon, with the spread of military regimes in the Third World, attention turned to Asia, Africa and Latin America. This had been accompanied by a shift on conceptual emphasis. From the traditional preoccupation with the expansionist and bellicose aspects of militarism, concern has turned to the internal space – the systemic disruption caused by militarism. Attention has moved to governmental rigidities, repressive measures and the seizure of civil competences by the military. Only slowly has the realisation been growing that contemporary militarism is a malady of far wider scope, intertwined with the current world military and economic order.

Today militarism has become clearly visible as never before. The military establishment and armaments have outgrown all proportion to the rationale of security. This holds true not only in global dimensions but also for most of the state members of the international community. The lead has been given by the superpowers with nuclear arms and a war machinery far in excess of any deterrence needs. Even the most economically weak countries are following suit, devoting to the acquisition of modern weapons resources much above their material capabilities and security requirements. While the great powers are using armaments mainly as an instrument of politics and diplomacy, most of the developing countries use them mainly as a tool of domestic suppression and to assert their status in international relations. The fever of the arms race has infected all continents, pushing up armaments expenditures to the staggering figure of US $400 billion annually – the equivalent of a yearly national income of the poorer half of the world population, and expanding the ranks of the armed forces around the world to 22 million people – almost as much as the world number of teachers. Objective conditions have been created for the enhancement of the military establishment and its activation in political life.

The nature of contemporary militarism differs from the previous manifestations of militarism, mainly in its current global reach and a dynamic rooted in a new world hierarchy, the controlling position of the superpowers, the dominance-dependence relationship between the great powers and developing nations, the socio-economic predicament of most of the Third World countries, and the impact of the technological revolution. Militarism today has a changed attribute and role. Without losing the aggressive traits of the past, it has become channelled into a fierce struggle of the giant nuclear powers for world predominance. Expanding beyond open imperial adventures, it has established a military-economic neo-colonial presence around the world. Militarism today has unleashed a world-wide arms race unparalleled in history, it has supplied arms for dozens of local wars, it has distorted development priorities in the Third World, and with ever-new weapons of mass destruction at hand has been playing with the very survival of mankind. The shadow of militarism today looms longer and more widespread than ever. It lurks behind most of the world conflicts and violations of human rights. It is undermining human integrity and the moral standing of an ever-greater number of governments in the world community.

2.2 *The Socio-political Dynamics*

Any discussion of militarism and militarisation must take as its point of departure the primary role of the military in society. By definition, military organisations are called to apply organised violence in defence of the state, mainly in foreign affairs. The state, it is generally recognised, has the right and duty to employ violence in support of constitutional law or to shield itself against external danger. Internally, this task is usually left to the police, while external protection is the domain of the military.

In a very general sense, militarism and militarisation start with the abuse of the military by its legitimate function and its encroachment on political affairs, internally and externally. Brought up to apply organised violence and professing to be the guardians of national survival, the military tends to usurp roles and prerogatives in society which go beyond democratic legitimacy, intervening in internal and imposing its will in external affairs. However, the term 'excess' often used in scholarly sociological literature to denote militarism may not be the best way to define the problem. Rather than clearly brand militarism, it may blur the issues. It makes the very phenomenon of militarism liable to subjective interpretations. Instead of a focus on excess, militarism needs to be defined in clear socio-political terms. It is a phenomenon well embedded in societal dynamics, it has a clear political profile, uses specific means and adheres to definite goals. It has a structure, ideology and line of conduct.

Militarism is a socio-political phenomenon which draws its vitality from a complex set of sources – national and social, material and spiritual. However, its foremost breeding ground is to be found in state formation and the military profession.

With some simplification, one may trace the problem complex of militarism back to the definitional task of the soldiery, their relation to the state, their way of life, behavioural habits, values and outlook. Decisive for a militaristic posture is the belief in organised violence as an indispensable instrument to uphold the state and to regulate human relations. It is the conviction that human beings and society can be manipulated by the application of force, and that violence is the ultimate expedient for the control and solution of conflicts. In the final instance, this view holds that human behaviour can be corrected and held in check only by the employment of organised violence. As a corollary to this belief comes the tenet of authority and discipline with a proneness to authoritarian rule. Militarism, then, tends to curtail democratic interplay, replacing it by drill and regimentation. It tends to display a bellicose activism and a predilection to impose solutions. Finally, placed strategically in the web of state and government bureaucracy, and entrusted with the management of the instruments of violence, the military develops a propensity to intervene actively in politics, foreign and domestic.

The above abstractions are not absolute, and should serve only to elucidate a certain behavioural dynamic. In reality militarism defies any simplistic definition. It is multidimensional and varied, with different manifestations in various circumstances, dependent on the historical background, national traditions, class structure, social conditions, economic strength, acute problems faced and the vigour of the officer corps. Thus a grasp of militarism in contemporary international relations requires much concrete analysis with reference to both local and international developments and trends. Any generalisation has to be broad and inclusive, with special consideration for the particular and exceptional.

Militarism has many faces today. There is the great power reliance on force in international relations. There are the repressive authoritarian regimes backed by the military. There is an exploitative world order with spheres of influence and dependencies sustained by a combination of economic and military power. In some cases, the government may be directly in the hands of the military. In others, civilian rule is retained while the military exerts predominant influence. In some countries, military influence coexists with representative democracy, while in others the military shares power in a one-party system. Each of the manifestations of militarism may be different. They have in common strong reliance on organised violence, a privileged position of the military establishment, consistency in the build-up of the war machine, nationalistic attitudes, and a proneness to the limitation of democratic freedoms. Needless to add, the cancerous spread and growth of militarism in our times are fraught with danger for peace and impede efforts for any progressive transformation of the international community.

2.3 Indicators of Militarism and Militarisation

We may try now to draw up a set of indicators helpful for recognising and discerning different manifestations of militarism and militarisation today. Not all the symptoms may be present simultaneously, and their degree of intensity may vary. But the discovery of only some of these symptoms, to a certain extent, may be sufficient to suggest the hypothesis about a militaristic evolution. To encompass all shades of militarism, three groups of indicators would be required, pointing to: (1) structural systemic features; (2) elements of ideology; and (3) policy orientation and execution. The following is a list of these indicators compiled with an eye to contemporary variants and manifestations of militarism:

(1) Systemic features:
   (a) Position of the military in state and government: ruling force, decisive influence, co-partnership or high authority under civilian supremacy.
   (b) Deviation from democratic rule: dictatorship, authoritarian government, denial of democratic freedoms, repressive measures. Special case: governments established in the wake of a *coup d'etat*.

(2) Elements of ideology:
   (a) nationalism, chauvinism, ethnocentrism, xenophobia;
   (b) expansionism, aggressiveness, bellicosity;
   (c) glorification of power, of the army and the military establishment;
   (d) stress on hierarchy, discipline, regimentation and

redistributive authority;
(e) ideological dogmatism: political, religious or tribal-traditional.

(3) Policy orientation and execution:
(a) high military expenditures and preferential treatment of the armed forces;
(b) military build-up and application of military strength as an instrument of politics and diplomacy;
(c) participation in military alliances;
(d) imperial and neo-colonial postures;
(e) care for police forces and participation of the army in internal security operations;
(f) military interference in shaping socio-economic goals and policy;
(g) arbitrary decision-making process.

2.4 Variants of Militarism

The plurality of symptoms of a structural, attitudinal and political nature subsumable under the notion of militarism/militarisation points to diversity in form and substance. Indeed, there are no two identical cases of militarism with the same scope and features, and the study of particular cases requires a grasp of the specifics as well as their relation to the global structure. The kind of mix of the above indicators displayed in a particular case may define the type of militarism.

With this diversity and singularity in mind, we may attempt to arrive at a general typology and classification of contemporary variants of militarism. In general, we may differentiate between two prime manifestations of militarism today: mainly outward-oriented and mainly inward-oriented. Though seldom occurring in a pure form, these two variants correspond to the more traditional great-power militarism on the one hand, and the military regimes of developing countries in the process of nation-building and socio-political transformation on the other. While both variants lavish attention on the armed forces and rely on them to achieve political objectives, they differ in essential traits.

Great-power militarism is distinctly expansionist, seeking aggressively to expand its power and influence beyond its borders, to other states and nations. In the case of the superpowers, this policy aspiration has a global reach. Great-power expansionism to date need not necessarily mean actual pursuit of territorial conquest. It can mean an offensive drive to uphold and broaden spheres of influence, a struggle to maintain imperial or neo-colonial positions, or efforts sustained by military power to gain new political and economic footholds in even most distant continents. On the other hand, the internal influence of the military in such cases must not appear in open form. The military can hold authority and exert pressures behind the scenes, showing formal respect for a civilian form of government, either within the framework of a representative democracy or a system dominated by a single political party.

Currently, military influence and predominance within the great powers rely on a well-knit and vigorous alliance of the military establishment, the war industry, the military research and development establishment and the state bureaucracy. Some time ago, President Eisenhower in his farewell message warned against the growing influence of what he coined 'the military-industrial complex' in the councils of the state. A deeper insight into the decision-making processes within the great powers points to a much broader coalition behind the vested military interests. Two further links, in addition to the military establishment and the industrial circles, are of basic importance: (a) the large army of scientists and engineers – numbering together about half a million in the United States and the Soviet Union – employed in military research and development; and (b) the state bureaucracy vitally interested in the strength of the armed forces as a key instrument in the diplomatic game. Altogether, the military-industrial-technological-bureaucratic complex represents a powerful political force. It has a crucial influence on the direction of the foreign policy of the great powers. The way this influence is exercised and the mode of operation may differ in the capitals of East and West, as they are naturally tailored to systemic particularities. Yet the outcome seems the same. No basic move in the field of foreign relations touching on long-term engagements or strategy can be initiated and adopted without the approval of this alliance. Moreover, it is actively engaged in shaping foreign policy and has a decisive voice in its execution.

Great-power militarism in foreign affairs has also its internal repercussions. It imposes an atmosphere of security-mindedness and political warfare verging toward extreme police rigour and deprivation of human freedoms. Especially large prerogatives and authority are granted to the security services. We can easily discern a linkage between the outward imperial thrust and the internal rigidity. As an example, we may cite the interrelationship between the actions and covert operations effected by the United States in the Vietnam adventure and the methods employed in the Watergate affair. Domestic repression in the

Soviet Union is another manifestation of this reality. State authorities are eager to shore up internal support for their policies and to silence as far as possible voices of opposition.

The other variant of militarism – the mainly inward-oriented – is characteristic of military regimes in the Third World. Here the presence of the military on the political scene is much more visible and of wider internal implications. The military becomes not only engaged in the management of the means of organised violence but seeks also to shape the domestic development strategies of the society. It tries to determine socio-economic priorities and to set systemic guidelines – always in line with its own interests and with a view to consolidating its power. These regimes are usually openly repressive, and the military tends to become actively involved in the maintenance of internal security. In specific local situations, with tribal tension or other conflict in the air, such regimes tend also to embark on foreign ventures, sometimes to boost their power, in other cases to divert attention from internal troubles.

The military establishment in Third World countries usually finds allies in conservative forces fearful of population radicalisation, and relies frequently on the middle classes eager to seize positions in state and government left vacant after the departure of the colonial administration. In foreign relations, such militarily dominated countries tend to turn into peripheries of the great powers. They become dependent on those powers not only for arms supply, but also economically: trade relations, financial handicaps, transfer of technology, etc. The phraseology of extreme nationalism frequently goes hand in hand with an activation of the centre-periphery dynamics. This seems also the case where the military, either acting on its own or in alliance with revolutionary movements, chooses to introduce radical reforms. The social effects, of course, are then different, and the reliance is on socialist powers. But common to both types of military intervention is domestic repression. Whatever the banner under which the military comes to power, after the seizure of government the military tends to consolidate the rule of violence.

From a dialectical point of view, militarism, especially in the Third World, can be seen as essentially a response to weakness: social, economic or political. The military seizes power either at moments of political stress or in times of crisis. It tries then to discipline society and impose solutions in line with its socio-political outlook. Use of violence acquires central importance. The outcome is seldom successful: socio-political problems are not amenable to resolution by force.

In both variants of militarism, the great-power and Third World categories, the critical variable is the importance attached to the armed forces and armaments. Wherever the armed forces receive favourable attention and armaments are going up, militarism is either present or just round the corner. This is also true of armaments of a defensive nature. A growing military establishment, in an atmosphere of security fixation, tends to expand its influence into civilian spheres. This dynamic may pose serious dilemmas for nations really threatened by outside forces. Defence is a just and legitimate concern. It may then be worthwhile in such situations to contemplate precautionary measures against the growth of militarism. One way could be to introduce more democratic and participatory organisational forms of defence. Another move could be to invest in strategies of peaceful political solutions, i.e. to take a risk for peace instead of becoming resigned to the perpetuation of conflict. Enhancing the position of the military in situations of protracted conflicts is fraught with injury to democratic values.

Without any doubt, militarism is an ugly and dangerous socio-political malady in whatever form it may appear. But we should differentiate between the two main variants of militarism mentioned above. There is a distinct quality to the great-power militarism on the one hand, and the militarisation of weak developing countries on the other. Not only is great-power militarism far more potent, more aggressive and with wider international implications, it is also largely the root cause and the driving force behind the global spread of militarism. The great powers produce the weapons, pave the way and set patterns for the militarisation of the international community.

2.5 Military Attitudes and Ideology

The strength of militarism in our times derives not only from the material base of the state organisation and the support of powerful social groups within the state, but also from an ideological super-structure pervading society. Postures and attitudes developed by the military, and sustained largely by the state organisation and the educational system, tend to infect larger strata of the population which then actively back the military designs. There is now an international climate to this development. With the explosion of the national state system in the wake of decolonialisation, the ideology propounded by the military finds fertile ground in the minds of many people who apparently conclude from recent history that force is one of the decisive factors in assuring sovereignty and security in the life of a nation. An affinity has developed between the political and ideological outlook of the military, and the perceptions inspired by the state on the one hand, and the notions of broad strata in society on the other. The state has become associated with national values, and the military with their guardians. Rising nationalism on a global scale has served to reinforce militaristic tendencies and the influence of the military.

But military thinking is not freely or independently shaped. The military mind and militaristic attitudes are conditioned by a long socialisation process effected through professional training and indoctrination. The attitudinal backbone is formed by the military's specific function of employing organised violence to achieve specific goals. The military doctrine attaches then special attention to organisation, the ideal of organisation being of an authoritarian nature. Moving from form to substance, the military tends to identify state and nation, and develop nationalistic attitudes served to the public as patriotic national postures. Frequently, religious fervour is added to reinforce the effect. The outcome is a simplistic and often dogmatic black-and-white image of human relations, national development and international interaction. It would seem that organisation and force are able to move mountains. A posture ensues which generates ethnocentrism, favours coercive action, sanctions uncritically all means to achieve chosen ends, embraces centralisation of authority and stratified hierarchy, and evinces a proneness to intervene in most affairs of the state – whether political, social or economic.

At the same time, the focus on the state organisation does not prevent the military from developing close ties with related military entities abroad. Attitude and ideology, together with specific state security interests, generate alliances across borders. In fact, military bodies all over the world think and tend to act within a similar conceptual framework born out of their professional routine, life-style, mode of operation and career socialisation. It is then easy, when policy interests coincide, to develop associative relations between allied military establishments. Professed nationalism is brushed away, to be replaced by ideological conformity.

Today, with armaments accorded the highest priority and developed on the basis of the most advanced technology, the military feels more competent than ever to govern and rule, and aspires to ever-greater influence in the affairs of the state. Backed by an enormous military research and development establishment, the military profession can boast a controlling position at the wheels of the highest contemporary technology and development potential. It feels expert in organisation, the application of modern technology, technical advance and the safeguarding of state interests.

We should not underestimate the pervasiveness of the militaristic ideology in society at large. There are many channels of public socialisation. One is the system of universal conscription, another is the state educational organisation, a third the mass media. Universal conscription is often presented as an instrument of participatory democracy and identification between army and nation. But in real life, when subjected to the control of the army, it becomes rather an instrument of nationalistic and militaristic indoctrination. Conscription may not win over all the recruits to militaristic convictions, but it does leave a deep nationalistic imprint on a large number of soldiers. Of a much greater impact is the kind of 'patriotic' education generally served in schools, in the teaching of history, 'civics', or international relations. National aggrandisement, exceptional and unique national qualities, as against feelings of ties and solidarity with other nations, and enemy images are inculcated and ingrained in the citizen from early childhood. Taken up later by the mass media, they become a powerful material force in the daily political life of states and nations.

Thus, as important as it is to grasp the substantial foundations of contemporary militarism and to strive for structural change in the material base, it is equally vital to try to come to grips with the attitudinal and ideological dynamics in the superstructure, and try to erect barriers against their inflation.

3 The World Military Order

3.1 Structure and Hierarchy

At a time when the concept of a new international economic order stressing the need for more justice in relations between the rich and the poor nations is getting broad currency, it is pertinent to investigate the impact of militarism and armaments on the international set-up and the interrelationship between the economic and military international dynamics. We need not dig very deep into books and data to state the obvious: there is an enormous waste of human and material resources diverted from development to military purposes. The recent report of the UN Consultant Experts on Social and Economic Consequences of Armaments sums this up in the following way:

> The social, political, technological and industrial options of

> countries are affected by their participation in the arms race. International policies, not only in the military field, but also in fields of international trade and of cooperation and exchanges generally, are influenced by the climate of confrontation and apprehension engendered by the arms race. Many of the major problems faced by the world community, problems of development, of economic imbalance and inflation, of pollution, energy and raw materials, of trade relations and technology and so forth, are enhanced and exacerbated by the arms race. Progress in other areas such as health, education, housing and many more, is delayed due to lack of resources.

The detrimental effects of armaments and the rise of military influence are felt throughout the globe, especially in countries where these processes have assumed sizeable dimensions. But most important are the international cumulative effects. No single central field of development and human relations remains untouched. If we extrapolate from present trends, humanity is on a collision course against its own survival. It is indeed difficult to imagine how the hungry can be fed, economy improved, ecology saved, peace established and war avoided – with present trends continuing into the future, with such an essential part of resources devoted to armaments, and with a majority of world nations subjected to military regimes.

There is structure and hierarchy to the world military order, best seen in the flow of armaments around the globe. On the top of this structure, as pacemakers in armaments, military technology and international arms deals are the two superpowers, the United States and the Soviet Union. Together they stand for half of world military expenditures, they concentrate in their hands up to 90 per cent of global military research and development, and command 70 per cent of the world arms trade. They are then followed in the vertical and horizontal proliferation of arms by the second-rank powers: Britain, France and China, with aspiring powers such as West Germany and Japan on their heels. While the superpowers and China are motivated in their arms deals mainly by political considerations, the others trade in weapons mainly for economic reasons. For the secondary powers, the arms trade serves also to uphold an economy of scale in military research and development and modern weapon production.

Across the dependence line are the arms receivers, with a diversity and differentiation of their own. There are those oil-rich countries which can easily pay for arms and are in a position to strike a good bargain. There are the poor Third World countries which are much more dependent on political favour of the big. There are countries with sub-imperial ambitions, or which, because of involvement in local conflicts, seek to develop domestic arms production or to enter into co-production with the big suppliers. There are other states deprived of resources where a relatively small influx of weapons may decisively influence the internal relations of forces.

Inevitably, arms transactions contribute to the establishment and consolidation of a patron-client relationship. Modern arms require high technological know-how, maintenance capabilities and a developed infrastructure. As technology is making fast strides, and as its mainstay rests with the great powers, those receiving the arms become dependent for a long time on the flow of spare parts, technical assistance and training. This process is reinforced by parallel economic pressures. At the same time, military supplies and aid serve to sustain friendly or allied local regimes and to further the process of militarisation in the Third World.

One indicator to this evolution is the trickle-down process of military power and the spread of modern weapons to the Third World. According to SIPRI data, the number of Third World countries with supersonic aircraft increased between 1955 and 1975 from 1 to 21, while the number of these countries with long-range surface-to-air missiles grew between 1958 and 1975 from 1 to 18. In 1976, altogether 75 Third World countries were importing major military equipment of some type.

Military power has, of course, its uses both in war and peace. The application of military power as an instrument of politics and diplomacy in the post-World War II period is an established fact. A recent study by the Brookings Institution, *The Use of the Armed Forces as a Political Instrument* (Blechman, and Kaplan (eds.), 1976) cites 215 incidents between 1 January 1946 and 31 October 1975 in which the United States utilised her armed forces for political objectives. During the same period, the study notes, the Soviet Union deployed its forces in a similar way on at least 115 occasions. The incidents with US involvement, the study states,

> ranged from a visit to a foreign port by a single warship, to the deployment of major ground, air and naval units against a backdrop including the mobilization of reserves and the placing on alert of strategic nuclear forces . . . Throughout the post-war period, the United States has turned most often to the Navy when she has

> desired to employ components of the armed forces in support of political objectives. Naval units participated in more than four of every five incidents. Land-based forces were used in much fewer incidents, and rarely without the simultaneous participation of naval units. Land-based air units participated in roughly half the total number of incidents. Ground combat units took part in only about a fifth of the total. Strategic nuclear force units were used alone or together with conventional force units in a tenth of the incidents.

The list of armed conflicts and incidents with direct to indirect involvement of the great powers is long: a hundred local wars in the Third World, mainly of a neo-colonial character and intended to stem the anti-colonial tide; the Korean War; the Indo-China conflict; the Middle Eastern wars; Soviet interventions in Hungary, Poland and Czechoslovakia; US interventions in Latin America and Lebanon; the Cuban conflict; the Anglo-French-Israeli Suez expedition; the Indo-Pakistani wars; the Indo-Chinese clashes, etc. Whatever the local components and factors of these conflicts, they were fuelled by arms supplied by the great powers. They reflected an international climate of power politics intended to threaten, deter and coerce by the force of arms, and to uphold existing structures.

This kind of power relationship tends not only to expand geographically in horizontal directions and maintain a feudal hierarchical subordination, but serves the internal role expansion of the military as well. Parallel to the rush to arms and to the new military technology, and parallel to the growth in complexity of the world military web, there is also an increase in military prerogatives in the councils of the great powers, and an expansion of military influence and its manipulatory power in society at large. This sort of internal dynamics is clearly felt in developing countries with weak democratic traditions and weak modern institutions. The officer class finds there far more leeway for intervention and social space to move from low to high autonomy.

In sum, the military and militarisation today rely on a strong international structure and a well established hierarchy. There is specific order in this structure and hierarchy, rank being dependent on military and economic strength, and mobility on the mastery of the application of violence.

3.2 Militarism Dynamics and Armaments Dynamics

Militarism dynamics and armaments dynamics are closely interrelated.

No military regime could survive long without the supply of arms, and no military establishment could flourish in an environment without arms. And vice versa: the threat system established by the arms race and violence in international relations serves to promote the interests of the military and to encourage militaristic tendencies. Whatever the local and subjective grounds for militarism and militarisation in the Third World, the aspirations of the military in these countries find a favourable breeding ground in the rush to armaments initiated by the great powers. Weapons instrumentation is readily at hand. Moreover, armaments in the developed world induce the developing countries to follow suit. In a world where weapons invest states with power, prestige, status and authority, even states devoid of militaristic tendencies become inclined to enter the race.

To confront militarism requires then a grasp of contemporary armaments dynamics. This subject has been widely treated in the peace research literature. It should therefore suffice to point to the main elements of these dynamics.

First come the international conflict formations. The political roots of the contemporary arms race lie in great-power rivalry, their security concerns and ideological confrontation. Essentially, after World War II this boiled down to a struggle for reshaping the world political map. The emergence of two superpowers with world-wide ambitions led to claims for special spheres of influence and a struggle for economic, political and military positions around the globe. These developments coincided with the anti-colonial revolution, resulting in (a) the emergence of a hundred new states seeking to acquire arms as a symbol of sovereignty and as an instrument for solving a number of local residual problems, internal and external; (b) an effort by the defeated colonial powers to regain some of the lost ground by military, economic and political means. The ensuing competition between the powers has added fuel to the conflicts. No struggle against militarism can possibly succeed without trying to bring all these conflicts under some control, under the aegis of the United Nations or peaceful co-existence, and unless the political will for disarmament can be generated.

Second, as armaments impelled by the conflict formations have started to expand and escalate, a specific dynamic has come into play: the pattern generated by the momentum of action and reaction. In an atmosphere of suspicion, mistrust and secrecy, every upward step by one side tends to produce reaction and over-reaction by the other. The result has been a chain reaction of constantly moving up the armaments ladder, intensifying the arms race. The only possible remedy lies in a reduction of tension, in greater openness in security matters, and in improving the political climate between states – leading to concerted disarmament.

Third, an increasing impact on the armaments dynamics comes from the burgeoning modern technology and the mode of operation of military research and development. Three regularities in this mode of operation are of decisive importance: (a) the impulse to technological competition stemming from the fact that hundreds of thousands of scientists and engineers employed by militaristic R&D and dispersed in a multitude of research centres and laboratories compete with each other, both across borders and on the national level; (b) the long lead-times, up to ten years, for the development of new weapon systems which assure stability and continuity for the war effort and uphold the armaments momentum; (c) the urge constantly to improve the old and introduce new technology, as well as the need to keep the production lines open, produce the 'follow-on' imperative which impels uninterrupted expansion and growth of military R&D establishment.

While the action-reaction pattern mentioned above stimulates the armaments dynamics on the inter-state level, the mode of operation of military R&D actuates also an internal – autistic – momentum exerting powerful pressures and invigorating the arms race immensely. Together, the internal and external thrust have accorded armaments dynamics an impetus of their own. Consequently, a basic pre-condition for restraining the arms race is to impose control and progressively dismantle military R&D.

There is no easy way to fight armaments and militarism. Powerful forces stand behind. A long historical process has brought us to present realities of militarism and militarisation. Time and persistence are required if we are to reverse this process. The issues are of a political, social and economic nature, affecting almost every aspect of modern life. Confronting militarism clearly demands a response in all these spheres.

3.3 Military Regimes and Militarism in the Third World

Any sickness, even when of a social nature, will hit hardest the weak and the feeble. This is indeed the case with militarism and militarisation. Like a contagious disease, military regimes have spread in the Third World. It is not that militarism and militarisation in the developing countries affect international relations more strongly than do the arms race, East-West rivalries or the growing gap between the rich and the poor nations. The malady affects and has struck foremost the Third World nations themselves, interfering with development, corrupting the political process and destroying human values. This is the more so as the malady afflicts the young nations in their formative stage. The derangement of the democratic development may have far-reaching consequences for the future as well. Obviously, because the international community is interdependent and also because of the numbers involved, the way these countries behave and develop will affect international relations and the socio-political shape of the globe.

With hindsight, we can say that the defeat of colonialism has not led, in most cases, to a radical progressive socio-political transformation in the Third World. After a period of confusion, armed struggle and the emergence of the many new sovereign states, a co-ordinated effort of neo-colonial forces in the metropoles and conservative social strata in the peripheries has succeeded largely in imposing regimes which fit a structure and hierarchy favouring the great powers. The centre-periphery dynamic which serves well both the metropoles and the elites in the peripheries has come into being. Militarism in the Third World is in fact a dependent militarism carried largely by the centre-periphery dynamics. Acting on behalf of the elites in the peripheries or constituting themselves as the very elite, the military has become a vehicle for this evolution.

Circumstances have been favourable for military intervention. An interlocking of social and national issues has created an explosive atmosphere, while the structure of state and society has remained weak, lacking consolidation. In such conditions the military has been able to justify their intervention by the need for:

- organisational effectiveness and discipline;
- enhancing national sovereignty and security;
- promoting national integration and nation-building, against ethnic and tribal fragmentation;
- dismantling feudal interests and elimination of corruption;
- advancing social mobility in the interest of the middle classes/to which the officers themselves belonged/and lower social strata;
- technological modernisation;
- overcoming legitimacy strains and enforcing political stability.

This has essentially been a response to social conflicts in the new class configuration after liberation, aiming to surmount political crisis and socio-economic difficulties by a combination of force, repression and modernisation. At the same time, incentives for intervention have been great. State bureaucracies in developing countries usually enjoy far larger privileges and have more direct access to the nation's wealth than in developed countries. The military have simply desired to usurp a lion's share in this exercise.

Though the list of self-justifying arguments for military intervention in Third World countries is long and impressive, there is good reason to question its utility and social benefits. Against the arguments of the military as being an energising and modernising force stands the reality of its inability to tackle successfully the social and economic problems of developing nations.

Basic tension exists between the pursuit of efficiency and modernisation in the military style and the inherent socio-political weakness of a military regime (as reflected in the suppression of participatory democracy, the structural dependence on foreign powers, the inability to apply modern social theory within the rigid framework of military thinking, and the search for technical solutions when structural change is imperative). The organisational abilities of the military get lost in the wilderness of conceptual confusion and the propensity for rigidity and excess.

As an example of the negative effects of the 'modernisation' sought by Third World military regimes we may cite the complex consequences of according high priority to military purposes and the procurement of modern military technology. Large military spending is naturally unproductive. The money is lost for development – even if a degree of spill-over to civilian economy is taken into consideration. But far more detrimental long-term effects come from the acquisition of modern military technology basically extraneous to the needs of a developing society. Not only does this divert scarce human talent and material resources to fields of little use for the country's economy, it also generates a dynamic which restrains an autonomous development oriented towards human needs and directs it into systemic channels patterned by the metropoles. There is now near-unanimity among economists specialising in Third World problems that economic patterns of the developed nations are at variance with the needs and conditions of the developing nations; as far as technology is concerned, the exigency is for intermediate technology adapted to local conditions, requirements and capabilities. But modern military technology is quite the opposite: it means reproduction of an alien metropolitan system aimed to serve the perpetuation of the dominance-dependence relationship and impairing efforts at self-reliance.

By far the greatest harm military regimes inflict on Third World countries lies in the undermining and corruption of democratic development and in violation of basic human rights. The creative energy of young nations is suppressed at the very start of sovereignty and nationhood. The experience of the Latin American countries where the military has long since won a strong foothold should serve as a warning here. For the international community, such a development is not only a tragedy in human terms but a real stumbling block for global progressive change.

3.4 *Combating Militarism*

Considering the size of the problem, we will see that a strategy to combat militarism and militarisation must encompass a wide range of actions, national and international. There is a systemic, social, political, economic and human rights context to such a strategy. To be effective, it would have to focus on the human being and human values, and of crucial importance is the activation of public opinion.

Without going into detail, we may draw up a general list of steps to undertake and fields to cover.

(1) Conceptual clarification of the terms and scope of contemporary militarism and militarisation. This calls for critical interdisciplinary research on the organisation, behaviour, attitudes, role in state and international impact of the military. Both case studies and research on international linkages are important. A good mapping of military regimes and the extent of militarisation in the international community would be most helpful.

(2) In-depth study and analysis of the interrelation between militarism dynamics and armament dynamics. A better comprehension of these issues is basic for devising ways and means for a successful anti-militaristic strategy. In the final instance, disarmament should be one of the most effective ways to combat militarism.

(3) In-depth study of the interrelation between militarism dynamics and problems of development in the Third World. There is a need to make the interrelation clearer, and to develop intellectual tools for a fundamental critique of military regimes in developing countries.

(4) Most of all, together with studies to broaden our knowledge and understanding of the phenomena of militarism and militarisation, we need a world-wide educational campaign which can shed light on the essence and consequences of militarism, and which aims

actively to engage broad strata of citizens all over the world against the evil of military rule. A coalition of concerned organisations – political, religious and professional – is urgently needed to undertake this task.

2 MILITARISM: THE ISSUES TODAY*

Michael T. Klare

1 Defining Militarism

For the purposes of discussion, we can define 'militarism' as the tendency of a nation's *military apparatus* (which includes the armed forces and associated paramilitary, intelligence and bureacuratic agencies) to assume *ever-increasing control* over the lives and behaviour of its citizens; and for *military goals* (preparation for war, acquisition of weaponry, development of military industries) and *military values* (centralisation of authority, hierarchisation, discipline and conformity, combativeness and xenophobia) increasingly to dominate national culture, education, the media, religion, politics and the economy at the expense of civilian institutions. This definition is consistent with Marek Thee's picture of militarism as subsuming 'a rush to armaments, the growing role of the military (understood as the military establishment) in national and international affairs, the use of force as an instrument of dominance and political power, and the increasing influence of the military in civilian affairs'.[1]

Common to these and other definitions of militarism is the notion of *excess*, of the growing *encroachment* of the military over civilian institutions with a concomitant decline in individual freedoms and democratic forms of decision-making. Militarism, then, is a *dynamic condition* characterised by the progressive expansion of the military sphere over the civilian – rather than a static, fixed phenomenon whose contours can be accurately mapped.

2 Forces which Generate and Promote Militarism

It follows from this that if we are to be effective in combating militarism, we must first identify those forces and conditions which generate and promote militarism in any given society. For to stop the *spread* of militarism, we must attack those phenomena and structures which are the driving force behind that expansion. To begin this process of analysis, it is useful to divide these generative forces into *internal factors* (those indigenous to the society in question) and

*This paper was originally presented to the Consultation on Militarism held by the World Council of Churches at Glion, Switzerland, 13-18 Nov. 1977 (hereinafter cited as the WCC Militarism Consultation).

external factors (those practices which promote and sustain militarism across international boundaries).

2.1 Internal Factors

Among the internal factors which generate and nurture militarism are the following:

(1) *Unjust class structure:* in any society where a small segment of the population owns (or reaps the benefits from) a large share of the nation's wealth, that privileged minority is likely to rely on the use of military force to deter or overcome any threats to the prevailing order. This tendency results in what has been termed a system of 'economic apartheid', wherein the privileged few live in 'sanctuaries of wealth' surrounded by and protected from the impoverished masses.[2]

(2) *Unjust racial structures:* similarly, in any society wherein the people of one race are subordinated and exploited by people of another race, the dominant racial grouping tends to rely on military force to discourage and overcome rebellion on the part of the oppressed.

(3) *Institutionalised military industries:* as demonstrated by the US experience since World War II, the creation of large-scale military enterprises is likely to result in the formation of a self-perpetuating industrial combine that will take independent measures (propaganda and 'scare' campaigns designed to create a perpetual crisis-type atmosphere; lobbying efforts, bribery and intrigue, etc.) to ensure a continuing demand for its products. Although we can surmise the existence of such institutional pressures also in the major socialist states, this phenomenon is obviously most pronounced in the advanced capitalist countries where institutional ambitions are reinforced by the profit motive.

(4) *The military's self-aggrandisement:* once a society has created a powerful military apparatus in response to some real or imagined threat, this institution will often seek to expand and enhance its prerogatives at the expense of civilian institutions. In the advanced countries, this drive is often linked to and fed by the self-perpetuating mechanisms of the military industries; in the poorer countries, it is sometimes produced by the desire of the officer class (which is often composed of middle- and even lower-class persons) to enhance their status *vis-à-vis* the traditional ruling elite.

(5) *The 'national security' syndrome:* all four previous items take an ideological cast through the 'national security' syndrome: the

tendency to expand the definition of 'national security' to require ever-greater military control over national life. In the Third World, this is most often expressed in 'developmental' terms, whereby the military affirms that it is the only institution capable of managing rapid econometric growth, while in the advanced countries it is often predicated on the existence of a 'Cold War', i.e. the existence of an intense global struggle encompassing all forms of human activity (culture, education, religion, science and technology, diplomacy, etc.).

(6) *Cultural prejudices and stereotypes:* despite all that has been said about global interdependence and ecumenicism, cultural prejudices and stereotypes remain deeply engrained. This is particularly true in the less developed countries where ethnic religious and tribal animosities are often highly pronounced, but it is hardly absent from the most advanced societies. In the United States, for instance, some prominent officials and scholars have organised a multi-million dollar 'scare' campaign to persuade the general public that the Russians – unlike the Americans – are emotionally capable of planning a thermonuclear war that would result in the death of at least 40 million people, by conservative estimates.[3] Such attitudes are easily manipulated by the military authorities for their own purposes, and hamper the efforts of peace-minded people to work against militarism. Such efforts are also impeded, of course, by popular attitudes which equate 'masculinity' and 'patriotism' with aggressiveness, chauvinism and indifference to the suffering of others.

(7) *Perceived insecurity in the face of external threats:* countries surrounded by hostile neighbours will often develop a 'siege' mentality which views any unusual external move (troop movements, military exercises, major arms purchases) as a signal of impending hostilities requiring appropriate counteractions. In such countries – Israel, South Korea and Taiwan are perhaps the outstanding examples – preparation for war often becomes a *permanent way of life*, and any demands for relaxation of military authority and martial law are viewed as tantamount to treason. In some cases, as a result of the impulses described in (3) and (4) above, this condition persists long after the initial threat has disappeared.

2.2 *External Factors*

Among the external factors which promote and sustain militarism we can identify:

(1) *Imperial intervention:* throughout history, imperial powers

have sought to expand or guard their empires by displacing hostile leaders and replacing them with local warlords who agree (or can be compelled) to serve the imperial cause. This practice underlies, for instance, the formation of the prevailing political order in the Persian Gulf, fixed by British colonial agents in the nineteenth century. Although most formal arrangements of this sort have now disappeared, the practice persists in the efforts of the major powers to promote the rise of friendly military elites in client states. Such efforts have long constituted a major component of US policy in the Third World, and represent the core of the 'Nixon Doctrine'. US support for friendly military forces typically includes cash subsidies, arms deliveries, military sales at subsidised interest rates, free military training and technical assistance, political recognition and other benefits. In some important cases (Iran 1953, Guatemala 1954, Brazil and the Dominican Republic 1965, and Chile 1973), US aid and personnel have been used to help engineer the collapse of civilian governments and their replacement by pro-US military governments. And even when US involvement does not extend to such direct intervention, it is obvious that the transfer of such resources (particularly of arms and equipment for internal repression) will contribute to the ascendancy of the military sphere at the expense of competing civilian institutions.

(2) *International arms marketing:* many of the advanced nations have concluded that they must export arms in order to retain a domestic munitions industry at a time of rising military costs, and/or help reduce balance-of-trade deficits brought about by the rising cost of raw material imports. And since many nations now possess the capacity to produce weapons, there has been a growing competition between the arms exporters which in turn has led them to use a variety of conventional and unconventional techniques to induce increased military spending by the arms-importing countries. According to the US Arms Control and Disarmament Agency, the volume of arms imports by the developing countries has risen fourfold over the past ten years, from about \$ 2 billion per year in the mid-1960s to \$ 8 billion annually today.[4] And, as competition between the major exporters has increased, they have offered increasingly more lethal and sophisticated weaponry to prospective buyers, leading to a steady increase in the war-making capabilities of the poorer countries.

Linked to the trade in conventional weaponry are several other factors which also contribute to the spread of militarism: (1) the growing trade in *police weapons and other repressive technologies* (surveillance devices, torture equipment and techniques, computers used to identify and track victims for torture, assassination or imprisonment, etc.) whose use tends to parallel the encroachment of the military over the civilian sphere; (2) the sale of *arms-making technologies* by the advanced countries to the less developed countries, thereby permitting an increasing number of countries to become self-sufficient in war-making commodities and to enter the arms trade on their own; (3) the sale of *nuclear power technologies* which, as demonstrated by the case of India, has led to the proliferation of nuclear weapons; and (4) linked to all of the above, the sale of *military technical services*, which has resulted in the formation of a new corps of 'white-collar mercenaries' who sell their technical skills to Third World governments which have imported large quantities of advanced weaponry that they cannot adequately maintain, support and operate using indigenous labour. All of these factors obviously enhance the power of the state – and particularly of the military sector – *vis-à-vis* the population at large and tend to promote the use of force to solve internal and international disputes.[5]

(3) *Big power involvement in local conflicts:* since the major powers tend to view local power shifts in critical areas, whatever their cause, as enhancing or damaging their global strategic interests, they often attempt to influence the outcome of a struggle or rivalry by providing their clients with arms, training, advisory support, etc. As soon as any such support is provided, all other parties to the dispute will almost automatically seek similar assistance from a competing great power. And since the major powers tend to equate *their* security and prestige with the fortunes of their clients, they are usually quick to match or outstrip any arms deliveries made by another great power to their clients' rivals. Obviously, this process tends to intensify the local arms race and increase the risk of great power involvement in any war that does erupt.

(4) *Cross-national ideological/religious struggle:* as recent history demonstrates, national leaders sometimes feel compelled by ideological or religious ties to provide military assistance to like-thinking governments (or, in some cases, minority or separatist groups) under attack elsewhere. The division of the world into pro- and anti-Communist alliance systems is, of course, the most obvious example of this phenomenon; but recently we have seen the socialist world itself rent by ideological struggle between supporters of Moscow and Peking. In the Third World, we see that Saudi Arabia is subsidising the 'front-line' Arab states battling Israel, that South Africa is arming the white minority government of Rhodesia, and that Brazil is aiding the military

regimes of Chile, Uruguay and Bolivia. Such linkages ensure that even the poorest nations have access to modern military equipment and obviously complicate the job of negotiating a peaceful solution to local conflicts.

(5) *Alliance politics:* military alliances are presumably forged in response to clearly perceived dangers, but often these linkages develop a life of their own long after the original danger has passed. In such cases, various governments and/or powerful interest groups perceive a vested interest in the survival of the alliance as a *system*, and thus will intervene in the political process of member states to assure their continued adherence to the pact. Thus the Soviet Union intervenes regularly in Eastern European politics to assure the stability of the Warsaw Pact system, while the NATO powers have provided financial support to centrist parties in Portugal to prevent the Communist Party from winning control of the government. Furthermore, since the survival of many of these alliances appears to depend on the perceived 'steadfastness' of their most powerful member(s), they sometimes trigger military actions whose major purpose is to demonstrate a nation's 'commitment' to the alliance; this, indeed, was the principal reason cited by US authorities for continued involvement in Vietnam after it had become apparent that a US victory was unattainable.

3 Interdependencies

Although it is helpful to separate out internal and external factors for the purposes of discussion, we must always remember that these factors normally work together and *reinforce each other*. Indeed, analysis suggests that it is the very *mixing* of these factors, each of which tends to nurture and support the others, which underlies the current world epidemic of militarism. Thus we see that the strategic and economic interests of the great powers, as represented in arms deliveries or arms sales to clients, often promote the rise of military institutions within recipient countries. By the same token, the desire of military elites in Third World countries to strengthen their position *vis-à-vis* competing civilian institutions often leads them to seek alliances with the military of the great powers in order to obtain the arms, equipment and funds to carry out their political designs. All this suggests that there is an *interdependence of militarism* between the industrial and non-industrial nations, and that this interdependency intersects and distorts all other relationships between the nations. This interdependence has been characterised by some analysts as constituting a *world military order*, whereby military developments in any one nation or bloc of nations tend to produce parallel or related developments in all other nations.[6]

4 Threatening Trends

Clearly the growth of militarism and the formation of a world military order is having a profound impact on contemporary human life. Their consequences for the future are likely to be even more devastating, unless we are able to overcome this modern scourge. Of the most threatening trends associated with militarism, we can identify the following:

(1) *The superpower arms race:* of all the trends associated with militarism today, none is more costly in the short run and as potentially catastrophic in the long run than the nuclear arms race between the United States and the Soviet Union. The desperate efforts of the US leadership to retain its nuclear lead over the USSR, and of the Soviet leadership to narrow that lead, are leading to the development and deployment of ever more potent and provocative weapons. Furthermore, with the development of precision-guided *counter-force* weapons (weapons designed to destroy an enemy's strategic military forces, rather than its cities), it is becoming increasingly possible to conceive of 'first-strike' scenarios. Thus both sides will be under ever-increasing pressure to launch a pre-emptive strike of their own during a crisis, to preclude the threat of a similar attack by their adversary.

To 'deter' such strikes, both sides are now introducing new types of delivery systems (mobile ICBM launchers, 'cruise' missiles, etc.), which will further burden already heavily militarised economies in the USA and USSR, while increasing the risk of thermonuclear holocaust. These trends have not, moreover, been appreciably slowed by the SALT negotiations between the superpowers. Given the facts that: (a) the rivalry between the superpowers tends to poison relations between other countries and to lead to big-power involvement in local rivalries (with sometimes devastating consequences), (2) war preparation in these two countries consumes enormous resources that could be otherwise used for global development; and, most serious, (3) *any* nuclear exchange between the USA and USSR will almost assuredly cause enormous destruction elsewhere, it is obvious that *all* peoples in the world have a vital stake in first controlling and ultimately abolishing the superpower arms race.

(2) *Authoritarianism in the Third World:* on the grounds that 'national security' requires a high degree of economic 'modernisation',

and that high growth rates are possible only in tightly disciplined societies, more and more Third World military leaders are assuming control of the governing institutions of their countries. In some cases this process leads to the violent overthrow of civilian governments (as in Brazil, Argentina, Chile, Uruguay and Thailand), while in others it is characterised by the progressive emasculation of civilian institutions at the expense of military agencies (a process not unknown in many of the advanced countries as well). In carrying out their 'developmental' programmes, the military tend to impose centralised, hierarchic forms of decision-making on all government institutions, and to place all other national institutions – the press, schools and colleges, the church, trade unions, peasant organisations, etc. – under central state control. Any institutions, social groupings, organisations or individuals which resist such control are considered a threat to national security and are forcefully dissolved, restricted, purged or neutralised by state agencies. Non-conforming ideas, values, religious or political beliefs, artistic styles or ethnic identities are considered subversive and adherents thereof are punished accordingly. Furthermore, to obtain the external financing, technology and investment considered essential to promote the Western-sponsored 'developmental models' most Third World juntas have adopted, more and more governments are imposing punishing 'austerity' measures which cause disproportionate hardship and suffering for the poorest and least poweful sectors of the society.

(3) *Armamentism and local conflict:* in order to enhance their own self-image as powerful, modern institutions, to intimidate or suppress competing civilian institutions, and/or to counter real or imagined external threats, the military forces of most countries are diverting more and more resources to the acquisition of advanced weaponry. This phenomenon is most marked in the Third World, where spending on imported weapons quadrupled between 1965 and 1974, from $2 billion to over $8 billion. At the same time, in order to assure a high degree of popular support for the national development programmes and/or for increased military spending, military regimes tend to exaggerate external threats and to encourage nationalistic and xenophobic feelings. Both of these trends tend to generate local arms rivalries, since any military build-up in one country will naturally cause insecurity and thus matching military spending in neighbouring or rival countries. This process is most visible in the Middle East, where every new arms purchase by Israel is almost automatically followed by comparable acquisitions by the front-line Arab states (and vice versa),

but it can also be detected in South and South East Asia, North and East Africa, and South America. The principal victims of this phenomenon are the poorest sectors of all these countries, who must watch needed development projects be scrapped in order to release scarce funds for military purchases. In the long run, however, we all stand to lose since such local rivalries, fed by the aggressive posturing of the reigning military and the arms marketing of the great powers, can easily explode into armed conflict and conceivably trigger a global war.

(4) *Internal violence and terror:* since all of these developments are occurring at a time of generally rising expectations – both for improved material conditions and increased personal freedom – on the part of the world's peoples, and since the military's goals (whether in the advanced or underdeveloped areas) tend to be achieved at the expense of the most disadvantaged sectors of the population, there is a growing divergence of interests between the military authorities and the disenfranchised masses of poor people that tends to result in ever-increasing repression of the latter by the former. And since in many countries the poor have obtained a degree of power or at least self-expression through the formation of unions, peasant and farmers' organisations, neighbourhood and *barrio* committees, and, in some cases, political parties, the ruling authorities often feel compelled to employ indiscriminate terror and brutality to deter popular resistance. This process is perhaps most advanced in Chile and Indonesia, where the military leadership has attempted to eradicate – through mass executions – an entire generation of political activists, but it can be seen in many other societies where martial law has become a permanent way of life. The desire for increased freedom and self-development has emerged with particular force among the minority peoples whose sense of 'nationhood' is denied by existing political boundaries (which were established, in most cases, by the colonial powers), and this has led to intense and often bloody conflicts with the prevailing authorities (hence the Biafran War, the Kurdish uprising, the conflict in Northern Ireland, the Palestinian struggle, the Moslem insurgency in the Philippines, and dozens of similar conflicts). Although militarism (in its modern guise) is not always the cause of these conflicts, it is obvious that the military mission – whether 'national security' or economic 'development' – tends to preclude a search for a just and peaceful solution. All this is even more true, of course, in southern Africa, where minority white regimes rely on superior force to dominate majority black populations. (In this case the issues of

militarism, human rights and racism are all inextricably linked.)

(5) *Misuse of resources and technology:* it is becoming increasingly obvious that many of the earth's critical natural resources will soon be depleted if present-day rates of consumption prevail. At the same time, it is clear that changes in the global 'ecosphere' – many of them produced by human activity – threaten to limit the supply of food-stuffs at a time of rising birth-rates throughout most of the Third World. These developments suggest an urgent need for international action to conserve critical resources, protect the environment, and develop new sources of food and other vital products. However, not only is the epidemic of militarism making such co-operation appear increasingly unlikely, but it is also hastening the advent of global catastrophe by consuming enormous quantities of scarce and non-replenishable natural resources. It has been estimated, for instance, that the US Defense Department accounts for 14 per cent of US consumption of bauxite and copper, 11 per cent of zinc and lead, 10 per cent of nickel, and 7.5 per cent of iron.[7] This pattern of waste is not confined to material resources alone, but extends to human resources as well: according to SIPRI, over 400,000 scientists and engineers were committed to weapons research and development (R&D) work in 1970, representing a large fraction of the world's total R&D work-force.[8] If these scientific resources were freed from military work, we would have a much better chance of solving the world's food, shelter and health problems.

5 Concluding Remarks

Surely it is the conjunction of these trends – their propensity to nurture and reinforce one another across international boundaries – that makes militarism such a great danger today. As noted by Marek Thee with devastating eloquence:

> The nature of contemporary militarism differs from the previous manifestations of militarism mainly in its global *reach* and a dynamic rooted in a new world hierarchy, the controlling position of the superpowers, the dominance-dependence relationship between the great powers and the developing nations, the socio-economic predicament of most of the Third World countries, and the impact of the technological revolution . . . Militarism today has unleashed a worldwide arms race unparalleled in history, it has supplied arms for dozens of local wars, it has distorted development priorities in the Third World, and with ever-new weapons of mass destruction at

hand has been playing with the very survival of mankind.[9]

This is a frightening picture indeed of the menace we face, but what must be added to it is an appreciation of the *time factor* at work. For, as we noted earlier, militarism is a progressive disease, whose crippling effects accumulate and accelerate with time. If left untreated, it will surely end, as in 1914 and 1939, in the outbreak of world war – perhaps, this time, leading to the annihilation of all human life.

Our task now is to pinpoint the most potent internal and external factors promoting militarism, to develop programmes to counter those factors, and to build alliances with other concerned groups and people to counter these factors. Our analysis suggests, moreover, that we are at a critical junction in time, and that every moment we postpone action now will make our job infinitely harder later.

Notes

1. Marek Thee, 'Militarism and Militarization in Contemporary International Relations', paper submitted to the WCC Militarism Consultation; *Bulletin of Peace Proposals*, vol. 8, no. 4 (1977).

2. Peter Lock and Herbert Wulf, 'The Dialectics of Rearmament and Dependence', paper submitted to the WCC Militarism Consultation.

3. See Richard Pipes, 'Why the Soviet Union Thinks it Could Fight and Win a Nuclear War', *Commentary* (July 1977), pp. 21-34.

4. US Arms Control and Disarmament Agency, *World Military Expenditures and Arms Transfers* (Washington, DC, 1977), and earlier editions.

5. For further discussion, see the following articles by the present author, 'The Political Economy of Arms Sales', *Bulletin of the Atomic Scientists* (November 1976), pp. 11-18; 'Exporting the Tools of Repression', *The Nation* (16 Oct. 1976), pp. 365-70; 'America Exports its Know-How', *The Nation* (12 Feb. 1977), pp. 173-8.

6. Thee, 'Militarism and Militarization'. See also Jan Øberg, 'The International Military Order: Structural Militarism and Human Security', paper read at the Pugwash Symposium on Militarism and National Security, Oslo, Norway, 21-4 Nov. 1977.

7. Stockholm International Peace Research Institute, *SIPRI Yearbook 1976* (Almqvist and Wiksell, Stockholm, 1976), p. 97.

8. Stockholm International Peace Research Institute, *Armaments and Disarmaments in the Nuclear Age* (Almqvist and Wiksell, Stockholm, 1976), pp. 184-7.

9. Thee, 'Militarism and Militarization'.

3 THE NEW INTERNATIONAL MILITARY ORDER: A THREAT TO HUMAN SECURITY*

Jan Øberg

1 Introduction

World military expenditures passed $ 1 billion a day in 1977, reaching $ 400 billion a year, which is approximately $ 50 million an hour and roughly $ 100 for each human being on Earth. This was the price of what is usually termed security.

This price increased thirty times in real terms throughout this century. However, the twentieth century is probably the most war-ridden of all in Western history; at least 100 million human beings lost their lives in war – on average 3,500 a day. Since 1945, there have been 120 wars all over the world, primarily in the periphery of the global system.[1]

In the name of security, armament spreads its branches horizontally to ever more nations and peoples and at the same time tends to root itself ever more deeply into social formations – by maintaining or destroying old ones or constructing new ones.

Although virtually impossible to grasp in its absurdity, we shall try to approach the phenomena related to these developments within a conceptual framework of a New International Military Order (NIMO). Gaining momentum as it is as a result of the so-called legitimate security needs of all nations, it represents probably the largest single threat to human security and the survival of mankind. To counteract it effectively is a challenge only comparable in scope and depth with that of creating a truly equitable New International Order meeting the needs of the structurally underdeveloped majority of peoples. And – as so strongly emphasised by the non-aligned nations – the establishing of a New International Economic Order (NIEO) will not stand a chance unless the armament trends are effectively reversed.

This chapter[2] attempts, first and foremost, to give the *concept of the NIMO* a reasonably precise content away from the status of a mere slogan. In this respect it is considered especially relevant to relate the 'hardware' developments with those of social and economic driving

*Revised and shortened version of a paper presented at the 28th Pugwash Symposium, 'Militarism and National Security', Oslo, November 1977.

forces and consequences, i.e. the transnationalisation of arms production and the militarism which is a phenomenon at the level of social structure.

Second, there is the idea that the *concept of militarism* can be usefully employed not only as a descriptive concept but as an analytical tool which partly relies on already existing theories of militarism, partly on updating and renewal. If so, there is a possibility that militarism can serve as a bridgehead to a deeper understanding of the very important ways in which social and military structures interact.

2 The New International Military Order (NIMO)

Table 3.1 outlines the New International Military Order as conceived of in this essay; it has *three main dimensions* making up building blocks each of which has a number of elements and sub-elements.

It may be asked, *what is new about this order?* Elements 1.2-1.6 are all phenomena that are qualitatively or quantitatively new in the world system compared with the arms trend of 1950. In other words, the globalisation of hardware is new and, it may be added, it is here that the largest expansion in consumption of military arms is taking place.

The increasing emphasis upon economic driving forces signified

Table 3.1: The New International Military Order (NIMO)

Dimensions	Elements	Focus
1 Globalisation	1.1 Centre armament	arms
	1.2 Arms trade	
Politico-military	1.3 Peripheral arms production	'arms control'
	1.4 Nuclear technology	
	1.5 West European MIC	
	1.6 Atlantic defence market	
2 Transnationalisation	2.1 Arms capital integration	arms production
	2.2 Arms project management	
Economic	2.3 R&D and planning	
	2.4 Armament economics	'conversion'
	2.5 Arms interest integration	
3 Militarism	3.1 Civil-military isomorphism	social and military structures
	3.2 Military monopoly	
Sociological	3.3 Social vulnerability	
	3.4 Insecurity	'social transformation'

specifically by the transnationalisation of arms production (also related to elements 2 and 3) is also new in the sense explained above. It is a post-World War II trend. This is also the case with merging of major civil and military interests under the heading of the military-industrial complex which was first mentioned by Eisenhower in his farewell speech. Finally, we tend to argue that these developments challenge old concepts of militarism and have gained such a momentum that one could actually speak of a 'new militarism' of the post-World War II period. This argument will be developed below.

It could also be argued that this order is not 'military' but *military-industrial*. This is partly correct. Our main point is that it is within the military-economic or military-industrial field that we first find, in general, indicators of things to come. A typical example would be present developments in Western Europe, where it is obvious that – while most of the political focus is upon the integration of military policies, foreign policy and the possibility of a 'European army' – these are features of much less significance than the pace with which the idea of a unified European military-industrial co-operation is being developed. If this trend continues we would predict the rest – policies, armies, strategic thinking, etc. – to follow almost 'automatically'.

Then of course there is the problem of the word *order*: isn't it simply the old disorder? How should we speak of order when there is such an obvious lack of control in this field?

The word 'order' does not signify that these developments are under political control. What we suggest is a degree of regularity which, at least in certain areas, makes prediction possible.

But there is an equally important idea behind 'order' – that, of course, of its relationship with NIEO as a concept. We here lean on the idea of verticality, of exploitation and penetration – even of isomorphism between the present international economic order (PIEO) and NIMO. Many of the structural features pertaining within the civil order are also found within the military order; this argument will also be developed below.

2.1 Globalisation

The catchword of this dimension of the NIMO is the changing 'geographics' of armament, its global reach. Advanced weapon systems flow around in increasing amounts and the military-industrial capacity of nations likewise is intensified. This is the most conspicuous manifestation of the order, and its main elements are the following:

2.1.1 Centre armament dynamics. The NIMO originates in the overdeveloped, overarmed centre nations – especially within the superpowers. The two main military pact systems consume around 70 per cent of world military expenditures combined. They prepare for the 'worst case' over the entire weapons spectrum – strategic as well as conventional – and their developments spill over into trade expansion supporting civil trade patterns, investment or the acquisition of strategic raw materials and energy.

The global strategies contain, of course, the building up of allies, pact systems, bases, infrastructure and the militarisation of oceans and space – as well as the continued threat of using force, intervention or invasion. The capacity to operate weapons is spread to more and more peoples, and the centre nations function fundamentally as pace-setters as well as technological models.

2.1.2 Arms trade to the periphery. This is probably the element in the NIMO which, in fixed prices, has increased most rapidly during the last 25 years. The main exporters are the United States, the Soviet Union, the United Kingdom and France, which export arms to about 100 peripheral nations, of which roughly 50 per cent are in the Middle East.

The export of weapons – larger as well as smaller, the first representing the larger share – serves several purposes: to 'police' an area as sub-imperialist in harmony with centre interests, to open up or maintain civil markets, to support investments, the existence of certain loyal local elites or to secure supplies of raw materials and energy – apart from purely strategic purposes. More fundamentally, it should not be forgotten that a rather important function is to 'facilitate' specific socio-economic systems within peripheral countries through a number of civic actions undertaken by local military forces which mould society to be receptive for investment and trade favourable to multinational companies, for example.

2.1.3 Peripheral arms production. About 35 peripheral nations are now engaged in local production of advanced weapons systems – Israel, India, South Africa, Brazil and Argentina being the largest. Roughly 20 are manufacturers of major weapons. Recent developments also point to a number of Arab countries, Iran, Indonesia, South Korea, the Philippines, Taiwan and Pakistan embarking on the same course. With the development of a militarised infrastructure and a potentially very serious distortion of civil development priorities – not least because domestic arms production within this type of economic structure will not only draw heavily upon scarce resources, but is also likely to lack any beneficial spin-off effects upon social development.

2.1.4 Nuclear technology. The export of nuclear facilities for peaceful purposes may very well have military implications, especially when entire fuel cycles are exported. The most probable nuclear powers in the periphery are all among those which have imported most conventional weaponry during the last 25 years. There is, therefore, the direct possibility of diversion of fissile materials for military purposes, and there is the indirect effect of the expansion of nuclear energy technology – not least through the possible next step, the breeder reactor – that increasing amounts of highly dangerous materials will flow around the global system. This development, in general, already causes great concern with respect to stopping nuclear proliferation. The call for control systems, at the national as well as the international level, may imply, in their extreme, a repression and social control of populations and the boosting of security forces even to the degree that the 'police state' emerges – in the name of security.

2.1.5 A West European military-industrial complex. As a part of the overall integration into the European Community, there seems to follow a slow but increasing integration of foreign policies, defence policies and – especially – a new type of military-industrial co-operation. Integration of procurement, military research and development (R&D), production and export is on the programme within various EEC bodies, represented in a number of reports during the last few years (related to names like Gladwyn, Spinelli, Tindemans, Normanton), as well as within NATO – the latter still holding for standardisation.

The Independent European Program Group (IEPG), with its close EEC and NATO ties is, by far, the most significant and successful, as the United States has accepted this body as the main negotiation partner across the Atlantic concerning future military-industrial co-operation.

2.1.6 An Atlantic Defence Market. The United States definitely prefers a militarily-industrially integrated Western Europe to deal with in the future – securing continued US technological superiority on the way to standardisation within NATO. Huge new armament projects are likely to take place across the Atlantic, the co-production scheme of the F-16 fighter aircraft being the most significant indicator of developments likely to become more typical in the future.

2.2 *Transnationalisation*

The catchword of this building block of the NIMO is the changing economics of armament. It represents the step from the arms to the economics of their production, to the economic driving forces underlying armament.

2.2.1 Arms capital integration. On top of the international military production structure, armament capital is increasingly concentrated in a few hands. Modern armament production is outgrowing national boundaries, many are merging and others become state-owned in order to be able to bear still larger projects, share the burdens and counteract the consequences of the rapidly increasing costs of modern weapons systems.

Vertically integrated development-production-export programmes are appearing more frequently and add to the number of subordinated co-producers taking part in various types of co-production schemes. Rich countries 'push out' parts of their armament manufacturing in order to exploit lower wages, evade environmental restrictions or arms export regulations.

What seems to develop these years is a fundamentally new international division of military-industrial labour with a top-heavy control and management and still fewer main producers competing on a world 'market'.

2.2.2 Arms project management. Where armament capital does not merge, integrated project management represents a lower degree of unification – a form of co-operation which takes place, most typically, among governments, ministries, military bureaucracies and industries at the international level.

The structure of this type of co-operation is tied together by means of co-ordinating groups and committees often established on a more or less *ad hoc* basis and functioning at a transnational level which defies national parliamentary, democratic control, as well as public insight. The transatlantic co-operation and management structure of the F-16 fighter aircraft, which is the largest of its kind ever undertaken, is an example of this particular element of the NIMO.

2.2.3 R&D and planning. Together with capital and management, research and development, as well as overall military planning, are significant driving forces behind world armament. R&D continuously add to the sophistication of military technology, making systems more and more rapidly obsolete and contribute, thus, to cost increases.

Various planning tools with various time horizons tend to fix military activities increasingly to non-military, non-security-related factors. This, again, makes for the possibility of over-reacting when facing 'real' threats.

These factors also contribute to lengthening the cycles of arms generations now taking five to ten years from development to phasing out, making it increasingly difficult to counteract armament projects efficiently.

2.2.4 Armament economics. This element is based on the idea – or rather experience – that more and more security and defence decisions are taken on the basis of economic considerations and less and less on actual security analyses.

System cost explosions, standardisation, saving of taxpayers' money, combating unemployment, acquiring the newest technology, offsetting balance of payments problems, civil spin-off effects, regional development potential and the survival of individual companies are all arguments exemplifying this trend.

Disarmament proposals are more often turned down on such economic grounds than on reasoning in terms of an endangered security position.

2.2.5 Arms interest integration. There is a rich variety of theories concerning armament 'complexes'; the main interests seem, however, to be the military, the industrialists, the bureaucrats and the scientists (MIBS). Each of them has a substantial interest in armament versus disarmament and they belong to the category of 'top dogs' in most social formations. As such, they possess the potential for monopolising security policies as well as the development, production and use of the means of destruction.[3]

2.3 Militarism

The catchword of this building block of the NIMO is the changing sociology of armament. While the two former blocks primarily represent reasonably visible phenomena, this one attempts to outline features of armament which are much less transparent – the structural 'roots'.

2.3.1 Civil-military isomorphism. The basic idea behind this conceptualisation of militarism is that of isomorphism between civil and military spheres of society – an idea expounded by such different writers as Nisbet, Galtung, Senghaas, Kaldor, Liebknecht, Engels and Abrahamsson.[4] Isomorphism suggests a fundamental, continuous correspondence between the two 'spheres' of society. In principle, the notion applies both to the national and the international level of analysis.

Thus we assume a basic correspondence between social, economic and political structures on the one hand and the way in which the society defends itself. Something like: 'Tell me which kind of society you are, and I shall tell you the general outline, at least, about your military apparatus and the character of the social forces which promote your ongoing armament!' It suggests that the two spheres reflect each other, that there is a structural similarity between *social formation and military formation* or, to stay within the base, between *poles of production and modes of destruction.*

In this way we attempt to avoid speaking of a mere military and civil 'sector' – which only signifies (often in statistics and political analysis) the result of the social forces behind armament and not the social forces themselves. The term 'sector' also gives the false impression that it is possible to draw a clear-cut line between what is civil and what is military. The point about 'sphere' is that this illusion is broken down, indicating that the same interests are often active in both civil and military activities – in changing alliances and with different caps on, so to speak.

It also indicates the intention here to speak of *structural causation* instead of merely relying upon a factor analysis. This is in harmony with the fact that there is no clear boundary between empirically distinguishable sectors, but rather a multitude of systems and actions relating in constantly varying ways to each other – in correspondence with the changes taking place in the social formation of society at large.

It may be argued here, however, that although there exists quite a number of social formations – or national orders – and different socio-political systems, we find a rather high degree of similarity among military systems and armament trends all over the world.

First of all, this may only seem to be so. Armed forces in a peripheral, capitalist and structurally underdeveloped nation do not automatically resemble those of an overdeveloped centre nation – neither do they serve the same functions. It may well be so, on the contrary, that there is a two-way process going on, leading to the increasing isomorphism mentioned.

On the one hand, there is the case where the civil sphere has the upper hand and is in the process of transforming and adapting the military – e.g. if there is an effective parliamentary control and a low-politicised military sphere or where the 'party is in command'.

On the other hand, one may imagine the case where the military sphere may have acquired the upper hand and attempts to transform and adapt the rest of society – as may be the case in some military regimes, in nations with armed forces of the new, so-called 'new professionalism', in extended civic action programmes or where external forces, through *coups d'état*, intervention or intelligence operations, succeed in installing a loyal regime beneficial to such external interests.

In these cases, militarism will not imply the same socio-military profile; *militarism will vary according to social formation, specific circumstances, history and level of overall development.*

The force at play – which should definitely not be ignored – is, of course, that centre nations (or interests) may have a constant interest in influencing peripheral societies for their own purposes. Thus, the transfer of technology – civil as well as military – will have substantial effects upon social structure. Only in this sense would it be meaningful to speak of a global military 'monoculture'.

Depending on the stage of development and the other factors mentioned, isomorphism will vary – in some social settings it may be stronger than others at a particular point of time. This does not invalidate the basic hypothesis that *isomorphism increases over time* – as an effect, one may add, of militarisation of the civil sphere and civilianisation of the military sphere. The point is that all nations, all social formations, may not have proceeded equally far in this process. Those having a high degree of isomorphism are likely to try to influence those at a lower level.

Finally, it deserves mention that the conceptualisation does *not* imply identity, but, as mentioned, similarity, affinity, mutual reflection. This is the reason that there is no adherence to, for example, a 'garrison state' model here.[5] The idea should help us to understand why a society may be militaristic although it is not experienced that way by the citizens. Militarism, especially in Western democracies, does not exhibit itself through large military parades, militaristic attitudes, charismatic military leaders or a militaristic education system, etc. *But it is there* – in a most sophisticated manner, less open, less transparent and less stamped on people's consciousness. If it wasn't there, these democracies would hardly be so over-armed or so deeply stuck with consuming ever more resources for armament – which has long ago stopped adding to security, but rather resembles the situation of a drug addict.

We shall now proceed to examine the concept of civil-military isomorphism itself.

Liebknecht should be quoted at some length, as he seems to have produced one of the oldest and still most fruitful points of departure for an understanding of militarism:

> Militarism is not specific to capitalism. It is moreover normal and necessary in every class-divided social order of which the capitalist system is the last. Capitalism, of course, like every class-divided social order, develops its own special variety of militarism; for militarism is by its essence a means to an end, or to several ends, which differ according to the kind of social order in question and which can be attained according to this difference in different ways.

and:

> A history of militarism in the deepest sense discloses the very essence of human development and its motive forces, and a dissection of capitalist militarism involves the disclosure of the most secret and least obvious roots of capitalism. The history of militarism is at the same time the history of the political, social, economic and, in general, the cultural relations of tensions between states and nations, as well as the history of the class struggles within individual states and national units.[6]

Thus militarism reflects social orders – there may be feudal, capitalist and socialist militarism (would Liebknecht agree today?).

It would be typical Western thinking to ask: What is the basic driving force behind militarism? To give such a cause would violate the idea expressed earlier of structural causation versus factor causation (or explanation). Anyhow, Liebknecht argues his case in favour of *division of labour* and the *role of technology*:

> The natural process of development is of course that the division into classes, which is the consequence of the economic-technical development, runs parallel with the cultivation of the technique of

> arms, including the fortification and strategy. The production of arms therefore becomes to an ever greater degree a professional skill. Further, since class domination as a rule is constituted precisely by the economic superiority of one class over another, and since the improvement of the technique of arms leads to the production of arms becoming ever more difficult and expensive, the production gradually becomes the monopoly of the economically dominant class. The physical basis of democracy is thus removed . . . The general and equal arming of the population only becomes a permanent and irreversible characteristic when the production of arms itself is in the hands of the people.[7]

and:

> In the lower cultures which know no division into classes the weapon serves as a rule also as a tool for work. It is at the same time a means of acquiring food (by hunting, by cultivation, etc.) and a means of protection against wild beasts and of defence against hostile tribes, as well as a means of attacking them. The weapon has such a primitive character that anyone can easily acquire it at any time (stones and sticks, spears with stone tips, bows, etc.) . . . If the lowest form of culture employs the weapon inside the community at most to settle individual conflicts, the situation changes when a division between classes appears together with a higher development in the technique of arms. The primitive communism of the lower agricultural peoples in which women were dominant knows no social and therefore normally also no political relation of class domination. Generally speaking, militarism does not occur.[8]

There are a number of important catchwords here – class domination, monopoly, technique of arms, a tool for work, etc. The general point to be brought out here seems to be that the structural similarity of spheres within total social formations evolved around technology as a main factor – but not the only one. The higher the level of sophistication, the larger the probability of division into classes and the likelihood that centre-periphery structures develop and – consequently – that the need for armament (especially within the dominant classes) emerges and starts gaining momentum, needing ever more armament, which again deepens social divisions, etc.

In other words, *mode of production determines mode of destruction – the focus being upon the production, distribution and use of the means of destruction*. It is pretty obvious, however, that technology should not be seen as an independent variable. As techniques develop – civil as well as military – so does social formation, and division into classes emerges or develops further.

Another dimension to be noted is the *internal/external* one; as pointed out by Leibknecht, militarism is at hand as well within states (the class struggle) as between states (the imperialist perspective), which Lenin has expressed in the following way:

> Contemporary militarism is the result of capitalism . . . In both its forms it is a 'vital manifestation' of capitalism: as a military force utilized by capitalist states in their external clashes . . . and as a weapon serving in the hands of the ruling classes to crush all (economic and political) proletarian movements . . .[9]

Following the idea of the close interaction between military and civil spheres – of militarism being a structural phenomenon – the question of course occurs: to what degree is militarism primarily *a function of the base* and to what degree *a function of the super-structure* of society? Engels here provides an insight:

> Militarism dominates and is swallowing Europe. But this militarism also bears within itself the seed of its own destruction . . . The second moral . . . is that the whole organization and method of warfare, and along with these victory or defeat, prove to be dependent on material, that is economic conditions

and:

> Nothing is more dependent on economic prerequisites than precisely army and navy. Armament, composition, organization, tactics and strategy depend above all on the stage reached at the time in production and in communication.[10]

At the same time as Engels emphasises the priority of the base in the armament process, he also – elsewhere – stresses that the military and the whole field of warfare activities belong to the superstructure. There is no effort here to try to 'solve' this problem. Our main point would be that one should not take for granted any kind of automatic change of superstructure as a consequence of changes in the base.

First of all, the material production for military purposes

substantially influences the economic base – especially in a number of Third World countries – and military technology is often ahead of civil technology – especially in the over-armed superpowers.

Second, one of the main issues (later to be taken up) is precisely the fact that the superstructure organisation – organisation for war preparation, military indoctrination, attitudes, politics, national interests, alliances with church, schools, etc. – may gain such influence *vis-à-vis* the civil sphere that one could maintain that 'superstructure functions as the base' – to borrow a perspective from the anthropologist Godelier – signifying the 'nation in arms'.[11]

The preliminary conclusion to be drawn concerning this dimension is the following: militarism cannot be understood simply by relying on the classics; it cannot be attributed exclusively to the superstructure as a 'cultural', attitudinal phenomenon – neither can it be automatically derived from the socio-economic base. Rather, warfare, the military sphere, the economics of armament exercise *such deep influences upon social formations at large that militarism as a structural phenomenon must be ascribed both the base and the superstructure*. As pointed out again and again by Nisbet:

> It would be possible to write the history of postmedieval western Europe in terms of what happened to the feudal military community and then to the whole military sector of Western society. Capitalism, nationalism, the territorialization of power as well as the centralization, large-scale organization, mass society, technology; all of these make their first appearance in the modern West in circumstances strongly characterized by war and the military. This fact has received far less attention from the historians than it deserves. Much that is said to have been caused by capitalism, nationalism, the middle class, and technology might better be thought of in terms of pressures for war and of a rapidly expanding military force in modern Europe.[12]

Thus, it is not sufficient to outline the characteristic of militarism simply from the base – although the isomorphism exists at this level, too. This kind of determinism should be avoided when meeting the extremely broad concept of militarism. Trying to do so anyway – leading to, among other things, a denial of any non-capitalist militarism – could be said to represent the major, classical mistake of the more or less Marxist-oriented school on militarism theories.

On the other side, of course, we find a number of liberal-oriented conceptualisations which, in general, tend to detach militarism from socio-economic structures and leave it entirely as a way of thinking, a reminiscence from pre-capitalist or pre-industrial periods, etc. – much like the whole discussion of imperialism between these two main schools around the turn of this century. Names of relevance here would be Vagts, Proudhon, Ferrero, Lee Bernhard, Hinze, Spencer, Miller, Radway and, more contemporarily, Radway, Eckhardt, Thee, Lumsden.[13]

An ideal combination of classical approaches may therefore be the following: the basic idea of isomorphism between civil and military structures is derived from primarily Marxist-oriented thinking, but – to avoid any kind of determinism or selectivity as to social formations which *can* be militaristic – we shall try to put much 'liberal' heritage into this framework on the following pages.

It remains to be mentioned that the military-civil isomorphism can be traced over time, i.e. that there is *a dimension of history* not to be forgotten.

The *feudal military structure* is characterised by the local decentralised activities of the knights and their warriors with large differences in terms of status and armament; it was a temporal affair in the sense that, when the fighting was over, the knight rode back to his castle and the warriors dispersed. It was based on relatively simple armoury and on men fighting face to face. The nobility had the monopoly of command, and, sometimes, also of the weapons.

The social hierarchy at that time reached from the serf who was tied to the land, over the feudal master of the estate – the basic economic unit – above which again we find the counts, dukes and, on top of it, the king and the Church; all were vertically related to each other through economic and military rights and duties.

Essentially, this formation represents an exchange between classes: the primary economic duty of the vassal to his superior and the protection he received in return.

In the towns, of course, other values were defended than in the countryside – trade, markets, roads and cities with their handicraft. The burghers found out that the 'reserve army' coming into town from the countryside could be employed to fight for them as *mercenaries* or soldiers (*solidus* = heavy coin), organised by the war entrepreneurs – the *condottieri*. In Germany, for instance, the system of princes and war lords having colonels to organise regiments for them of 'Landsknechte' was fully developed around 1500.

But technology enters the picture; as Kaldor has pointed out, 'it took the introduction of mercenary soldiers, financed by the new bourgeoisie on behalf of the emerging absolute monarchy, before guns – the products of bourgeois technology – could be accepted into the armed forces'.[14]

Vagts, in his classical *A History of Militarism*, has the following to say about the transition to the formation of *merchant capitalism*:

> With the introduction of artillery, the antagonism of bourgeois and noble increased. The devices were the products of urban arts and crafts; they resulted from the economic, social and intellectual changes that disintegrated feudalism and were manufactured by the foes of feudalism – the city bourgeois and the artisans. In a strict sense, gunpowder, muskets and cannons did not 'smash feudalism'; plebeian foot soldiers without firearms had already beaten chivalric bodies before their introduction; moreover, the last feudal armies had themselves employed guns . . . the weapons themselves were the fruit of a long period of development in which urban independence was growing and money-economy spreading, challenging the old social system based on soil. Artillery was made and introduced, however, by antifeudal classes, it is true, and it remained in bourgeois hands henceforth.[15]

In other words, technology is introduced at the same time as social formation at large is changing fundamentally. It implies a transfer of the means of destruction from one class to another, an enlargement of armies, and increasing need for knowledge and skills, an increasing mercenarisation and – in general – a trend towards professionalisation.

However, in the same way as the warfare system may indicate fundamental future changes in social formations – not least through the development of new military techniques – there are also indications of its ability to sustain outmoded social groups. In this period, the bourgeois did not want to be soldiers nor to lead the soldiers it bought. That was still the task of the now otherwise rather redundant nobility:

> Although the bourgeois left the direction of war to the princes, the princes did not themselves control their armies in the beginning: rather they contracted with private entrepreneurs for the collection, organization, disciplining and feeding of forces. Thus the bourgeois financed wars they did not start – kings started wars they did not fully manage.[16]

The nobility did not rely on education but on social status, but gradually they were forced to enter the military academies which were set up during the latter half of the eighteenth century.

The next phase is represented by the increasing *nation-state formation* and *nationalisation of warfare.* It is excellently described by Nisbet in the following manner:

> But *Gemeinschaft* in war is succeeded everywhere in the West by *Gesellschaft*; that is, by increasing use of the wage system (even the economic-oriented Karl Marx wrote that the wage system in the strict sense began in the modern West with the military), by ever-larger social units of war – national armies instead of feudal militias, by a constantly improved technology along with a constantly improved system of military accounting in matters of supplies and weapons, and finally by all the attributes of secularism, impersonality, and contractualism that were later to be found in almost all parts of Western society . . . the passage of Western warfare, beginning in the late Middle Ages, from traditional Gemeinschaft character to a Gesellschaft one is scarcely less than a preview of a similar passage to be observed in economy, polity, and many other areas of society.[17]

This kind of development put increasing demand upon society's resources at the national level. Centralisation, bureaucratisation and specialisation became central features. Again there was an interplay with the factor of technology, and from around the French Revolution it is probably correct to speak of the *industrialisation of warfare* – parallel with changes of the overall social formation towards modern industrial capitalism.

The idea is to rely exclusively upon mass conscription and mass-produced weapons – making warfare economically cheaper but much more costly in terms of casualties. With more complicated weaponry go larger wars, a need for higher education and training, much more emphasis upon logistics and a substantial reliance upon resources of the whole society. The main group benefiting from this particular stage were the capitalists producing the weapons as well as the general supplies. With rising levels of the means of destruction go, furthermore, the organisational differentiation as well as overall planning. A new type of officer appears on the stage – *the military manager* – expert and highly professionalised.

From now on, warfare becomes rapidly more capital-intensive

needing relatively fewer and fewer people to service the weapons systems and needing more and more for 'software' occupations and infrastructural development.

Abrahamsson has summarised well the emerging stage of *totalisation of warfare* which dates back to the beginning of this century:

> Today, the enormous expansion of the logistic functions of armed forces *has made the military establishment almost a replica of civilian society*. Further, the invention of the aeroplane and, later, the ballistic missile created a new concept – total warfare. Total warfare brought total defence; this, in turn, meant closer integration between the military and civilian sectors.[18]

In other words, the total warfare trend contributed to *militarisation of the civilian society* and, at the same time, the structural similarity between the two spheres increases. The other side of the coin, of course, is *civilianisation of the military* – a trend which, as pointed out by Abrahamsson, signifies integration, but at the same time also fertilises the ground for a dangerous autonomy of the military *vis-à-vis* the rest of society. To grasp the implication of this feature, one may speak of an *asymmetric integration* which is increasingly characterised by the military sphere acting as a 'centre' while the rest of society serves as its 'periphery'. Abrahamsson expresses it in this way (borrowing from Janowitz):

> Thus, it is not only the case that some such tasks have civilian counterparts but, more importantly, the military establishment *as a whole* shows a notable similarity with civilian society. Military training and practice today give the military elite the experience and managerial expertise to run something which is, with few functions excepted, a replica of civilian society . . .[19]

The military runs legal systems, education, communication, transport systems, health services, engineering, etc., and contributes to infrastructural development and, more often than not, influences overall political management. Through this 'taking over' of civil functions, the military sphere has become more and more self-sustaining and independent *vis-à-vis* civilian society, while the latter has become still less able to survive without a huge military apparatus – for economic, political, social and so-called security reasons:

> The only functions which are not readily included into the military organizational structure are, first, production of base materials like iron, coal, oil, textile fibres and grain; and, secondly, the reproduction of men. Were it not for these basic needs, military society could exist entirely on its own.[20]

And he might have added, 'as long as the civilian society is willing to pay for its own subordination', i.e. as long as it is politically accepted that the military sphere exploit ever-larger civil resources in order to deliver a product called security, while *civil society is rapidly losing every kind of inner strength and non-military defence capacity*.

It is a tragic fact that this short summary of the history of civil-military isomorphism points to the following conclusion: with the totalisation of warfare we also face a fundamental *de-democratisation*. It is so excellently expressed by Reynolds that his account will round off this section:

> The nuclear powers are bound together in a system which virtually ensures reciprocal strikes in the event of any one state taking a nuclear initiative. Communications between nuclear powers have been developed in order to preserve some element of choice in crisis situations. Never have potentially belligerent states been so closely linked in terms of communication.
>
> The point here is that the political element is removed from this area of decision and is insulated from domestic politics. *Public opinion and the political process* can only have influence on the question of capacity, that is, on expenditure during the initial stages of defence policy. *Once a nuclear capacity exists then they become irrelevant*. Thus the possibility of nuclear war and the nature of a nuclear strike *remove the area of foreign policy and national security more completely from national politics* than ever before.[21]

2.3.2 Military monopoly. The idea of a military 'radical monopoly' is, of course, borrowed from Illich, who defines it in this way – although only in relation to the civil sphere:

> The establishment of radical monopoly happens when people give up their native ability to do what they can do for themselves and for each other, in exchange for something 'better' that can be done for them by a major tool. Radical monopoly reflects the industrial

> institutionalization of values. It substitutes the standard package for the personal response . . . Against this radical monopoly people need protection . . . The cost of radical monopoly is already borne by the public and will be broken only if the public realizes that it would be better off paying the costs of ending the monopoly than by continuing to pay for its maintenance.[22]

Illich does not mention the military, but there is hardly any doubt that it fits into this conceptualisation. It has succeeded in taking the security and means of security out of the hands of people and – with the over-armament we are facing today – the people need protection against this monopoly because it increases insecurity.

But there is a terrible difference – the military radical monopoly holds the power to exterminate all living things on Earth and leave us with a nuclear desert. In this sense, the military radical monopoly is the most dangerous of all; therefore, no institution or individual, no single nation and no ministry should be given the sole responsibility for the actions of such a monopoly.

The monopoly has *deprived people of much*: the right to define their own security, the opportunity to develop local defence measures as well as the opportunity of choice concerning the means to satisfy their security needs. Likewise, people at large have been deprived of the control over development, production, distribution and use of weapons.

Of course, it may be asked: how is it that people have tolerated this monopoly by an alliance of elites concerning their own security? One explanation is given by Lang:

> The monopoly that the military claim over military expertise has naturally thrust them in their capacity as technical advisors into important policy roles. Since the military sense a strong identification between their own professional commitments and the national interest, disputes inevitably arise over how much say they or civilians should have over certain national security matters.[23]

This *identification of elite interests with national interests and security* is of primary importance – employed as it is by the military, the industrialists, the bureaucrats and the scientists (MIBS). However, it is only possible to exercise this monopoly if there is: (a) a sufficient amount of information or propaganda material issued from the military sphere; if (b) the general popular knowledge concerning military matters is low in comparison with that of the monopoly; and (c) that alternative security and defence concepts and policies are virtually non-existing – i.e. that the *status quo* of pact membership, high technology, modernisation and enemy images are presented as the constants of the only possible policy.

In other words, the managers of the military sphere must seek *to narrow the political battlefield* and have the discussion taking place on their territory – employing the old Clausewitzian idea that defence (in this case the military sphere) has superiority through choosing the mode of the struggle.

Thus there is a fundamental difference between accepting the military because it is found right, and accepting it because it is found right – through socialisation, indoctrination, mass media and experts' work – to accept the military as it is. 'Ex-doctrination' and much consciousness-raising may certainly be needed to change the most traditional military security thinking among people at large. The 'military-mind' installed in much popular thinking would then be broken up, too.[24]

It is certainly not enough to show, as we have attemped to here, the structural similarity between the civil and the military sphere; neither to maintain that the military has acquired a monopoly position over the parts of human life which have to do with security.

We would also have to take a closer look at the *interaction between the two spheres*. Formerly, we have argued that much of the tendency towards militarism is signified by the increasing civilianisation of the military and militarisation of the civil sphere, i.e. a deeper and more fundamental *integration*. On the one side, the military sphere has become more dependent upon the civil resources and skills; on the other, civil society is now more dependent for its security and would be virtually left vulnerable and helpless if general and complete disarmament arrived tomorrow.

Thus the aggressive potential of the military sphere has increased beyond human imagination, while the defensive capacity, the inner strength and cohesiveness of societies have rapidly declined. The only appropriate term for this is *asymmetrical integration* – suggesting an element of exploitation by the military sphere of the civil society around it, a type of 'internal imperialism'. This is, indeed, one of the results of the increasing structural similarity of the mutual adaptation over time.

To examine this idea a bit more, let's make use of an *interaction budget* and ask: who benefits from what? The first thing to do would be to try to assess the flows of resources from the military sphere to the civil and the other way around.

What seems to be happening is that the civil sphere contributes more and more and receives less and less. A tremendous amount of resources are poured into the military sphere with hardly any positive effect upon security. Rather, it may actually be more precise to state *that never before could so many people feel so insecure with so much weaponry.* In other words, here – as with energy, capital, raw materials, manpower, medicine – the value added by one unit more of resource investment decreases or turns negative. The system is becoming less and less able to handle resource investments in an effective manner – while at the same time 'needing' still more, in this case, for its security. The quality of the throughput is declining, and in consequence society is not only facing *the 'poverty of power'* in terms of energy, but also in terms of its security policy.

2.3.3 Social vulnerability. The idea behind this third dimension of militarism is easily understood by means of a very simple dichotomisation which makes us come out with the *typology of threats* of Table 3.2. It will immediately be clear that the main security interest is related to *type I.* Of military expenditures in total it is not unusual that 95-98 – if not 100 – per cent is poured into purely military defence measures. Depending on the overall social setting these measures may be directed primarily towards external threats or primarily towards internal threats (type II).

Table 3.2: A Typology of Threats

	External	Internal
Military/violent	I International warfare	II Civil war
Civil/non-violent	III Economic warfare	IV Social warfare

Type II threats are exemplified by revolts, guerrilla warfare, liberation movements which are obviously considered threats to centres – but not necessarily to the people. *Terrorism* may also be placed here with specific reference to a number of overdeveloped Western societies which have proved virtually unable to deal with this security challenge in a meaningful way.

Type III threats have to do with pressures from outside which are not military or directly violent. It may be the threat experienced during an oil crisis, the threat from certain nations running an economic war or boycott of one's products, it may be the threat experienced from global economic problems or that perceived through the demand for a New International Economic Order which – if properly realised – is likely to cause rather fundamental changes within the centre economies and demand that they become more self-reliant instead of exploitative.

Here there are *no threats against territory*, rather against a life-style, against a structure, against a culture and – in the final analysis – against an historical stage of a particular social formation. It will hit countries which are highly other-reliant particularly hard – nations which are especially dependent upon trade and mobility of production factors in large economic cycles and it will hit those nations which are increasingly unable to satisfy the basic human needs of their population by means of their own resources. For national as well as international peripheries (whether in economic or military matters) the solution may very well be to withdraw from the interaction and extend collective self-reliance.

Type IV threats are exemplified by the increase in *social problems* within societies. It may be centralisation (of people, capital, transport, communication) which increases vulnerability – according to traditional centre-oriented strategic thinking. It may be that ever more people are pacified, that commitment and creativity are not needed as much as before, or it may be a sign of social disintegration – like criminality, corruption, decreasing health standards, lack of value orientation, decreasing social solidarity, individualism, pollution, lack of general happiness, etc. It may be the situation where an increasing number of social groupings are left idle, superfluous – in other words, the society which faces the consequences of a deep economic crisis where system maintenance cannot be taken for granted any more.

To summarise this point of militarism, it is probably true to say that the maldeveloped, militaristic society keeps on accumulating military means to meet threats of type I and, to a certain low degree, type II. While it grows increasingly vulnerable socially and insecure militarily, threats are misperceived, the military sphere becomes ever more powerful and civil society is left torn apart, defenceless and fundamentally threatened. The point is well stated by Huddle:

> National security requires a stable economy with assured supplies of materials for industry. In this sense, frugality and conservation of materials are essential to our national security. Security means more than safety from hostile attack; it includes the preservation of a system of civilization.[25]

2.3.4 Insecurity. It will hardly surprise anyone that militarism embraces the feature of insecurity – apart from the idea of structural similarity, military monopoly and social vulnerability. The NIMO as such increases human insecurity, as we have already touched upon.

This point is by no means new – but it deserves mention again. Even in 1916, the historian Edward Krehbiel wrote in his most visionary and well documented study, *Nationalism, War and Society*:

> It is to be noted that the cost of insuring peace by competitive armaments has in the last decade risen very rapidly and out of proportion to the increase in population, wealth or prosperity. If armaments insured peace all nations should be more secure than formerly. On the contrary *no nation feels one whit more secure*. Even if a nation outruns all competitors it gains no security, as fear impels other nations to make new alliances which change the balance of power . . . Thus uncertainty, suspicion and fear are abroad and are subject to the exploitation of the unscrupulous.[26]

And a modern analysis by Reynolds substantiates this view in the following way:

> Thus all statesmen prepare for the eventuality of war, and the history of the nation-state has also been the history of warfare. War thus appears not as abnormal but as being pre-eminently normal in international politics. However, the paradox which makes this apparently sensible policy create the condition which it most wishes to avoid *stems from the notion of security*.* Security only exists when a state possesses the capacity to fight successful wars against any potential aggressor, and defence policy is concerned in the main with relative military *capacities* and not the *intentions* of other nations. Clearly, if all nations share this concern then *the result is a condition of permanent insecurity in the world.**
>
> To refer to a point made earlier, the central problem is that one state's security is another state's insecurity. The consequence is a competition between states which takes the form of arms races,

> treaties for mutual defence, and social and economic preparation for war, *which can only be finally resolved by war itself*.* In attempting to achieve security the nation-states of the world succeed instead in creating anarchy and violence. Yet war can decide the question of national security or, to be more precise, *which* nation is secure, only if that nation succeeds once and for all in *monopolising violence in the world, in the same way as its government has monopolised violence within the state*.*
>
> In theory, security can be achieved through world hegemony or empire, or by creation of a one world state. None of these possibilities has been realised. No state has ever won a war, for victories and defeats have never been total. The end of every war has been the beginning of another power stuggle [*italics added].[27]

Reynolds has been quoted here at some length because few analyses express the features of what could properly be called the *security crisis* of the world system so well. It is a problem in which all nations share a part.[28]

What is not explicitly stated above is the fact that this security crisis naturally violates *human security* – a circumstance which reflects the fact that 'security' is almost exclusively thought of in terms of 'national security'. Thus, security – in this field – is never seen as *a basic human need*, which may very well be one reason why there is so little popular debate and protest against the armament developments in general. It may be added that other means of controlling the populations are also influencing human life today – although of a more civil orientation they are often managed by military, paramilitary or intelligence apparatuses as well illustrated by LeMond and Fry, Ackroyd *et al.* and Hedrick Smith.[29] In other words, national security may no longer be *able* to deliver the goods, it may no longer be the *purpose* of it; rather it seems that a substantial part of all security investments are directed *against* the people. The world of 1984 may thus be closer than is realised.

Notes

1. The estimate of the number of people killed in wars stems from Milton Leitenberg, R. Kalish and D. Lombardi, *A Survey of Studies of Post W.W. II Wars, Conflicts and Military Coups* (Cornell University, Ithaca, New York, 1977), p. 1. Concerning the number of wars since 1945, see Istvan Kende, 'Wars of Ten Years', *Journal of Peace Research*, no. 3 (1978).

2. I am particularly indebted to Johan Galtung, with whom many of the ideas in this essay have been developed during my participation in the World Indicators Program at Oslo University. I am also grateful to Dieter Senghaas for discussion and much help during two research visits to Frankfurt. Being a part of the research programme of the Department of Peace and Conflict Research at the University of Lund, I am happy to thank Håkan Wiberg for much good advice through several years.

3. There exists a very large literature on the so-called military-industrial complex and related conceptualisations; for an overview which applies the concept to both East and West – although with various contents and proliferation – see Steven Rosen, *Testing the Theory of the Military-Industrial Complex* (Lexington Books, D.C. Heath, Massachusetts, 1973).

4. See, e.g., R. Nisbet, *The Social Philosophers* (Paladin, Herts, 1976), Chapter 1, pp. 21-100 for an excellent historical account of the use of this idea; Galtung in a forthcoming book from the World Indicators Program (WIP); D. Senghaas in his *Abschreckung und Frieden. Studien zur Kritik organisierter Friedlosigkeit* (Fischer Taschenbuch Verlag, Frankfurt am Main, 1972), touches upon the idea of isomorphism in the use of the concept of 'organized peacelessness'. It is also penetrating the same author's *Weltwirtschaftsordnung und Entwicklungspolitik. Plädoyer für Dissoziation* (Suhrkamp, 1977) (see especially Chapter 9, pp. 223-61 on the New International Military Order – here borrowed by the author); Senghaas' article, 'Military Dynamics in the Context of Periphery Capitalism' in *Bulletin of Peace Proposals*, vol. 8, no. 2 (1977) also deserves mention here.

M. Kaldor, 'The Military in Development' in *World Development*, no. 6 (1976) (especially p. 467), and in 'The Significance of Military Technology' in *Bulletin of Peace Proposals*, vol. 8, no. 2 (1977); Liebknecht, *Militarism and Anti-Militarism* (1907) (Rivers Press, Cambridge, 1973); F. Engels, *Anti-Dühring* (Lawrence and Wishart, London, and Progress Publishers, Moscow, 1975), especially Part II, Chapters II-IV.

The idea of isomorphism is also strongly present in B. Abrahamsson, *Military Professionalization and Political Power* (Sage Publications, Beverley Hills, 1972).

5. See H.D. Lasswell, 'The Garrison State Hypothesis Today' in S.P. Huntington (ed.), *Changing Pattern of Military Politics* (Free Press of Glencoe, Glencoe, 1962), pp. 51-71.

6. Liebknecht, *Militarism and Anti-Militarism*, pp. 17 and 9.

7. Ibid., pp. 11-12.

8. Ibid., pp. 12-13.

9. From Milovidov and Kozlov, *Problems of Contemporary War* (Moscow, 1972), p. 65. Notice that Lenin sees capitalism as the *only* militaristic social order and as a 'weapon' – not as a structural phenomenon pertaining to various social orders throughout history. This makes Lenin's conceptualisation much more limited than the other mentioned above.

10. Engels, *Anti-Dühring*, pp. 204-5 and 200.

11. See M. Godelier, *Bas och överbyggnad* (Norstedts/Pan, Stockholm, 1975), pp. 16-21 and 55-7.

12. Nisbet, *The Social Philosophers*, pp. 63-4.

13. *Proudhon* was probably the first to use the word 'militarism' (in 1864) to describe 'Das Heer-wesen eines monarkish und zentralistisch regierten Staates sowie die damit verbundenen Finanzlasten' (here quoted from the excellent anthology by Volker Berghahn, *Militarismus* (Kiepenheuer and Witsch, Koln, 1975, p. 10). Berghahn also notes that the word was found in a German dictionary in 1870, defined as 'das Vorherrschen und die Bevorzugung des Soldatenwesens' (ibid., p. 10). There is a clearly *liberal-oriented tradition or school* on militarism; *Guglielmo Ferrero* in his *Militarism* from 1902 (Garland Publishing, New York, 1972) defines militarism in relation to war which serves (a) to provide civilisations with sufficient capital and bring it into circulation and thus imparting new life to decadent societies, (b) to accumulate land and (c) to secure a supply of slaves in the ancient world.

Hirtze in 1904 related militarism to feudalism and, where it existed in his time, it was considered 'a feudal reminiscence' (see Berghahn, *Militarismus*, p. 13). This draws closely upon *Herbert Spencer's* distinction between the warfare-oriented society and the industrial society. These two could have nothing in common. This is also the view of the American liberal *Joseph Miller*, according to whom 'the military spirit is always on the side of reaction – always allied with the non-progressive and anti-liberal movements of the time' (quoted by Berghahn, *Militarismus*, pp. 12-13). *Lee Bernhard* in his *War and its Causes from 1944* (Garland Publishing, New York and London, 1972) defined militarism as

> that personal attitude and collective practice which develops in connection with a highly organized and self-conscious profession or arms, whether it actually dominates society or merely seeks to do so. It looks upon the military as the most important and essential phase of the total social organization and regards all government as in the last analysis necessarily dependent upon military support and control (p. 91).

In his famous work, *A History of Militarism* (Hollis and Carter, London, 1959), *Alfred Vagts* distinguishes between the 'military way' which he perceives as a specific concentration of military strength to achieve a clearly defined goal in an effective manner, limited in scope and time, and, on the other hand, 'militarism', which he sees as customs, interests, prestige, etc., associated with wars and military actions which transcend any true military purpose and permeate all corners of society for its own irrational purpose (p. 13).

Of the more recent conceptualisations, *S.P. Huntington's* description of *civil-military relations* should be mentioned (David Sills (ed.), *International Encyclopedia of the Social Sciences*, vol. 2 (Macmillan and the Free Press, London, 1968)) together with *Laurence I. Radway*, who defines militarism as

> a doctrine or system that values war and accords primacy in state and society to the armed forces. It exalts a function – the application of violence – and an institutional structure – the military establishment. It implies both a *policy* orientation and a *power* relationship (David Sills (ed.), *International Encyclopedia of the Social Sciences*, vol. 10 (Macmillan and the Free Press, London, 1968, pp. 300-4).

The World Council of Churches in a recent *Report of the Consultation on Militarism* (Glion, Switzerland, November 1977) distinguishes between *militarisation* 'as the process whereby military values, ideology and patterns of behaviour achieve a dominating influence on the political, social, economic and external affairs of the State' and *militarism* as 'one of the more perturbing results of this process' (p. 3).

William Eckhardt, in an article titled 'The Causes and Correlates of Western militarism', maintains that

> militarism as an attitude, then, is the readiness or willingness to engage in behaviours which have been authorized and institutionalized by a government for the purpose of using or threatening to use destructive weapons against the people and property of another nation, or even against the people (but seldom the property) of one's own nation (paper presented at the Pugwash Symposium on Militarism and National Security, Oslo, November 1977, p. 2).

In his article, 'Militarism and Militarization in Contemporary International Relations' in *Bulletin of Peace Proposals*, vol. 8, no. 4 (1977), *Marek Thee* has the following broad collection of symptoms:

> Under the term 'militarism' I subsume such symptoms as a rush to armaments, the growing role of the military (understood as the military establishment) in national and international affairs, the use of force as an instrument of prevalence and political power, and the increasing influence of the military in civilian affairs. Seen from this angle, militarism has indeed become a global phenomenon. I understand 'militarization' as being the extension of military influence to civilian spheres, including economic and socio-political life (p. 1).

Finally, it should be mentioned that *Malvern Lumsden* has recently attempted to distinguish clearly between militarism and militarisation. He defines militarism as 'the military exploitation of "mythology" in order to "legitimise" the expropriation of surplus for illegitimate microparasitic purposes' (Militarism – Cultural Dimension of Militarisation', paper presented at the above-mentioned Pugwash Symposium). Thus he links militarism to the superstructure and militarisation to the socio-economic base.

These conceptualisations – no matter how different they otherwise are – closely resemble the liberal-oriented way in which the concept of imperialism was formerly treated, i.e. as something alien to capitalism as such but primarily serving as 'reminiscences' or as 'attitudes' or 'ways of thinking' (the military mind, etc.). They are, in this respect, in sharp opposition to most Marxist-oriented conceptualisations which, on their side, are extremely limited in seeing militarism as pertaining to only one social formation.

14. M. Kaldor, 'The Significance of Military Technology', *Bulletin of Peace Proposals*, vol. 8, no. 2 (1977).

15. Vagts, *A History of Militarism*, pp. 44-5.

16. Ibid., p. 47.

17. Nisbet, *The Social Philosophers*, p. 65.

18. Abrahamsson, *Military Professionalization and Political Power*, p. 23 (italics added).

19. Ibid., pp. 35-6.

20. Ibid., p. 36.

21. Charles Reynolds, *Theory and Explanation in International Politics* (Martin Robertson, London, 1973), pp. 210-11.

22. I. Illich, *Tools for Conviviality* (Harper and Row, New York, 1975), pp. 58-60.

23. Kurt Lang, 'Military' in David L. Sills (ed.), *International Encyclopedia of Social Science*, vol. 9 (Macmillan and the Free Press, London, 1968).

24. See, for example, Abrahamsson, *Military Professionalization and Political Power*, pp. 81-129, for an account of the 'military mind'.

25. Franklin P. Huddle, director of the US Congressional study, *Science,*

Technology and American Diplomacy, is here quoted in Lester R. Brown, *Redefining National Security*, Worldwatch Paper 14 (October 1977) of the Worldwatch Institute, Washington (p. 41).

26. Edward Krehbiel, *Nationalism, War and Society* (1916) (Macmillan/ Garland Publishing, New York, 1973), p. 48 (italics added).

27. Reynolds, *Theory and Explanation in International Politics*, pp. 178-9. See also the UN study on the *Economic and Social Consequences of the Armaments Race and of Military Expenditures* (United Nations, New York, 1977).

28. The reader should also be referred to Reynolds's analysis of the territorial vulnerability built into strategic doctrines and the nuclear hostage function which the non-nuclear nations in Europe play. See, for example, pp. 184-6 – an aspect which has been dealt with in detail by Alva Myrdal in *The Game of Disarmament* (Pantheon, New York, 1976).

29. See Alan LeMond and Ron Fry, *No Place to Hide* (St Martin's Press, New York, 1975); C. Ackroyd, K. Margolis, J. Rosenhead and T. Shallice, *The Technology of Political Control* (Penguin, Harmondsworth, Middlesex, 1977); and Hedrick Smith, *The Russians* (Sphere Books, London, 1973) for numerous examples of the violation of human integrity, privacy and rights within different social settings.

PART III

MEANING OF MILITARISM

4 MILITARISM, ITS DIMENSIONS AND COROLLARIES: AN ATTEMPT AT CONCEPTUAL CLARIFICATION*

Kjell Skjelsbæk

1 Introduction

The news media today are replete with accounts of military *coups d'état*, deployment of new weapons systems, advances of military technology, new forms of military-industrial co-operation, militant nationalism, etc. Politicians, scholars and others are becoming more attentive to, puzzled by and occasionally worried about the strength of military concerns and interests in our societies. There is every reason to be alarmed by the speedy growth of the military sector in most countries, a large number of them being poor, and by the increase in destructive capability everywhere.

These phenomena are regularly referred to as 'militarism', a term 'thoroughly pejorative in tone' (Erickson and Mommsen, 1973, p. 436). The term militarism seems to have gained currency in political debate. It is applied to a growing number of phenomena and situations. Obviously, the term can be applied to discredit political opponents. Then it is regularly linked to other negative words like authoritarianism, xenophobia, imperialism, etc. But the term 'militarism' is also used sometimes as an explanatory concept. For instance, a war is supposed to have been the result of the militarism of country x, or of the competing militarisms of two adversaries. The propagandistic and the scientific usages of the term are not necessarily contradictory. A scholar should not avoid calling a spade a spade.

On the other hand, value-loaded and diffuse terms seldom make good analytical tools. The emotional content invites political quarrel rather than scholarly discourse. Vagueness and generality cause

* This study is derived from my response to a letter from the Commission of the Churches on International Affairs (CCIA) of the World Council of Churches. At its Fifth General Assembly in November-December 1975 several delegates voiced the opinion that the churches should devote more attention to the perils of modern militarism. The letter from the CCIA posed the question: what do peace researchers mean by militarism? This paper contains my personal thoughts. However, I am grateful for comments on earlier drafts from Ulrich Albrecht, Marek Thee and Jan Øberg, and from students participating in a seminar at the Department of Political Science at the University of Oslo. The paper is identifiable as PRIO-publication S-5/79.

misunderstanding. Therefore, one could reasonably argue that terms like *militarism* should be deleted from the scientific vocabulary. Instead one should develop neutral terms, less general and less susceptible to varying and possibly contradictory interpretations.

In practice, it is impossible to do without broad and popular political terms like militarism, democracy, imperialism, etc. Replacements are artificial and impede communication between the scientific community and people at large. It should also be noted that some of the opposition to using loaded, political terms is based on an old-fashioned concept of 'value-free, objective social science'. When this concept is rejected, it is easier to accept 'militarism' as a useful and challenging term. A value-conscious scientist focuses attention on desirable and undesirable aspects of society. Therefore he cannot avoid using loaded, political terms. Problems exist, but assigning artificial terms for the sake of objectivity has little meaning.

The second argument against using the term *militarism* carries greater weight. The term is very diffuse, it is defined in a variety of ways in the literature, and it is often used interchangeably with similar terms like 'militarisation' or 'militarised'. It is like a big bag into which one can put a number of 'bads' – militaristic thinking, the arms race, militant chauvinism, the military-industrial complex, military juntas, gunboat diplomacy, etc. From one point of view it is unreasonable to subsume all these different things under the same heading. An indiscriminate use of the term 'militarism' causes confusion. It refers to a problem area so enormous that we are forced to split it up and define sub-categories before it can be meaningfully applied in theoretical models.

Despite these problems, the term is still regularly used in the singular and without modifiers. It seems that the reason for this is to be found in one attribute shared by all the phenomena mentioned above: their relationship to the military. They are consequences of the existence of a military establishment. Although they are qualitatively different, they are linked to each other through the presence of the military. It is therefore possible and meaningful to analyse and discuss them together and to explore their direct and indirect relationships to one another.

We agree with those (e.g. Albrecht, 1977, p. 124) who maintain that a universal definition of militarism is likely to be meaningless. No brief sentence could cover all the different consequences of military which possibly could be called *militarism* while effectively excluding those things which should not be given that name. There are important differences in time and place. Militarism in industrialised countries is different from that in traditional societies. Soviet militarism is significantly different from French militarism, etc. In addition, there are of course ideological discussions about the definitions and understanding of militarism at a particular time and at a particular place.

Although a universal definition of militarism is likely to be meaningless, this does not render the term totally without heuristic and scientific value. Many terms frequently used by social scientists do not meet the criteria of having universally meaningful definitions.[1] They have survived nevertheless because they are indispensable. The term *militarism* belongs to this category. It serves a function by pointing to the propensity of the military for creating problems and causing damage. It can be used as a general reference to these phenomena just as the word cancer is applied to a number of different but related diseases.

The purpose of this article, then, is not to define militarism. Our objective is more modest: we shall attempt to present some of the more important aspects of modern militarism. It will be seen as a set of 'diseases', and we shall take a look at the symptoms. We do not proceed to the more ambitious task, namely to explain how different forms of militarism emerge (Senghaas, 1977, p. 103), but there will be causal references in this volume to explanatory theories. Our objective is this: to try to list some of the more important elements of that which should be explained. This will be done after a brief presentation of some of the definitions of militarism found in the literature.

2 A Preliminary Discussion of Terms and Concepts

Like the term imperialism *militarism* gained currency as a political slogan in the anti-Bonapartist polemics of republicans and socialists in France under the Second Empire (Erickson and Mommsen, 1973, p. 436). The term military is much older, of course.[2]

It will be useful for our purposes to distinguish between two different usages of the term military. *First*, the term can be used in a technical, legal sense, pertaining to uniformed personnel in the armed forces. This definition seems simple, but is not without problems. Different countries have different traditions of classifying supportive personnel as either military or civilian.[3] The problem becomes acute in war because of the very different legal status of uniformed and non-uniformed combatants.

Second, we shall take a look at Lang's more sociological definition. He writes that

> as a sociological category, the term 'military' implies an acceptance of organized violence as a legitimate means for realizing social objectives. Military organizations, it follows, are structures for the co-ordination of activities meant to ensure victory in the battlefield (Lang, 1968, p. 305).

The organised and legitimate use of violence is the essence of this definition.

The legal and the sociological definitions are not necessarily congruent with each other. There are groups and institutions which are military in the first sense, but not in the second, and vice versa.

Thus there are many countries in which some military units have significant, if not predominant, civilian functions. (The term civilian is defined here as the opposite of military in the sociological sense, i.e. as an adjective meaning 'not pertaining to organised violence'.) A coastguard can be an organisational unit within the navy, but its functions are to a large extent civilian. Military units in some areas are frequently charged with responsibilities for disaster relief, etc. The United Nations Peace-Keeping Forces are expected to perform police and humanitarian functions and to use arms only in self-defence. These examples indicate how military forces can be 'civilianised' and given non-violent functions. It would be useful if plans for the civilianisation of the military were included in schemes for disarmament.

On the other hand, some units and organisations which do not administratively and legally belong to the military establishment may nevertheless have military functions. We are faced with the problem of drawing a line between those who actually do the killing and those who have a supportive function, the chauffeur of an armed vehicle, the cook who prepares food for the troops, the engineer who designs the submarine. As mentioned already, in different societies there are different legal classifications of personnel doing essentially the same things. The problem of drawing a line between military and civilian is made difficult by the close integration of the military in society at large. An operational definition of military and civilian cannot be made without a large measure of arbitrariness.

Lang's definition is so general that it covers police forces in many countries. Some sections of the police force are often trained for large-scale violence against terrorists, striking workers and students, rebellious farmers and ethnic groups, etc., depending on the local circumstances. The militarisation of police forces is a problem to which peace researchers should pay more attention.

While police violence is supposedly legitimate, there are two other kinds of organisations which could be regarded as military, but whose legitimacy is contested. The armed, political – primarily fascist – groups in many European countries in the inter-war period are examples of one type. Frightening and intimidating the population was one of the main functions of the Italian and German Blackshirts and Brownshirts. They did this both before and after the establishment of Fascist governments in these countries.[4] Similar groups are active in some countries today.

National liberation movements constitute another type of war-fighting organisations whose legitimacy is contested. Their aim is to gain undisputed political power within a territory. They are in many instances well organised and can become a difficult match for regular troops.

The subsequent discussion of militarism bases itself on a sociological rather than a legal/administrative understanding of the military, as we bear in mind the difficulties often involved in making clear distinctions between the terms 'military' and 'civilian'.

3 Some Definitions of Militarism

3.1 The Western, Liberal Tradition

In his classic study of the history of militarism, Vagts wrote that

> militarism has connoted a domination of the military over the civilian, an undue preponderance of military demands, and emphasis on military considerations, spirits, ideals, and scales of value, in the life of states . . . In the international sphere militarism has provided fuel for those recriminations which were supposed to find a solution and end in the war-guilt paragraph of the Versailles Treaty – recriminations in which each nation charges another with building up disproportionate armaments that threaten peace and force pacific nations to follow suit (Vagts, 1938, p. 12).

It is worth noting that Vagts attributes both national and international aspects to militarism. The rise of militarism in one country provokes a response in other countries. However, the notion of excess is the most important idea in his definition. Vagts is opposed to militarism, but he is not a pacifist. He does not object to the military as such, but only to its domination under certain circumstances. He is concerned with 'disproportionate armaments that threaten peace'.

Radway, in an encyclopaedic article, expresses the same idea: 'in ordinary usage "militarism" has a derogatory meaning. Like legalism or clericalism it suggests excess: a lack of proportion in policy or, when warriors, a disregard for appropriate professional bounds' (Radway, 1968, p. 300). Another paragraph of the same article gives some indication of the nature of the excess of militarism:

> Militarism is a doctrine or system that values war and accords primacy in state and society to the armed forces. It exalts a function – the application of violence – and an institutional structure – the military establishment. It implies both a *policy* orientation and a power relationship (ibid).

In another encyclopaedic article, Erickson and Mommsen list a number of aspects of militarism:

> The term's polemical ancestry endows it with a broad range of meanings. 'Militarism' is used to designate, *inter alia*, the mentality characteristic of the age of imperialism . . . which glorified warlike attitudes . . . In the period preceding World War I the advance of military interests was directly reflected in arms races between great powers, in growing expenditure on armaments and the spread of military conscription. The influence of military leaders on domestic and external policy was sustained by widespread military propaganda . . . From these many senses three definitions emerge: militarism as a specific feature of government policy, as a product of certain concrete power structures, and finally – the original interpretation – as an ideology in its own right (Erickson and Mommsen, 1973, pp. 436-7).

Numerous other citations of this sort could be given (cf. the Appendix). There are great variations in scope and emphasis. Some authors stress the size and the role of the army or other armed forces in a society. Others focus their attention on values and attitudes. Still others are preoccupied with the economic underpinnings of a strong military apparatus. However, there is one notion which seems to be shared by most Western writers critical of and concerned about militarism. It is the idea of *excess*. Synonymous words like domination, preponderance, primacy and exaltation are often used, but the emphasis is the same: militarism is seen as the expansion of the military beyond certain, usually not very well defined, bounds. Correspondingly, their recommended cure is a policy of restraint and control of the military. For the sake of simplicity we shall call this line of reasoning the liberal critique, bearing in mind that great diversities exist within this tradition.

The notion of excess is central, but very imprecise. The liberal tradition is essentially preoccupied with the question: how much is enough? (Enthoven and Smith, 1971.) But this question should be split into two subsets of problems. First, one must ask about the objectives for which the use of the military – or the application of violence – supposedly is justified. This question regularly causes great controversy. Second, even if the first question could be answered unequivocally, one has to estimate whether the strength and influence of the military establishment is insufficient, sufficient or redundant relative to the accepted objectives. Redundancy is equivalent to militarism.

It is not the purpose of this article to solve the dispute about defining excesses. In our opinion, it is futile to discuss the notion of excesses on the abstract level only. The question of how much should be enough must be answered with reference to specific situations. It seems, however, that the response to this question reflects our ideological biases more than careful situational analysis. For the pacifist, everything military is equivalent to militarism. For the super-hawk, no amount of military power and influence would be too much. And those in between tend to argue for their respective positions in a stereotyped manner regardless of time and place (Hoffmann, 1970). Fortunately, one does not have to take a firm stand in this dispute in order to map some of the important dimensions of the disputed term.

3.2 Militarism in Marxist Theory

Marxist-Leninist theory employs a completely different concept of militarism. Each class society is, according to this theory, by definition militaristic (Jahn, 1975, p. 187). The following citation from a publication for the armed forces of the USSR is typical:

> Imperialist militarism is a complex social phenomenon which comprises a system of economic, political, ideological and directly military measures taken by aggressive capitalist nations and directed toward preparing for and conducting imperialist wars. It is utilized by the finance oligarchy to consolidate and expand its domination, to preserve the capitalist system on the one hand and to generate big profits on the other.

> Militarism as a social phenomenon was born with the split of society into classes, with the appearance of the exploiter state. Inheriting militarism from other class-antagonistic societies, the bourgeoisie took over the most reactionary elements in it and adapted them to its interests and needs. Under capitalism, particularly at its monopolist, imperialist stage, militarism has reached an unprecedented scale and has assumed a truly ominous character (Milovidov and Kozlov, 1972, p. 58).

Almost all states have military forces, but not all are militaristic. According to the Marxist school of thought one can speak about militarism only when the governing, exploiting class consciously increases armaments, armed forces and preparations for predatory wars (Lider, 1977, p. 7). Bourgeois militarism has an internal aspect as well. The military establishment in capitalist countries can be used for the suppression of working-class opposition. The military is a conscious instrument of the monopolist bourgeois to give it more power and profit. 'Monopolies universally strive toward profit, while militarism rests on the monopolies as its economic base' (Milovidov and Kozlov, 1972, p. 60).

Bourgeois militarism is aggressive. For this reason, writers in Eastern Europe hesitate to qualify small, especially neutral, countries as militaristic. But in principle, according to this theory, militarism also plays an important role in countries like Sweden, Austria, Luxembourg and Liechtenstein (Jahn, 1975, p. 187).

War was originally seen as a method of resolving antagonistic conflicts based on private ownership (Milovidov and Kozlov, 1972, p. 72). However, after the October Revolution, and especially after the emergence of the socialist camp, the militarism of competitive, capitalist war has been replaced by an anti-socialist militarism, not only on the national level, but also internationally. Although inter-capitalist wars cannot be ruled out, the main objective of present-day militarism in the West is to check and conquer the forces of socialism.

Because the fundamental class antagonisms have vanished in Eastern Europe, there can be no militarism in these countries. No social group can find itself basically in opposition to another social group. The various groups which exist are linked to each other through the Communist Party (Jahn, 1975, p. 188). This applies to the armed forces, the arms industry and to military R&D institutions as well. Therefore the military has become an instrument of the whole people and cannot be used to oppress it. Socialist militarism, according to this theory, is a contradiction in terms. Consequently, it becomes difficult to explain violent struggles between countries which call themselves socialist. Such encounters, and the preparations for them, are explicable only if at least one of the parties to the conflict is not really socialist, i.e. domestic class antagonisms are not solved. This is a central theme in the ideological quarrel between China and the USSR, which mutually accuse each other of elitist tendencies.

3.3 The Liberal and the Marxist Critique Compared

Neither the liberal nor the Marxist tradition is pacifist. Both accept the military as having an important and legitimate role in national and international affairs. According to Marxist thinking, armed forces are one of the determining factors of social development. They also have a role to play in defending the revolution against external imperialist forces. The notion of defence of the socialist fatherland is strikingly similar to the Western concept of national security. Liberals in Western countries may be critical of the role of the military and the size of the military establishment, but they generally support the amount of military preparedness needed for 'adequate defence'.

The term 'militarism' is used pejoratively in both traditions, but for different reasons. In the Marxist tradition, the use of violence becomes militaristic in so far as it is used for the wrong objectives, i.e. for the maintenance and expansion of capitalism and the suppression of progressive forces. Revolutionary violence is condoned, and often glorified. One seldom, if ever, poses the question of whether revolutionary violence and the preparation for it can be overdone. In brief, the Marxist critique of militarism is directed at the political interests for which the military is an instrument, and it is less concerned with the conduct of violence.

The liberal tradition, exemplified by Vagts and Radway, is the opposite of this. It does not take class interests as a point of departure. In general, it is vague about the objectives for which the maintenance and use for a military establishment could be justified. It is true that one sometimes finds discussions of illegitimate political ends, for example, the occupation of neighbouring territory or other forms of imperialism. But their main preoccupation is with the following questions: who defines the ends for which the military is used, the political organs of the state or the military establishment itself? Who determines the amount and kind of violence to be used for a particular purpose, the government or the generals? To the Marxists this distinction between civilian and military authority is deceptive because both authorities are instruments of the ruling class.

The two traditions are often presented as opposites, as being mutually exclusive. In our opinion it is possible to try to combine, in an undogmatic way, elements of both. The emphasis on the class functions of the military is the strength of the Marxist approach. But liberal critics of militarism more often ask the question: who benefits? A weakness of the Marxist approach is found in its disregard for important group or class criteria other than the relationship to the means of production. Because the means of production are collectively owned in socialist countries, there could be no class antagonism. The conflicts which nevertheless exist within and between these countries are therefore either denied, or blamed on imperialist subversion, and in any case poorly understood.

The ambiguity and diffusiveness of the term 'excess' is one of the main weaknesses of the liberal tradition. It is implied in this term that there exist certain objectives that could justify the use of certain amounts of violence. These objectives should be spelled out and linked to a theory of the functions and consequences of violence. As mentioned above, the theory must then be applied to concrete situations.

A final important difference between the two traditions should be noted. In Marxist theory one distinguished between the basis and the superstructure. Accordingly, some dimensions of militarism are basic while others are mere derivatives. Militaristic ideology, for instance, cannot be separated from its socio-economic roots. It is used to justify the use of military means for the protection of the ownership patterns of capitalist societies. The development of military technology is similarly a consequence of the efforts of the ruling class to maintain its hegemonic position. Thus capitalist militarism has many faces, but one main root.

Within the liberal tradition, there are many different schools of definitions of militarism. Some emphasise ideology, others stress the role of the military in the economies of various countries, still others consider the dynamism of the arms race the core of the problem. There is very little unity but a plethora of hypotheses about the ways in which the various dimensions are connected.

In the following pages we shall try to systematise and describe some of these dimensions. While the Marxist proposition of one root cause is rejected, we do not make the simplistic assumption that everything is equally important. But we feel that in order to make a judgement, one should first make a map of factors or dimensions to be considered.

4 The Dimensions of Militarism

The dimensions of militarism will be presented under three broad headings, corresponding to three fundamental aspects of human existence. First, our attention will be directed towards the behavioural aspect of militarism, and the way it is acted out. Second, we shall discuss the militarism of the mind, its attitudinal and ideological components. Third, militarism will be looked at in the context of the social structure of our societies. According to many observers, they are becoming increasingly militarised, and we shall discuss what that means. Because this point is so encompassing, it will be split into two subsections. The national and international levels will be presented separately.

4.1 Militarist Behaviour

Behaviour, unlike attitudes and to some extent social structure, is in principle directly observable. Militarist behaviour is, simply defined, the excess use of violence. Violence may be directed against military installations, human beings, or against objects which are important for their survival. The latter form of destruction is often called sabotage.

From one point of view, behaviour is the most central dimension of militarism. Militarist social structures and militarist ideology are worrisome factors primarily because of their conditioning of behaviour, their incitement of violence. This is not to say that other negative effects of, for instance, excessive military spending should be overlooked. The strain on the economy can in itself be a very serious problem. But the actual use of an excessive military apparatus in war may be considered the more central issue.

However, this dimension becomes more complicated if one introduces the distinction between latent and actual use of weapons. The use of threats, the policy of brinkmanship and the strategy of deterrence 'would be, in effect, a theory of the skillful nonuse of military forces' (Schelling, 1963, p. 9). The strategy of latent use of arms 'is not concerned with the efficient application of force, but with the exploitation of potential force' (ibid., p. 5). Obviously, both actual and latent use of violence may be excessive. To the extent that threats are made explicit, they are probably exaggerated in the sense of indicating a level of violence which is not really seriously contemplated by the threatening party. The more asymmetric the relationship in military capabilities between two parties, the more likely use of excess threats by the stronger one.

There is no consensus, either in principle or in historical situations, about the divide between excess and non-excess violent behaviour. However, the identification of some points along the pacifist-militarist dimension may be helpful in the discussion.

(1) Pacifism, particularly in its Gandhian version, means no violent action ever, under any circumstances, not even in self-defence.
(2) Conditional pacifism is less absolute. Adherents of this doctrine accept the application of small-scale violence in self-defence and usually some forms of police violence. But they are opposed to the establishment of military apparatuses for the ostensive purposes of achieving political objectives like 'national liberation' or 'defence against threats from abroad'.
(3) Then there are those who accept a military apparatus on the national level to protect their national independence or neutrality. Military alliances are avoided. In some cases, particularly destructive and/or offensive types of weapons are avoided.
(4) Many, if not most, nations acquire arms not only to protect themselves but also to change their military potential into political currency. In a number of situations, conventional arms are more useful because of the greater possibility of their actually being employed. But the superpowers also resort to threats of nuclear strikes in critical situations in attempts to influence each other's politics.
(6) Surprise 'preventive' attacks in order, for instance, to eliminate the military capability of an opponent, or to topple an unfriendly neighbouring regime, are the next rung on the ladder. A combination of the first-use and the counter-force doctrines could easily lead to actions of this sort in the relationship between the superpowers. Both major and many smaller powers actively involve themselves in domestic wars in countries in Asia, Africa and Latin America.[5]
(6) A large-scale attack to capture territory and to destroy an enemy's military installations, population centres and economic potential is a still more militarist action. It can be construed as revenge, or justified in terms of a supremacist ideology, such as the Nazis'.
(7) Finally, through the ages there are many examples of wanton killings. Some atrocities take place in all wars, even in those which are fought on a limited scale for limited objectives. But in some wars, killing and the extermination of peoples and groups

become an end in themselves. This is the ultimate militarism.

The above description of the pacifist-militarist behavioural dimension is very crude. It could easily be divided into a number of sub-dimensions on the basis of which it would be possible to construct a behavioural index. Although such an instrument can be elaborated and refined, it does not represent an answer to the political question: given certain historical and political circumstances, where is the line of excess?

4.2 Militarism of the Mind

According to the Constitution of UNESCO, 'war starts in the minds of men'. Like all other one-factor theories of war, this one is inadequate – but it contains an important point. Unlike natural catastrophes, wars are the results of human decisions. Human decisions are conditioned by any number of factors, and many of these are external to the human mind. But some of the conditions are found within the mind itself. It is generally accepted that some individuals are more likely than others to promote and become engaged in warfare. But there is disagreement about the extent to which differential 'war-proneness' of individuals is explained by social factors, or by inborn attributes. One school of social psychology linked with K.Z. Lorenz relates aggression to a psychologically programmed fighting instinct. An instinct is understood as rigidly stereotyped innate movements which are co-ordinated in the central nervous system (Kim, 1976, p. 254). Others contend that the biological potential of man does not *ipso facto* explain human behaviour any more than one's IQ could predict one's behaviour. As already mentioned, Marxists maintain that attitudes and ideologies belong to the superstructure, i.e. they are derivatives of the structure of economic, social and political relations.[6]

Regardless of the cause of militaristic attitudes, it is necessary to define what they are. In principle this can be done by two different approaches, deductive and inductive. A deductive research method can be applied to a group of persons who perceive themselves, and/or are being perceived by others, as being militarists. By questionnaires, interviews or other methods one can obtain information about their beliefs and attitudes. Their attitude patterns can be compared to that of a general population sample, and some distinguishing features will hopefully appear. There are a great number of attitudinal studies which directly or indirectly tap the dimension of militarism.[7] However, most of the studies known to us are done with only Western respondents and this is a serious shortcoming. Militarist beliefs and militarist cultures outside the West probably take different forms, although we also expect to find some striking similarities.

The other approach is inductive. We can classify sets or attitudes and beliefs according to the degree in which the use of violence is accepted and people and communities capable and efficient in the application of violence. For instance, we reason that an authoritarian personality is more likely to use physical violence as a means of punishment, and is less likely to disobey an order to apply excessive violence against an enemy. We also reason that nationalism, tribalism and other forms of group identification may become so strong that violence against members of other groups (nations, religions, families, ideologies, etc.) is readily accepted at a means of defending the group and/or expanding its power.

The two approaches, the deductive and the inductive, should lead to similar results. The kinds of mind which theoretically are conducive to militarism should not be significantly different from the ones which reportedly are typical of acknowledged militarists.

So far the terms 'ideology', 'attitude', 'belief' and 'mind' have not been defined, and no attempt has been made to distinguish them from one another. For simplicity we shall refer to all of this as ideology, but there will be an emphasis on four elements which seem to be of particular importance from the point of view of militarism.

4.2.1 Values. In all ideologies, distinctions are made between good and bad, right and wrong. Societies, situations and actions are rated on value scales. We can be more or less conscious about our system of values, and our judgements may be more or less consistent. Nevertheless we spend our lives making choices, i.e. comparing alternatives on our value scales. Groups and individuals are frequently described and explained in terms of their positive and negative values.

It is outside the scope of this paper to discuss thoroughly the complexities of militarist value systems, but a few observations are necessary for illustration. For instance, we assume that the value one attaches to the life of human beings is a factor of major importance. Disregard for human life and human suffering is an 'excess' which most likely is correlated with other ideological and non-ideological dimensions of militarism.

The moral imperative, or at least acceptance, of revenge is another value to be considered in this connection. An obsession by the thought of revenge can feed on other militarist attitudes and motivate violent actions.

As mentioned above, various forms of group identification can become strong enough to justify hostile, violent actions towards other groups. Ethnocentrist ideologies frequently have religious underpinnings, but they can also be fuelled by modern 'isms' from anti-Communism to anti-imperialism. A strong conviction about the righteousness of one's own group or cause, combined with a low regard for human life, or with an attempt to 'dehumanise' the enemy, is conducive to violence. Thus there is a link between militarism and racism.

In most societies, participation in military life is positively valued as a sign of masculinity. It implies strength, endurance, in some cases chivalry, loyalty to comrades in arms, etc.[8] The notion that struggle and conflict give life meaning is linked to the masculinity syndrome. This notion is often based on religion – Norse mythology being an historical example. In modern times, bravery itself does not seem to suffice as a motivating force. It must be linked to a cause, be it 'freedom', 'socialism', '*der Führer*' or 'my' country. The number of associations formed to commemorate and glorify the struggles of past wars (and prepare mentally for new ones) is but one indication of the importance of this variable.

Finally, we should not forget that military symbols have great value for some people, and this is the reason they are being used. The veneration of medals, banners, insignia, badges, etc., may seem ridiculous, and it is not easy to explain the psychological mechanisms at work. But this form of 'petty militarism' has an important function in fostering loyalty and dedication. Uniforms enhance discipline, and drills and parades are training in co-ordination.

4.2.2 Beliefs about Human Nature and Social Relationships. Ideologies not only distinguish between good and bad, they also contain premisses and propositions about 'reality'. Some ideological propositions are little more than beliefs. Others are to some extent confirmed or disproved by empirical research. But unfortunately, most ideological propositions are of such a general nature that they do not lend themselves to scientific tests.

We propose that there are certain beliefs (be they true, partly true, false, conditional or self-fulfilling) which are associated with and conducive to militaristic behaviour. For example, several authors suggest that a pessimistic view of human nature is typical of the military profession (Abrahamsson, 1971, pp. 102-5). When man is considered essentially egoistic, the perceived need for defence is easily understood. As a corollary, the international system is conceived as essentially anarchistic, i.e. each nation strives to protect its own interests and takes immediate advantage of possible weaknesses of its neighbours. Thus a strong military posture is seen as essential for survival.

In a different version of this theory the world is divided into two or more camps, some of which are inherently evil, aggressive, etc., while others, and specifically one's own group, do not entertain such feelings. Needless to say, the latter version forms the basis of more intolerance than the former, which can accept that potential opponents also may have reason to fear. The division into different camps can be based on national, cultural, religious, racial and other criteria.[9]

A number of other propositions follow from these perceptions of human nature. If all human beings and, as a consequence, all nations are basically aggressive, the best one can hope for is a system of balance of power, or more specifically, a system of mutual deterrence. Needless to say, this idea is widely accepted and central in the thinking of many of those who actually shape the 'international military order'.

Another consequence of this philosophy, particularly in its second version, is found in the theory of punitive, military action. A raid, a limited engagement, a selective strike, etc. are methods which some circles contemplate, plan and occasionally apply in international politics.

Militaristic attitudes do also come in a defensive mode, for instance in the form of constant alarmism. Regardless of objective changes in the military postures of relevant nations, some leaders unceasingly emphasise the need for preparedness. This is not to say that nations have not been caught unprepared. But the unfailing, sometimes apparently neurotic demands by some groups for more defence spending is at times more easily explained by psychological variables than by political, diplomatic, economic or military factors.

4.2.3 Central Concepts. The militaristic mind can probably be distinguished by its choice of certain concepts and its exclusion of others. Ideologies have emotional as well as cognitive elements.[10] Some of the concepts presumably typical of the militarist mind have already been alluded to. Threat, revenge, military strength, order, warning, morality (in the military sense), obedience, loyalty, balance of power, brinkmanship, tension, capabilities, victory, defeat, supremacy, challenge, destruction, etc. are concepts that seem congruent with militaristic thinking. Other concepts seem non-congruent: accommodation, forgiveness, trust, reconcilation, persuasion, isolation, suffering, construction, etc. It is not implied of course that the use of these terms is limited to militarists or non-militarists respectively. But we do propose that persons with a militaristic inclination are more likely to make use of the first set of concepts in their thinking, and not to use the second set. More research is needed to determine the validity of this proposition.

4.2.4 Emotional Characteristics. In studying the mind of the militarist, we are concerned about what he or she values, believes and thinks, but we should also take into consideration what the militarist feels, i.e. the affective or emotional aspects. The militarist has been described as an emotionally blunt personality with high scores on scales like extraversion (meaning dependence on the social environment for the guidance and motivation of behaviour), misanthropy, social irresponsibility, neuroticism, lack of empathy with others, impulsivity and egoism (Eckhardt, 1977, p. 9). In short, the militarist is portrayed as emotionally damaged and/or underdeveloped. This is related to frustrating childhood disciplines and family discord which often is carried over from one generation to another. Although this may be true statistically, this author feels that many of those national leaders who actually plan and carry out rather militarist domestic and foreign policies do not conform to this description. We may be in need of theories which distinguish between leaders and followers.

4.3 *Structural Militarism*

4.3.1 The National Level. National governments have a near monopoly on the legitimate use of violence – against each other or against their own citizens. But although the legitimate use of violence is an essential element in the definition of 'nation-states', they differ widely in the organisation of civilian-military relationships. Some of these structural aspects will be discussed in the following paragraphs.

A social structure is made up of units (actors, organisations, sectors, etc.) and their interrelationships. If, for the sake of simplicity, we consider the military establishment as one sector or unit, two questions emerge: (1) what is the size of the military sector relative to other sectors of a particular society, and (2) what are the relationships between the military sector and others?

The size of the military sector can be determined by a number of different indicators, the amount of military spending compared to the gross national product, the number of personnel, the percentage of an educated elite which chooses careers in the military rather than in civilian sectors, the consumption of commodities like fuel, metals and food, etc. Regardless of which mix of indicators one chooses, one does not avoid the problem, referred to in section 2, of the arbitrariness of the distinction between military and civilian. This arbitrariness makes comparison across nations difficult.

Although an oversized military sector undoubtedly is a significant aspect of militarism, more attention has been devoted to military-civilian relationships.[11] We shall focus particularly on the relationship of the military to political institutions and to the industrial sector.

Two main questions can be posed regarding the relationship between the military and national political institutions, especially the government. First, it is important to ascertain the degree to which a government (presumably based on popular support) is able to control and direct the military, as prescribed by democratic theory. The second problem can be stated as follows: the military is sometimes used by governments for unacceptable, and hence excessive, purposes, for instance for the suppression of democratic forces, of ethnic or religious minorities, etc.

With regard to question one, national traditions vary considerably. A number of different patterns of control, integration and infiltration are observable. In extreme, but not unusual cases, civilian governments are removed by the military and often replaced by juntas of professional soldiers.

One author, who did a comparative study of military-civilian relationships, concluded that

> the militaries of Prussia-Germany and Japan have both hindered and enhanced the establishment of a stable political order . . . The military elites of Latin America, Africa and the Middle East have challenged the political order and rendered it permanently unstable . . . While French corporatism enhanced military docility, it also encouraged conspiracy against political orders that did not conform to the military's concept of Frenchmen and France . . . In Stalin's day the military of the USSR was a frustrated professional group with no identity of its own. Although its efforts to rise were brutally crushed by Stalin, his successors were unable, even if willing, to tyrannize society or the military (Perlmutter, 1977, pp. 284-5).

It is beyond the scope of this chapter to discuss the many forms of deviation from the democratic ideal of political control with the military.

But a couple of general points should be emphasised. *First*, in many countries, particularly among those which relatively recently have gained their independence, the military exerts a considerable influence, directly or indirectly, on both the composition and the policies of the government. The power of the military is the key political factor as to whether the generals and colonels themselves staff the Cabinet or not.

Second, in most countries where the government is based on approval by a popular majority, the relationship between the military and the government is most often relatively harmonious. Officially this is frequently explained by the acceptance of the political control doctrine by the military leadership. Such an official attitude does not, of course, prevent parts of the military establishment from promoting, through bureaucratic and other less visible channels, their own views on national and foreign policies. The relationship may also be harmonious because the majority of the population accept and promote the strengthening of the military, the application of violence to subdue and possibly exterminate minority groups, an aggressive foreign policy, etc. In Nazi Germany, Hitler was in charge of the military and not the other way around, and after 1933 he had little problem getting popular approval. Another example: a Leninist party may control a nation, including its armed forces, but this does not preclude militarist ventures nationally and internationally. It also does not preclude the development of a tightly knit military-industrial structure.

The relationship between the military and industry has been receiving more attention from scholars and politicians. The rapid development of military technology has made this relationship more and more important. The dominant norm in most countries is that the industrial sector (or more generally, the production sector) should serve approved military objectives, and not the other way around. In other words, the level of military spending should be determined by 'defence needs', and not by the economic needs or interests of individual firms or of the business community in general.

According to popular theory, military production provides jobs, relatively high profits for the firms, technological development which also advances the manufacturing of non-military goods, etc. It is difficult to make unconditional generalisations in this field, and all of the above hypotheses have been contested.[12] Much more research is needed. However, it is an indisputable fact that the level of military spending and the output of military-industrial products have not been reduced in spite of the thaw in East-West relations. On the other hand, the level of armaments increases all the time. It is difficult to account for these contradictory trends without taking into consideration the economic functions of military production.

The existence of common interests between military and industrial leaders (including the top of the trade union hierarchy) does not in itself account for military procurement and spending over and above 'real' defence needs. One must also take into account the role of the political institutions, particularly high government officials whose careers and interests are tied to military expenditure and legislators whose districts benefit from defence procurement. They are also core members of the so-called military-industrial complex, a term which unfortunately tends to obscure their role. The complex may also be supported by voluntary groups like the veterans and military service associations, and by scientists and engineers engaged in defence-related research (Rosen, 1973, p. 3). According to the theory, these groups promote armamentism not primarily for defence reasons, as they purport, but in order to increase their own economic benefits and status in society.

The socialist governments in Eastern Europe deny the existence of a military-industrial complex or its equivalent in their societies. Because these countries are impervious to critical research, we know very little about the domestic role of military interests. However, there can be little doubt that military production is very privileged relative to other sectors of the economy (Halloway, 1974).

The central role of the military in many developing countries is sometimes defended on the basis of the assumed contribution of the military to nation-building and development. From the military point of view, backwardness is seen as threat to national security. Furthermore, if a strong military influence is conducive to the achievement of certain generally acceptable societal goals, such as order or development, then the notion of excess military influence will be changed accordingly.[13] Needless to say, this optimistic evaluation of the role of the military has been very much disputed by analysts who make a contrary argument 'that political intervention by the military should essentially be seen as a conservative or even reactionary activity by the defenders of the status of entrenched elite groups, designed to inhibit economic and social change' (Jackman, 1976, p. 1078). Still others have suggested that the social and economic policy consequences of military rule vary according to the type of society being considered (ibid.).[14]

4.3.2 The International Level. The militarisation of social structures is perhaps most easily seen on the national level. The international level is significantly different. With the exception of the minuscule peace-keeping forces of the United Nations, which mostly have a police function, the international community as such does not maintain a military sector.

However, there are several aspects of the structure of the international community which can be discussed in terms of militarism or militarisation. The international community is organised very much according to military logic or, more specifically, according to the logic of military alliances. According to this logic, intra-alliance disputes should be avoided and economic, logistic, technological and political bonds between the alliance members should be encouraged and developed. Because of the rapid advancement of military technology, it becomes increasingly difficult for the smaller and middle-size countries to develop and produce their own arms. Therefore intra-alliance arms trade is increasing. Co-production schemes involving several alliance partners are the next step in this development. By means of such schemes, both the economic and military sectors become more integrated across national borders. Joint manoeuvres, standardisation of equipment, joint commands and sharing of intelligence information are also part of the picture. In spite of the attempts of some countries, for example France and Romania, to reduce their alliance commitments, it can safely be concluded that the present alliances among advanced industrial nations are far more integrated, and probably also more stable, than the alliances of, for instance, nineteenth-century Europe.

Conversely, the relationships between members of opposing alliances are restrained and regulated. During the Cold War, the United States in particular has tried with varying degrees of success to prevent its alliance partners from selling strategically important products to members of the Warsaw Pact (Adler-Karlsson, 1968). The movement of persons and ideas has been effectively curtailed, particularly by the WTO side. In short, several forms of international interaction are patterned after the alliance system; the international interaction structure is significantly militarised.[15] It has been proposed that the greater the correlation between the alliance structure and the interaction structure, the more conflict-prone the system. In other words, the weaker the positive and beneficial bonds between the two, the less costly the initial stages of an escalation process which often involves economic and political 'warfare'. This is, of course, another version of the traditional functionalist theory which proposed the establishment and development of a network of international co-operation, particularly in the field of welfare, as a means to prevent war.[16]

There are also some other factors on the international level which have gained considerably in importance since World War II. The increase in arms transfers from industrial to developing countries, particularly after 1973, has been astounding. There has been an almost exponential growth both in demand and supply. Although some of this increase must be understood on the basis of the very low level of military spending in many newly liberated countries, and by the withdrawal of imperial armies, this in itself does not explain why, according to Øberg's calculations, military spending in the so-called Third World grows faster than the gross national product, which again is surpassed by the growth in military import (Øberg, 1975, p. 215).

The transfer of military technology is another crucial aspect of the military relationship between industrialised and non-industrialised countries. Such transfers take many different forms, and it is not easy to describe the trend in simple, quantitative terms. But there can be no doubt that this transfer contributes to the militarisation of international relations and also the strengthening of the military *vis-à-vis* the political and economic sectors both in producing and recipient countries, but most importantly in the latter.

The transfer of arms and arms technology is paralleled by the internationalisation of military expertise and training programmes. The purchase of a batch of arms or a package of technology often necessitates training of local personnel. This can be done both in the exporting and importing country, and the kind of training may range from purely military to mainly technological.

The combination of factors like the three mentioned above has been called 'the New International Military Order' (Øberg, 1977). Increased dependence on development by 'advanced' countries is a result of this new order, a result which contradicts the objectives of the new international economic order. It may be hypothesised that maintenance of the old current international economic order is one of the aims of many of those who press for the further development of the military order. Military links are established in order to protect friendly regimes, which often means regimes which accept substantial foreign economic influence, if not foreign economic dominance. This relationship between international military influence and economic interests is not new. As one observer writes:

> The 'old' international economic order was established largely

> through the direct application of military force; it was maintained and consolidated by the direct and indirect use of military power. Although the colonial period has formally ended (with a number of minor exceptions), the present world economic order is in many respects a continuation of the colonial economy, maintained to a considerable degree by global military power systems analogous to those of the colonial period (Lumsden, 1976, pp. 26-7).

The history of colonialism and the recent development of neo-colonial relationships in the military field provide an abundance of examples of excessive use of the military, including the instigation of and direct interference in violent domestic conflicts.

5 Summary and Conclusion

Militarism is a many-faceted phenomenon, deeply ingrained in many minds and embedded in many societies. For some purposes it seems appropriate to consider militarism as several different but related phenomena.

This has not been an investigation of the causes of the various forms of militarism. But we have noticed some strong indications of links, direct or indirect, between the different dimensions. If the dimensions really are loosely connected, two conclusions follow. First, anti-militarism strategies must be directed specifically at each of the various dimensions and sub-dimensions. Second, the various strategies must be co-ordinated. For instance, educational approaches should be paralleled by efforts to change the interaction patterns in the international system (including educational exchanges) to exert political control with the military, and to resist the temptation to threaten with the use of arms in order to enhance one's diplomatic position, etc. Different anti-militarist groups will naturally stress different strategies and dimensions depending on their ideological orientation. But it is their combined efforts which count. It would increase the effectiveness of the anti-militarist struggle if the various groups and movements could see their aims and methods as complementary, at least to some extent, rather than competitive.

It would also be helpful if such groups could tolerate a certain amount of disagreement about the notion of excess. As mentioned several times already, the dividing line between adequacy and excess cannot be scientifically determined, either in theory or in specific historical situations. It is essentially a political and ideological issue. But there ought to be a basis for tolerance and hopefully for co-operation between those who accept a limited role for the military and those who reject all forms of organised violence regardless of the circumstances under which it is applied. Both categories of anti-militarist face powerful groups which hardly ever open their eyes to the danger of military excesses, particularly in their own environment.

Appendix

In preparing for this paper, I was curious about the way 'militarism' was presented in different encyclopaedias. In the 1967 edition of *Encyclopaedia Britannica* there was no entry at all, and the word was used only once in a peripheral way in an article on World War II. *The Encyclopedia Americana*, international edition of 1968, carried a twenty-line article in which militarism was defined as 'a term applied to the policy of giving exalting emphasis to military preparedness, exalting the military virtues, and relying on force in international relations'. The article recognises both domestic and international aspects of militarism, but the emphasis is on the preparation for international war. The *Grand Larousse Encyclopédique*, 1963 edition, does not differ very much: 'Préponderance exagérée de l'élément militaire dans une nation. Système politique qui s'appuie sur l'armée . . . Sentiment, doctrine de ceux qui sont partisans de cette préponderance de l'armée.' Considering that the term originated in France, this article is remarkably short.

Two German encyclopaedias, however, contain more compehensive presentations. *Brockhaus Enzyklopädie* writes that the term

> Militarismus . . . bezeichnet das Vorherrschen militären Formen, Denkweisen und Zielsetzungen in Staat, Politik und Gesellschaft. Während Verteidigungsbereitschaft, Wehrpflicht, Soldat Ethos, militärisch . . . Disziplin in allen zivilisierten Staaten als Notwendigkeit anerkant werden, haben sich in der Geschichte zu allen Zeiten Staatstypen herausgebildet deren Organisation durch die Vorherrschaft militärisch-kriegerisch . . . Prinzipen geprägt wurde . . . Merkmale des Militarismus sind die Überbetonung militärischer Formen und des militärischen Machtprinzips im offentlichten Leben, die Ausbreitung militärisch-autoritärer Ordnungsformen (Personlichet Gehorsam, Disziplin) im zivilien Bereich, die Einwirkung entsprechender Prinzipien auf das Erziehungswesen wie die Einordnung des Heeres als Erziehungsinstitution, die Bevorzugung und elitäre Sonderung der militarischer Führungsschicht (Offizierskorps), die Priorität und Staatsrechtliche Sonderstellung des Militärhaushalts.

Meyers Enzylopädisches Lexikon from 1976 states more briefly that militarism is characterised by

> drückend empfundenen Militärverfassung . . . einer forcierten Rüstung, hoher finanzieller Militärlasten, der innenpolitische Stabilisierungsfunktion der bewaffneten Macht in konservativen Gesellschaften und schliesslich . . . der Überfremdung des zivilien Lebens durch militärischen Formen und Gesinnungen sowie der Dominanz militärisches Denkens in der Politik.

Both of the German encyclopaedias have a short outline of the development of militarism.

Finally, the Russian *Malaya Sovietskaya Entsikopediya* (*The Little Soviet Encyclopaedia*) of 1959 has a relatively long article on the subject. It defines militarism as (author's translation)

> the policy of enhancing the military power of exploitative governments in order to prepare for aggressive wars and suppress opposition from the exploited masses within nations. Modern militarism – Lenin points out – 'is the product of capitalism. In both of its forms, [militarism] is a vital manifestation of capitalism: as military power applied by capitalist governments against their foreign opponents . . . and as a weapon in the hands of the ruling classes for the suppression of any form (economic or political) of movement of the proletariat.'

In the remaining part of the article, militarism is linked to monopoly capitalism and imperialism.

Notes

1. Examples are: government, democracy, political power, socialism. We have a universal declaration of human rights, but it is doubtful whether human rights could be considered universal even on the prescriptive level.
2. It stems from the latin word *milit* meaning soldier.
3. In connection with the MBFR negotiations in Vienna, the WTO side has been pointing out that it dresses more supportive personnel in uniform than do the members of NATO.
4. 'Mussolini was the first man to see that militarism is a powerful weapon of political propaganda in a modern democracy' (Crossman, 1969, p. 265).
5. For some interesting statistical information, see Kende, Ch. 15, in this volume.
6. Lumsden (1977) suggests that the word 'militarism' should be applied at the

level of the superstructure, while the word 'militarisation' should refer to problems at the level of structure. Although he takes Marxist categories as his point of departure, he does not accept the view that problems on the attitudinal or cultural level are merely reflections of problems at the structural level (see Ch. 19 of this volume).

7. Several such studies are reported in Abrahamsson (1971). The Canadian Peace Research Institute in Oakville, Ontario, has made extensive opinion studies on militarism and related problems. For a recent summary of these studies, see Eckhardt, Ch. 18, in this volume.

8. It will be interesting to see whether the feminist movement can challenge and change this definition of masculinity. So far there is little evidence of such a change taking place.

9. Russell (1971) notes that militarism in North America is linked to religious orthodoxy, i.e. conservative theology. This is not surprising because conservative theologians tend to emphasise the sinfulness of man.

10. Eckhardt writes that 'cognitively, the militarist is likely to be anti-intellectual, dogmatic, intolerant of ambiguity, rigid, ego-defensive, less intelligent (including knowledge of foreign affairs), and positivist (vs. humanist) in one's philosophy of human consciousness, knowledge, science, truth, etc.' (Eckhardt, 1977, p. 11). However, all human beings, be they 'anti-intellectual' or belonging to the intelligentsia, make use of certain concepts which are part and parcel of their *Weltanschauung.*

11. See, for instance, van Doorn, 1968 and 1969; Janowitz and van Doorn, 1971; Rosen, 1974; and Perlmutter, 1977.

12. Some studies indicate that defence production is so capital-intensive that more jobs would have been created by alternative forms of investment. See, for instance, Albrecht, Lock and Wulf, 1978, and Melman, 1978. Rosen concluded, on the basis of a series of studies of the United States military-industrial complex, that the majority of US corporations which have Defense Department contracts derive only the smaller part of their sales from these contracts, and defence profits are not a disproportionate share of corporate earnings (Rosen, 1973, p. 23). The appropriateness of military technology for civilian production is discussed and refuted by a group of experts appointed by the Secretary-General of the United Nations (General Assembly Official Documents A/32/88, para. 99 ff.).

13. In a somewhat dated but influential article, Lucian W. Pye concludes that 'the military in the underdeveloped countries can make a major contribution to strengthening essentially administrative functions. If the new countries are to become modern nation-states they will have to have a class of competent administrators. They will also have to have responsible and skilled politicians. In cooperating with the military in these countries, we should recognize that they can contribute to only a limited part of national development' (Pye, 1962, p. 89).

14. Perlmutter writes:

> [The] 'progressive officer' theorists have argued that that the military is a modern bureaucracy and that the military elites in developing countries are inclined to emulate modern organizational forms which ipso facto will rationalize society, institutions, and politics. In actuality the military has failed . . . This failure has stemmed not so much from the military's inability to internalize, improvise, and orchestrate the fundamentals of modern organization. It is true that in some developing polities the military has scored high on the Weberian scale of rational bureaucracy . . . Nevertheless, several 'modern' military establishments in developing nations have

contributed little toward expanding the political system and widening the political participation of their respective polities (Perlmutter, 1977, p. 287).

Cf. also Dieter Senghaas, Ch. 10, in this volume.

15. This was one of the main findings of a number of related studies at the International Peace Research Institute in Oslo in the late sixties. See for instance Galtung (1966), Gleditsch (1967), and Skjelsbaek (1972).

16. Cf. David Mitrany, 1966. For a recent discussion of the state of functionalist theory, see Groom and Taylor (1975).

References

Abrahamsson, Bengt. 1971. *Militärer, makt og politik.* Stockholm: Bokförlaget Prisma. An English version is titled *Military professionalization and political power*. London: Sage Publications, 1972

Adler-Karlsson, Gunnar. 1968. *Western Economic Warfare 1947-1967: A Case Study in Foreign Economic Policy*. Stockholm: Almqvist and Wiksell

Albrecht, Ulrich. 1977. Technology and militarization of Third World countries in theoretical perspective. *Bulletin of Peace Proposals,* **8**, 2, 124-6

Albrecht, Ulrich, Lock, Peter and Wulf, Herbert. 1978. *Arbeitsplätze durch Rüstung? Warnung vor falschen Hoffnungen*. Hamburg: Rowolt Taschenbuch Verlag

Crossman, R.H.S. 1969. *Government and the Governed: a History of Political Ideas and Political Practice*. 5th edn. London: Chatto and Windus

van Doorn, Jacques (ed.). 1969. *Armed Forces and Society, Sociological Essays.* The Hague: Mouton

van Doorn, Jacques (ed.). 1969. *Military Professions and Military Regimes.* The Hague: Mouton

Eckhardt, William. 1977. The causes and correlates of western militarism. Paper presented at the Pugwash Symposium on Militarism, Oslo, Norway. 21-25 November 1977 (cf. Ch. 18)

Enthoven, Alain and Smith, K. Wayne. 1971. *How Much is Enough? Shaping the Defence Program, 1961-1969*. New York: Harper and Row

Erickson, John and Mommsen, Hans. 1973. Militarism. In C.D. Kernig (ed.), *Communism and Western Society: a Comparative Encyclopedia*, Vol. 5. New York: McGraw-Hill

Galtung, Johan. 1966. East-West interaction patterns. *Journal of Peace Research,* **3**, 2, 146-77

Gleditsch, Nils Petter. 1967. Trends in world airline patterns. *Journal of Peace Research,* **4**, 4, 336-408

Groom, A.J.R. and Taylor, Paul (eds.). 1975. *Functionalism: Theory and Practice in International Relations.* London: University of London Press

Halloway, David. 1974. Technology and political decision in Soviet armaments policy. *Journal of Peace Research,* **11**, 3, 257-79

Hoffmann, Fredrik. 1970. Arms debates: a positional interpretation. *Journal of Peace Research,* 7, 2, 219-28

Jackman, Robert W. 1976. Politicians in uniform: military governments and social change in the Third World. *American Political Science Review,* **70**, 4, 1078-97

Jahn, Egbert. 1975. The role of the armaments complex in Soviet Society (Is there a Soviet military industrial complex?). *Journal of Peace Research,* **12**, 3, 195-214

Janowitz, Morris and van Doorn, Jacques (eds.). 1971. *On Military Intervention.* Rotterdam: Rotterdam University Press

Kim, Samuel. 1976. The Lorenzian theory of aggression and peace research: a critique. *Journal of Peace Research,* **13**, 4, 253-76

Lang, Kurt. 1968. Military. In David L. Sills (ed.), *International Encyclopedia of the Social Sciences*, Vol. 10. London: Collier-Macmillan

Lider, Julian. 1977. The critique of militarism in Soviet study. Utrikespolitiska instituet, Stockholm (cf. Ch. 9)

Lumsden, Malvern. 1976. The role of the military in the world economic order: perspectives for peace and development research. Opening plenary lecture at the 7th Nordic Peace Research Conference, Silkeborg, Denmark, 26-29 July 1976

Lumsden, Malvern. 1977. Militarism: cultural dimensions of militarisation. Paper presented at the Pugwash Symposium on Militarism, Oslo, Norway, 21-25 November and the Seventh General Conference of the International Peace Research Association, Oaxtepec, Mexico, 11-16 December 1977 (cf. Ch. 19)

Melman, Seymour. 1978. Inflation and unemployment as products of war economy; the trade union stake in economic conversion and industrial reconstruction. *Bulletin of Peace Proposals,* **9**, 4, 359-74

Milovidov, A.S. and Kozlov, V.G. (eds.). 1972. *The Philosophical Heritage of V.I. Lenin and Contemporary War.* US version published as no. 5 in the series of *Soviet military thought* by US Government Printing Office (original USSR version by Voyennoye Jzdatel'stvo, Ministerstvo Oborony, Moscow)

Mitrany, David. 1966. *A Working Peace System*. Chicago: Quadrangle Books

Øberg, Jan. 1975. Arms trade with the third world as an aspect of imperialism. *Journal of Peace Research,* **12**, 3, 213-34

Øberg, Jan. 1977. The new international military order, structural militarism and human security. Paper presented at the 28th Pugwash Symposium, Militarism and National Security, in Oslo, Norway, 21-25 November 1977

Perlmutter, Amos. 1977. *The Military and Politics in Modern Times: on Professionals, Praetorians, and Revolutionary Soldiers.* New Haven and London: Yale University Press

Pye, Lucian W. 1962. Armies in the process of political modernization. In John J. Johnson (ed.), *The Role of the Military in Underdeveloped Countries.* Princeton, New Jersey: Princeton University Press

Radway, Lawrence I. 1968. Militarism. In David L. Sills (ed.), *International Encyclopedia of the Social Sciences*, Vol. 10. London: Collier-Macmillan

Rosen, Steven (ed.). 1973. *Testing the Theory of the Military-industrial Complex.* Lexington, Massachusetts: D.C. Heath and Company

Russell, Elbert W. 1971. Christianity and militarism. *Peace Research Reviews,* **4**, 3

Schelling, Thomas C. 1963. *The Strategy of Conflict.* New York: Oxford University Press

Senghaas, Dieter. 1977. Militarism dynamics in the contemporary context of periphery capitalism. *Bulletin of Peace Proposals,* **3**, 2, 103-9

Skjelsbæk, Kjell. 1971. Shared memberships in intergovernmental organizations and dyadic war, 1865-1964. In Edwin H. Fedder (ed.), *The United Nations: Problems and Prospects*. St Louis: University of Missouri

Skjelsbæk, Kjell. 1972. Peace and the structure of the international organization network. *Journal of Peace Research,* **9**, 4, 315-30

United Nations. 1978. *Economic and Social Consequences of the Arms Race and of Military Expenditures*. New York: United Nations

Vagts, Alfred. 1938. *A History of Militarism: Romance and Realities of a Profession.* London: George Allen and Unwin

5 MILITARISM AND UNDERDEVELOPMENT*

Ulrich Albrecht

The militarism paradigm has been largely ignored since the publication of Vagts's famous book forty years ago.[1] The West German debate on Prussian militarism in the fifties apparently had no wider repercussions,[2] and as Volker Berghahn notes in his recent reader on the problem, has not contributed to a consenus about what the term really could mean today.[3] The term 'militarism' is additionally denounced as being highly controversial, politically one-sided, and hence not useful for scholarly debate.[4] It should be noted, however, that analytical terms in political science *per se* are controversial (take such notions as 'democracy', 'legitimacy', etc.), an issue in which authors on all sides of the political spectrum apparently agree.[5]

The recent rise in the importance of the militarism paradigm is apparently due to the action of social (not scientific) forces. There are three strands of criticism of militarism to be identified, which have been carried on since the middle of the last century.

(1) *The tradition of political liberalism*. Nineteenth-century liberalism basically considered the society to be divided into two segments: a civilian sphere and a military sphere. The major tenet in this tradition was that there was an inherent tendency of the military segment of society, after the establishment of a permanent military force, to spread unduly into the civilian sector. Authors like Janowitz still adhere today to this notion when they introduce refinements like the existence of paramilitary forces which might conceal the actual militarisation of society. In a militaristic society, according to the liberal notion, the formerly civilian segment has accepted military values, ways and means for political decisions, and military conduct of political life. The actual purpose of this notion is to exert control of the military on the side of the civilians, and to contain the military sector in a kind of permanent struggle. Also in this tradition is the claim that today's armed forces in industrialised countries must be considered to be highly civilised, i.e.

*The paper is based upon discussions with a number of friends and colleagues during the last two years. A first version appeared in German, 'Der Zusammenhang zwischen Militarismus and Unterentwicklung', *Internationale Entwicklung (Österreichische Forschungsstiftung für Entwicklingshilfe)*, no. IV (1977), pp. 19-26. The usual disclaimers apply.

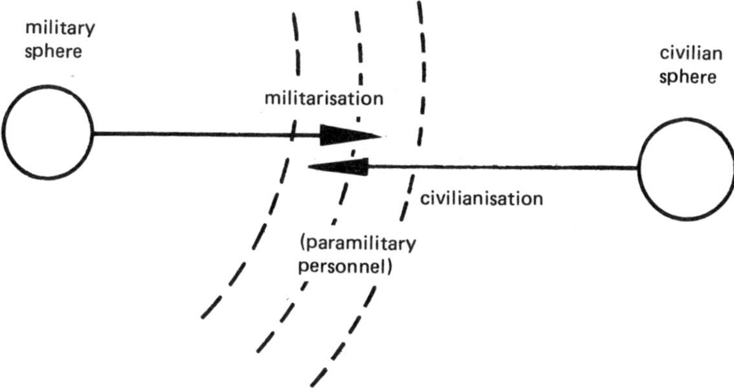

penetrated by civilian values, ways and means of decision-making, and conduct of daily affairs.[6]

(2) *The socialist tradition.* According to Assmus,[7] the French socialist Proudhon was the first to use the term 'militarism', in 1864. All critics in the socialist tradition start from the point that the liberal division of society into the civilian and military spheres is utterly misleading, and that militarism as a symptom should be studied in a way that considers the development of society as a whole. Liebknecht went as far as to state that militarism can be found in all class systems,[8] and Luxembourg was the first who linked explicitly military production with the problem of armed forces in society.[9] In sum, the socialist tradition explains militarism as one of the manifestations of capitalist societies, i.e. that militarism arises from the nature of the capitalist mode of production.

The question whether the development in countries of 'real socialism' in Eastern Europe is to be criticised by the notion of militarism is beyond the scope of this contribution. Because Joseph Stalin himself in his criticism of Marshal Tuchachevsky spoke about the dangers of 'Red militarism', there is no doubt about the possibility of such an approach.[10]

(3) *Parochial traditions*. Finally, there is a tradition of analysis in Continental Europe arising from the churches' concern with the problem. Analysts close to the churches in the last century, like

Wasserburg[11] or Pachtler,[12] argued against the etatisation of social life, particularly in the *Kulturkampf* against Bismarck in Germany. Since then, a tradition of opposition against the rise of militarism can be traced which today culminates in the project of the World Council of Churches to have a 'programme to combat militarism'.[13]

The subordination of individual authors to these three strands appears as somewhat confused in the literature (Berghahn, for instance, sees Dieter Senghaas and Monika Medick in the Luxembourg tradition, while a more precise account would put them under the liberal label).[14] As a point of departure for a better understanding of the notion of militarism, Berghahn's final statement about the requirements for further investigation shall be adopted:

> We shall have a more precise understanding of the term if one puts equal emphasis upon manifestations as well as functions of militarism, and if one cares as well for the character and structure of the order which gives rise to militarism.[15]

If Berghahn's third aspect gets a little bit generalised, the following division of labour for a better attack on the problem remains: militarism ought to be studied by its

manifestations;
functions; and
contributing factors.

The liberal tradition of criticism tends to concentrate on the manifestations of militarism, i.e. that the military sector affects the civilian sector to an intolerable extent. The functions of militarism are present more in the light of the socialist tradition. The major charges are that militarism contributes to preserving existing modes of production and relations of dominance, and perpetuates existing class relations. Because the literature about the functions of militarism is redundant, it shall not be repeated here at length.[16] The concern of this contribution is rather to overcome the inadequacies of present concepts in the current state of social, political and economic affairs in order to give a proper understanding of what militarism is today. Hence the reference to analytical traditions is not only to place their understanding of militarism into its historical context, and to find out the proper connotations of their respective approaches. Because the criticism of militarism also today is vitally dependent on the social groups which carry it forward, the reflection of the historical strands is mandatory.

The conceptual clarification of the role of the military in contemporary societies is based upon three premisses. *First*, a general definition would be grossly meaningless. Militarism is 'multidimensional and varied, with difference manifestations in various circumstances, dependent on the historical background, national traditions, class structure, social conditions, economic strength, acute problems faced, and the vigor of the officer corps'.[17] *Second*, a complete atomisation into aspects and individual manifestations of militarism won't do justice to a phenomenon which is, after all, coherent. Despite variations in outer appearance, particularly in different social systems, systematic causes and factors contributing towards militarisation as well as the impacts of such development will offer generalisations. *Third*, militarism is, despite all historical evidence, no phenomenon which acts unabated in history. There are obvious waves of militarisation, and the Third World of today appears as moving on the apex of her military penetration.[18]

There is a widespread consensus in the literature that, militarism in the Third World is distinct from militarism in industrialised countries.[19] This provokes the question of how to define coherently militarism as a global phenomenon, i.e. how to find the common features of militaristic developments between such country groupings, and finally how to trace the specific ways of militarisation in different parts of the world. *The coherent element in my view of any militarism rests with its functions in the industrialised and the less developed world, while the manifestations and contributing factors may differ considerably.*

Based upon these premises, the phenomenon of militarism will be approached on three different levels:

(1) manifestations of militarism in specific regions of the world shall be inspected by resorting to selected indicators in a descriptive way;
(2) the meaning of certain functions of militarism shall be analytically separated from the delineation of descriptive indicators;
(3) contributing factors shall also be distinguished from the assessment of manifestations and functions.

After the classification of these aspects, one should be prepared to deal with the 'ism' in the meaning of militarism, the self-sustaining element in the developments that the socialists, liberals and some Christians have been criticising for the last hundred years.

1 Militarisation and Militarism

The role of armed forces in development – or, as critics maintain, continued underdevelopment – recently became the focus of increased debates. The topic has long been dominated by authors drawing on the modernisation theory approach of American vintage,[20] accompanied by the closely related concept of the 'national democratic revolution' in Soviet writings.[21] There is only a small minority of analysts writing about the military in the Third World who do not adhere to one of these two strands.[22] The majority of Third World countries are now under military rule, and a couple of them reigned over by pseudo-civilian governments, and growth rates of military budget outlays have reached levels unknown before; hence the claim for a re-assessment of past analytical evidence about the positive contribution of the military to civilian development has been brought forward outside the scientific community. Studies by expert groups launched by the United Nations and, apart from those diplomatically mitigated texts, ambitions by the World Council of Churches to arrive at a 'Programme to combat militarism' have promoted a number of case studies which reach conclusions with results, to put it mildly, quite contradictory to the propositions of modernisation theories. Various expert meetings convened by those distinguished bodies apparently contributed considerably to a revival of the debate, which soon concentrated upon efforts to arrive at new conceptualisation of the militarism paradigm. These shall be examined in the following. Additionally, new approaches to assess the impact of militarisation on development processes shall be reconsidered. Despite the fact that this debate is far from producing results, and despite some confusion with respect to manifestations, indicators and meanings of militarisation, some major progress is apparent. The recent study of the militarism phenomenon, particularly in the Third World, has demonstrated the usefulness of a strict analytical separation between militarisation and militarism. The evident advantage of the notion of militarisation is that it offers all attractions of operational empirical research: if militarisation is defined as the process of enlargement of the military establishment within a society, indicators of a quantifiable kind could be brought to bear. This approach would move the study of the militarism phenomenon on to the qualitative level.

The quantitative understanding of the militarisation phenomenon does not necessarily provide for a negative judgement. During World War II, the societies of the anti-Hitler coalition were highly militarised, and today a number of liberation movements in the Third World are also strongly militarised, but these developments ought not to be condemned as indicating militarism *per se*. One should speak about militarism and militaristic development if the process of militarisation is turned into a self-perpetuating, autonomous development which detaches from the forces promoting militarisation (which can be assessed, for example by means of interest analysis), and which continues unabated by internal constraints. Needless to say that such a kind of militarism contradicts any meaningful development strategy.

Recent efforts to define militarisation and militarism are all apparently tied to the historical tradition. Skjelsbaek selects as the point of departure the long-standing definition by Vagts, stemming from the year 1937 (in the meantime, no major effort has been undertaken to define militarism). He quotes: 'Militarism has connoted a dominance of the military over the civilian, an undue preponderance of military demands, and emphasis on military considerations, spirit, ideals, and scales of value in the life of states.'[23] Skjelsbaek suggests using two aspects of this definition for a new understanding of militarism. First, Vagt's definition is an open one – it is not tied to specific societies or the role of the military under given conditions. Hence one could use this definition also under present circumstances. Second, Skjelsbaek stresses the aspect of exaggeration in this definition. Militarism is not seen as a necessary consequence of the establishment of military independent states of the Third World. The term is rather focused on excess impacts of this development – 'a militarised society is then equivalent to a society with strong militarism – a *militaristic* society.'[24]

Skjelsbaek's proposal is addressed towards a problem of enormous significance for development strategies: he raises the question of how the size and function of newly established military apparatuses can be determined on the normative level. If there is no yardstick, it will be virtually impossible to assess military influence as disproportionate. If a measure of appropriate size of the military establishment is lacking, then the notion suggested by Vagts will provide only for a rather vague assessment that in comparison to other institutions the military is exerting excessive, proportionate or insufficient influence in society (formally speaking, one is operating with a one-point scale).

An expert group convened by the World Council of Churches prefers a narrower definition, because such an approach appears more promising. This concept also distinguishes more clearly between a static and a process-oriented fixation of the phenomenon:

> Militarisation should be understood as the process whereby military values, ideology, and patterns of behaviour achieve a dominating

> influence on the political, social, economic and external affairs of the State, and as a consequence the structural, ideological and behavioural patterns of both the society and the government are 'militarised'.[25]

Militarism is seen as the result of the militarisation process: 'Militarism should be seen as one of the more perturbing results of this process'.[26] This concept appears as usable for an empirically oriented research on development strategies, hence it provides for quantification and the definition of indicators. The aspect of exaggeration also appears as measurable with respect to the militarisation concept. The approach towards 'militarism' is, however, much less telling, comparable in this respect to Skjelsbæk's proposal. It is hard to see how much an approach can be converted into operational reseach concepts.

Other concepts also look for a narrower definition of the older militarism concept in a vein comparable to the expert group statement of the World Council. Marek Thee defines:

> Under the term 'militarism' I subsume such symptoms as a rush to armaments, the growing role of the military . . . in national and international affairs, the use of force as an instrument of prevalence and political power, and the increasing influence, of the military in civilian affairs.[27]

Under 'militarisation' Thee defines 'an extension of military influence to civilian spheres, including economic and socio-political life'.[28]

The argument against this suggestion is less that the concept of militarisation is largely contained in the militarism concept and hence is made redundant. It must be stressed that reference to the manifestations (or, as Thee calls it, 'symptoms') of any phenomenon restricts insight to the descriptive level; certain aspects of society may be identified as 'militaristic' or not. The definition of any entity through its impact remains always unsatisfactory in social science and excludes theoretical reasoning: a definition should aim at the essence or the structure of a phenomenon rather than giving mere hints for a proper identification. Thee believes that with his approach one can circumvent the normative problem (where does 'excess' start?); on the other hand, his colourful delineation of manifestations of current militarism remains the most comprehensive approach on this level.

By comparison, a slightly older piece by Dieter Senghaas is rather close to the catalogue offered by Thee on manifestations of current militarism. Senghaas wrote five years ago about appearances of militarism in international and national politics:

> (1) in a continued quantitative and qualitative nuclear strategic armaments policy;
> (2) in a continued quantitative and qualitative conventional armaments policy;
> (3) in a high rate of innovation in so-called counter-insurgency warfare.[29]

Senghaas continues to list ten points where according to his view one can trace militarism, which led a German military journal to one conclusion: 'In this view, militarism appears as a global movement for the destruction of social and economic progress.'[30] At the other extreme, distinctly narrow concepts are propagated. Alexander Kirby submits the following definition: 'I take militarism to mean the willingness by a state to achieve the realisation of its policies through the deliberate and organised use of physical force against the frontiers.'[31] Kirby suggests an interesting combination of his militarism concept with the concept of racism; because of the one-dimensionality of such approaches, this track shall be neglected here.

In contrast to such definitions based upon a group of actors, two different approaches ought to be mentioned before a conclusion can be drawn. The first views militarism in a certain country as a quality of the political attitudes of the population. Empirically, this approach is based upon the well known techniques of attitude analysis. In this respect, the Canadian researcher William Eckhardt holds a long-standing reputation for ten years and more of extensive empirical research. His definition:

> Militarism may be studied as an attitude or set of attitudes in the minds of people, as a behavior or set of behaviors in which people engage, or as an institution or set of institutions which people establish to facilitate or to organize such behavior.[32]

Despite the impressive results of this methodologically fruitful approach, there remains a definite gap between the delineation of military attitudes and the explanation of the rise of militarism. Approaches of this kind tend to describe the phenomenon from peripheral aspects, in particular because they do not study militarism as an outcome of processes of domination and the enforcement of political will upon society. It appears that militarism in the Third World is even less a problem of mass political attitudes than it might be in the industrialised world.

Finally, there are structuralist approaches of the study of militarism. The most radical concept to the best of my knowledge has been put forward by Malvern Lumsden: 'Militarisation is primarily a problem at the level of social structure whereas militarism is a problem at the level of superstructure.'[33] Albeit definitions of this type tend to describe the genetic place of the phenomenon rather than the problem itself, this approach entailed impressive explanatory value in the recent debate. In keeping with the intention stated at the beginning of this chapter, we shall focus more on the essence than on contributing factors to the militarism problem.

2 The Normative Problem

The comfortable distinction between militarisation as a process and militarism as one perturbing result leads into considerable methodological problems. Despite all difficulties of drawing a borderline, however, the distinction is considered to be an achievement in itself.

Reference to the qualitative conversion of militarisation processes into the excess development, as it is approached by a number of the definitional efforts quoted above, entails an answer to the following principal question: how can one arrive normatively at a measure of 'proportionate' size and influence of the military in a given society? The literature contains four answers to this question.

First, there are normative derivations based upon competitive analysis: one compares the military effort of various states and tries to assess whether the military effort of a specific government is 'too high' or not. The very character of the comparative approach used rules out such normative concepts producing evidence about absolute sizes of military effort. The choice of yardsticks also handicapped the usefulness of past elaborated proposals in this vein. The English economist E.A.G. Robinson, for instance, has submitted a catalogue of four categories based exclusively on the physical nature of a country, which, according to his claim, lead to the necessary conclusion that smaller states need to spend more on the military than bigger ones in order to arrive at the same level of outer security. His hypothesis meets strong contradication from empirical evidence both from industrialised and developing countries.[34]

Second, the work of military planners is usually based on normative aspects. In such computations one can find statements about how much is militarily needed to compensate for a given hostile potential. This strictly comparative approach is much more open with respect to amounts compared, and hence it is even less suitable for the assessment of absolute requirements for military preparedness in a society.

Third, there are efforts based upon impressive theoretical thrust, to establish within alliances criteria for 'fair' sharing of military costs among members. Oriented towards the 'theory of collective goods', all these efforts have in fact been based upon factual military outlays rather than normative approaches. Outside NATO, such concepts apparently play a minor role, and can be neglected here.[35]

A fourth normative concept is fuelled into the debate by the critical literature, which focuses upon the legitimacy of military spending. Specific military budgets are criticised as not supported by the legitimacy beliefs of the population. This hypothesis is regularly not put to empirical test (it would be hard to isolate a special issue like military effort methodologically from the real belief in legitimacy of a given government). Regularly, there are only appeals to the plausibility of the argument. In developing nations with their different approach to participation and legitimacy of government, this concept would also be frustrated to deliver a normative hint for the calibration of military budget outlays.

In retrospect, there is no normative assessment of military effort seen as fit for providing even vague hints about the proper dimensioning of military budgets and military apparatuses. The conversion of militarisation into militarism is hence to be approached by rather complex methods of descriptive evaluation – if simple landmarks can not be enumerated.

3 Contributing Factors

Assessing current developments, a specific set of factors can be traced which contribute to militarisation or even militarism in a decisive way, but which are not necessarily military in nature themselves.

For the analysis of the interrelations between militarisation and underdevelopment, there are different constellations of factors seen in the literature, and the following conceptualisation is but one of a number of possible approaches.[36] Generally, one may distinguish between global structural factors and singular factors.

It must be stressed that the factors which can be identified as furthering militarism and the arms race are not to be seen as an array of otherwise singular elements. Their combination forms a kind of system, for which the label *new Military World Order* has been suggested.[37]

Making an analogy to the combined effort of economic development everywhere in the world, which has recently been understood as functioning by rules of its own in addition to economic policies pursued by individual national governments, military transfers and policies, like economic interactions, are considered in this view as being highly determined by the environment in which a national government makes decisions on military policies. While some authors describe an 'old' military world order reaching far back into history,[38] the coercive force of this system is certainly felt to be much stronger in our times, for example in developing countries building national institutions, including armed services. The systemic approach stresses the overall international aspects of militarisation, its structure and its dynamics. It cares for the roots and interrelations of militaristic developments with the current international political, social and economic set-up. Militarism in the industrialised world is regarded in this perespective as a systemic function of bipolar superpower struggle for predominance and control, while Third World militarisation appears as a dependent process enforced by the set-up of the system by new members acquiring their respective international roles.

Dieter Senghaas, who first argued the issue with Jan Øberg, observes initially an 'uneven attention directed on the one side towards the debate on the "new international economic order", and on the other side the spread of militarism'.[39] He speaks about the 'internationalization of militarism', and urges a comprehensive conceptualisation of global militarism. This notion was quickly accepted by other scholars. Marek Thee, again particularly interested in the manifestation of the phenomenon stresses:

> there is structure and hierarchy to the world military order, best seen in the flow of armaments around the globe. On top of this structure, as pacemakers in armaments, military technology, and international arms deals, are the two superpowers . . . Together they stand for half of world military expenditures, they concentrate in their hands up to 90% of global military research and development and command 70% of the world arms trade.[40]

On a more general level, Thee defines:

> In sum, the military and militarization today rely on a strong international structure and a well-established hierarchy. There is specific order in this structure and hierarchy, rank being dependent on

> military and economic strength, and mobility on mastership in the application of violence.[41]

A study group convened by the International Peace Research Association is more precise in its definition. The group indicates that militarisation has hitherto predominantly been studied as one aspect of national development (or maldevelopment), and confronts this common view with the following statement:

> When examining the military structures from a global point of view, much of past thinking and analysis of the military turns outs to be conventional and untenable wisdom. The global military structure is historically developed, it is an outgrowth of patterns of dominance and dependence, it contains the sediment of past conflicts, it is undergoing a self-sustained and irrational growth in organizational bureaucracy as well as aimless technological transformations.[42]

The group uses the phrase 'condominium' of superpowers for its portrait of hierarchical structures in this world military order in which the military establishments of the various countries find their respective ranks:

> These give them different functions depending upon the positions they hold. At the highest level, i.e. at the level of the superpowers, the military serves functions of international control of established dominance. In addition, they also serve the general purpose of internal legitimation of the established political systems. As we move from the superpowers to the more peripheral actors, the role of the military becomes increasingly subordinate and dependent, not only in terms of technological dependence on armament imports, military training, and advice, but dependent also with regard to the functions served by the armed forces.[42]

Like economic exchanges, military processes in this view are highly dependent on the structures of the global system. The structuralist approach stresses the historical basis aspect as well as the impact of economic, social and political arrangements on the nominally independent decision in a new nation-state to have its own military establishment. According to this approach, the world-wide phenomenon of militarisation is a function of superpower rivalries, linked to the much more broadly discussed issue of industrialisation.

Besides the general structural aspect as circumscribed by the notion of a world military order, there is an array of singular factors which contribute significantly to Third World militarisation.

First, a major factor contributing to the rise of militarism is to be found in the social history of the former colonies. All colonial regimes were based upon brute force. Without military forces, the exploitation of Asia, Africa and Latin America would have been impossible. When the colonial armies were disbanded, they left societies marked by the experience of exploitation guided by force as the basis of their economic reproduction. Colonial infrastructures had been built to transport goods extracted from the country as directly as possible to the coastline, and to safeguard these transport lanes. Because all colonial powers were sea powers, administrative infrastructures (most prominent: the site of one's capital) were oriented towards the sea, to provide military access in the case of uprising. The handicaps which such colonial heritages represent for an optimum allocation of national resources for general development are usually vastly underrated. Today the military element in the given infrastructures together with the lack of civic traditions will certainly favour recent trends towards militarism.

Second, we must mention the enormous influx of relatively modern weapons from US supplies into the best of so-called 'forward defence countries' surrounding the socialist part of the world after World War II. With respect to the general level of global armaments, this transfer of arms may be judged negligible. With respect to the domestic situation in those 'forward defence countries', however, the impact upon the future path of political development was tremendous. The armed forces experienced a thrust of modernisation unrivalled by any other branch of the society.

Third, the crisis of development policies in the sixties enhanced a tendency to transfer responsibility for planning and other state functions towards the armed forces, as the least poorly functioning branch of government. This touches the question of how forced development should be politically organised. Authoritarian patterns of guidance, not necessarily directly commanded by the military but similar to military systems of obeying orders, appeared better suited than the import of Western democratic institutions. The model of authoritarian guidance as offered by Eastern European societies was not without attraction in this situation.

The implementation of this choice led to a massive yet hardly visible transfer of software technology based upon military systems developed in industrialised countries, ranging from communication patterns to the imitation of bureaucratic decision-making and non-civilian administration.

Fourth, the increase in hard currency resources in the hands of a number of Third World governments (created by the massive increase of the price of crude oil as enforced by the OPEC cartel) enabled certain governments to divert additional money for arms purchases. Civilian alternatives for public spending – for which the government could have opted – were apparently not as attractive (at least in the short run) as the absorption of the new wealth by military procurement. The military therefore experienced an additional and unexpected modernisation thrust, again unchallenged by civilian development.

Fifth, the increased social role of the armed forces in many Third World countries would remain but an episode without sustained support from industrialised countries. In the West, dominant agents of this support have been the huge production enterprises which invest in peripheral countries, while in Eastern Europe centralistic state parties are striving for political allies, even if these wear uniforms. Both types of agents from the industrialised world are characterised by the fact that they do not protect against authoritarian forms of power. (It is also more attractive from the viewpoint of a multinational firm if political life in a country is free from political clashes or labour disputes, if the labour force is disciplined by powerful elements of law and order, and if reliable partners for investments are available, in the form of the military as a stable authoritarian government.) The huge multinational enterprises have recently begun to exploit wage differentials and other relative benefits in several Third World countries for weapons production – in countries which, without such foreign initiatives, would not see such production for some time to come. The impact of this recent development is rarely fully understood: today we observe the passing of a threshold in militaristic industrialisation in which excessive arms requirements, to be optimally fulfilled by domestic arms production, mean that leading munitions makers can gain a composite edge by transferring part of their production activities into Third World regions.

4 Regimes of Militarisation

In any society, and in developing systems in particular, development is shaped by the result of the struggle for the distribution of resources. Military effort can contribute to development – if development is understood as a specific road to an industrial state (based upon macroeconomic growth, forced stabilisation of industrial relations, etc.). A forced orientation on militarily induced growth influences predominantly three regimes relevant to development.

4.1 The Regime of Technology

The development path and industrialisation of a given society are dependent on the accumulation of technology in the country. Military technology may impose important landmarks in this respect by forming import patterns of technology transfers, by the demand for particular servicing or production technology, and predominantly by the attraction of numerous accompanying technology inputs which would not be necessary if there were no military technology of an advanced kind. Military and civilian accumulations of technology are regularly opposed as alternatives. The well known 'spill over' argument in favour of military technology appears as – to say the least – exaggerated in a Third World context, and there is no empirical foundation which would support this apologetic view outside the industrialised centres of the globe. Even the staunchest proponents should reconsider whether a militarily oriented technological development of the Third World is the requirement of the day.

4.2 The Regime of Political Administration

The establishment and growth of political institutions in developing nations is severely affected by militarisation. Two aspects exert a decisive influence:

> A high level of authoritarian rather than participatory decision-making, and a high reliance on coercion to enforce decisions . . . A participatory democratic system will lead to decentralization . . . the military represents an entirely different organizational structure, with a high degree of centralization and hierarchy.[44]

Even if there has been no *coup d'état* by the armed forces, a disproportionate influence from the military will deform any development path (it needs to be stressed, however, that simple indicators for such trends are not available).

4.3 The Regime of Personnel Resources

The visible impact of militarisation is to be found in the manpower regime, i.e. the ways and means of how manpower is recruited and qualified. The armed forces, in the first round, are competing with other institutions for personnel and educational capacities. With that special potential for achieving given goals in those rivalries, the military are likely to attain preferential treatment, and later to become dominant in recruiting the necessary cadres. It is no illusion that elites in a large number of Third World countries are predominantly replenished from military institutions.

The three regimes may be affected in the same way by a process of militarisation; they may interact with each other, and they may enforce the tendency towards militarism among themselves – they may also contradict it in specific cases. Among others, Marek Thee refers to cross-relationships among, as he calls it, 'militarism dynamics and armaments dynamics'.

> Whatever the local and subjective grounds for militarism and militarization in the Third World, the aspirations of the military in these countries find a favourable breeding ground in the rush to armaments initiated by the great powers. Weapons instrumentation is readily at hand. Moreover, armaments in the developed world induce the developing countries to follow suit. In a world where weapons invest states with power, prestige, status, and authority, even states devoid of militaristic tendencies become inclined to enter the race.[45]

As the pillars of militarisation, Thee closes in upon the officer corps in Third World armed forces. Based on his long-term experience in international military commissions,[46] he refers to the remarkable aspect that 'the military all over the world think and tend to act within a similar conceptual framework born out of their professional routine, life-style, mode of operation, and career socialization'.[47] Civil servants in Third World bureaucracies appear as much less similar in this respect. Furthermore, the modern officer 'feels expert in organization, the application of modern technology, technical advance, and the safeguarding of state interests'.[48]

After the delineation of these premisses, Thee describes the impact of militarism upon a developing society:

> In a very general sense, militarism and militarization start with the abuse by the military of its legitimate function and its encroachment on political affairs, internally and externally. Brought up to apply organized violence and professing to be the guardians of national survival, the military tends to usurp roles and prerogatives in society which go beyond democratic legitimacy, intervening in

> internal and imposing its will in external affairs . . . Finally, placed strategically in the web of state and government bureaucracy . . the military develops a propensity to intervene actively in politics, foreign and domestic.[49]

Mary Kaldor has proposed, with impressive theoretical nerve, to break through such descriptive approaches, which are tied to mere appeals of evidence in order to be commonly accepted, to analyse the rise of current militarism. Her proposal is to link the understanding of the militarisation process directly with the general pattern of industrialisation, as it is offered in parallel by the industrial centres in the East and the West. She speaks about the 'model form of force' which is represented by the 'industrial army':

> This is based on the weapons system concept which strictly limits the room for variation in the relations of force. With some qualification, the form of force thus becomes a reflection of the form of force prevailing in the metropolis. The rise of such armies is associated with the beginning of industrialization, and the need to create or preserve a social structure in which the industrialization process can take place . . . The industrial armies, like their progenitors in the metropolis, are rarely used directly, except in external war . . . The true significance of the weapons system concept is political; it creates a commitment to industrialization, and, more particularly, to a model of industrialization that is decadent by the standard of the most advanced industrial societies. The primary function of the industrial army is not so much combat as political intervention.[50]

Kaldor foresees much analytical potential if this approach is accepted, particularly in overcoming contradictory findings by empirical studies:

> This political tendency would explain the positive findings of the 'modernizers' measured in terms of attitudes towards growth and modern industry and, at the same time, it would explain the negative findings of those who emphasize the wasteful nature of militaristic industrialization and the importance of non-growth goals.[51]

Robin Luckham suggested the first fully-fledged analytical tableau to link development patterns (e.g. 'petty capitalist commodity production', 'enclave commodity production', 'import substituting production' and 'export-promoting industrialization') with the development path of the various military establishments which can be traced in the Third World.[52]

5 What is Militarism?

After the delineation of concepts and the separation of militarisation processes from the phenomenon itself, we finally turn to answer the question of what the ideological content of militarism is today – what the 'ism' in the term actually means. As well as all the materialistic elements on our concept, ideology also contributes to the developments one deplores, particularly and most visibly in the Third World. There ideologies illuminating militarism demonstrate impressive materialist force.

It appears that on a general level militarism can be traced in the following aspects: First, relatively militant patterns of political processes can be observed in the countries in question. Governments try to mobilise masses by militancy. This ought not to be judged negatively with respect to development impact: but the dangers of such political styles are obvious. Second, in most Third World countries the political decision-making process is influenced by means of force, i.e. the physical suppression of opposition. Policy patterns are similar to military modes of reaching a decision, although they are not necessarily to be blamed on militarism. Third, a nationalistic attitude in foreign policies can be noted in a majority of Third World governments, often supported by claims to use military force in order to promote specific ends. The borders established by former colonial powers created ethnic minorities in many of those countries, and a nationalist emphasis has been organised in order to integrate the society.

It appears that based on such conceptual clarifications an analytical level of understanding of the nature of the militarism problem has been reached, and that further progress in this field should be expected from case studies which verify the concepts. Given the traditional gaps between empiricists and the theoretical schools (to which most of the literature quoted above belongs), one hesitates to utter such an assessment without pragmatic hints on how to organise progress. Methodological debates about the fitness of certain empirical approaches will certainly be required, as well as some continued thrust from political bodies like the UN expert panels or the World Council of Churches, in order to integrate the participants in the debate into the scientific community again. The effort appears to be justified: it is only by such procedures that one can hope for an action-oriented concept to halt or even to reverse global militarisation trends, and for hints on how meaningful development can be achieved by converting current misallocations of physical and immaterial resources.

Notes

1. Alfred Vagts, *A History of militarism. Romance and realities of a profession* (New York, 1937, revised edition New York, 1959).

2. An excellent introduction to this debate, together with a presentation of principal papers, can be found in Volker R. Berghahn (ed.), *Militarismus* (Cologne, 1975).

3. Ibid., p. 9. Cf. also the instructive account by John Erickson and Hans Mommsen, 'Militarism' in C.D. Kernig (ed.), *Marxism, Communism and Western Society* (New York, 1973), Vol. 3.

4. Cf., for example, *Militarismus*, p. 9. A dramatic illustration of this point was given by the West Berlin teacher examination board in 1978, when a political science professor was attacked for putting forward a topic 'neither acceptable to the examination committee nor the candidate' – the candidate's presentation was formulated 'The position of the SPD in the remilitarization question in West Germany'. Eventually, the authorities interfered and changed this examination topic completely.

5. Ekkehart Krippendorf, ' "Imperialismus" in der Friedensforschung' in *Friedensanalyse. Für Theories und Praxis*, no. 3 (Frankfurt am Main, 1976), p. 68. Krippendorf quotes the conservative German political scientist Wilhelm Hennis (ibid.) as holding the same view.

6. Especially Harold Lasswell, 'The garrison-state hypothesis today' in Samuel P. Huntington (ed.), *Changing Patterns of the Military in Politics* (Free Press, New York, 1962), para IV.

7. E. Assmus, 'Die publizistische Diskussion um den Militarismus unter besonderer Berücksichtigung der Geschichte des Begriffs in Deutschland und seine Beziehung zu den politischen Ideen zwischen 1850 und 1950' (unpublished PhD dissertation, University of Erlangen, 1951), p. 36. Berghahn, *Militarismus* p. 32, quotes additional sources in support of this finding.

8. Karl Liebknecht, 'Militarismus und Antimilitarismus unter besonderer Berücksichtigung der internationalen Jugendbewegung', Address to the Mannheim Youth Congress, October 1906. Various printings, e.g. *Gesammelte Reden und Schriften*, Vol. I (Berlin, 1958), pp. 247-456.

9. Rosa Luxemburg, *Die Akkumulation des Kapitals* (Berlin, 1913), especially Chapter 32.

10. Cf. Erickson and Mommsen, 'Militarism', p. 247.

11. P. Wasserburg, *Gedankenspäne über den Militarismus* (Mainz, 1874).

12. G.R. Pachtler, *Der europäische Militarismus* (Amberg, 1875).

13. E.G. Jose-Antonio Viera Gallo (ed.), *The Security Trap. Arms Race, Militarism and Disarmament. A Concern for Christians* (Rome, 1979).

14. Berghahn, *Militarismus*, p. 14.

15. Ibid., p. 31.

16. The economic functions in particular have been extensively studied, for example, in all the literature of the military-industrial complex; the repressive functions are also widely discussed in the literature on the military in the Third World.

17. Marek Thee, 'Militarism and Militarization in Contemporary International Relations', *Bulletin of Peace Proposals*, no. 4 (1977), p. 298 (cf. Ch. 1).

18. This view has been extended into the notion that militarism is tied to cultural cycles (e.g. Arnold Toynbee, *War and Civilisation* (London, 1951)), or that it is tied to a stage of decay in society (among more recent writings, Fritz Vilmar maintains this view, cf. *Rüstung und Abrüstung im Spätkapitalismus. Eine sozio-ökonomische Analyse des Militarismus* (Frankfurt am Main, 1965)).

19. There is a number of writers holding this view; one of the most systematic views is given by the Syrian analyst Bassam Tibi, *Militär und Sozialmismus in der Dritten Welt* (Frankfurt am Main, 1973).

20. In the German literature, the most comprehensive criticism of the modernisation theory approach is found in Tibi, *Militär und Sozialismus*. I tried to contribute to this debate together with others in 'Armaments and Underdevelopment' in *Bulletin for Peace Proposals*, vol. 5 (1974), pp. 173-85, and in more elaborated form, in the introduction to the book with the same title, *Armaments and Underdevelopment* (forthcoming English version of *Rüstung und Unterentwicklung* (Hamburg (Rowohlt), 1976), under preparation with MIT Press).

21. Cf. R. Ulyanovsky, *Socialism and the Newly Independent Nations* (Moscow, 1974); A.A. Iskenderow, *Die nationale Befreiungsbewegung, Probleme, Gesetzmässigkeiten Perspektiven* (translated from the Russian) (Berlin, 1972); or more recently, K.N. Brutents, *National Liberation Revolutions Today* (Moscow, 1977); I. Andreyev, *The Noncapitalist Way: Soviet Experience and Liberated Countries* (Moscow, 1977). A detailed case study, by the Cuban Raul Valdes Vivo, *Ethiopia's Revolution* (New York, 1978) (originally *Etiopia, la revolucion desconocida* (Havana, 1977)), received a detailed criticism by John Markakis, 'Garrison Socialism: the Case of Ethiopia' (unpublished paper, Institute for Development Studies, University of Sussex, 1978). Critical comments (also about Tibi's assessment, cf. note 1) can also be found in Salim Ibrahim's contribution in *Das Argument*, vol. 16, no. 88 (December 1974), Parts 10-12, p. 127.

22. In the Anglo-Saxon context, one should refer to work done at the Institute for Development Studies at the University of Sussex (cf. the contribution by Mary Kaldor in this volume), contributions from Scandinavia, particularly the debate in the IPRA study group on militarisation and the Third World. From the US Miles Wolpin and Eric Nordlinger ought to be mentioned.

23. Kjell Skjelsbaek, 'A Dictionary of Terms for the WCC Consultation in Militarism' (mimeo.), *inter alia* to be found in *Preparatory Materials for the Consultation on Militarism* (Glion, Switzerland), 13-18 November 1977, no. 2 (edited by the Commission of Churches on International Affairs, World Council of Churches, Geneva), p. 30.

24. Ibid., p. 31.

25. Consultation on Militarism, World Council of Churches, Glion, Switzerland, 13-18 November 1977, 'Report of Working Group III' (mimeo.), p. 1. Cf. also Gallo, *The Security Trap*, p. 117.

26. Ibid.

27. Thee, 'Militarism', p. 296.

28. Ibid.

29. Dieter Senghaas, *Gewalt-Konflikt-Frieden* (Hamburg, 1974), p. 55. Senghaas first presented these views under the title *Rüstungsdynamik und Abrüstung* to the Conference Ökonomische und Soziale Aspekte der Abrüstung (Berlin, 1973).

30. Dr Seidler, 'Militarismus' in *Informationen für die Truppe*, no. 11 (1976), p. 62.

31. Alexander Kirby, 'Militarism and Racism' (mimeo.) in *Preparatory Materials for the Consultation on Militarism* (Glion, Switzerland), 13-18

November 1977, no. 1, p. 4.

32. William Eckhardt, 'The Causes and Correlates of Western Militarism', paper presented at the Pugwash Symposium on Militarism and National Security, Oslo, November 1977 (mimeo.), p. 1 (cf. Ch. 18).

33. Malvern Lumsden, 'Militarism: Cultural Dimensions of Militarisation', paper presented at the Pugwash Symposium on Militarism, Oslo, Norway, 21-5 November 1977, and the Seventh General Conference of the International Peace Research Association, Oaxtepec, Mexico, 11-16 December 1977, p. 3 (cf. Ch. 19).

34. A discussion about Robinson's concept can be found in my piece, 'Die Struktur von Rüstungsausgaben', *Leviathan*, vol. 1, no. 1 (1973), p. 46.

35. The justification of this statement can be taken from the numerical results by Bruce M. Russett, *What Price Vigilance? The Burdens of National Defence* (New Haven, 1970), Ch. 4.

36. Skjelsbaek (cf. n. 23), for example, distinguishes the indicators behaviour, attitudes, social structure and technology.

37. The term 'World military order' has apparently been fed into the debates of the peace research community by the Danish expert Jan Øberg and Dieter Senghaas, who had a direct exchange on this subject.

38. Cf. Malvern Lumsden, 'Social and economic consequences of the world military order' (mimeo.) (Stockholm, 1977).

39. Dieter Senghaas, *Weltwirtschaftsordnung und Entwicklungspolitik. Plädoyer für Dissoziation* (Frankfurt am Main, 1977), p. 223.

40. Thee, 'Militarism' (n. 4), p. 303.

41. Ibid., p. 304.

42. 'The Impact of Militarization on Development and Human Rights. Statement by the Study Group on Militarization of the International Peace Research Association' in *Bulletin of Peace Proposals*, no. 2 (1978), p. 170.

43. Ibid., p. 171.

44. Ibid., p. 176.

45. Thee, 'Militarism' (n. 4), p. 304.

46. Cf. his report, *Notes of a Witness. Laos and the Second Indochina War* (New York, 1973).

47. Thee, 'Militarism' (n. 4), p. 302.

48. Ibid.

49. Ibid., p. 298.

50. 'The Military in Third World Development' in R. Jolly (ed.), *Disarmament and World Development* (Oxford, 1978), p. 70.

51. Ibid., p. 71.

52. Robin Luckham, 'Militarism and International Dependence' in Jolly, *Disarmament* (cf. n. 32), pp. 35-56. Cf. also the *IDS Bulletin*, vol. 8, no. 3 (March 1977), pp. 38-50, for another version of this contribution.

6 WHAT IS MILITARISM?

Ernie Regehr

By the reckoning of the pacifist, violence is an absolute evil, unmitigated by circumstance. To the extent that the ultimate purpose of military activity is the effective application of violence towards particular ends, there is assumed to be little point in distinguishing between variations in military or 'militaristic' attitudes, styles, objectives or activities. Every act of a military nature is characterised as 'militaristic', in that it depends upon violence as the ultimate means of resolving conflict.

The purpose of the following, however, is to suggest that a distinction between 'militarism' and what has been called 'the military way' *is* relevant and useful in our attempt to confront the still burgeoning military establishment in North America. (The use of the singular in referring to the military establishment in North America is deliberate. The Canadian and US military establishments are arranged according to a single continental strategy. Canada performs certain specialised and regional tasks, but Canadian defence policy is consciously planned as part of a continental defence system.)

In pursuing a distinction between 'militarism' and the 'military way', there will be references to 'legitimate' and 'illegitimate' military activities, but not in the sense of moral or theological legitimacy. The distinction is made in terms of the stated national roles and objectives of military forces and, more important, in terms of historically recognised areas of legitimate military activity. Stated another way, the purpose of the distinction is to recognise that historically, and popularly today, there is widespread acceptance of the legitimacy of a defensive war as an extreme means of service to the general good; provided that such a war be declared as just by an authoritative sovereign, that is can be independently shown to be in pursuit of a just cause, that the intention of the participants is the pursuit of justice and not some ulterior goals, and that the methods adhere to accepted codes of conduct. I'm *not* suggesting a revolution in the pacifist's ideology or theology to embrace the just war theory, but I am suggesting that opposition to militarism and opposition to the military way confront and challenge different assumptions. Opposition to the military way challenges the 'legitimacy' of any military activity and, particularly, the above notion of the just war; opposition to militarism, on the other hand, does not challenge that notion.

It is, therefore, counter-productive to condemn the use of military force to restore fundamental human rights and to end the rule and violence of a tyrant, or, for that matter, to condemn the right of North Americans to use military force to resist aggression on their borders and on their institutions with the same moral argument that we invoke against the mad overkill of the nuclear deterrence system. In doing so, we simply allow both objections to be dismissed by the perfectly sincere and rational response that absolute opposition to the use of military force is naive and unrealistic. For it is 'unrealistic' (which, of course, has nothing to do with its moral validity) to say that force has no role to play in the defence of justice and the preservation of order. And to say that it is unrealistic is not to question the moral and theological validity of absolute condemnation of violence; but the point is that opposition to 'militarism' (in this case to nuclear overkill) need not engage that fundamental question. Militarism can be fully discredited in terms that do not question the legitimacy of a national defence force itself – in other words, militarism can be discredited in the military's own terms. The question of military violence *per se* must obviously still be confronted, and pacifists must continue and make more effective their historic role of challenging the legitimacy of the military, but it is useful to distinguish between the two questions.

To separate the two terms 'militarism' and 'the military way' – and to invest them with distinctive meanings, I refer to the work of Alfred Vagts, *A History of Militarism: Civilian and Military*. He says:

> Every war is fought, every army is maintained, in a military way and in a militaristic way. The distinction is fundamental and fateful. The military way is marked by a primary concentration of men and materials on winning specific objectives of power with the utmost efficiency, that is, with the least expenditure of blood and treasure. It is limited in scope, confined to one function, and scientific in its essential qualities. Militarism, on the other hand, presents a vast array of customs, interests, prestige, actions, and thought-associated with armies and wars and yet transcending the true military purposes. Indeed, militarism is so constituted that it may hamper and defeat the purposes of the military way. Its influence is unlimited in scope. It may permeate all society and become dominant over all industry and arts. Rejecting the scientific character of the military way, militarism displays the qualities of caste and cult, authority and belief.[1]

Note that the two categories of military activity not only differ, but are contradictory. The 'military way' pursues specific, limited objectives of physical power – no more. It has only one function. The emphasis is on efficiency and scientific method. Militarism, far from having specific and limited objectives, claims transcendent purposes. It rejects the scientific method and employs custom, ceremony and prestige for ends that actually undermine the effectiveness of the military way. Militarism's functions are many. While the military way is an element of service of the interests defined by the society at large, militarism employs military forms to itself define and shape the interests of society.

By this definition, not all military activity is an expression of militarism and one can indeed oppose 'militarism' without making a judgement upon the use of military means in any and all circumstances. In short, opposition to militarism is not necessarily an expression of pacifism. Militarism is not the opposite of pacifism; it is more properly the opposite of 'civilianism'. Militarism represents a system of thought and attitudes that places military institutions above civilian institutions and introduces the military mentality into civilian decision-making. Militarism, to go back to the conditions of a 'just war', obtains when the soldiers, and not the authoritative sovereign, declare whether or not a war is just and whether or not the military should participate. It is the extension of military thinking over civilian institutions and civilian planning and over civilian authority.

The measure of militarism, however, is not the extent of the direct *power* of the military over civilian institutions. The issue rather is the *prevalence* of military thinking and assumptions and the extent to which they are operative within civilian institutions (we may expect a high correlation between the two, but they are not identical). It is possible to conceive of a military government that is not militaristic. For example, a central military assumption is that the criterion for decision-making is the opponent's realistic military *capabilities*, with no regard for his *intentions*. In a normal situation, in which a proper balance between political authority and the military service exists, the military's planning in terms of the opponent's capability is modified and curbed by political attention to the opponent's intentions. It is not the function of the military strategist to assess the political or military intentions of the other state; the strategist's task is confined to plotting the most efficient military response (efficiency being the least expenditure of life and material) to a variety of possible situations. It is the role of foreign policy to assess the intentions of the other power and then to instruct the military to prepare for particular eventualities, but not to prepare for others. It is theoretically possible for a military government to keep these two functions, the military and the political, separate, just as it is possible for a civilian government to obscure the distinction between military and political responsibility. When the distinction is maintained, the problem of militarism is not present; when the distinction is blurred, militarism is present.

Again, the definition is not the extent of *power* of the military over political institutions. One need go no further than Canada to illustrate the point. In Canada the Defense Department and the armed forces certainly exert no power over civilian institutions, and they have precious little influence. The best way to demote a Cabinet Minister without actually firing him from the Cabinet is to make him Minister of Defense. Unfortunately, this has not been enough to ensure the absence of militarism in Canada. It is a point that will be pursued later, but it is clear that Canada is a full participant, for example, in the matter of nuclear deterrence and has consistently supported the expansion of America's nuclear arsenal, so that we North Americans now have the capability of destroying the Soviet Union's major civilian and military targets many times over. Nor is militarism defined by the size of the defence budget. Canada's defence budget is relatively small ($4.2 billion in 1978/9). The increase in the US defence budget from $500 million prior to World War II to something in excess of $100 billion today may be an expression of militarism, but it is not a definition of it.

The point is an important one and challenges the comfortable illusion that American's militarism, as evidenced by her wars abroad and her outrageous defence spending at home, is the result of the power of the Pentagon, which somehow holds the country to ransom. It is difficult to believe that America's civilian institutions and political leadership are the hapless victims of the Pentagon. That the Pentagon is powerful is hardly to be denied, that its influence is, to say the least, extensive, is also true, but that it has gained its power and continues to exercise it in defiance of the wishes of the constitutional authorities and of the American people is doubtful. The US congressional system, with its emphasis on congressional vigilance, provides many more opportunities for detailed examination of, and challenges to, military spending than the British parliamentary system does. How many congressional committees, never mind the two Houses of Congress themselves, have opportunities to examine and amend budget allocations and requests submitted by the Pentagon? In one sense, this may simply beg the question. The failure of Congress to curb militarism is itself an expression of the power of the Pentagon – of its ability to mobilise the mass media and public relations forces to convince the American people and their elected representatives that their way of life depends upon an ever-growing defence budget. We must, however, consider the possibility that the primary source of militarism is not the military, but the corporation, and that the Pentagon, instead of taking over government, has itself been taken over by the corporate interests and their allies in government.[2]

There is an intriguing account by the military historian, Stephen Ambrose,[3] which suggests that the military lobby in Washington, to the extent that one exists as distinct from the military-industrial lobby, is rather less of a monolith than we are sometimes led to believe, and that the President more often than not must choose between conflicting military advice. His description of the way in which the Eisenhower and Kennedy administrations differed, not in their relations with the military, but in the way they evaluated military advice, is provocative. The main thrust of the Eisenhower administration, he says, was to balance the budget and hold down or reduce taxes and that the only way to accomplish this was to curb military expenditure. Democrats soon charged that the Republicans were allowing their Neanderthal fiscal views to endanger national security and the Army – which took the brunt of the fiscal cuts – was so furious that its Chief of Staff, Maxwell Taylor, resigned to publish a blistering criticism of Eisenhower's defence policy. But the President ignored the critics, kept the Defense Department budget at around $40 billion for all eight years of his administration and carried on a relatively inactive foreign policy.

Ambrose argues that under Kennedy and McNamara, however, the military got all that it asked for, and then some.

When in late 1958 Khrushchev threatened to turn control of access to Berlin over to the East Germans, Eisenhower was under intense pressure from both the Democrats and the military to increase the armed services dramatically as a prelude to taking a hard line with Khrushchev over Berlin. But in March 1959, as Khrushchev's deadline approached, and the Pentagon prepared plans for mobilisation, Eisenhower dismissed demands that he stop reducing the size of the Army and asked instead what the United States would do with more ground forces in Europe. He suggested the greatest danger in the Berlin crisis was that the Russians would frighten the United States into an arms race that would bankrupt the country.

Two years later Kennedy faced a similar crisis. He received the same military advice Eisenhower received, but he took it. Kennedy put a $3.2 billion additional military budget through Congress, tripled the draft calls, extended enlistments, and mobilised 158,000 reserves and National Guardsmen. Altogether he increased the size of the armed forces by 300,000 men, sending 40,000 of them to Europe and making six 'priority divisions' in the reserves ready for quick mobilisation.

On the question of ICBMs, Ambrose says neither Eisenhower nor Kennedy faced any significant military pressure to increase the number of missiles. In general, the Army preferred putting any additional defence funds into its own ground strength build-up; the Navy wanted to use extra money to build aircraft carriers, other surface ships, and Polaris submarines; the Air Force argued that its bomber force ought to be modernised. Eisenhower refused to do any of these things on a scale remotely satisfactory to the three services, but he also refused to increase the ICBM force, despite the so-called missile gap. Throughout his second term, Eisenhower kept the number of ICBMs steady at around 200. Kennedy and McNamara multiplied the missile force by a factor of five (to 1,000 plus). Ambrose comments:

> those who wish to understand why they launched the greatest arms race in the history of mankind must begin their search outside the Armed Services, for the pressure for the buildup did not come from the Army, Navy or Air Force. Simultaneously with the missile program Kennedy did bolster the three Services and the military obviously benefitted from the arms race. Like all the bureaucracies, the Services were happy to grow and could find rationalizations to justify the growth, but they did not initiate the program. Kennedy and McNamara were the drivers; the generals and admirals joyfully went along for the ride.

The main point, whatever the merits of the particular historical examples cited by Ambrose, is that the military itself is not a convincing scapegoat for the rise of militarism in North America. The origins of militarism may lie instead in the civilian population, the economy and the governments. Final responsibility for decision-making in the military still rests in civilian hands and there is little evidence that the military, as distinct from the military industry, has gained a covert power (a kind of power behind the throne) to compel the civil authorities to do their bidding.

To return again to our attempts to define militarism, we said that the establishment of military forces capable of conducting war by the 'humane' use (to the greatest extent possible) of personnel and weapons is a function that does not come under the term militarism. (Clearly, to speak of 'humane' war is not to speak in the language of pacifism, but in the language of main-line Christian theology, under which terms the just war follows not only strict criteria for participation but also a strict code of conduct. The question of whether modern methods of warfare have made the traditional notion of 'humane' warfare obsolete ignores the fact that many modern wars, such as guerrilla wars of liberation, do not employ the more sophisticated and pernicious of modern weapons.) When armies prepare themselves for war decided upon not by themselves, but by civilian authorities, based upon questions of justice, they then play a legitimate role – a role which we who describe ourselves as pacifists will not accept as moral, but one that is outside the definition of militarism.

The problem with this definition, and one which we simply have to acknowledge, is that the point at which such a military function becomes 'militarism' must, in the final analysis, be an arbitrary one. There is likely to be little agreement on the precise point at which 'legitimate' military activity loses its 'legitimacy', particularly during peacetime. To what extent can a military train and arm itself in preparation for future military threats without resorting to propaganda campaigns to win political (and therefore budgetary) support? To some, any PR campaign will smack of militarism, while to others a substantial public campaign to win public support and to attract recruits will be recognised as essential to the maintenance of an effective fighting force. But there *is* likely to be much wider agreement that military influence over non-military areas of public policy and the mounting of military activity out of proportion to real military threats constitute militarism.

Now, the pacifist may argue that all promotion of the military is 'militarism' – but that then is a matter of redefining the term 'militarism' to include all military activity. A more logical approach for the pacifist is to allow the distinction between militarism and the military way to stand and then to assert that both are evil and must be combated and that there can be no justification for participation in either sphere. But in this instance, it would at least be clear that different arguments need to be offered against the two and the pacifist will at least be able to make common cause with the non-pacifist in opposing militarism. The pacifist and non-pacifist would clearly part company in the matter of 'legitimate' military activity.

A corollary of the phenomenon of military ways of thinking

becoming predominant in civil institutions is the misuse of military institutions by civil authorities. The purpose of the military is exclusively the deadly abhorrent business of fighting. Everything in an army that is not preparation for fighting – that 'transcends' this purpose – is militarism. A great deal of activity in modern armies is diversion. Air shows, pollution clean-up, ceremony – the purpose of these auxiliary roles is to take our attention away from the deadly business of killing. They are an attempt to place a gloss of respectability and honour on the matter of killing. Armies are for killing and nothing should be allowed to obscure that fact. By the reckoning of those who adhere to something like a just war theory, there exist circumstances in human affairs when killing is unavoidable, or even 'necessary' in finite terms. Necessity, however, does not imply justification. Violence may sometimes appear necessary in the finite, imperfect affairs of this world. The choice sometimes is not between violence and non-violence, but between two kinds of violence – hopefully of differing magnitudes. In such cases it may become 'necessary', but it is still not justified. It still debases the human condition, and the perpetrator bears the full guilt of his action. He cannot gloss over his action or avoid guilt by pointing to mitigating circumstances.[4]

We need to apply the same criterion to armies. If they are necessary then the brutal reality of their purpose must be kept prominently before us and not glossed over with diversions. Thus another prominent instance of militarism is really the opposite of the notion of the misuse of civilian institutions by the military – namely, it is the misuse of military institutions by the civilian authorities. When military institutions are used to foster nationalistic fervour, or, as in Canada, national unity, when the military is made the symbol of statehood and nationhood, that is civilian exploitation of the military. A Russian Grand Duke said it more effectively: he is reported to have admitted that he hated war 'because it spoils the armies'.

The Grand Duke would have found much to his liking in Canadian military policy. One important element of Canadian military policy is the manufacture and world-wide sale of military commodities. The only potential customers that are excluded as a matter of course are those behind Churchill's Iron Curtain, but, in an apparent effort to make this unsavoury enterprise more palatable, Ottawa added further conditions to the effect that we sell weapons as long as they are not used. The official policy is that Canada does not sell weapons to areas of military conflict. In other words, as long as the weapons and other military commodities are not actually used in war, then the whole exercise can be explained in terms of balance of payments, technological innovation, national security, etc., but when the war starts, that spoils it. So we sustain the myth that the sale of weapons really isn't so objectionable by insisting that we don't ship them to war areas. A former Minister of External Affairs even went so far as to deliver himself of the opinion that our weapons aren't for killing people.[5]

Canada abounds with examples of this kind of militarism. At the base of it is the myth that military production is good for the economy. We maintain a military research and development enterprise that integrates the Department of Defense, the Department of Industry, Trade and Commerce, Canadian universities and industry in a programme to develop new military technology; not for the purpose of improving the military capabilities of the Canadian armed forces, but for the purpose of competing more effectively in the international arms market. If the object of the research were to increase the destructive potential of our armed forces one could at least ask the question, 'For whose benefit?' or 'To meet what threat?' Instead we live under the illusion that our military commodities aren't really so bad because we don't send them to places where there is war, and that all Canadians benefit from this innovative enterprise. A civilian official of the Defense Research Board, in explaining the Board's work, pointed out that Canada could expect at least $ 24 in sales for every $ 1 invested in military research.

In 1969, not very long after he had told a delegation of Mennonite representatives that he hoped Canada could become a haven from militarism, Prime Minister Trudeau announced that the reorganisation of the armed forces, with new equipment and training, would give Canada 'a sense of purpose as a nation'. That is a new task for the Canadian military and one, one might add, it hasn't performed very effectively to date.

There are other ways in which Canada employs the military for illegitimate or non-military purposes. NORAD, for example, was formed in the late fifties in response to the Soviet nuclear bomber threat. Few people, and certainly not the Canadian government, any longer believe that there remains a Soviet bomber threat worth countering, but elements of the US Defense Department disagree and there are several reasons why Canada does not now wish to make trouble with the Defense Department or with the US government in general. In the first place, Canadian membership in NORAD is essential for the maintenance of the Defense Production Sharing Arrangements between Canada and the US whereby Canadian industry is given almost unrestricted access to the huge military market represented by the US Defense Department. Second, it is believed that such an arrangement makes it less expensive to equip Canadian forces – permitting Canadian forces to buy surplus production runs from US suppliers. Perhaps most important, there are a number of contentious non-military issues that currently occupy US-Canadian relations. Communications, environment, energy – in these and other issues Canada is sometimes seen by the US government to be uncooperative. The Canadian government, therefore, has been looking around for an issue in which it can demonstrate its willingness to co-operate and NORAD is just the thing. In 1975, the last time the NORAD agreement was renewed, there was less military justification for the pact than there has ever been since it began in 1958, but the renewal came off with the least questioning. It was a case of using the military to serve completely independent political ends.

Canada's situation in NATO is really about the same. Canada believes it to be an absurdity for Canadian troops to be stationed in Europe (although some do not agree), but the political costs of withdrawal are seen to be prohibitive. Canada has been seeking closer trade ties with Europe. Current military procurement programmes must be seen in the light not of defence needs, but of economic needs associated with her NATO and NORAD allies – Europe sought a demonstration of commitment from Canada before it could contemplate further trade and the US sought to have the huge imbalance in trade in military commodities across our border cut down as a prerequisite to continued access to the US market.

The size of the military budget, staggering as it may be in the US, for example, does not define militarism. As we said, we may expect to find a high degree of correlation between high defence spending and militarism, but other factors must be at play as well. One of the qualities of militarism is that while it employs thought and practice associated with armies, its purposes transcend those of armies. Militarism seeks to invest all international political disputes with a military dimension. An obvious doctrine of American militarism has been that the military can be used not only for the pursuit of specific military objectives, but also to restrain the spread of certain political ideas. (That, by the way, is a prominent view among some people in Ottawa as well. A senior official in the Canadian armed forces, serving as executive assistant to the Minister of Defense, said recently in conversation that NATO was essential to counter the threat of Communism in Europe. Asked where the biggest threat currently was, he replied that clearly it was in Italy and, to a lesser extent, in Portugal. When it was suggested that perhaps NATO was not a very effective instrument for stopping Communist there, both of them being member countries of NATO, he replied that this may be so, but that it only goes to show you that the threat of Communism has not decreased and that therefore the need for NATO is as great as ever.)

Perhaps one of the best examples of American militarism that seeks to inhibit the spread of ideas by military means is the Military Aid Plan. Referring to the failure of many Third World countries to achieve that quality of life desired by their citizens – one of the factors in this failure being exploitation of natural resources and the expropriation of any surpluses accumulated in the process by foreign (American) capital – and the tendency for radical groups to emerge as a result, a study of 'Military Aid and Counterrevolution in the Third World' (by Miles D. Wolpin) reports US efforts to strengthen local military establishments as a means of countering radical influences:

> Although military officers occasionally 'succumb' to such radical aspirations, in general they represent one of the more conservative elites to be found in underdeveloped areas. Most officers are recruited from the property-owning upper or middle class (teachers, clerks, etc.). Many in the last category are economically and socially privileged *vis-à-vis* workers and peasants. They often are disdainful toward the manual classes and feel threatened by radical elites who encourage mass demands for increased welfare and greater equality of opportunity, particularly in economies with marginal per capita growth rates. Hence, middle-class consciousness in these countries is frequently associated with hostility to radicalism.[6]

So the US military is enlisted to promote the military elites in the hope that they will prevent the rise of radical ideas and ensure a friendly climate for foreign commercial interests.

Another characteristic of militarism that emerges is that it actually undermines military security. While the methods of the military and of militarism appear to be the same, their objectives are very different. The objectives of the military are strictly the limited objectives of military security, but the objectives of militarism are whatever influential forces in the state, be they military or civilian, decide they should be – and because the pursuit of these transcendent goals involves and diverts the military, the result often is that the military objectives themselves are undermined. And there could be no more effective or frightening evidence of that than that of the mounting threat of nuclear accidents.[7] Not only do the design, construction and expansion of military systems *not* contribute to the maintenance and improvement of national security, but the relation between the two is inverse – i.e. the consequence of such systems is that national security is undermined rather than enhanced. If national security is defined in the military sense – 'the prevention of property damage, injury and loss of life caused by military means as well as the limitation of such damage, casualty and death in the event of war' – then one can point out four basic reasons why this objective is undermined by the further development of weapons systems: the possibility of nuclear accidents; the possibility of accidental nuclear war; limitations on the ability to control and safeguard nuclear inventories; and the large and widening gap between offensive and defensive military capabilities. A crucial point here is that this situation of risk, resulting from possible nuclear accidents and the other reasons just listed, has resulted *not* from the pursuit of strict military objectives, but from the pursuit of 'militaristic' objectives, which are very different.

One final reference to another characteristic of militarism is best introduced by the comment of Frederick the Great, whose great respect for and fear of the Russian soldier led him to explain: 'It is not sufficient to kill the Russians, one has to knock them over too!' North Americans seem to have a similar respect for the Russians. Not only is it necessary to be able to destroy all the urban centres of the Soviet Union, but we have to be able to do it 20 times over (we are expected to draw further comfort from the fact that the Trident and other new weapons systems will go a long way towards improving our overkill capacity.) Once again, overkill has nothing to do with military objectives – it has to do with the transcendent objectives of militarism.

I have tried to distinguish between 'militarism' and the 'military way', not because one is more serious than the other, but because they are different. To bring the principles of pacifism to bear upon questions of national security is to question military objectives, not the objectives of militarism. Militarism is an attempt to pursue by military means objectives that transcend military objectives, and an attack on militarism must be an attack on those transcendent objectives – including those of expanding our commercial interests to the ends of the earth, which in turn bring forth irresistible pressures to mount a military capable of protecting those interests, and of concentrating capital and public funds in industrial sectors that violate the interests of people within our borders as well as around the world.

Notes

1. Alfred Vagts, *A History of Militarism: Civilian and Military*, revised edition (The Free Press, New York, 1953), p. 13.

2. Seymour Melman elaborates this in his well known *The Permanent War Economy: American Capitalism in Decline* (Simon and Schuster, New York, 1974).

3. Stephen Ambrose (ed.), *The Military and American Society: Essays and Readings* (The Free Press, New York, 1972), pp. 3-18.

4. Jacques Ellul discusses the basis for seeing violence both as 'necessity' and human debasement in *Violence: Reflections from a Christian Perspective* (The Seabury Press, New York, 1969).

5. Former government House Leader, Mitchell Sharp, quoted in *Toronto Star*, 4 December 1975.

6. Miles D. Wolpin, *Military Aid and Counterrevolution in the Third World* (Lexington Books, D.C. Heath and Co., Lexington, Massachusetts, 1972), pp. 4-14.

7. Lloyd Dumas, 'National Security in the Nuclear Age', *The Bulletin of the Atomic Scientists* (May 1976).

7 NATIONAL SECURITY: PROPAGANDA OR LEGITIMATE CONCERN?

Robert D. Matthews

Many observers today view with alarm the world-wide trend of fast-growing military budgets and of increasingly sophisticated and destructive military equipment, for this massive expenditure in death and destruction has the probable effect of siphoning off badly needed funds from such important areas as social services, urban renewal schemes and cultural programmes. Worse still, it may reflect the growth of militaristic societies – what Harold Lasswell has termed the 'garrison state', in which those that specialise in the use of violence (the military and the police) dominate all aspects of society. And, internationally, the build-up of arms tends to exacerbate, if not to instigate, inter-state rivalries.

Few people regard this state of affairs with pleasure; indeed, most find it totally undesirable. However, wide disagreement exists over whether the actual outcome is inherent in the international system of sovereign states and thus impervious to human intervention or whether it is susceptible to change. For those who adopt the latter view growing expenditure on the acquisition of arms and on military research in developing and developed countries alike is portrayed as both harmful and unnecessary: harmful, because of the wasteful investment of resources in unproductive activities and the strong likelihood that the acquisition of arms by one nation will lead to an arms race with another and ultimately to war; unnecessary, because there exist alternative ways of organising society so as to provide for the peace and prosperity of a nation's citizens as well as the world at large.

But no society, even if it is undemocratic, can allocate its resources to the pursuit of an activity which is unnecessary and harmful without experiencing some, if not considerable, opposition. Faced with this potential or actual dissent governments have relied on the threat to their national security to justify their military budgets both to their own publics and to the international community. With the very survival of the country at stake and its territorial integrity under attack, those in power can easily explain away unpleasant policies and excesses of 'zeal' in carrying them out. According to this line of argument, 'national security' is but a term of rhetoric, a tool of propaganda employed by governments to camouflage oppressive policies and aggressive behaviour.

Like many arguments, the preceding one contains an important element of truth, but certainly not the entire truth. Some governments most of the time, and most governments some of the time, indulge in the use of propaganda and rhetoric to induce their citizens to accept, however reluctantly, unpalatable conditions and policies. As a vague and ambiguous symbol 'national security' is open to such exploitation. But it would be a serious mistake to conclude that the concern for security is nothing more than an artificial creation of technocrats, the armament industries and those that profit from them, and ruling elites anxious to hold on to the reins of power – in short, a modern-day version of the devil theory of arms and war.

To focus on the research, development and spread of armaments and on governing elites and their rhetoric as the principal sources of international disorder is to risk confusing symptoms for causes. Generally, states do not fight because they have arms but acquire weapons to resolve their basic conflicts of interest. Similarly, some governments may exaggerate intentionally the actual threat to their state's security or extend beyond reason the values they wish to protect. Rarely, however, do they succeed long in conjuring up an imaginary external enemy to displace the attention of their publics from the real domestic and international problems at hand. In short, for most states, most of the time, the search for security is not a false issue but involves a genuine effort to resolve an existing and persistent dilemma.

While avoiding the extreme pessimistic view to which I alluded before, that is, the view that international politics is an unmitigated struggle for power, equivalent to the Hobbesian state of nature in which life is 'nasty, brutish and short', an analysis of the present situation must be placed in the context within which international actions and reactions occur. Unlike politics in most national communities, *international* politics takes place in the absence of an overriding higher authority on which the nation-states can rely to perform the traditional functions of government. Without an accepted mechanism to reconcile conflicting interests, each of the actors in the international system is left to protect and further its own interests. In such a setting, particularly when the ultimate arbiter is the resort to arms, violence can and does occur. Although states do often resolve their differences short of the use of violence, international politics do take place in the constant shadow of war. States are therefore compelled by the very circumstances in which they find themselves to show a concern for their security and are generally prepared to allocate scarce resources to obtain it.

But, someone might respond, history is replete with examples of long periods of peace, of co-operative ventures undertaken jointly by several states, and of states that have neglected their security requirements without any evident injury to their independence and territorial integrity – the so-called core values. To such an observation I would make on objection. Although 'national security' is a recurring goal of unit-actors in an anarchical system, the particular shape it assumes in a given historical situation will vary from place to place and from time to time. The very general, vague and ambiguous quality of the term is itself a reflection of the diverse forms of behaviour that are encompassed by the idea of 'national security'. It is, of course, this ambiguity which, as Arnold Wolfers has written, permits 'everyone to label whatever policy he favors with an attractive and possibly deceptive name'.[1]

The task before us then, is a difficult one: on the one hand, how do we avoid the mistake of simply dispensing altogether with the concept of national security which, as I have suggested, does describe a continuing reality for most states, most of the time? On the other hand, how do we prevent those in power from misusing this concept as a form of moral justification for otherwise reprehensible purposes? On one level, the answer to this dilemma is really quite simple: if we wish the concept of national security to serve as a guide for action and as a benchmark against which to judge the country's policies, then it must be rendered more precise. In the last analysis, however, this will involve finding answers to the following questions with respect to each particular case: *what or whom* is a government seeking to secure? against *what kind of threat*? and by *what means*? And those answers are neither simple nor obvious.

Before turning to this task, however, I must hasten to add one caveat. No matter how precise the meaning ascribed to national security by either participant or observer, the actual reading of a particular situation may well vary from person to person, from regime to regime, and from state to state. Objectively, it may be generally agreed that a particular state is secure, that is, that it is able to defend its internal values against any conceivable external attack. But, subjectively, those in power may in all honesty fear that the security of their state is in jeopardy. The difference between France's and Britain's evaluation of the German threat in the inter-war period illustrates well what constitutes a genuine discrepancy between objective assessments and subjective perceptions of a state's national security.[2] In the last analysis, I suppose, whether or not a state is threatened cannot be measured objectively, except of course from the vantage point of hindsight.

Perhaps one thing on which we can all agree is that 'national security' does identify the *nation* as the unit to be preserved or secured. The interests of subgroups within the nation, such as business associations, tribes and classes, or groups that transcend the nation, such as multinational corporations and revolutionary movements, are subordinate to those of the nation. Thus, for example, any policy that serves to maintain a ruling elite in power or to favour a particular section of the population at the expense of the nation as a whole cannot be termed a policy of *national* security, unless it can be shown it is in the interest of the entire population that the present government stay in power or the privileged group continue to be favoured. Similarly, a policy designed to preserve an alliance of nation-states as such, but which does not add to, and may even detract from the security of the individual nation(s), cannot be labelled one of national security. In this regard, however, it is interesting to note that whereas in the inter-war period most Canadians considered that their security was best maintained by remaining aloof from European politics and the League of Nations, since 1945 they have subscribed to the view that their security is intimately tied up with that of the United States and Western Europe. The limits of the 'nation' to be protected were thus extended to include those other states with which Canada was allied.

This process of extension may even go so far as to embrace the entire globe, at which point 'national security' would be supplanted by 'collective security'. Under such a system all states in the system must consider aggression anywhere by any state as a threat to their own security and must be prepared to join in a collective effort initially to deter and, if necessary, to defeat any such aggression. Unfortunately, the histories of the League of Nations and the United Nations bear witness to the fact that most states have not been willing to identify their security with a global order. The sense of community on which such a system must rest does not seem to have existed in the past or, for that matter, to exist today.

But the question of who is to be protected does not end there. Up until now in our discussion, we have assumed that there was general agreement as to what a nation was, what clusters of people constituted a nation and that political, as distinct from geographical, boundaries between nations were universally accepted. Without getting into the hoary question of the meaning of 'nation', let me state from the outset that it is defined here as a group of people whose loyalty to the group transcends all other loyalties and that even if a nation has not achieved statehood, there will be a tendency for it to do so. Conflicts do arise then when a nation has failed to achieve its sovereign independence or when its people are living on different sides of a political frontier. When, as in the latter case, it is unclear where one state's population begins and another's ends, the situation can become tense, resulting sometimes in a confrontation, such as the one that Morocco, Mauretania and Algeria became embroiled in over the future of Spanish Sahara, or even in a war, such as the one that is presently being waged across the Horn of Africa. Similarly, disagreement over where the actual boundary falls can lead to conflicting or overlapping claims to a piece of real estate and the accompanying territorial seas. Thus legitimate differences over the exact definition of the nation to be defended can result in hostilities and outright war.

Even if we reach some tentative agreement on who is to be protected, it is much more difficult to arrive at a consensus as to what constitutes a legitimate threat. Differences in assessing the degree of danger confronting a particular state do arise from contrasting historical experiences. Thus, for instance, those countries that have suffered recently from attacks, such as the Soviet Union and France, are likely to consider the need for security much more intensely than those that have largely escaped the horrors of war.[3] Similarly, those states that have only just acquired their independence from colonial rule may be expected to view the world with more suspicion than those that have experienced a long existence as independent sovereign states. In this regard, it has always intrigued me to observe how little understanding the West has shown of the security concerns of independent African states in the southern portion of that continent. Given their geographical location and their recent colonial experience, it should not come as a surprise to anyone that the latter group of states would consider their independence in jeopardy as long as colonialism is still alive and white minorities continue to dominate life in Rhodesia, South Africa and Namibia.

It is also important to stress the changing nature of the security threat. Traditionally, the only threat that was considered worthy of that name was that of military attack and conquest. Thus national security policies focused almost exclusively on the development of a nation's coercive capacity. For reasons that can only be hinted at here, states have in recent years become more concerned with threats of a non-military character: external domination of a country's economy by citizens from another state or foreign corporations, total dependence on another country for scientific research and technological developments, unrestricted movement of ideas resulting sometimes in the erosion and eventual loss of national identity, and pollution of the seas and atmosphere leading to the upset of the globe's ecological balance. Who could question that an oil spill off the coast of a heavily populated area can do immeasurable harm to the well-being of that country's citizens, destroying their natural environment and reducing their fishing catch? Is this not as much a threat to that country's security, broadly defined, as an admittedly destructive war?

It is at this point that the nature of the threat and the values that the state desires to protect coincide. Increasing demands on non-renewable resources, the technological revolution in transportation and communications, expanding transactions between states and growing pressure from a wider public have together forced governments to pay heed to more than simply manning their battlements. In fact, governments can no longer prevent outsiders from penetrating the previously impermeable outer shell of the nation-state. They have been compelled by circumstances to attend to a wider range of activities. National security can therefore no longer refer only to the preservation of the independence and the territorial integrity of the nation-state. It must now also relate to the protection of a state's citizens, their distinctive institutions and values, and to the external environment (economic, cultural and ecological as well as military) within which each state must operate.

And finally, the question arises as to the means most likely to further a state's security ends. At one extreme, there are those who argue that 'a nation can be secure only if it increases its own power at the expense of another nation or nations'.[4] Accordingly, the only way to deter an attack or defeat one if it actually occurs is by establishing a position of strength from which to negotiate, by outclassing your enemy in every way, by providing for the worst conceivable situation. Bolstered by the obvious failure of appeasement in the inter-war period to dissuade the dictators from undertaking further aggression, this view of international politics and the consequent policy of national security have influenced many governments in post-World War II years.

Standing against this approach is one that depicts international politics as a mixed-sum game, that is to say, a game in which one state's security is not necessarily inconsistent with another's. Indeed, it is sometimes argued that one state's security depends upon the increase in the security of other states. Based on the idea of a harmony of interests, this perspective focuses on international co-operation through disarmament, arms control, international organisations and international law as the best way to achieve national security. National security and the establishment of world order are not only mutually consistent but mutually dependent upon one another.[5]

Obviously, the choice of means will have to vary in accordance with circumstance. Faced by an aspiring world dictator, any attempt to co-operate or negotiate is likely to prove disastrous. If, on the other hand, one's enemy is moderate, that is he is prepared to compromise on his goals, to emphasise only the stick is to miss any chance at negotiation. The most likely stance will be one in which differing mixes of promises of rewards and threats of punishment will be administered. Emphasis on what is expedient and a flexible approach as to means are likely to serve best a nation in its search for security.

By way of conclusion, let me recapitulate the argument I have sought to develop in the preceding pages. In the first place, I was anxious to offset the position adopted by some that national security is little more than a 'doctrine of military domination', a clever piece of propaganda devised to disguise a small ruling elite's grab for power. It is my contention that the concern for security was and remains a legitimate interest of states, an interest that is not likely to vanish as long as the international system is organised along semi-anarchical lines. Agreeing that the vagueness of the term is in part responsible for the different and contradictory ways it is used, I then attempted to provide more precision to the notion of national security. In doing so, however, I managed, hopefully, to demonstrate that only the broadest of generalisations about national security can be made. The assessment of a given policy or the evaluation of a leader's claim to be serving the national interest should only be undertaken on the basis of the specific circumstances of each individual case.

Notes

1. Arnold Wolfers, 'National Security as an Ambiguous Symbol' in his edited *Discord and Collaboration* (Baltimore, 1962), p. 147.
2. See, for instance, Wolfer's excellent study, *Britain and France Between the Wars* (New Haven, Connecticut, 1940).
3. For an elaboration on this point, see Wolfer, 'National Security as an Ambiguous Symbol', pp. 150-1.
4. Morton Berkowitz and P.B. Book, 'National Security' in David L. Sills (ed.), *International Encyclopedia of the Social Sciences* (London, 1972), Vol. 11, p. 41.

5. Although the Draft Document produced by the Preparatory Committee for the Special Session of the UN General Assembly Devoted to Disarmament does note that nations 'have for a long time sought to maintain their security through the possession of arms', it stresses the importance today of seeking 'security in disarmament, that is to say, through a gradual but effective process beginning with a reduction in the present level of armaments'. Admittedly, this portion of the draft document was not universally accepted. However, Prime Minister Pierre Trudeau of Canada did echo this theme in his remarks both at the Special Session and at a subsequent NATO gathering. At the latter meeting he was quoted as saying that 'the search for security can too easily be conducted only through armament improvements'. In fact, he went on to comment, 'the security of our countries and of our people will depend fundamentally on the strength of our collective conviction as free people that the values professed by our societies are sound and worth preserving'. Trudeau's comments were cited in an article in the *Sunday Star* (Toronto), 4 June 1978.

8 THE SOCIO-CLASS DETERMINANTS OF MILITARISM*

Ejub Kučuk

1 The Relation of Class Forces and Militarism

The differentiation of society into classes is essentially responsible for the development and constancy of the state military organisation. The relation of class forces is the primary social determinant of the historical types and forms of military organisation. When the bourgeoisie, for example, was compelled by historical necessity to rely on the oppressed classes for help in overthrowing the feudal system and, consequently, had to set up a class-heterogeneous military organisation, it could not adopt the feudal form of military organisation. The democratic social characteristics of the armed forces of the bourgeois revolution (the selection of officers, for example) vanished once the bourgeoisie established itself as the ruling class. When its allies in the struggle against the feudal forces became a potential or real danger to its system of rule, the bourgeoisie was compelled, again by historical necessity, to militarise the armed forces of the revolution. The same socio-political process repeated itself in the creation of the armed forces of the socialist state. Namely, the insufficiently favourable position of the working class of the first socialist country in the world and the need for consolidating the new social system influenced, to a decisive degree, the militarisation of the first victorious socialist revolution.

State military organisations can be militarised to varying degrees. When the relation of class forces is relatively favourable to the ruling class, the process of militarisation is not particularly intensive. But as soon as the slightest political crisis occurs, posing a real or even potential danger to the interests of the ruling class, this process is instantly intensified. In such a situation, not unnaturally, the emphasis in all state military organisations is on tighter military discipline, i.e. on the unconditional submission of individuals and whole social groups to the military organisation. In this manner, the army becomes a more serious threat or, indeed, a force better equipped for safeguarding the interests of the ruling class from the dangers inherent in what to it is

* Shortened version of a chapter from E. Kučuk's book *Militarizam*, ' "Rad" and Vojnoizdavački zavod' (Belgrade, 1977); reprinted from *Socialist Thought and Practice* (Belgrade), no. 11 (November 1977); translation by M. Hrgović.

an unfavourable relation of class forces.

Nevertheless, the militarisation of the armed forces of revolution, or complete militarisation of the already existing military organisation, does not mean in itself the alienation of the army from the ruling class. On the contrary, in this manner the army is made into an even more obedient instrument for protecting the general conditions of the class system suited to the ruling class. Nor does it mean the extension of the process of militarisation to the political, economic, educational and other spheres of social life.

Against a changed social background, the process of militarisation is not confined solely to the military and military activity. In circumstances of acute class antagonism, the principles of organising and the system of values of the state military organisation penetrate the political system and society as a whole. This process is largely determined by the need to protect the seriously imperilled vital interests of the ruling class. In such situations, not only does the ruling class rely, in a very great measure, on the strength and authority of the state military organisation, but it also fashions a whole series of spheres of social life in a manner typical of the state military organisation. The history of modern class society shows up the consistency of such processes in a very convincing light.

The bourgeoisie, in its campaigns of conquest, could never reckon on the loyalty of the colonial peoples. Its colonial rule was constantly confronted with a more or less vigorous resistance of the enslaved peoples. In such circumstances, the bourgeoisie could preserve its colonial holdings only by making maximum use of its state military organisation as a physical force and a social organisation.

The classical forms of Latin American imperialism are shown to have developed according to the same laws. Thus, during the indisputed rule of the big landowners, the state military organisation was the instrument by which the ruling class directly protected its class privileges and aspirations. The officer corps was exclusively recruited from the ranks of that class and, consequently, promptly reacted to any attempt to change the existing state of affairs in any Latin American society. The military, i.e., the aristocratic officer corps, had no other aspirations but to step on to the political stage through the strength of its organisation in any situation in which the interests of the landowners were in jeopardy. In the interests of, and on instructions from, that class it exercised permanent control over the pillars of political authority or took over all powers itself, setting up one or another kind of direct military government.

Consequently, the extension of the process of militarisation beyond the framework of state military organisation does nor signify in itself the alienation of the army or of the protagonists of militarisation in general from the ruling class. On the contrary, the military – both as a physical force and as an organisation whose structural principles pervade the political system and all of society – has an instrumental role to play in safeguarding the vital interests of the ruling class. But while this aspect of militarisation does not automatically lead to the estrangement of the army or the protagonists of militarisation from the ruling class, it does create real possibilities for the onset of such a process.

2 The State Military Organisation: From Instrument into Master

The possibility that a state military organisation or the protagonists of militarisation may become alienated from the ruling class is objectified in social situations in which there is a balance of forces of the main social classes, thus preventing any one class from becoming the dominant socio-political factor. In such a situation, the state military organisation or the factors of militarisation in general become alienated from the ruling class and are transformed from its instrument into its master.

Hitler's (civilian) militarism based its existence on a balance of forces of the main class groups of German society. It could consolidate itself only on a balance of forces of the bourgeoisie and the working class. True, this form of militarism manifested itself in the instrumental role of the state military organisation in the service of the militaristic civil oligarchy and in the alienation of both of them from the ruling class. Actually, the civil political groups used the army as a material force and as a social organisation for subordinating society, as a whole, including the ruling class.

Consequently, such processes of militarisation as shown up in the structuring of state military organisation and penetration of the principles of its organising into the broad expanse of the political system and overall society (with or without the alienation of the army or factors of militarisation from the ruling class) are largely brought on by the relation of class forces in a given social system. However, the relation of class forces can, to varying degrees, be favourable or unfavourable to the ruling class, thus determining the extent to which militarism finds scope in the social area. Namely, when the relation of class forces is relatively favourable to the ruling class, militarism finds expression, more or less so, in state military organisation alone. On the other hand, when the relation of class forces is unfavourable to the ruling class, the latter lays marked emphasis on state military organisation and fashions – by means of it and on its principles, the political system and a number of spheres of social life. In so far as such situations become more frequent, the military organisation (or the protagonists of militarisation) becomes alienated from the ruling class and, beyond the latter's control, enforces its principles of organising and system of values in overall social relations and processes.

These varying degrees of militarisation, however, are not isolated socio-political occurrences. A logical analysis can detect their existence and distinguishing features, but in the reality of political developments they are inter-connected and evolve into one another. Namely, the use of state military force and the application of its principles of organising are characteristic of every kind of class rule. The emergence of the state, with the monopoly of legitimate physical coercion, is primarily the result of society's class differentiation and of the need to ensure the functioning of a given class order. However, the ruling class protects and develops the class system suited to it with the help of other, non-violent means, too. In so far as its position in the structure of society tends to become more advantageous, and its vital interests are not in any particular danger, the need for it to rely above all on its state military organisation becomes less. And, conversely, in the event that its position has been undermined and its vital interests imperilled, the need for it to depend upon its state military organisation as a material force and as a social model on which the political system and a number of other spheres of social life are constituted becomes greater. For the purpose of satisfying this vital need, it strives to maintain control over the military organisation and penetration of its principles of organising into overall social life. However, if such a need arises frequently, the military organisation (or the factors of militarisation in general), in a particular constellation of class relations, becomes alienated from the ruling class by being transformed from its instrument into its master and by subjecting to its particular interests and aspirations all of society. Karl Marx indicates this law when writing about the state of siege:

> An excellent invention which has found periodic application in every successive crisis in the course of the French revolution. The barracks and the bivouac were thus periodically deposited on the head of French society in order to compress its brain and keep it quiet; the sabre and the musket were periodically made to judge and

> administer, to guard and to censor, to play the part of policeman and night-watchman; the military moustache and the service uniform were periodically trumpeted forth as the highest wisdom and the spiritual guide of society. Was it not inevitable that barracks and bivouac, sabre and musket, moustache and uniform, would finally hit on the idea of saving society once and for all by proclaiming the supremacy of their own regime and thus entirely freeing civil society from the trouble of ruling itself? They had the more reason to hit on this idea in that they could then expect a better cash payment in return for their elevated services, while the merely periodic states of siege and temporary rescues of society at the behest of this or that fraction of the bourgeoisie produced little solid payment apart from one or two dead and wounded and a few friendly bourgeois grimaces. Was the military not bound finally to play at state of siege in its own interests and for its own interests, and at the same time lay siege to the bourgeois purse?[1]

From what has been said so far it can be seen that the relation of the class forces of a particular social system lies at the core of different degrees of militarisation and of their interdependence and interconnection.

3 The State Military System

Beginning from the nineteenth century down to the present day the contradictions between the social character of production and the private way of appropriation have been growing ever sharper. On the political scene this has been manifest in an intensive class struggle (civil wars, revolutions and counter-revolutions) which has increasingly jeopardised the class rule of the bourgeoisie. In the interests of the preservation of the bourgeois exploitative system, the bourgeois class has been compelled by historical circumstances to rely on its own state more and more. Statism, which is distinguished by an ever more complete subordination of the once free social activities to the control and domination of the state, has grown on that basis. In that context, the political systems of bourgeois democracy have radically altered their structure. The supremacy of legislative power over the executive and over the military organisation of the state, which had been characteristic of the liberal phase of development of capitalism, was increasingly endangered or, indeed, brought into question. Under conditions of an intensified class struggle (a real or potential civil war between the antagonistic classes) the bourgeoisie abandoned the democratic organisation of the political system and constituted one or another form of autocratic government. On the other hand, the political systems of socialism and of a number of countries in the underdeveloped regions of the world arose under conditions of underdeveloped productive forces and in most cases in circumstances of a sharp class polarisation The inadequate economic and political strength of the working class and of the other progressive social strata could not guarantee the defence of the acquired social positions. Against this background, the state assumed a notable role in overall social development and in relations with the outside world.

The marked role of the state is evident not only in the internal set-up in global societies but in international relations as well. Moreover, in this century it has become the principal force that models all kinds of communication between individuals and peoples. Such a role is derived from the character of international contradictions at the core of which lie socio-class antagonisms. Although relations between capitalist and socialist states are not a class struggle in the sense of a direct conflict of antagonistic classes because states do not act on the international stage as pure expressions of the ruling political forces which stand behind state authority, they are nevertheless class creatures of a particular nation and it is precisely for this reason that they can behave as national states.

Consequently, the role of the state set-up in subordinating the once free activities of global society and étatisation of international relations are traceable to the intensified class antagonisms of the modern age. On the surface of political life these antagonisms take a broad variety of forms such as: liberation movements of peoples across the world and processes of decolonisation in general, socialist revolutions and the creation of socialist social systems, or profound political crises which hold out a realistic prospect of leading to the destruction of a bourgeois society based on private ownership and exploitation, different types of civil and international war between different factions of the bourgeoisie itself and between bourgeois classes of different global national communities, different kinds of counter-revolution on a national or international scale, etc. The role of the state military organisation in all these processes is of first-class importance. Both as a physical force and as a type of social organisation it becomes a first-rate support of progressive and reactionary social forces alike. These are all manifestations of the threat of war or types of war underlying which, to a large extent, are heightened class contradictions. They all determine the varying degrees and forms of militarisation of political systems, global societies and international relations.

The markedly exacerbated international contradictions around the middle of this century and the menace of a disastrous world war, a number of limited wars and the contradictions which came to the fore in the aspirations and strivings to develop socialist social relations, on the one side, and the desire and efforts to thwart them, on the other, resulted in national state and supranational military organisations becoming a first-class power in the protection of the 'free world' and in the development and defence of 'world socialism'. For as long as the menace of a total or limited war hovers over it, mankind must necessarily remain in a state of perpetual war preparedness, and military demands constitute the elementary ingredient of the foreign and internal policies of almost all states. All walks of social life become, in one way or another, an integral part of the state military system. Moreover, supranational military organisations comprise whole regions of the world in which national military organisations are treated simply as military units within the composition of international military formations. What is involved here is not the free military integration of the masses in defence of their economic and political achievements but the domination over the totality of national and international life of the military organisations or protagonists of militarisation in general, which have been alienated from society, and the penetration of the military-statist principles of organising and system of values into whole societies and the international community.

4 The Socio-political Status and Political Characteristics of the State Military Organisation

The profound socio-class changes of the social systems of the twentieth century and the changed character of combat actions and war in general have altered considerably the socio-political status and characteristics of the classical type of state military organisation. The most complete manifestation of these influences is its transformation from a purely professional-instrumental social force into a political one. In view of the intensity of its political indoctrination, the system of values fostered in it and its social role in this century, the state military organisation has become a notable political force which is constantly striving to extend the principles typical of its distribution of social power and authority to the political system and all of society. Thus its mere existence is a significant determinant of society's militarisation.

According to the classical laws of military organisation, the army is formally beyond the sphere of politics. This has never been so in reality. Concealed behind the classical values of military ethics (order, discipline, hierarchy, obedience and devotion to the interests of the homeland) have been the political interests of the ruling class disguised as concern for the protection of the general interests of the social community. Apart from this, there existed explicit class-political convictions which were not, however, evenly distributed throughout the military system. They were most completely expressed in the top echelons, but as they spread towards the lower ranks they became increasingly transformed into patriotism, strict obedience and loyalty to the military-hierarchical ethos. Such a system and type of politicisation of the army sufficed to place the military organisation in the service the service of the interests of the ruling class.

The intensity of the class contradictions of the twentieth century and the changes they brought into the character of war and military activity in general, led to the transformation of implicit political convictions among the military into explicit ones and to their spread to all levels of the military hierarchy. In order to be able to operate effectively in modern-day conditions, a professional soldier needs to be highly susceptible to the political implications of his activity. What is more, he is directly involved in the passage of political decisions. For regulating relations between the troops and the population of an occupied territory, waging a war against progressive national movements, membership of military alliances, participation in talks on armament control and direction of military aid programmes are political activities as much as they are military ones. On the other hand, success in a modern war is largely dependent on the political indoctrination of each fighter and each organisational-functional group within the military set-up. This accounts for its intensity and it is manifested in the endeavours of the army to prepare each citizen and soldier for 'ideological warfare . . . in the strengths of western values (justice, liberty, the rights of man)' and against 'the evils of communism' and its effects on family and on individual liberty.[2]

The same social process of political shaping of military personnel is highly conspicuous in the state military organisations of the statist socialist political systems and of the political systems in the underdeveloped regions of the world. In such military organisations as have grown out of revolution or of a struggle for national liberation, or from both, a profound politicisation of all organisational functional groups is the basis of their cohesion and combat readiness. As distinct from the armies of the political systems of bourgeois democracy, in the socialist armies the Communist Party wields a decisive influence on the formation of political convictions of all organisational-functional groups on the basis of a precisely elaborated programme. Moreover, it is the duty of each soldier constantly to expand his political knowledge.[3] On the other hand, in the vast area of the underdeveloped part of the world, the army (i.e. its commanders) does not merely adopt its political stand in regard to particular aspects of socio-political life, but often becomes the creator of integral political programmes of reconstruction and development of the political system.

Regardless of the fact that the state military organisation is a class institution *par excellence* and that it is imbued with the political values of the ruling class, it does not usually operate on the political stage in the name of these values and aspirations. In influencing the political authorities or in directly taking over state authority or else in enforcing the principles of state military organisation in the political system and global society in any way whatsoever, it does so, as a rule, in the interests of the nation as a whole in order to safeguard the constitution, the order of the 'free world', or to protect society against the danger of 'anarchy or communism'. In relation to the other political forces, it is presented as a non-ideological political force which is called upon to guarantee public order and national security.

This possibility of presenting class-political or even particularistic military interests as general ones is derived from the socio-political status of the army in the structure of the political system. Namely, it is formally outside the political parties and their struggle in the political system of bourgeois democracy or is the executor of the policy of a political party in the statist-socialist political systems. Its mission is to defend the constitutional order, i.e. a given class system. However, on the surface of political life, this mission of the army is manifested as patriotism, as an affection for the national community, for its scenic beauty and culture. Thus, the military organisation is imbued with patriotism more than any other political force. What is more, its creation is closely related to the struggle of peoples for free and independent development and for the formation of national states. For this reason it has come to symbolise independence, sovereignty and equality with other peoples more so than has any other institution of the political system.

Such a status and social role enable the army, under cover of a struggle for general national interests, to meet the interests of the ruling class or else its own particular interests and aspirations. They also enable it to present its desire to structure the political system on principles specific to its social being, or the reality of this, as a reflection of its concern for the well-being of the entire national community.

This way of presenting things can inspire a widespread belief amongst soldiers and civilians in a special political mission of the state military organisation in political and social life.

On this basis beliefs are formed about the special value of military life, about the superiority of the military bureaucratic organisation to the democratic, about the inferior value of politics as an activity and of politicians as its protagonists. For

> military authority is not only indispensable, it is probably in itself more good than bad. It is also a producer of good. It sets an example and establishes desirable standards of conduct. Those who live an ordered life usually find that it is a good life. To be one of those set in authority with men under command is a liberating experience. The acceptance of the role seems on the whole likely to make better people.[4]

Or 'in military honour there is a breakwater which does not yield to confusions of opinion'.[5]

On the other hand, in extreme cases, entirely different beliefs are inspired in relation to politics and politicians. Professional soldiers believe that politics are a dirty, unsafe game unworthy of a noble man, and that politicians are superficial and unprofessional people who exist in a world of their own full of uncertainties: 'civilians will never understand the greatness of our ideals. We shall therefore have to eliminate them from the government and give them the only mission for which they are suited: work and obedience.'[6]

5 Structure and Properties of the Military Organisation

A developed system of political indoctrination, the possibility of socio-class and military-particularistic interests being portrayed as general interests and a widespread belief in a special state mission of the army are not the only elements which make the army an important political force. Aside from them, the social structuring of the state military organisation and the means it employs are of the greatest significance. Namely, it is structured in a manner which makes it the technically most efficient organisation of the political system and society as a whole. On the other hand, it enjoys a monopoly over arms and war material. Centralised command, hierarchy and strict discipline make it the technically most effective force of the political system. A modern military organisation is a miniature state in itself. It has its own system of supply, engineering, communication and education. In insufficiently developed societies, the army is technically better equipped than any other social organisation. Its specific role makes it necessary also physically to separate the army from the rest of society (life in the barracks and separate military quarters). Its forces are distributed across the whole territory of the state community according to a plan drawn up beforehand, and are ever ready to go into action under a unitary command, using arms and other war material. Nowhere else are bravery, discipline, submission and self-denial cultivated and developed as much as they are in a military organisation.

Such of its technical and social characteristics are of great political consequence. Because

> the degree of predominance of the armed forces over the unarmed populace depends above all on the quality of the armament; a machinegun gives a far greater advantage to him who possesses it over the unarmed people than does the sword . . . We can say, therefore, that the predominance of armed forces over the populace grows as the armament becomes more elaborate.[7]

On the other hand, the helplessness of the populace in relation to the armed forces grows as the latter improve their organisation:

> It is a well-known fact, moreover, that as the size of a collectivity increases it can be dominated by a proportionately smaller minority; one policeman can hardly keep down 100 civilians but 1,000 policemen can easily keep down 100,000 civilians. This is because the advantage derived from being organized grows more than proportionately to the numbers involved.[8]

All these properties of state military organisation, which are derived from its socio-political status and from the political significance of its structural characteristics, find full expression under conditions of a particular relation of class forces. They then influence the political system and overall society in different ways, either on the ordinance and under the supervision of civil political institutions or on their own account, fashioning them in their own model. This influence can take different forms ranging from the demand of military commanders to decide intra-army questions independently to demands for the realisation, or actual realisation, of complete programmes of socio-political development, as happened at the time of the dictatorship of Primo de Rivera in Spain, or between the two wars in Japan, in Egypt in 1952, in Iraq in 1958, in Syria throughout the post-war period, in Turkey, Libya, Sudan, Burma and Ethiopia today, and in a number of other countries. Also, its properties can be used by both civil and civil-militarist groups for the development of the same socio-political processes, as happened in Spain, in the USA or in Hitler's Germany.

6 The Officer Corps

When discussing state military organisation as a political force and its place in the structure of the political system, one must consider the impact of the class composition of its officer corps on its political behaviour. It is commonplace to observe the phenomena of militarism and militarisation as reactionary socio-political manifestations. The conclusion derived from this is that those armies whose officer corps comes from the reactionary social classes are inclined towards intervention in politics and militarisation of the political system. But militarism is not, in itself, a reactionary social phenomenon, nor are the officers from the ranks of the reactionary classes the sole actors of militarisation. In order to prove this thesis we must analyse the class make-up of the officer corps of modern armies and its influence on processes of militarisation of the political system and society as a whole.

The far-reaching structural-class changes in the twentieth century have produced significant and in some cases radical changes in the class structure of the officer corps of state military organisations. Although it is difficult to offer a precise survey of these changes on the comparative plane, first of all because of the theoretically differing and hence incomparable conceptions of the social class, it is nevertheless possible to recognise some of their basic tendencies.

The socialist revolutions of the twentieth century in overthrowing the bourgeois state also destroyed its military organisation. In place of the bourgeois state military organisation with an officer corps coming for the most part from the ranks of the capitalist class or from the feudal or semi-feudal social strata, armies of the socialist states were created, whose officer corps came almost entirely from the ranks of the peasantry and the working class. So, with the most far-reaching revolutionary social transformation came the most radical socio-class changes in the composition of the officer corps.

In bourgeois social systems the military profession expanded recruitment to encompass in addition to a narrow, socially privileged stratum of the bourgeois class, the middle classes and social strata and, to a lesser extent, even the working class. True, members of the latter classes and strata do not enjoy equal opportunities in their military career to reach important positions in the military organisation. As a rule, only the chosen representatives of the ruling class make up the military elite which is trained in the best military schools (Saint-Cyr in France, West Point, Annapolis and the Military Academy in the USA). The armies of bourgeois political systems, moreover, comprise a considerable proportion of sons of professional soldiers who take up the military profession.

As for Asia, Africa and Latin America, their armies too have been subject to notable changes in the class structure of the officer corps. With the suppression of the political domination of the big landowners in Latin America, who enjoyed the monopoly over officers' positions, and with the emergence of the bourgeoisie on the political stage, bourgeois elements and elements of the middle classes began penetrating the officer corps. In the armies of the underdeveloped Asian and African countries, officers are recruited not only from the ranks of the feudal or semi-feudal class but also from the ranks of the middle classes and, in some instances, from the peasantry too.

Thus, the shifts in the relation of the class forces of overall society are shown to have produced more or less marked changes in the class composition of the officer corps everywhere in the world. Notwithstanding the fact that societies have differing economic, political and cultural characteristics and differing class structures of their armies' officer corps, in all modern-day state military organisations the officer corps have one common feature. In all of them a large proportion of the officers come from the rural regions and provinces.

7 Processes of Militarisation

How do these changes relate to the processes of militarisation? Are these processes less pronounced today than they were before? This is not a simple question to answer. Present-day political trends show militarism to be more developed today than it was in past epochs. Today it is not just a question of assaults by some military clique on the helm of state power, but rather it is a question of deep thrusts of the principles of state military organisation into the political system and totality of social life.

Consequently, the changes in the class composition of the officer corps have not led to the decline of militarism. On the contrary, each change on the political stage has been linked up, as a rule, both with the assaults of the military on political power and with the shaping of the political system, to a greater or lesser measure, on the model of state military organisation. The intervention of the army in Latin American politics from the 1930s down to the present and in Asian and African politics since the middle of this century, Nationalist Socialist militarism and the militarisation of the political systems in the highly advanced capitalist states provide sufficient proof in support of this thesis. In all these instances, the protagonists of militarisation, military and civilian, had little understanding for democratic rights and for the democratic institutions of the political system. What is more, they actually undermined or annulled them, constituting the political system to a greater or lesser degree on principles the same as those on which the state military system is based.

Such political behaviour is occasioned above all by the described historical relations of the class forces. Namely, these relations were crucial to both the emergence and maintenance of the undemocratic structural features of the state military organisation and also to their extrapolation into the political system and overall society. All the same, regardless of the fact that the non-democratic structural characteristics of the state military organisation are an effect produced by the class factor, they are not a passive but rather an active effect acting in return as a causal agent. In this sense they take on the role of a determinant of militarisation and militarism because 'in reality, independently of whether one wants it or not, there is an incompatibility between liberal customs and habits, as we practise them, and the behaviour of officers . . . who, in order to be efficient, must be authoritarian in their actions and thoughts'.[9] 'Whatever the nature of authority in the military institution and however it evolves it is certainly not the product of democratic processes.'[10]

For this reason the state military organisation usually acts in political processes in accordance with its own specific undemocratic values, regardless of the class origins of their officer corps. In this sense, M. Janowitz is right when he says that 'the social background [of officers – note by E.K.] emerges as progressively less important than professional experiences and personal alliances in fashioning the outlook of the military elite',[11] and so is R. Mils when he contends that the influence of the military organisation is decisive in the education of soldiers, 'no matter whether the future officer is the son of a woodcutter or a millionaire'.[12]

Yet the non-democratic orientation of the army and its officer corps does not reveal their essential political choice. That is, the introduction of the principles on which the state military organisation is set up and incorporation of its system of values into the political system does not show, in itself, the interests of the social class or force for which the process is being carried out. It can be developed by either progressive or reactionary social forces in the interests of either progress or regress.

In this context the class origins of the officer corps are of great consequence. In the course of the long-lasting militarisation of the political systems of Latin America, the military, in dependence on the class structure of its officer corps, developed this process both in the interests of the large-scale landowners and foreign capital and in the interests of the national bourgeoisie by assisting its resistance to the landowners and foreign capital. The changes in the class make-up of the officer corps of Egypt, Sudan, Libya, Portugal and Ethiopia were linked to the militarisation of the political system. This was the only way to free the country from the absolute domination of feudal and semi-feudal classes and from the big bourgeoisie which was closely associated with foreign capital. On the other hand, the middle strata, which predominate in the officer corps of the advanced capitalist states, aspire to militarising society in a manner which is seriously threatening peace and social progress.

8 Political Institutions, Political Culture and Militarism

The next important determinant of militarism is the given characteristics of the political institutions and political culture. Political institutions can be differently structured. Hence we distinguish democratic, bureaucratic and bureaucratised political institutions, which are incorporated into a given political system. Also, the political culture of different societies, just as of the same society in different periods, can be very different, depending on the level of development of democratic or autocratic values, greater or lesser devotion to civil political or military institutions (greater or lesser) presence of a tradition in the use of force, especially military force, in political relations and processes, etc.

There is no doubt that public attachment to certain civil political institutions and political systems which are characterised by the existence of well organised political parties, trade unions and economic associations can play an important part in preventing military intervention in politics. And, conversely, that a low level of public attachment can enable the army to become the dominant political force. All the same, a wide public attachment to any civil political institution is not in itself an obstacle to military intervention in politics. For civil political institutions, different kinds of political and social grouping, the same as the other components of the political system, are not spontaneous social phenomena, but are primarily conditioned by the specific class structure and relation of the class forces of a given social system. These essential factors, and their mutual relations which can be differently socially structured, shape the degree of militarisation of the political system.

The impact of political institutions and of the level of political culture in military intervention in politics can only be understood if their characteristics are analysed in the context of the class structure of a given social system. This is because civil political institutions and their domination (formal or real) over the state military organisation are not, in themselves, an obstacle in the way of the processes of militarisation of the political system, i.e. to military interventions in politics.

In the USA during the Second World War, there were highly developed political civil institutions which enjoyed supremacy over the military organisation, yet the role of the joint chiefs of staff of the armed services in matters of external and home policy was still very significant. During Hitler's reign, the power of the generals and admirals was greatly restricted. There was strict civilian political control over the state military organisation as embodied in the control of Hitler as chief of state and Federal Chancellor. Yet the whole of social life was subject to an unparalleled degree of militarisation. Whatever the case, the military do not exercise political power directly nor do they operate in political life as an autonomous political force. By the same token, the militarisation of the armed forces of revolution, or the militarisation of the colonial regions, is carried out on the ordinance of and under the direct control of civilian political institutions whose legitimacy is not brought into question since there is wide recognition of their existence and of their social role.

Hence, the sheer existence of civilian political institutions and their predominance over the military, as well as a wide public attachment to civilian forms of government, are not in the cited instances an impediment to the penetration of the principles of organising and set of values of the military into the political system and overall social life. However, in social systems with not much of a tradition of civilian political institutions, and with poorly organised political parties, labour unions and economic organisations, military intervention in politics is widely practised. What's more, the military are here most often the only organised political force capable of dominating political relations and processes.

Since the phenomenon of militarisation finds scope both in social systems with well rooted civil political institutions, developed political parties and other social organisations and in social systems lacking such elements, it is obvious that neither these nor a broad-based devotion to them are of significance in determining the penetration into the political system and overall society of the principles of organising and system of values specific to the state military organisation. But in no circumstances does this mean that the social character of civilian political institutions and political grouping, or their mutual relations, are of no relevance to the onset and development of individual forms of militarism. On the contrary, the specific social character of their shaping and their mutual relations become under certain conditions an important determinant of militarism.

9 Legislature and Executive Power and the Military

The undisputed class rule of the bourgeoisie presupposed the existence of democratic political supervision by legislative power over the apparatus of executive power. However, the later course of development of the political systems of bourgeois democracy showed up radical changes in relations between legislative and executive power. Theoretically speaking, legislative power defines national policy, executive power enforces it, and the state military organisation is simply an instrument of realising one aspect of that policy.

In reality, the relation between legislative power, executive power and the state military organisation is not as simple as that. Namely, neither under democratic nor autocratic forms of political organising of society are the relations between legislative and executive power, or between them and state military organisation, static categories. Indeed, the supremacy of legislative power over executive power and military organisation is constantly in the process of being impaired and re-established. In the course of this century, however, the predominance of legislative power has been called into question more and more often and gradually transformed into the predominance of the executive over legislative power. The subsequent evolution of the political systems of bourgeois democracy attained a stage in which the traditional demarcation lines between political and military institutions and between the political and military spheres, in general, were erased.

This had the effect of transforming democratic political institutions of bourgeois democracy into institutions and a political system structured in a bureaucratic manner. In the context of such changes, civilian control was deprived of all meaning. So, not only are such political institutions and such a political system not a barrier to militarisation, but they are actually one of its more significant determinants. Such political institutions, moreover, themselves initiate and develop processes of militarisation of political systems and international relations. Incorporated into them are the executive bodies of the political parties and even of the labour unions. The party and labour union bureaucracies in the USA, for example, are closely associated with government agencies and military institutions and participate together with them in integrating all walks of social life into the state military system.

In the vast area of the one-time colonial empire, political institutions used to be traditionally autocratic; the state absorbed all the administration functions of society and eliminated all independent centres of political power. At the time when the large colonial powers were enslaving the peoples of Latin America, Asia and Africa, the strength and authority of the state provided a first-class instrument for pursuing such activity and constituting colonial power. The setting up of new, independent national states in the course of the long period of decolonisation usually did not result in the creation of really democratic political institutions and political systems. The root causes of such a course of political development should be sought, first of all, in the socio-class characteristics of the majority of the social systems in Asia, Africa and Latin America. In all of them the resilient vestiges of archaic social and political relations are vigorously opposing the new economic relations and political institutions of modern society.

The existence of social classes which are typical of varied socio-economic formations finds expression in the political sphere in the existence of different and opposed conceptions of society's political organisation and prospects of social development in general. In some of these societies we find political institutions of bourgeois democracy, or rather their imitations. These, however, have not manifested a desirable degree of political efficiency in directing social development. This is why they are being displaced with others, conforming to the character of economic and class relations. Where they still survive they serve as a screen behind which the strength of the executive or the state military organisation is at work.

The development of the political systems of socialism has been closely connected from the start with the power and influence of the state. In the distorted forms of its development, the state has been proclaimed the motive power of the development of national and world-wide socialism. It has grown into an omnipotent 'Leviathan' who submits to his control and domination the entire social life of the largest socialist country and the entire 'socialist camp'. In such circumstances, the executive organs of the highly developed political parties (i.e. the parties) are intertwined, personnel and institution-wise, with the organs and institutions of political authority. In view of the fact that the ruling forces of statist socialism operate within the social system and in international relations by virtue of the strength and authority of the state, in the first place, the state military organisation becomes a pre-eminent means of reinforcing this type of socialism and promoting its development on a world scale. Out of this spring different kinds of civilian or civil-military militarism.

The existence of democratic political institutions, developed democratic political systems and a wide approval of them and of their social role undoubtedly play a part in restricting the process of militarisation in the social sector of the state military system. In other words, they prevent the penetration of the principles of organising and system of values, peculiar to the state military system, into the political system and global society. Yet they play this part only to a certain degree. Democratic institutions in Chile, and their existence, did not prevent an army, traditionally excluded from active political life, from grossly intervening in politics, from quelling all democratic forms of organising, and from militarising Chilean society to a large measure. Actually, in the case in point, militarisation was carried out just because of the existence of democratic institutions of the political system, since they had become highly suitable instruments of bringing about the socialist transformation of society and had thereby become a direct threat to the vital interests of the wealthy classes and foreign capital.

It is therefore if capital importance to stress that by proxy of both types of political institution, of both sets of value of political culture, and their influence, the strength of class determinism creates scope for a greater or lesser degree of militarisation. When the position of the ruling class in the structure of society is advantageous and, in consequence, its rule undisputed, it develops democratic political institutions and a democratic structure of the political system. On the other hand, when its position becomes unstable and when, in consequence, its rule and the legitimacy of its political institutions are called into question, the ruling class begins increasingly to rely on the strength and authority of its state.

In this way, the executive branch of state power grows stronger and more influential, and the democratic character of the political institutions and the whole political system are eroded and destroyed. In order to defend the class interests of the ruling class, imperilled by an intensified class struggle which is threatening to destroy the very foundations on which the given class system is based, the executive branch of power makes use of the state military organisation both as a material force and as a social organisation more and more often. This can be done by the class itself, directly, if it assesses that the executive is not a convenient intermediary between itself and the army. This is what inspires in military commanders an exaggerated sense of the army's social importance. Under specific conditions, such a feeling materialises in the direct usurption of state power by the state military organisation (or by military commanders) and in its alienation from the ruling class itself.

10 The Socio-political Meaning of Militarism

Investigations of the determinants and social characteristics of militarism confirm that militarism is a social relation between the military organisation of the state and the rest of society occasioned by a historically determined class structure and distinguished by the fashioning of the political system, global society and international relations on principles of organising specific to the state military system. They also make it possible to envisage the socio-political meaning and future of militarism.

One may ask: is militarisation of military activity, political relations and processes, of the economic, educational and other spheres of social life a progressive or reactionary social phenomenon? It is not at all easy to answer this question. The results of the investigation show that militarism, as a specific way of fashioning social relations and processes, is not, in itself, either progressive or reactionary. Namely, it takes on a definite social meaning and sense only in dependence on the socio-political conditions in which it finds expression. To be more precise, one must know in whose interests particular spheres of social life are being more or less militarised.

The militarisation of the armed forces of revolution (to a certain degree) and that of the political systems and social structures of a number of underdeveloped countries (Egypt, Burma, Libya, Ethiopia today, etc.) represent progressive socio-political processes. This is because they have an instrumental role to play in the defence of the achievements of the revolution or in initiating progressive social transformations. By contrast, Hitler's National Socialist militarism, modern-day militarism in the USA and the militarisation of contemporary international relations are deeply reactionary phenomena. They are instruments in the hands of reactionary social forces which, by modelling political systems, global societies and the international community in a militaristic fashion, strove or are striving to preserve their privileges and to suppress progressive social forces and are not strictly separated from each other in real movements.

The progressive and reactionary forms of militarism, however, are also not separated from each other in real political life. That is, progressive forms of militarisation of society can become transformed in the course of time into reactionary ones. And, conversely, certain reactionary forms of militarisation can evolve with the progress of time into progressive social phenomena.

The militarisation of the armed forces of revolution, as a progressive social process, for example, and the creation of the military organisation of the bourgeois and socialist states can be transformed in the course of time into military organisation of the bourgeois state (in the course of the militarisation of the armed forces of bourgeois revolution). Its social role is progressive while the bourgeoisie itself is a progressive social class, while it is fighting to stabilise capitalist social relations against the opposition of the feudal social forces. But when the bourgeois class turns into a reactionary social force, the military organisation of its state becomes a first-class instrument of protecting and advancing its class interests and aspirations. In such circumstances, the originally progressive militarism is converted into reactionary militarism (more or less marked militarisation of the political system, global society, colonial regions and international relations). Similarly, the creation of the military organisation of the socialist state, after the victory of the socialist revolution, represents a progressive kind of militarisation, considering that it springs from the need of the working class to defend and preserve the newly constituted socialist social relations. The fact is that, directly after victory, the working class is not yet capable of stabilising the socialist social system by itself. Consequently, this is done by its state, i.e. the military organisation of the socialist state, in the name and in the interests of the working class. But once the working class has grown strong and once the conditions have been met for it to manage all social activities directly, the further maintenance of the exclusive monopoly of the state, i.e. its military organisation, over military affairs becomes a reactionary social manifestation. It usually leads to all the most important social activities being integrated into the state military system and to relations not just between socialist and capitalist states but also between socialist countries themselves being militarised.

Similar tendencies are perceived in the evolution of reactionary forms of militarism into progressive ones. The state military organisations across the broad expanses of Asia, Africa and Latin America were for years the mainstay of the reactionary forces and a model according to which these forces structured their political system with a view to safeguarding their class privileges. In some of these countries, the army became, in the course of time, the force that upheld progressive social aspirations, since, in developing military organisations, i.e. in creating ever larger and stronger supports of their class rule, the ruling social forces were historically compelled to recruit part of their officer corps from the ranks of the lower social classes. And precisely these changes in the class structure of the officer corps helped to revise its political outlook and political orientation. They usually led to the alienation of the military organisation (complete or partial) from the ruling class and to the militarisation of social relations and processes, with the result that the military organisation became an instrument of progressive social forces by which more or less radical changes in the social system were carried out in a number of underdeveloped countries. In this manner, what was originally a reactionary type of militarism was transformed into a progressive or even revolutionary brand.

11 Future Prospects

In the end, something should also be said about the future of militarism. This analysis has shown that its onset is causally related to the existence and social role of the state, i.e. to the class-structural characteristics of a given social system. Hence the prospects of militarism, too, are closely linked to the prospects and social role of the state. In other words, for as long as society is differentiated into classes there will be a more or less marked tendency towards the alienation of the military organisation from society and from the ruling class and/or the practice of structuring the political system, all of society and international relations on the lines of a distribution of social power and authority typical of the state military system. This stems from the contradictory nature of the state military organisation as the most complete social substitute for the state. Under conditions of the class differentiation of contemporary society, the state military organisation plays an important part and its existence has a historical justification. To insist, therefore, on its abolition would be anarchic subjectivism. For, the fundamental problem is not in abolishing the state military organisation but in preventing the political system, global society and international relations being fashioned on its specific principles of organising and its system of values. Without entering into a polemic with anarchical conceptions, according to which the mechanical abolition of the state military organisation is the only way to transcend militarism, we shall examine some theoretical and practical possibilities of preventing the spread of the system of distribution of social power and authority peculiar to state military organisation to the political system and all society. In this respect, contemporary sociological theory offers us the following solutions.

(1) The militarisation of the political system and the rest of society can be rendered impossible by establishing civil political supervision over the state military organisation which should be constituted and developed as a professional, non-political force. This conception has been materialised in the political systems of bourgeois democracy, and it is theoretically explained, in particular by S. Huntington.[13]

(2) The militarisation of the political system and the rest of society can be rendered impossible primarily through the strength and stability of civil political institutions and by political consensus which lies at their core. This conception is theoretically endorsed by S.E. Finer.[14]

(3) Militarisation of the political system can be rendered impossible through the transformation of the state military organisation into a modern civil militia such as was the militia of local self-government before the nineteenth century. 'Direct participation of the citizen in the running of the country in all kinds of ways should be revived and extended in modern form.'[15] In the past, local self-government implied the right to defend one's family and property, one's land and its allies. The revival of these rights in modern form is essential to the modern military organisation.

(4) The militarisation of the political system and international relations can be rendered impossible by strengthening the national and supranational state military organisations of the socialist states. The exponents of this theory proceed from the thesis that militarism is exclusively the product of capitalism. In other words, militarism does not exist in socialism. On the other hand, socialism opposes militarism and is conducive to its historical transcension primarily through the strength of its state military organisation and the supranational military state structures of the socialist countries. This conception is advocated by Soviet authors, and is elaborated in particular by A.P. Zalyetnii.[16]

Real participation of citizens in the management of social affairs can only be developed in a socialist social system. But it is not characteristic of every form of socialist organisation of society. Namely statist socialism tends to reinforce the social role of the state military organisation and to incorporate the free social activities into the state or a supra-state military system, as shown earlier on. Consequently, not only is statist socialisation of military activity not an impediment to the penetration of the principles of organising and system of values specific to state military organisation into the political system, global society and international relations, but it is an indicator of their presence and greater or lesser development. We can talk about direct socialisation of military activity only under a form of socialist organisation of society based on social ownership of the means of production and self-management. Namely, as the statist structure of the socialist social system is transcended and as it is shaped ever more completely on the lines of self-management, self-management relations are increasingly extended, besides others, to the sphere which through a long period of human history had been the exclusive monopoly of the state. In this manner, for the first time in the history of class society, the process of direct socialisation of military activity is carried out on the basis of social ownership of the means of production and military activity in the context of a self-management political system and a military organisation specific to it.

The military organisation of a socialist self-managed society dialectically surpasses the techno-bureaucratic organisation of military activity peculiar to capitalism and statist socialism. In this manner, a socio-political system based on social ownership of the means of production and self-management provides the historical framework for, and is the determinant of, the transcension of militarism as a social phenomenon.

Notes

1. K. Marx, 'The Eighteenth Brumaire of Louis Bonaparte' in *Surveys from Exile, Political Writings*, Volume 2 (London, 1973), p. 163.
2. John Steward Ambler, *The French Army in Politics 1945-1962* (Ohio State University Press, 1966), p. 195.
3. *Rule of the Internal Service of the Armed Forces of the USSR*, p. 7.
4. J.N. Wolfe and John Erickson (eds.), *The Armed Services and Society: Alienation, Management and Integration* (Edinburgh University Press, Edinburgh, 1970); the quotation was taken from the writings of Sir John Hackett, pp. 27-8.
5. Charles de Gaulle, *The Army of the Future* (London, 1940), p. 85.
6. H. Perón, cit. according to Wolfe and Erickson, *Armed Services and Society*, p. 28.

7. S. Andreski, *Military Organization and Society* (University of California Press, Berkeley and Los Angeles, 1968), p. 35.

8. Ibid., p. 95.

9. *Le Monde*, 12 May 1961.

10. Sir John Hackett, cit. according to Wolfe and Erickson, *Armed Services and Society*, p. 27.

11. M. Janowitz, *The Professional Soldier* (The Free Press, New York, 1971), p. 427.

12. R. Mils, *Elita vlasti* (Kultura, Belgrade, 1964), p. 253 (translated from Serbo-Croatian).

13. S.P. Huntington, *The Soldier and the State* (Harvard University Press, Cambridge, Mass., 1957).

14. S.E. Finer, *The Man on Horseback* (Praeger, New York, 1962), pp. 24, 28.

15. W. Correlli Barnett, 'The Military Profession in the 1970's' in J.N. Wolfe and John Erickson (eds.), *The Armed Services and Society*, p. 14.

16. A.P. Zalyetnii, *Militarization of the Federal Republic of Germany* (Academy of Sciences of the USSR, Institute of Military History of the Ministry of National Defence of the USSR, published by 'Nauka', Moscow, 1969) (in Russian), pp. 400-15, 452.

9 THE CRITIQUE OF MILITARISM IN SOVIET STUDIES

Julian Lider

> [By militarism] we mean simply an acceptance of the values of the military subculture as the dominant values of society: a stress on hierarchy and subordination in organization, on physical courage and self-sacrifice in personal behaviour, on the need for heroic leadership in situations of extreme stress; all based on an acceptance of the inevitability of armed conflict within the state-system and the consequent need to develop the qualities necessary to conduct it [M. Howard, *War in European History* (London, 1976), pp. 109-10].

> The militarised state-apparatus is the weapon of the whole monopoly bourgeoisie. Although it is only a small group of monopoly capitalists that is deriving direct benefit from militarisation, the scale and scope of militarisation, the state armaments programme and military policy are dictated by the political and military strategy interests of the whole of monopoly capital [*Problems of War and Peace* (Moscow, 1972), p. 103].

The striking difference between these two descriptions of militarism, its very concept, essence and functions, illustrates the deep difference between the Soviet approach to the subject and an approach (political realist) widespread in the West. The different outlook persists even if other Western assessments (including the frequent critical comments on the military-industrial complex) are taken for comparison. The critical assessment of militarism is one of the most important subjects in Soviet studies.[1] In Soviet theory criticism of other views is considered a means of developing and presenting one's own. It requires that each theory in social science develops through the criticism of so-called bourgeois views and thereby, at the same time, contributes to the ideological struggle. The criticism of militarism is a case in point. It is regarded as one of the main topics in Marxist-Leninist political economy which, together with the philosophy and theory of the political struggle (so-called scientific Communism), constitute the three component parts of the Marxist-Leninist ideology. Critical assessment of militarism is considered essential to the concept and assessment of contemporary imperialism, international relations and war.

I have tried to sketch such an assessment, starting with the review of the Soviet conceptual apparatus applied in the criticism; there follows a brief description of the functions attributed by Soviets to militarism, and of the ideology which is said to underly it, and a few comments on the differences between the position of the critics and the criticised. The final comment is on the equation of militarism with modern capitalism, which seems to be characteristic of the prevailing Soviet position on the subject.

1 The Concept

To begin with the concept applied in Soviet literature, there are many different presentations which put emphasis either on the political instrumentality of militarism (policy, complex of measures, instrument, function), or on the aim of militarisation (external wars, internal suppression, both), or on the social forces whose instrument militarism is said to be (financial capital, military establishment, bourgeoisie as a whole, imperialism as a whole, capitalist states, great powers, etc.). These are usually brief definitions, afterwards complemented and explained by long descriptions.

Let us look at some of these definitions. In one Soviet approach, militarism is presented as the *function* of the state-monopolist capitalism that is defending its class interests by means of armed violence.[2] In another, it is called the most important *instrument* of the monopolistic bourgeoisie, whose reactionary policy aims at strengthening and extending its dominance by means of armed violence.[3] A third definition states that militarism is a kind of *policy* aiming at increasing the military power and preparing predatory wars.[4] Militarism should be regarded as a *system* of economic, political, ideological and direct military measures undertaken by aggressive capitalist states aimed at preparing and conducting imperialist wars.[5]

All descriptions emphasise the internal aspect of militarism. It leads to the domination of the military and to the subordination of the entire policy, economy and culture of a given country to the imperialist military aims.[6] It is used by the financial oligarchy to consolidate and expand its domination. It reflects a complex of many measures in all fields of internal and external social activity: militarisation of the economy, science and education; arms race; building up military blocs, growth of the armed forces, intensification of the preparation for wars; suppression of workers' movements and national liberation struggle, spreading militaristic propaganda, etc.[7]

In a few studies, these broad definitions are in some sense complemented by the emphasis on the 'economic' aspects: militarism is considered an economic activity, aiming at ensuring extremely high profits.[8]

The common denominator of all these various definitions and descriptions is the treatment of militarism as a class phenomenon. Militarism is not discussed 'in general', nor is it confined to the growth of the role of the military: it is a conscious instrument of the monopolist bourgeoisie, to enable it to attain more power and more profits. As such, it is considered nothing new in history: militarism as a social phenomenon was born together with the emergence of class society, and was always characteristic of it; in the monopolistic stage of capitalism it has reached a size and an intensity without precedence in history.

One definition, complemented by a description, may perhaps be quoted to exemplify this approach; it starts a chapter devoted to militarism in a collective study by a group of well known Soviet theorists:

> Imperialist militarism is a complex social phenomenon which comprises a system of economic, political, ideological and directly military measures taken by aggressive capitalist nations and directed toward preparing for and conducting imperialist wars. It is utilized by the financial oligarchy to consolidate and expand its domination, to preserve the capitalist system on the one hand, and to generate big profits on the other. Militarism as a social phenomenon was born with the split of society into classes, with the appearance of the exploiting class. Inheriting militarism from other class-antagonistic societies, the bourgeoisie took over the most reactionary elements in it and adapted them to its interests and needs.[9]

According to the Soviet presentation, the necessity to expand and intensify militaristic policy is rooted in the *general crisis of capitalism*. The imperialist bourgeoisie has exhausted the economic means provided by the capitalist system of economy for the exploitation of workers, and the unhindered exploitation of the colonies as sources of raw material and markets has also come to an end. *Non-economic measures of compulsion*, both internal and external, have been assessed as necessary to a much greater extent than ever before. This has led to world wars and is now creating the danger of a most destructive war encompassing the whole globe.

As we see, in the Soviet approach, militarism is one of the essential attributes of the pre-socialist class state. Such a state always tends to expand its armed forces and to use them in the pursuit of an aggressive foreign policy and an oppressive domestic policy. The definitions either focus on the external aspect, or internal, or both, but – as mentioned before – they always stress that the defence of class rule underlies each kind of militarism.

In contrast, there are several definitions of the term in the Western literature. Some of them focus on militarism as a kind of political *structure*, in which the military run the government. In another approach, militarism is considered an *ideology* which either glorifies war or maintains that the military should hold a dominant, or at least an independent, position in society. The evaluation of the policy pursued by the military is considered a separate question, which depends on the concrete circumstances in the particular countries.

From this general assessment, Soviet political thought presents its view of the functions, ideology and institutional setting of contemporary militarism.

2 The Functions

The criticism focuses on the functions of militarism, which are said to spring from the main functions of state and are described similarly to those of armed forces. The internal one is the function of preserving and strengthening the existing system, keeping the exploited masses in subjugation and obedience and suppressing their struggle for liberation. The external function consists in promoting and defending the interests of the ruling class outside the country. Both functions are interrelated, and both aim at preserving or increasing the power of the ruling class and securing its profits. While they are a constant and conceptual characteristics of armed forces, as regards militarism they constitute a variant linked to the period of aggravation of all class contradictions, internal and international, in the imperialist world. Continuing to defend the interests of the ruling class, militarism is assigned the task of preserving its *threatened* rule. For this aim, it must use not only armed forces, but the whole state apparatus, the whole of its administrative, economic and ideological power (including the use of police).[10]

No wonder that in such interpretation both functions expand and become more intense. The internal one becomes more cruel, resorts more frequently than ever before to terroristic methods, and the ideological indoctrination uses Fascist and racialist ideas. The external function, now more important, acquires quite new features. First, whereas at the beginning of this century it was applied in inter-imperialist competition, after the October Revolution, and especially after the emergence of the socialist camp, it became an anti-socialistic militarism. Since internal oppression has always been its determining characteristic, it has today become *counter-revolutionary both in the internal and international aspects*, with emphasis on the destruction of the socialist system.

> Imperialist politicians and ideologues do not hide the fact that the principal goals of militarism today are destruction of the world socialist system, the international labor and liberation movement, and reestablishment of the domination of capital throughout the world. Calling for unlimited nuclear world war against the socialist nations, the militarists declare that the aim of such war should be victory at any price over the nations of the socialist community.[11]

The second feature is that militarism has now encompassed all imperialist countries and 'tied them into a common knot', which enables the United States to impose its will on both its allies and competitors. Third, war and the threat of war have now become the main instruments of militarist external policy.

Parenthetically, Soviet scholars complement this description with the comment that the very dangerous character of militarism involves an increased resistance of peoples against it and 'ties the hands of militarists'.

3 The Ideology

Militarism is said to include ideological justification and indoctrination. It must be justified in order to infect the population and to gain its acceptance and the backing of the military build-up and policy.[12]

The basis of the ideological outlook which underlies militarism is the proposition that armed force is one of the determining factors, if not the determining one, of social development. It is said to assure sovereignty, to be the motive force of progress, and to serve as the indispensable means of resolving all political disputes. In other words, it is both necessary and inevitable.[13]

According to Soviet scholars, all reactionary bourgeois theories of the roots of wars are resorted to in order to justify these assumptions, from biological to 'technico-industrial'; the latter, the most recent, is said to state that contemporary wars are generated by the industrial, scientific and technical progress which both creates fierce competition and a means of struggle favouring its armed resolution. The constant underlying philosophy is the political realism which regards search for power and resort to war as a normal and necessary means of conducting international relations. War and threat of war, arms race and shows of force – these means of policy are at the same time presented by modern militarism not only as inevitable but also as the engines of technical and scientific, and consequently of social, progress.[14]

The apologia for the militarisation of the economy occupies a special place here.[15] It is justified and praised for the following alleged social and economic merits:

(1) militarisation of the economy increases the entire national product;
(2) it diminishes unemployment;
(3) it diminishes the costs of production and increases consumption;
(4) it improves the distribution of the national product;
(5) since the role of the state grows, and private ownership of the means of production shrinks, social inequalities and conflicts diminish.[16]

Interrelated is the apologia for the militarisation of science.[17] Western theory is charged with attempting to justify the militarisation of science by the alleged needs of contemporary wars, and the alleged natural interaction of the economy, science and military affairs. It is said to contend that the growth of the size and intensity of wars involves the development of science and techniques connected with fighting and their increased engagement in military affairs. Needs of war stimulated the development of many sectors of science and the creation of many technical devices (ballistics, probabilistic theory, radar, automated systems, aerodynamics, missiles, etc.). The enormous requirements of the military machine have then made it necessary to divert a large portion of scientific discovery and enormous material resources to military purposes and to create an enormous military-industrial apparatus with its own relatively independent economic base.

Finally, the intrinsic feature of the ideological arsenal of militarism which is said to underlie all its apologetic expositions is the presentation of it as of a non-class phenomenon. Militarism is either treated as an external phenomenon and defined in a way concealing its class nature, or presented as quite a new phenomenon generated by the modern conditions and unusual for the classical capitalistic system. In using the former method, scholars present militarism as a regime based on military force, or emphasising armed violence, without providing any indication of whose policy this military force and armed violence are instruments.[18] In the second approach, militarism is presented as the outcome of the modern military technical revolution and modern specific conditions, unusual in the previous stages of history of Western powers.[19]

The criticism of all above tenets of the ideological apologia of militarism – as Soviet scholars term it – is contained in the very *way* of its presentation in the Soviet literature: all features attributed to it, its genesis and role in society, classify it according to the Soviet political, ideological and scientific criteria (which are strictly interconnected) with the most reactionary and anti-scientific ideas. The criticism of particular aspects of militaristic ideology is therefore similar to that of the critique of Western philosophies of war and armed forces, which have been reviewed in many studies (also by me in *On the Nature of War* (1977) and in *The Political and Military Laws of War* (1979)). While it seems to me unnecessary to remind the reader of this criticism, some points may be added here since Soviet scholars also take issue with the following assumptions which they consider to be characteristic of the ideological justification of militarism.

With regard to technical and scientific progress as the modern root of war: these achievements do not provide impulses to armed violence *per se*, they may as well be placed at the service of peace; the way they are used depends on the interests of the class which has them at its disposal.[20]

As to the proposition that militarism and war economy are quite new phenomena: they accompanied all class societies, and especially the capitalist system.[21] The increased interventionism of the state apparatus, now more than ever subordinated to the ruling class and strengthening its rule, is a quite logical and natural development of the capitalist system in its monopolistic stage. Thus the development of militarism is in full accord with the development of capitalist society.[22]

As to the alleged non-class character of militarism: all states have military forces, but not all are militaristic. It is only when the governing exploiting class consciously increases armaments, armed forces and preparations for predatory wars, and also increases internal oppression, that one can speak about militarism. Naturally it is a phenomenon inherent in the essence of class societies only.

As to the alleged merits of the militarisation of the economy; three main objections may be raised. First, militarisation is always performed at the cost of the working classes, and results in the deterioration of their material conditions. Second, it is not only unproductive but also counter-productive: it takes material resources and human talents from the fields crucial for economic and social development and diverts them to fields of little use for the country's economy. Finally, Soviet criticism of the apologia for the militarisation of science assumes that, contrary to Western views, the whole process of interaction of science, technology and military affairs, involving the militarisation of science and technology, is socially caused, since the use of all of them is determined by social, i.e. class, interests.

The critics say that the use of scientific and technical achievements in military affairs is determined primarily by the narrow class of monopolistic capital which needs them for gaining extraordinarily high profits, preparing aggressive wars and countering the acute class struggle.[23]

Being socially caused, the militarisation of science also has social *consequences.*[24] While providing temporary additional sources and incentives for economic development, it strengthens its rottenness and parasitism. The increased production is used not in the interests of all society as a whole, but against it.

The social inequality increases; the production of weapons of mass destruction swallows up an enormous part of the national income, and the growing production enriches a handful of monopolists, while the number of unemployed workers and intellectuals and ruined peasants grows. The extreme aggravation of the internal social contradictions makes the economic and political development of particular countries ever more uneven. The adverse psychological consequences of militarisation and of the constant preparedness for war and fear of war are enormous and difficult to be estimated.

4 The Military-industrial Complex

The criticism of militarism commonly leads Soviet scholars into talking about the so-called military-industrial complex. This is defined by them as the alliance between the imperialist monopolies and the reactionary military in the state apparatus; it is presented as *the highest form of modern militarism.*[25] The top echelon of the state bureaucracy joins the monopoly groups and the military hierarchy, and the whole gigantic military machine serves as its material basis.

The military-industrial complex exerts great influence on the whole policy-making process, on militarisation of the economy, and on scientific-technical research. Two consequences are singled out for criticism: one is the growth of the danger of war, and the other is the further concentration of capital and the increase in social inequality. The former may be expressed by the following short quotation: 'Having come into being, the military-industrial complex is, to some extent, acquiring a dynamism of its own, becoming the motor of further militarisation of the economy and a serious obstacle to detente and disarmament.'[26]

The criticism of the MIC is not confined to the United States, but includes West Germany, the United Kingdom and other countries, and also includes the impact of the military-industrial complex on military alliances, in particular on NATO's armament build-up.

5 The Differences in Approaches

There are principal differences between the Soviet and Western approaches to the concept and practice of militarism. The main point of disagreement rests on its very concept.

In the West the term is interpreted so variously by different schools and scholars that it 'has become a term of such general illiterate abuse' (Michael Howard) and so many symptoms of structural, attitudinal and political nature have been subsumed under this notion[27] that in fact any political or economic policy, or any theory of war and armed forces, can be termed militaristic.

In the Soviet approach, all connotations with which militarism has been used can be reduced to a common one: it is a *conscious activity on the part of the monopolistic bourgeoisie, aimed at increasing its own power and intensifying its reactionary external and internal policy; it uses the increase of the role of military and armed violence as an instrument of such a policy.*

For the sake of analysis, this principal difference can be presented as a set of points of disagreement.

(1) While in the Western approaches the departure is the increasing role of the military and its tendency to become relatively autonomous without, however, any pointing to its role as defender and instrument of the exploiting classes – in the Soviet literature the emphasis is not on the military regarded solely as the *instrument*, but on the *subject* who uses it – i.e. on the monopoly bourgeoisie. In other words, although there are many national forms of militarism, its class essence is always the same; the increasing role of the military cannot be the

deterministic characteristic of militarism; its essence is determined by the character of policy, and of the socio-economic system which generates it.

(2) Thus, while in some Western approaches militarism is treated as the *abuse by the military* of its legitimate function, usurpation of roles and prerogatives which 'normally' are not theirs (implicit: by diminishing the power of the 'normal' rulers),[28] in the Soviet approach it is precisely *the rulers who use the military* to increase their own power. Militarism does not mean the change of the main actor or the ruler, but only the change of methods; and the change is not qualitative, but is more a matter of degree, of intensity, and of emphasis.

(3) An interrelated difference is that distinctly from the Western interpretations, the Soviet concept of militarism places it *in the framework of class struggle* between the two antagonistic classes, the exploiting class and the exploited masses, and emphasises the internal function of militarism as aiming at increasing and making more effective this exploitation by using non-economic means. This stems from the fact that, distinct from Western interpretations, in the Soviet concept militarism and the military are but instruments of the policy of the governing class.

(4) The next difference is a corollary. In many Western approaches the external function of militarism is mainly a consequence of the primary status of the military and it partly serves as a justification and rationalisation of their privileged position. In the Soviet approach, *both internal and international functions are closely bound up with each other* as serving the same class and the same class interests. Which of them comes to the fore depends on the period and situation; at present the external function of militarism and its aggressive tendencies are receiving very great attention.

(5) Since in the Western approaches the growth of the role of the military is usually the deterministic characteristic of militarism, or of the process of militarisation, they include the significant role of the military in the Soviet Union (constantly growing, as many Sovietologists assert) into the concept. The armament policy on an enormous scale, which characterizes the Soviet military build-up after World War II, is used to confirm this approach. One writes therefore about the 'global reach of militarism' as caused by the competitive military policy of the superpowers. Soviet scholars not only reject such a standpoint, which is quite natural, but sharply criticise it as *anti-Soviet propaganda*. To equate the two military policies means *to equate two contrary foreign and internal policies*, the policy of the United States

which is bellicose and directed against the working masses, and the peaceful and progressive policy of the Soviet Union. The similarity in symptoms is similarity in form, but not in essence. One cannot equate the world-wide arms race unleashed by the United States with the defence effort of the socialist states, or the dominance-dependence relationships between the imperialist powers and developing countries with the relations between the Soviet Union and countries of the Third World, and the domestic suppression aggravated by militarism in the capitalist countries with the close ties between armies and people in the socialist societies, etc.

(6) A corollary is the difference in assessing the so-called military-industrial complex. In the West this is also criticised by many, and is related to the phenomenon of militarism. It is charged with the extension of influence of bellicose forces on society, with plundering the natural and human resources for the sake of superfluous military measures, with corrupting the state apparatus, and with excessive profits.[29] While agreeing with these charges, as directed against the Western military-industrial complex, Soviet scholars take issue with the assumption that it is an abnormal phenomenon which can be liquidated by improving the existing capitalist system: this is not a disease which can be cured by reforms, but, as militarism itself, *it is a natural and inevitable product of the imperialist system*, to be liquidated with the liquidation of the system itself. And naturally, any subsuming of the Soviet military organisation under the common concept of the military-industrial complex can be regarded only as a conscious distortion of the political reality, and anti-Soviet propaganda.

(7) As to the ideology of militarism, while in the West it is often regarded as a deviation from democracy, and even a departure from it, Soviet scholars point out that it does not constitute any new quality, since *the bourgeois democracy* – which never was democracy proper – in its imperialist variant *has always been militaristic*, with its absolutisation of the role of force and violence in history and in contemporary international relations, as well as in domestic affairs. Such ideas underlie the traditional theory of balance of power, in which violence and war are declared to be supreme arbiters, and normal instruments of policy justified by the 'interests' of nations. Militarism only means that this apologia for war and its externalisation have become more open and explicit.

(8) Soviet scholars also take issue with the frequent attempts to present militarism as a kind of ideology, or 'subculture', where it is

described as a set of values dominating society. It is usually based on an acceptance of the inevitability of war and presented as including such values as emphasis on hierarchy and discipline, on physical courage and self-sacrifice in personal behaviour, on the need for heroic leadership in situations of extreme stress, on the readiness to fight for one's country, etc.[30] However, militarism cannot be reduced to ideology, nor can ideology which is really connected with it include such positive values as many of those mentioned above. On the contrary, only highly reactionary anti-human ideology can underlie the aggressive militarism. Nor can such ideology be presented as national and equated with patriotism, which its adherents attempt to do. However, *no ideology can be separated from its socio-economic roots*, and from the interests of the class which tries to impose it on society. Militarism has nothing in common with patriotism and with the readiness to fight for country's true interests; on the contrary, it justifies the necessity to fight for the interests of the monopolies, which run *against* the true national interests.

(9) Finally, a special point of disagreement seems to be the presentation of militarism in the countries of the Third World. While in the West it is sometimes considered one of the two main variants of militarism, Soviet scholars seem to give it quite a different quality. The emphasis on the necessity for strengthening armed forces is rooted in weakness and in an undetermined way of development, and not, like imperialistic militarism, in a conscious tendency to suppress, exploit and profit all the more. It can, with time, become an instrument of imperialistic militarism, as its ally and servant, but *it cannot be termed a variant of the same order*. This principal difference in interpreting the military build-up in the Third World is reflected in the way the external policy of the Third World countries is presented.[31] Here the most distinctive feature of militarism, as Soviets describe it, disappears. Although the young states can be differently classified with regard to their internal development – the division into the progressive and reactionary groupings being the usual one – 'the connection between the nature of the ruling class forces and their diplomatic activity is not mechanical'; in the very complex situation in the particular countries of the Third World it can happen that social forces which hinder internal progress at the same time aim at strengthening the newly acquired sovereignty of the state against the neo-colonialist endeavours of the imperialist states.

This leads to the general assessment that progressive anti-imperialist tendencies 'are characteristic of the foreign policy of the developing countries belonging to all the groups',[32] and to the general conclusion that the position and politics of these countries are a major and important 'factor of democratization of international relations'.[33]

Soviet scholars and politicians naturally point to the frequent changes in the foreign policy of certain young states, mentioning that the latter not only make use of inter-imperialist contradictions, but also play on the contradiction between socialism and capitalism, and on the balance between imperialist and socialist countries in order to get some material benefits. However, it is held that this cannot change the main tendency to strengthen the alliance between the national liberation movements and the socialist states, since without such an alliance the young states cannot cope with the machine of imperialism and neo-colonialism, or in other words with modern militarism.[34] To recapitulate, instead of speaking of bellicose militarism in the Third World, Soviet studies emphasise the contrary, *the anti-militaristic role played by the developing countries taken as a whole*, as one of the main forces of our world.

Both the direct exposition of the Soviet view of militarism and its indirect complement in its criticism of the opposite view allow us to make some concluding comments.

In the Soviet presentation the functions and role of militarism become hardly distinguishable from that of the 'normal' functions and role of the imperialistic state and its armed forces (military power).[35] In the military encyclopaedia militarism is defined as a system of political, economic and ideological means used by the exploiting classes for the purpose of accumulating military power; the latter is, in turn, necessary for attaining the basic reactionary aims of the internal and external policy. Militarism appeared together with the first class-antagonistic formation – the slave-owning society. It has taken its most extreme form in the imperialist system.[36]

Consequently, the criticism of the political nature of militarism and its aims is a repetition of the criticism of the whole of the so-called imperialistic policy; the assessment of the ideological apologia for militarism is similar to that of the so-called bourgeois theories of the genesis and nature of war, and of theories of violence as the determining force in history.

In some recent publications, militarism is simply equated with 'modern capitalism'. 'Relying solely on military power, the bourgeoisie can secure the maintenance of its rule, and this should be said not only about the imperialistic giants but also about the medium-sized and small countries, although to a different degree.'[37]

Thus the difference between militaristic theory and practice on the one hand, and the whole of what the Soviet term imperialistic ideology and policy on the other, seems if not obliterated, at any rate reduced in degree. And this is natural, if militarism is presented in Soviet teaching as only one of the natural stages in the development of militarism.

Notes

1. V.I. Skopin, *Militarizm*, 2nd edn. (Voenizdat, Moscow, 1957); Yu.M. Sheinin, *Nauka i militarizm v SShA* (Izd. Akademii Nauk, Moscow, 1963); *U poslednei cherty. Vliyane krizisa mirovogo kapitalizma na voenno-ekonomicheskie pozitsii imperialistischeskogo lagerya* (Moscow, 1964); S.A. Dalin, *Voennyi gosudarstvenno-monopolisticheskii kapitalizm v SShA* (Izd. Akademii Nauk, Moscow, 1961); A.A. Kornienko, *K kritike sovremennyth teorii militarizatsii Ekonomiki* (Voenizdat, Moscow, 1961); *Dvizhushchie sily vneshnei politiki SSha* (Akademiya Nauk SSSR, Institut Mirovoi Ekonomiki i Mezhdunarodnykh Otnoshenii, Izd. 'Nauka', Moscow, 1965), Chs. 1-4; P.A. Faramazyan, *SShA: Militarizm i ekonomika* (Izd. 'Mysl', Moscow, 1970); A.A. Mugolatyev, *Eskalatsiya militarizma* (Voenizdat, Moscow, 1970); V.M. Kolakov, *Ideologiya agressii* (Voenizdat, Moscow, 1970), Chs. I, V; *Problems of War and Peace* (Progress Publishers, Moscow, 1972), Ch. 5, 'Monopolies and Wars'; *Filosofskoe nasledie V.I. Lenina i problemy sovremennoi voiny* (Voenizdat, Moscow, 1972), Ch. IV, 'Leninskaya Kritika burzhuaznogo militarizma i sovremennost'; V. Dimitriev, 'Molokh militarizma', *Mezhdunarodnaya Zhizn*, no. 3 (1967); G. Korozkov, 'The Dangerous Grip of Militarism', *Soviet Military Review*, no. 12 (1972); P. Zhilin and Y. Rybkin, 'Militarism and Contemporary International Relations', *International Affairs* (Moscow), no. 10 (1973); Y. Rybkin and A. Migolatyev, 'The Ideology of the Present-Day Militarism', *International Affairs* (Moscow), no. 7 (1974); Y. Rybkin, 'Ideology of Militarism Serving the Opponents of Détente', *Soviet Military Review*, no. 9 (1977); D.A. Volkogonov, 'Militarizm i vneshnyaya politika imperializma', *Voprosy filosofii*, no. 10 (1974); Jerzy J. Waitr, 'Militaryzm: Pojecia i problematyka socjologiczna', *Studia socjologiczne-polityczne*, no. 6 (1960); his *Militaryzm a demokracja* (Izd. MON, Warsaw, 1966); D.A. Volkogonov, A.S. Milovidov and S.A. Tyushkevich (eds.), *Voina i Armiya* (Voenizdat, Moscow, 1977).

2. *Deutsches Militär Lexikon* (Deutscher Militärverlag, Berlin, 1961), pp. 272-3.

3. Migolatyev, *Eskalatsiya militarizma*, p. 43.

4. *Politicheskii slovar* (Gosudarstvennoe Izdatelstvo Politicheskoi Literatury, Moscow, 1958), p. 333. It is also asserted that militarist policy leads to the subordination of the whole policy, economy and culture of any given country to the imperialist miliary aims.

5. *U poslednei cherty*, p. 19; *Filosofskoe nasledie*, p. 78.

6. In some studies, the whole policy and economy of the imperialist powers are said to be subordinated to the system of measures aiming at preparing predatory wars (L.M. Gromov, V.I. Straigachev, *Problema razoruzheniya – glavnyi vopros sovremennosti* (Socekgiz, Moscow, 1963), p. 7).

7. In some definitions militarism is equated with military power; it is said to exist as 'war-power' ('Kriegsmacht') used by the capitalist states for external conflicts and as a weapons and a terror instrument for the suppression of each progressive movement within society (Sheinin, *Nauka i militarizm v SShA*, pp. 15-16).

8. Militarism is 'the main instrument of war, colonialist and internal policy, serving to ensure maximal profits' (S.M. Vishnew, *Sovremennyi militarizm i monopolii* (Izdatelstvo Nauk SSSR, Moscow, 1952), p. 17).

9. *Filosofskoe nasledie V.I. Lenina i problemy sovremennoi voiny*, p. 58.

10. Migolatyev, *Eskalatsiya militarizma*, pp. 55-60; *Filosofskoe nasledie*, pp. 65-70.

11. *Folosofskoe nasledie*, p. 67.

12. Kornienko, *K. kritike solvremennykh teorii*, writes that one should fight not only against the warmongers, but also against their scientific defenders, the apologists of militarism (p. 6). This sharp criticism, especially of the apologia for the militarisation of the economy, is the main theme in his book. Cf. Rybkin, Migolatyev, 'The Ideology of the Present-Day Militarism'.

13. This criticism is frequently presented as a set of objections against the so-called theory of violence, which is said to underlie the ideology of militarism:

(1) The theory of violence holds that the use of violence is a law of history. Violence is considered to be a primary force rooted in human nature, the main means by which men defend their rights and fight for their interests, and by which states try to impose their will upon other states.

From this premiss, the search for power becomes the first principle of the internal and international violence, since to possess power means to be able to use violence for the pursuit of one's interests. The criticism holds that violence cannot be regarded as the primary force in human and social life, nor as an inherent feature of humanity or the nature of the state, since it is the product of social forces. Its use cannot be considered a law, an inevitable necessity, since it is only an instrument which the reactionary or progressive forces may or may not use in the class struggle, depending on historical circumstances.

(2) Concomitantly, the theory of violence wrongly interprets the roots of violence: it is not human nature or the nature of the state, but the character of the class socio-economic and political system which is the basic root of all violence. All other 'explanations' divert the attention of peoples from this root.

(3) The theory of violence does not distinguish between revolutionary and counter-revolutionary violence, which is of extreme importance not only for the explanation of the origin of particular kinds of violence, but also for their consequences. The outcome of any violent action – victory or defeat with their social consequences – is highly dependent on the character of the social forces which apply it.

(4) The theory of violence in fact equates violence with armed violence; it does it by the way of its presentation in which the terms are used and conceived interchangeably, by quoting historical examples of using armed violence for confirming the theory, etc.

(5) A complex of ideas is interconnected with this theory and three of them are at fault for their unscientific character:

5.1 the idea that armed violence is the only means of resolving international conflicts, and armed forces the main factor of international relations;

5.2 the idea of the inevitability of war as a direct consequence of treating the use of violence as a law and universal phenomenon;

5.3 the belief that the socialist system of states can be destroyed by means of armed violence as well as the similar conviction that revolutionary and national liberation movements can be suppressed by such means.

Some items of the voluminous literature: A. Karenin, *Filosofiya politischeskogo nasiliya* (Izd. 'Mezhdunarodnye Ornosheniya', Moscow, 1976), Ch. I; *Marxism-Leninism on War and Army* (Progress Publishers, Moscow, 1972), pp. 47-50 ('The Theory of Violence'); *Voennaya Sila i Mezhdunarodyne Otmosheniya* (Izd. 'Mezhdunarodnye Otosheniya', Moscow, 1972); I.A. Grudinin, *Dialektika i voennaya nauka* (Voenizdat, Moscow, 1971); *Voina, Istoriya, Ideologiya* (Izd. Politischeskoi Literatury, Moscow, 1974); B. Shabad, *Imperializm i burzhuaznaya sotsialno-politischeskaya mysl* (Moscow, 1969); V.M. Kulakov, *Ideologiya agressii* (Voenizdat, Moscow, 1970); S.A. Tyushkevich, *Filosofiya i voennaya teoriya* (Voenizdat, Moscow, 1975); M. Yasyukov, 'Obshchestvennyi progress i voennoe nasilie', *Kommunist Vooruzhennykh Sil*, no. 12 (1973).

14. Rybkin, 'Ideology of Militarism'.

15. Keynes, R.W.B. Clark, K. Knorr and William F. Ogburn are among the most frequently criticised scholars. 'The whole bourgeois military-economic literature reflects and defends the political line of the governing imperialist groups directed towards a whole-encompassing preparation for a new world war' (Kornienko, *K. kritike sovremennykh teorii*, p. 28). Each war is claimed to be the last one (p. 29).

16. Keynes's ideas are criticised here (Kornienko, *K. kritike sovremennykh teorii*, pp. 49 ff.).

17. *Nauchno-tekhnischeskii progress i revolutsiya v voennom dele* (Voenizdat, Moscow, 1973), Ch. VIII; *Marxism-Leninism on War and Army* (Progress Publishers, Moscow, 1972), Ch. Six, section 3.

18. The definitions of militarism, presented in *Nouveau Larousse, Encylopedia Americana* and similar publications are frequently criticised.

19. According to the Soviet presentation, such theories state the following differences between the contemporary and previous states in the economic system: (1) the private ownership of means of production is being gradually transformed into state ownership; (2) the state controls the whole production, distribution of the national product and consumption; (3) the private profits are being transformed into social ones. Soviet scholars say that such a standpoint masks the fact that the state is class state, and that its control means the control by the governing class.

20. Rybkin and Migolatyev, 'The Ideology of the Present-Day Militarism', pp. 56-7.

21. 'No, militarism is not "new" to America. American militarism developed over a long time – in the course of predatory wars, punitive expeditions and interventions. During 100 years of its existence the USA triggered off more than 100 wars and interventions' (Korotkov, 1972, p. 47).

22. Kornienko, *K. kritike sovremennykh teorii*, p. 53.

23. In contradistinction, socialist states are forced to use science for military affairs in order to provide the necessary conditions for defending peace, democracy and carrying out the development of the socialist and Communist construction (*Naucho-tekhnicheskii progress*, pp. 267-8).

24. *Naucho-tekhnicheskii progress*, Ch. X; *Marxism-Leninism on War and Army*, Ch. 1, section 3, pp. 33-7.

25. A. Migolatyev, 'The Military-Industrial Complex and the Arms Race', *International Affairs* (Moscow), no. 11 (1975); Y. Rybkin, 'Pravda o voine –

oruzhie sil mira', *Kommunist Vooruzhennykh Sil*, no. 10 (1977), p. 13; O. Voine i Armii, pp. 977, 167 ff.

26. Ibid., p. 63.

27. For a comprehensive analysis of contemporary militarism, see Marek Thee, 'Militarism and Militarization in Contemporary International Relations', paper prepared for the Pugwash Symposium on Militarism and National Security, Oslo, 21-5 November 1977, and the 7th General Conference of the International Peace Research Association, Oaxtepec, Mexico, 11-16 December 1977.

While in Michael Howard's definition of militarism its aspect as a *system of values* has been emphasised, in other studies two aspects are stressed: militarism implies a *policy* orientation (focus on the application of violence) and a *power relationship* (the crucial role of military establishment). (Laurence I. Radway, 'Militarism' in David Sills (ed.), *International Encyclopaedia of Social Sciences* (Collier-Macmillan, London, 1968), Vol. IX, pp. 300-4.) And the third main variant seems to consider militarism at the same time as a specific feature of *policy*, as a *power structure*, and as an *ideology* (J. Erickson and H. Mommsen, 'Militarism', in C.D. Kernig (ed.), *Marxism, Communism and Western Society* (McGraw-Hill, New York, 1973), Vol. V, pp. 436-55).

28. 'Militarism is a doctrine or system that values war and accords primacy in state and society to the armed forces. It exalts a function – the application of violence – and as an institutional structure – the military establishment. It implies both a *policy* orientation and a *power* relationship' (Kurt Lang, 'Militarism', in David L. Sills (ed.), *International Encyclopaedia of Social Sciences*, Vol. IX, p. 300).

As we see, distinct from the Soviet concept of militarism, the above emphasises the extraordinary 'primacy' in the socio-political structure, an unusual policy and power relationship; the Soviets stress that militarism is a 'normal' institution with 'normal' functions, a 'normal' development of the capitalist system. Cf. John Erickson and Hans Mommsen, 'Militarism', pp. 436-55; here it is denied that militarism dominated the policy of any of the great Western states.

29. Cf. Egbert Jahn, 'The Role of Armament Complex in Soviet Society', *Journal of Peace Research*, no. 3 (1975).

30. Cf. Michael Howard, *War in European History* (1976), pp. 109-11. Even in studies which do not reduce militarism to an ideology, it is held that: '[the militarist] ideology rationalizes its use primarily in foreign affairs. War is held to be a divine commandment or an experience that ennobles by developing courage, patriotism, honour, unity and discipline. Militarists seek to universalize such values by precept, symbol, and ceremony' (Lang, 'Militarism', p. 300, comp. note 22a).

31. *Diplomatiya razvivayishchikhsya gosudarstv* (Izd. 'Mezhdunarodnye Otnosheniya', Moscow, 1976); G.I. Mirskii, *'Tretti Mir', Obschestvo, vlast', armiya* (Izd. 'Nauka', Moscow, 1976); G. Kim, 'Sotsjalizm i sovremennye natsionalno-osvoboditelnye revolutsii', *Mezhdunarodnaya Zhizn*, no. 7 (1977); A. Iskenderov, 'Revolutsiya, probudivshaya Aziyu i Afriku', *Mezhdunarodnaya Zhihn*, no. 10 (1977); SSSR i strany Afriki (Izd. 'Nauka', Moscow, 1977); B. Gafurov, 'Veliki katalizator natsionalno – osvoboditelnoi borby', *Mirovaya Ekonomika i Mezhdunarodyne Otnosheniya*, no. 9 (1977); E.I. Dolgopolov, *Natsionalno – osvoboditelnye veiny na sovremennom etape* (Voienizdat, Moscow, 1977).

32. *Diplomatiya razvivayushchikhsya gosudartsv*, pp. 21, 13.

33. The main conclusion in *Diplomatiya razvivayushchikhsya gosudartsv*. Cf. the review of this book by V. Sofinsky, 'An Important Factor of Democratization of International Relations', in *International Affairs* (Moscow), no. 9

(1977). Brezhnev is quoted: he stressed that the steadily growing influence of the developing countries on international affairs is 'a convincing manifestation of the current deep-going democratization of international relations', the transformation of peoples, 'which for centuries were objects of colonial policy into full-fledged participants and architects of international life'.

'In the contemporary period of development, the young national states of Asia and Africa increasingly actively appear as an influential force on the world arena, and – objectively – this is in principle a progressive, revolutionary and anti-imperialist force' (Kim, 'Sotsjalizm', p. 75).

And in a programmatic article devoted to the impact of the October Revolution on the national liberation movement, it is stated:

> The liberated countries play an increasingly active role in international life. They persistently fight for the restructure of international economic relations on the basis of equality and democracy, for the liquidation of all forms of imperialistic aggression, dictate and pressure, for the peace and security of nations (Yu. Sumbatyan, 'Sotsializm i natsionalnoosvoboditelnoe dvizhenie', *Krasnaya Zvezda*, 25 August 1977).

34. *Diplomatiya razvivayushchikhsya gosudarstv*, one of the main themes. *SSSR i strany Afriki*, one of the main themes. Cf. L. Zevin, G. Prokhorov, '*Ekonomicheskoe sotrudnichestvo sotsialistischeskikh i razvivayushchickhsya stran: novye tendentsii*', MEMO, no. 3 (1977).

35. Another symptom of the obliteration of differences between variations of what is by Soviet scholars called militarism is the inclusion in this concept of all political and social forces which they regard as anti-Soviet ones. For instance, in Rybkin and Migolatyev, 'The Ideology of Present-Day Militarism', the term 'militarists, reactionaries' include capitalist monopolies, political circles of NATO and other alliances, ideological centres in the West, Maoists and Israeli extremists; their political programme is presented as encompassing arms race, policy from the position of strength, liquidation of *détente*, socio-economic demagogic propaganda, 'exploiting' Keynes's theories, which are said to state that militarism and the arms race are necessary for economic welfare, the imposition on the socialist countries of cultural exchange based on the bourgeois principles and norms, which aims at counter-revolution, etc.

Numerous studies and articles contain sharp criticism of Chinese 'militarism'. Militarism in contemporary China represents a reactionary military system, assigned the task of securing by means of violence the political power in the country and of creating favourable internal conditions for the attainment of hegemonial external political aims.

'The Chinese armed forces which constitute the basic element of militarism are the mainstay of the Maoist regime in its pursuing these aims' (B. Gorbachev, 'Pekin: stavka na militarizm', *Krasnaya Zvezda*, 21 November 1978). Cf. *Opasnyi kurs. Kitai posle Mao Tze-duna* (Politizdat, Moscow, 1978).

36. 'Militarizm' in *Sovetskaya Voennaya Entsiklopediya* (Moscow, 1977), Vol. 5, pp. 281-5.

37. The main theme of Volkogonov, 'Militarizm'.

> A profound tendency toward armed violence is *characteristic of the present era of imperialism*: militarization of the economy and a military mode of action in policy, the establishment of international aggressive military alliances and a headlong arms race in the principal capitalist nations, the ignition of local and small-scale aggressive wars with vigorous preparations for unleashing a world nuclear-missile war at the appropriate moment (*Filosofskoe nasledie*, p. 13).

Militarism, armed forces constitute the most important instrument of the class domination of the monopolistic bourgeoisie, the instrument of political oppression of the proletariat, peasants, urban petty bourgeoisie, and intermediate strata. The role of monopolies is *unthinkable* without militarism, violence, predatory wars and attempts to expand the sphere of the gigantic capitalistic syndicates, financial and industrial magnates (*Problemy voiny i mira* (Izd. 'Mysl', Moscow, 1967), pp. 104-5).

PART IV

THE MILITARY IN THE THIRD WORLD

10 MILITARISM DYNAMICS IN THE CONTEMPORARY CONTEXT OF PERIPHERY CAPITALISM

Dieter Senghaas

In recent years, an increasing body of theoretical and empirical knowledge has been accumulated on processes of development and underdevelopment. Of particular importance are

theories related to accumulation processes on a world scale;
theories of metropolitan capitalism as the dominant factor of world accumulation processes;
theories of periphery capitalism related to processes of dependent reproduction

Within this debate – which has undermined the legitimacy of modernisation theories – the analysis of militarism has not been prominent, although the role of force within metropolitan and peripheral accumulation processes has generally been well perceived.[1] Historically oriented analyses have documented the role of force and violence in the development process of metropolitan capitalism, and they have naturally emphasised the role of violence in the subjection of distant societies and cultures, and in their restructuring into peripheries.

This chapter is not related to these macro-theoretical topics: its focus is more specific. We are concerned about the increasing *militarisation* of Third World countries. On the basis of proceding analysis we assume that this process of militarisation is to be understood within an *analysis of militarism*. Whereas an analysis of the process of militarisation is related to the phenomenology of the military (its obvious role and function within society), an analysis of militarism is more deeply rooted. This is because it is intrinsically related to the analysis of the reproduction dynamics of total social formations. Conceptually, the analysis of militarisation and the analysis of militarism could be located as the extremes of a broad spectrum, ranging from descriptive studies to theoretically well founded explicative assessments. This would mean that at some point a good study on militarisation process gradually merges towards a theoretically better-founded study of militarism. Whereas the first might be useful and descriptive, but still relatively 'superficial', the latter would be far better founded within a more comprehensive theory of the reproduction dynamics of total social formations.[2]

To what does the notion of *reproduction dynamics of total social formations* refer? Basically, it refers to the prevailing pattern of capital accumulation within a given society, its institutional framework and its characteristic conflict potentials. No modern society characterised by a relatively high degree of complexity and differentiation has been able to sustain itself *consensually* as a self-steering community. Should such an entity ever exist, there would be no basis for militarism. In reality, modern societies are antagonistically structured, held together by varying mixtures of force and more or less voluntary compliance. Within such a framework, the legitimised use of force by central institutions like the state is of key salience in upholding law and order.

The role of the use of force within the reproduction dynamics of societies is the true subject of any analysis of militarism.[3] Therefore, such an analysis has to be linked to the political economy of such societies.

In the following pages we, however, shall presuppose the analysis of periphery social formations as this has been developed over the past ten years. We do not wish to elaborate once more its key findings here. In summary, then, the analysis of periphery social formations has clearly worked out the notion of *dependent reproduction* as a fundamental structural characteristic of the societies and economies of Third World countries. It has demonstrated the structural defects of periphery economies: their lack of coherence and homogeneity – their increasing structural heterogeneity. And it has been shown that out of such heterogeneous socio-economic structures the instability of political regimes and political systems emerges. Their fragility is not due to political inexperience: rather, it is a reflection of a relatively frail underlying socio-economic fabric.

Within such a context, processes of militarisation and militarism are intrinsically built into the reproduction dynamics of the prevailing social order.[4] However, the function of the military, and of militarism, within dependent reproduction processes cannot be reduced to one general denominator, since the reproduction dynamics of peripheral capitalist social formations is different, due to differing profiles of the various peripheries. This is why a well founded politico-economic typology of periphery social formations would be useful in analysing militarisation process and militarism as related to periphery capitalism.

The military as an institution usually operates in periphery social formations within a political constellation defined by the existence of a landed obligarchy; a commercial or comprador bourgeoisie; a petty bourgeoisie (consisting of intellectuals, small traders, state bureaucrats, etc., who very much fought for political decolonisation); and furthermore the mass of the peasants, who are usually deliberately subject to political apathy; and finally the urban proletariat, who has hardly ever become a strong class of its own. Within that political constellation, the state apparatus and the state bureaucracy have become increasingly important, especially since political independence within the past twenty to thirty years. The occupation of the state not only leads to control over the means of force (the military and the police), it also means the most direct access to the national economy and its pay-offs.

Within such a constellation of political power and social forces, we may observe specific types of intervention and specific functions of the military – and thereby *specific articulations of militarism within the prevailing development process*. In the following, we delineate some of the most important of these types. We would like to emphasise, once again, that no analysis of militarism can be conceptually defended without being interlinked with the analysis of the different concrete profiles of dependent reproduction.[5]

Whenever the *traditional landed oligarchy* and the *traditional comprador bourgeoisie* have been *opposing impending changes of the prevailing* status quo, the military has functioned as an unambiguous instrument of law and order, discipline and repression. The history of nineteenth- and twentieth-century Latin American politics is full of such interventions. Sociologically, these interventions have been based on the high social and political synchronisation of the dominant economic classes and the representatives of the military appartuses.[6]

The *intervention of the military in factional disputes* within the oligarcy represents only a variety of the type of intervention just mentioned. This holds true both for such disputes among the representatives of the landed oligarchy, as well as for those between the landed oligarchy and the comprador bourgeoisie. In times of such political and socio-economic crises, the military has been used as an *instrument of social upward mobility* for members of social classes discriminated against within the prevailing oligarchial order; this has been the time for adventurers-caudillos to come forth as dominant political figures within an oligarchial social order in crisis.[7]

The fragility of the local political order, for example the lack of consolidated local dominant classes, has often allowed *foreign powers* to use the military together with some faction of the dominant classes as a means to promote their own interests. In Latin America, for example, this constellation was prominent in the late nineteenth century when an emerging industrial bourgeoisie vigorously tried to develop their productive forces and thus challenged the predominant oligarchial order. The military was then, together with parts of the comprador bourgeoisie and the landed oligarchy, a major *bridgehead* without which foreign interests could not have made themselves as much felt as they actually did.

Another constellation for the intervention of the military in the development process is the following: in most developing countries, the first phase of a vigorous industrialisation (import-substitution industrialisation) led to tremendous social and economic mobilisation of the urban growth poles out of which many political conflict potentials emerged. Under such conditions, neither the oligarchy nor the emerging new forces of state and private administrators of a not-too-well-organised urban proletariat and of an embryonic industrial bourgeoisie were strong enough to stay in power unchallenged, or to attain new political hegemony over the old dominant forces. In such political bottleneck conditions, the prevailing political regimes have been regularly subject to *political crises*. The military often had an open *reactionary* function by repressing the newly emerging social forces and their political aspirations; but it also happened that the military intervened *to the advantage of those new social forces* (small industry capital, small-scale agro-business enterprises, urban proletariat, public officials). In this way, those forces gained more political power than they would have without such a politically congenial military intervention.[8] Such intervention usually required the partial political mobilisation of newly emerging social strata as the prerequisite for the political destabilisation of the traditional oligarchy. The limits to such a political mobilisation have been evident very early in most cases; *demobilisation* or *pseudo-mobilisation* has been deliberately used to check the increasing political and social aspirations of newly emerging strata.

The seizure of political power leading to the total mobilisation of a society and the *total restructuring of periphery social formations* was not to be observed often in past decades.[9] When such a breakthrough did happen, it usually resulted from a long and enduring conflict between revolutionary nationalist forces on one side and intervening imperialist powers on the other (as in the case of Vietnam).

On average, the direction of military intervention has been quite different. The result of such intervention has been a *mixture of dynamic and reactionary policies*. In the 1950s and 1960s, the military was labelled as the only social force able to modernise periphery societies.[10] In countries with sufficient foreign exchange earnings the military often implemented public programmes, after their *coup d'état*, to improve existing transport, communication and administrative systems. Such measures have often been considered as prerequisites for increasing private capitalist activities. With respect to private foreign interests (investments by foreign multinational corporations, etc), military regimes differ slightly from one another, particularly with respect to the scope and the seriousness of the 'rules of the game' to be imposed on foreign capital. Whether such differences within the context of periphery capitalism really matter, is quite doubtful, as it is doubtful whether the differentiation between authoritarian civil regimes and openly military regimes is of any use in this repect. Both authoritarian regimes and military dictatorships have created dependable conditions for private investments, which are considered a major prerequisite for an attractive investment climate.[11] Economics under such political and military conditions frequently show quite high growth rates, the reverse of which can be observed in the political *demobilisation* and the *depolitisation* of the poor peasants, the proletariat and the critical intelligentsia. In such a political context, investment projects may become politically possible, although outside such an authoritarian political pattern they would be highly contested. The disciplining of the urban and agrarian proletariat (e.g. by the systematic repression of their trade unions and collective interest organisations) and a deliberate policy of decreasing real wages are considered, within such authoritarian and military regimes, as prerequisites for the *implementation of new phases of accumulation and industralisation.*[12] This is evident in the case of the build-up of export-oriented free production zones (South Korea, Singapore, etc.) as well as in cases where raw material extraction activities have been much increased on the basis of further metropolitan investments (Indonesia, the Philippines, Bolivia, etc.).[13]

The intervention of the military in the development process of a periphery-capitalist society is of key importance whenever a specific development phase becomes exhausted, and whenever *a political fight over the further direction of the development process* emerges. The options are usually of fundamental dimensions. On the one hand, there is the prospect of a development which would be very much nationally oriented and where the mass of the local population would be integrated in a coherently structured reproduction process; important social needs could thus be satisfied. On the other hand, there is the prospect of a development leading to further privileges for already privileged social strata, particularly as a result of the build-up of an industry for production of durable luxury consumer goods. The Brazilian model clearly shows how the build-up of such a production structure accentuates an unequal distribution of income, and how such inequality induces a demand structure for luxury consumer goods on the part of an old and new middle class.[14] *The military dictatorship and the authoritarian character of the political regime, under such circumstances, serve as the political midwife of a structurally expanded capitalist accumulation.* Thus, the accumulation structure of the contemporary Brazilian economy cannot be compared with that of twenty or thirty years ago, which at that time was still very much identical with that emerging out of the first phase of an import-substitution industrialisation. The present accumulation structure could, however, have been achieved only on the basis of tremdendous political and social costs. In Brazil, military intervention has undermined the objective possibility of an alternative development path at the cost of a further loss of national identity. It might be that the authoritarian and repressive character of such regimes will become less rigid once such a new and expanded capitalist accumulation consolidates itself. The Brazilian case, however, shows that, under present Third World conditions, such a limited 'liberalisation' – or what is within Brazil called '*decompression*' – is by no means certain. On the contrary, it seems clear that even a touch of an internal *détente* policy may easily threaten the prevailing *status quo* in general.

In summary, the *dynamic* function of the military intervention in such a case consists in the *vigorous promotion of a further capitalistically defined accumulation process*, in a tremendous, though distorted, development of the productive forces, and the further differentiation of the industrial and agrarian profile of the economy – with an increasing heterogeneity as a result. The *reactionary* function of such a vigorous accumulation process consists in the fact that its pay-offs are largely consumed by the dominant internal and external classes, and that the price of such a growth model necessarily has to be paid by the general mass of the population, a large part of which (according to the empirical assessments of the World Bank) continues to live at or below the subsistence level.

From such a situation we should differentiate the *reactionary intervention* of the military under conditions where, within a relatively mobilised society, the needs of the middle class and the proletariat used to be recognised at least partly; and where, as a result of the military *coup d'état*, the traditional dominant classes vigorously try to regain their old privileges. This is the *coup à la Pinochet*. This type of military intervention is reactionary in a twofold sense;[15] first, already-achieved standards of needs satisfaction and civil liberties for the masses are drastically suppressed; and second, not even those minimal state controls against national and international capital remain implemented which, under many military dictatorships of the last twenty years, have been implemented to increase the regime's internal legitimacy.

There is yet another type of military *coup d'état*: it occurs where the political strength and vigour of the military is the obverse side of the deficiencies and the weakness of the civilian society. Frequently, military internvention in such a context has been interpreted as a reaction to the 'decay of the political regime'. Such an interpretation necessarily remains superficial, since the crisis prone-ness of such political regimes is highly correlated with *the weaknesses and the structural fragility of the underlying social and economic orders*. This structural fragility and its concomitant high propensity for political crises are based on the sociological fact that no single class can become predominant within such a society and economy.[16] Post-colonial societies of Black Africa are examples: neither those social strata which have promoted the process of political decolonisation nor the representatives of private enterprises are powerful enough to pursue political and economic aims as a predominant class. The same holds true for the landed oligarchy and the urban petty bougeoisie. The mass of the peasants and urban proletariat are, in most cases, prevented from fully participating in politics, so that the state apparatus has become the only efficient political and social organisation, more important than non-governmental organisations and institutions. Control of the government and the state bureaucracy serves at the same time as direct access to the economy in general; this control is thus also a vital source of capital accumulation. Under such conditions, the military frequently have the undisputed ability to cope effectively, in the short run, with a political crisis which threatens to become chronic; they are often also able to eliminate some traditional antagonisms within the social and economic structure by eliminating the predominance of particular old-fashioned interests. After the military *coup d'état* the petty bougeoisie frequently becomes privileged, and often the state bureaucracy itself aspires to become the dominant class. For a while, local private enterprise, able to accumulate, is protected against the usually easily implemented economic and financial machinations of foreign capital.

Thereby, part of the locally produced surplus becomes available for the state economy and for local private capital. But experience shows (and one might today look particularly at the Peruvian model, of which so much was expected with respect to enduring structural reforms) that without a clear-cut policy of dissociation from the prevailing capitalist world market, such attempts are doomed to failure. Also here, the military usually shows a clear contempt for the broad mass of the population which (as Black Africa clearly shows) represents no serious threat to the predominance of the military nor to the state bureaucracy and their highly sophisticated instruments of violence. Having control over a large part of the local resources makes possible the build-up of a publicly administered industrial sector which, even in cases of military dictatorships, paves the way for the propagandistic rhetoric of local versions of socialism.[17]

In all the cases mentioned so far, we may observe that after the military *coup d'état* the interests of the military are very much promoted, generally receiving more resources than under civilian regimes. Inescapably, the pursued development policy becomes subject to the primacy of military aims. A high share of the state economy is militarily administered, and investment policy is pursued under militarily perceived imperatives.[18]

Given a sociological understanding of the cases debated so far, it is obvious why such regimes are so politically fragile, and why one military *coup d'état* follows another. In the same light we should view the tremendous and endemic role of *corruption* which is a side-effect of the inflated size of the state apparatuses and the state economy. Military *coups d'état* frequently function to reduce the burden on public finance and the total economy which results from corruption and which becomes dysfunctional by its sheer size. The military *coup d'état* as a *corruption regulator* ought to attract more attention. The same is true for the military coup as a means of *social upward mobility*, promoting members of these social strata which neither had a particular role in the decolonisation process, nor were beneficiaries and profiteers of the first phase of national independence. In this context one author rightly speaks of the observable re-traditionalisation of the military and of politics within the African context.[19]

The militarisation of periphery capitalist social formations can further be documented in the massive build-up of the military's ability for *counter-insurgency* warfare. Military containment of social conflicts is on the political agenda in all varieties of periphery-capitalist social formations. The predecessors of these local programmes can be found in the various projects of military aid and military training programmes as they have been pursued by the USA, England and France within their own armies for the fight against national liberation movements, but also within the armed forces and the police of the peripheries.[20] Preparation for the *social war* and its practice is no less an expression of militarisation than the *increased import of armaments* and the *build-up of a local armament industry*. Militarisation in the macro-area is very much in correspondence with the militarisation of those social forces against which authoritarian civil or authoritarian military regimes wage internal war. This *militarisation of social conflicts* can even be observed where the military has not yet formally seized power. This was the case for many years in Lebanon, which in recent years has been an incomparable theatre of internal disputes with military means, without the open intervention of the official military forces for a long time (*micro-militarism*).[21]

In summary, then, the military are likely to intervene in politics when social orders become unmanageable. If the prevailing *status quo* is threatened by new social forces, there is the possibility of a *static-reactionary intervention*: the *status quo* is to be simply preserved. In social formations with a higher degree of differentiation and social mobilisation, a *dynamic-reactionary intervention* is more likely; its aim is the further dynamisation of existing economies to the advantage of already privileged classes, including those which become co-opted during such a process (*new* middle class). Since most Third World economies are, on their own terms, quite dynamic with respect to the development of their productive forces (though these may remain highly incoherently structured), such dynamic-reactionary intervention has been far more prominent in the ten to twenty years than has the static-reactionary type which, for example in the nineteenth century Latin America, often merely reflected the circulation of elites within a *given* political *status quo*.

Under prevailing conditions, militarism within the Third World is more and more an inherent and constitutive dimension of growth-oriented accumulation processes. The more Third World economies are mobilised, the more social conflict potential will there be, and the more social warfare will there be waged to preserve the general political pattern. Prospects for more militarism are bright, indeed. In addition, any political forces and movements able to break with the existing *status quo* and wishing to pursue a need- and man-oriented development process have usually to take refuge in the military for protection. Without such military back-up they would probably be lost very early, being under attack both by external and by hostile internal forces. Unless an alternative development strategy, at a *very early* stage, attains self-sustained, coherently structured and internally balanced growth, it is highly probable that the potential progressive function of the military apparatus will easily recede, and that the military will become mainly their own protectors and that of the new dominant class. Under such conditions of an abortive progressive movement there might be still more social pay-offs for the mass of the people, compared to the social costs to be paid by the masses under dynamic-reactionary conditions. Obviously, however, these would certainly not be the ideal living conditions peace researchers have in mind when thinking about alternative development strategies.

Notes

1. This paper is related to the analysis of *militarism dynamics*. Peace research has so far very much dealt with *armament dynamics*, e.g. the analysis of the determinants of armament policies and arms races, predominantly confined to current armament processes. Such analyses have less deliberately reflected upon the *conflict formations* within which armament processes take place. There is an analytical need to enlarge the analysis of armament dynamics, and to relate it systematically to the analysis of conflict formations. See my paper 'Peace Research and the Analysis of the Causes of Social Violence', *BPP*, vol. 7 (1976), pp. 64-8. More specifically, Dieter Senghaas, *Gewalt - Konflikt - Frieden* (Hamburg, 1974), pp. 55 ff.; Johan Galtung, 'Das Kriegssystem' in Klaus Jurgen Gantzel (ed.), *Herrschaft und Befreiung in der Weltgesellschaft* (Frankfurt, 1975), pp. 68-114.

2. Cf. Dieter Senghaas, *Rüstung und Militarismus* (Frankfurt, 1972).

3. Interesting new conceptualisations have been suggested by Mary Kaldor in two recent publications: 'The Military in Development', *World Development*, vol. 4, no. 6 (1976), pp. 459-82, and 'The Arms Trade and Society', *Economic and Political Weekly*, vol. 11, nos. 5-7 (February 1976), pp. 293-301. Important in this respect is Ulrich Albrecht, Dieter Ernst, Peter Lock and Herbert Wulf, *Rüstung und Unterentwicklung* (Reinbeck, Hamburg, 1976).

4. Cf. Alain Joxe, 'Evolution des états et des coups d'état', *Le monde diplomatique* (July 1975), pp. 9-11.

5. For a general assessment see Bassam Tibi, *Militär und Sozialismus in der Dritten Welt* (Frankfurt, 1973), ch. 1; see also the excellent reports in the monthly *Le monde diplomatique*, on the military in Asia (February 1975), on the military in Latin America (July 1975), and on the military in Africa (December 1975 and January 1976). For a general treatise see also Katherine Chorley, *Armies and the Art of Revolution* (Boston, 1973).

6. Elena de la Souchere, 'Les trois ages du militarisme', *Le monde diplomatique* (July 1975), pp. 7 ff.; also I. Sotelo, K. Esser and B. Moltmann, *Die bewaffneten Technokraten. Militär und Politik in Lateinamerika* (Hanover, 1975).

7. Ibid.

8. Peru, for instance, would probably fall into this category.

9. Somalia may be seen as a case in point. Cf. Basil Davidson in *Le monde*

diplomatique (August 1975), pp. 18-20.

10. For a critical discussion of the approaches based on modernisation theories see Tibi, *Militär und Sozialsmus*, footnote 5; Volker Matthies, 'Militärische Staatsstreiche und Militärregimen südlich der Sahara', *Afrika Spectrum*, no. 1, (1971), pp. 5-33; Albrecht, Ernst, Lock and Wulf, *Rüstung und Unterentwicklung* (in English: 'Armaments and Underdevelopment', *BPP*, vol. 5 (1974), pp. 173-185); Eric Nordlinger, 'Soldiers in Mufti: The Impact of Military Rule upon Economic and Social Change in the Non-Western States', *The American Political Science Review* (December 1970), pp. 1131-1148; Uma Eleazu, 'The Role of the Army in African Politics. A Reconsideration of Existing Theories and Practices', *The Journal of Developing Areas*, vol. 7 (January 1973), pp. 265-86; Richard Rankin, 'The Expanding Institutional Concerns of the Latin American Military Establishments. A Review Article', *Latin American Research Review*, vol. 9, no. 1 (Spring 1974), pp. 81-108; Reinhard Korner, 'Unterentwicklung, Abhängigkeit und Militärherrschaft', *Neue Politische Literatur*, vol. 21 (1976), pp. 217-25.

11. See, as a case study, Robert Stauffer, 'The Political Economy of a Coup. Transnational Linkages and Philippine Political Response', *Journal of Peace Research*, vol. 11, no. 3 (1974), pp. 161-78. Von Weizsäcker wrote in this context: 'Military dictatorships correspond to the objective economic interests of international capitalism, and this is why the symbiotic interrelationship with capitalism corresponds to the objective political interest of military dictatorships' (Carl Friedrich von Weizsäcker, *Wege in der Gefahr* (Munich, 1976), p. 76).

12. Cf. the special issue 'Accumulation et surexploitation', *Critiques de l'économie politique*, nos. 16/17 (Paris, 1974).

13. See especially *Le monde diplomatique* on various cases in Asia (February 1975, pp. 9-16).

14. Cf. Dieter Senghaas, 'Brasilien assoziative-kapitalistiche Entwicklung', *Weltwirtschaftsordnung und Entwicklungspolitik. Plädoyer für Dissoziation* (Frankfurt, 1977), pp. 129 ff.

15. For the case of Chile see James Petras, 'Economie et repression au Chili', *Le monde diplomatique* (January 1976), p. 13; also Andre Gunder Frank, 'Economic Theory and Political Reality' (Frankfurt, 1976) (mimeo.).

16. Cf., especially Ruth First, 'Les nouveaux masques', *Le monde diplomatique* (December 1975), pp. 7 ff.; Cathérine Coquery-Vidrovitch, 'Les limites de l'indepéndence économique', *Le monde diplomatique*, (January 1976), pp. 19-20. For a class analysis of the state apparatus, especially in Black Africa, see Jean-Pierre Olivier, 'Afrique. Qui exploite qui?, *Les temps modernes*, no. 347 (1975), pp. 1744-1755, particularly pp. 1753 ff.

17. Cf. the report on the Congo, *Le monde diplomatique* (December 1975), p. 12.

18. See Nordlinger, 'Soldiers in Mufti', as well as Esko Antola, 'The Roots of Domestic Military Interventions in Black Africa', *Instant Research on Peace and Violence*, no. 4 (1975), pp. 207-21.

19. Cf. Ali Mazrui, 'The Resurrection of the Warrior Tradition in African Political Culture', *Journal of Modern African Studies*, vol. 13, no. 1 (1975), pp. 67-84; and Ali Mazrui, 'Soldiers as Traditionalizers', *World Politics*, vol. 28 (January 1976), pp. 247-72.

20. Cf. Miles Wolpin, *Military Aid and Counter-Revolution in the Third World* (Lexington, 1972), and by the same author: *Social Revolution and Military Subordination in the Third World* (forthcoming).

21. The same is true for the Argentine before the *coup* (1976), which – according to an analysis by Horacio Godoy – reflected a 'structured chaos'. On

the role of the 'industrial guerilla movement' and the respective new role of the Argentine Military for the social war, see Alain Labrousse, 'Les militaires devant les desordres et la crise économique., *Le monde diplomatique* (January 1976), p. 12.

11 MILITARISATION AND HUMAN RIGHTS IN THE THIRD WORLD

Richard Falk

1 Introduction: the Socio-Economic Setting

The current global focus on human rights prompts a search for an explanation for the spread of repression in our world. This article considers a part of this overall picture, by focusing on escalating repression in the capitalist portion of the Third World. It examines, in particular the socio-economic setting of capitalist Third World countries in which repressive regimes emerge and stabilise themselves. The perspective taken here is that this setting is being fundamentally shaped by a crisis in capital formation that exists in a variety of forms for all but a few of the resource-rich Third World countries. The crisis is generated by a series of factors. Perhaps the most significant of these is the inability of moderate political elites to maintain stability without redistributive and welfare programmes to pacify the poor, and their consequent inability to sustain growth via re-investment if adequate programmes of this sort are established. There is not enough capital to go around. In these circumstances, attempts at compromise tend to satisfy neither end of the political spectrum. As a result, discontent, instability and economic chaos emerge, creating a context that invites a take-over by those social forces (the military and its allies) willing and able to impose 'discipline' upon the polity. This dynamic is generally played out against an ideological backdrop in which Cold War themes, images and interventionary pressures are manipulated by the participants, as well as by the leadership of multinational corporations.

To provide the grounds for this analysis we first sketch the main dimensions of the setting from which militarised governance arises and the repressive patterns that result; second, we show the extent of the geographical diffusion of repression throughout the Third World during the period 1960-76; and third, we offer some tentative conclusions about the wider impact of this trend for world order values, especially peace and human rights.

2 Forms of Repressive Governance: Militarisation

The pattern of repressive governance is exhibited in forms corresponding to the exceedingly diverse situations of Third World countries. These variations reflect differences in size, level of economic development, resource endowment, political culture, geopolitical salience and foreign penetration. Nevertheless, despite these diversities – in fact, all the more remarkable because of them – there is an emergent form of militarised repression that shares sufficient features to justify being clustered into a pattern.

2.1 Militarised Governance

The state apparatus is controlled directly or indirectly by the military establishment; military officers are the key leaders and civilian institutions are subordinated, if not altogether eliminated. Typically, control of the state by the military is initially attained by extra-constitutional means, normally by a *coup d'état*. The *coup* is not, however, merely a means of achieving political leadership for military factions of the elite; it represents a long-term commitment, more or less permanent, to restructure state power, even though such restructuring may pass through a number of phases.

2.2 Rightist Ideology

Although some militarised governing systems are leftist in outlook (e.g. Iraq, Libya, Ethiopia) most are anti-leftist which, in contemporary terms, means anti-Marxist in orientation. Therefore, these rightist military regimes identify their countries' social-political futures with the security and prosperity of the urban upper classes working in collaboration with the state bureaucracy. Rightist leaders view the popular sector, or the masses, and sometimes the traditional rural elites, as potential or actual hostile social forces to be demobilised and controlled. Internationally, such regimes are anti-Soviet, anti-Communist in world view, and look to the United States for diplomatic and economic support, as well as for arms.

2.3 Capitalist Development Strategy

The main explanation of rightist militarisation is to overcome obstacles to national economic development through capitalist means. The pretext for military take-over is normally justified by the inability of civilian leadership to maintain order sufficient to check inflation, labour unrest and political turmoil. These social conditions destroy investor confidence and make it difficult to attract capital from abroad in the form of private investment, bank loans or international economic assistance. The military leadership declares its mission as saving the country from radical and destabilising demands for greater 'equity'. Such a role for the new military leadership presupposes the capacity and willingness of government to discipline the poor to accept low wages or acquiesce in unemployment without disrupting productive processes. The economic goal of militarisation in a capitalist context is a high rate of growth in gross national product, regardless of distributive consequences at least for the near term.[1] The poor are 'squeezed', or their expectations 'contained', to assure revenues and stability that benefit the state bureaucracy and most of the privileged classes. Rightist militarisation may produce dramatic results, at least for a time, with respect to economic growth: Brazil, South Korea and Taiwan have all had periods of high annual growth rates. Militarisation along these lines typically occurs because of a crisis in capital formulation.[2] Civilian leaders generally seek to steer a middle course between appeasing the poor and satisfying the rich, generating frustrations on both sides that may erupt into political violence. Civilian governments lack the capabilty to re-orient the economy to favour the popular sector, as the bourgeois elements in the state will resist such a mandate and are likely to be reinforced in their resistance by outside forces, especially the United States (e.g. Chile under Allende, 1970-3). As a result, constitutionally based civilian leadership lacks the capacity to achieve either *the efficiency* and *external support* of military governance or *the equity* and *participation* of left authoritarian regimes.

In this context, deepening polarisation of the left and right occurs, with important factions of the military being normally and coherently aligned with the right (although not invariably) and capable of tipping the domestic balance by seizing control of the state.

2.4 Militarist 'New Policies'

The leadership of military institutions in Third World countries has also been trained over a long period to regard the principal role of the military as 'internal security', guarding the polity against leftist radical forces eager to subvert the state. Such a role contrasts with the traditional domestic function of the military to act as arbiter among contending civilian forces or as temporary custodian of state power while the civilian sector sorts itself out; this new role involves accepting a more permanent mandate to safeguard the polity and manage the modernisation process. The United States, as part of its response in the early 1960s to the Communist endorsement of 'wars of national liberation', was instrumental, through its aid and training programmes, in orienting key sectors of many Third World military establishments to assume a counter-insurgency outlook towards their own populations. This 'new professionalism' of Third World military elites helps 'legitimise' seizures of power at least within the military establishment itself.[3]

2.5 Coalition with Technocrats

The main pretext of a military take-over is often to 'save' the country from political incompetence and radicalism, as well as to provide the discipline needed to increase economic and political power of the state by means of steady GNP growth, especially in the urban industrial sector. In order to assure realisation of these goals, the state must play a significant role. The military will not simply protect the traditional sectors of economic privilege from interference by the aggrieved sectors of the population; generally, its main objective is to stimulate and sustain economic growth by a sophisticated mixture of fiscal and regulatory policies that make the state an increasingly important participant in the economy. Administered capitalism is the result. Technocrats as expert administrators likewise play key roles. These civil servants share with their military colleagues impatience over the 'inefficiencies' of the conventional politicians who are distracted from true priorities by their search for popularity, their deference to tradition, and their tendency to support sentimental economic goals associated with equity. In the push towards modernity, the military provides a framework, while the technocrats supply planning and overview. Without the technocrats, the generals would be unable to rule for long; at the least, they would be unable to provide society with the kind of disciplined leadership that offers some prospect of restoring confidence in the functioning of a market-oriented economy linked through capital flows and exports to the world economic order.

2.6 Public Enterprise and Investments

As implied, the state enters the economy as principal investor in key industries. The growth-oriented ideology leads in a corporatist direction with the state constantly expanding its economic role.[4] Many basic industries like energy production and distribution, communications and transportation are state-owned in this recent form of militarisation in a Third World capitalist context. The move to the right does not attempt to establish a liberal economic order based on *laissez-faire* market conceptions, nor to supplement market dynamics merely by Keynesian 'fixes' intended to maintain 'full employment' at times when investment levels fall. The new focus is upon efficiency and growth of the economic aggregate, and the leaders accept high levels of unemployment and large-scale poverty for the indefinite future as an unavoidable side-effect of this search for economic viability based on keeping the engine of growth moving regardless of social and political adverse side-effects.

2.7 Ascendant Military Establishment

As might be expected, militarisation along these lines tends to increase defence spending and to diminish budgets for social welfare purposes.[5] By giving the military what it wants for defence expenditure, the governing elite mutes factional disputes within the military and helps to hold succession politics within reasonable bounds.[6] Perhaps most fundamentally, this model of militarised control produces strong states domestically and strengthens their participation in the world system. Statist aspirations for an enhanced status are usually associated with a dynamic military establishment. Hence, the military sector in this kind of polity is often the most dynamic, the most technology-modern, the most rapidly growing, as well as the inspirational source of continuing ideological leadership for the polity.[7]

The priority attached to a military build-up is related to the regional arms races that are aided and abetted by the sales policies of the developed world, especially the United States. These arms sales have been increasing at a dramatic rate during the course of Third World militarisation. Tables 11.1 and 11.2 show US military assistance and arms sales to the world and clearly reflect the strategic interests of the US during the relevant period of time. The figures for 1970 and 1975 and the percentage change between those two dates show that Latin America, the Middle East and Africa – all areas in which militarisation and repression are on the rise – have received substantially increased amounts of US military aid while the developed world, excepting Israel, has received no military assistance. A similar pattern is discernible for arms sales. Arms sales from the US to all parts of the world have increased between 1970 and 1975. But the most significant increase occurred in sales to Africa, with sales to South Asia and the Middle East following closely behind.

2.8 Repressive Policies and Apparatus

To assure the success of militarised governance under modern conditions requires the virtual absence of serious manifest political opposition. Given the reality of right/left splits in Third World politics, ascendancy to power by either the right or the left means intense opposition by the other. Harsh means are relied upon to quell opposition. To resist under such conditions requires desperate strategies – kidnappings, terrorism, armed struggle. A vicious circle of repression

Table 11.1: US Military Assistance for Years 1966, 1970, 1975 by Regions (millions of current dollars)

Regions	1966	1970	Per Cent Change	1975	Per Cent Change
Developing:					
Region 2 (Europe*)	281.3	295.0	+4.8	198.1	−32.8
Region 3 (Latin America)	131.4	26.4	−79.9	156.8	+493.9
Region 4 (Far East)	1,179.3	2,492.8	+111.3	1,243.2	−50.1
Region 5 (South Africa)	9.0	0.5	−94.9	0.6	+20.0
Region 6 (Middle East)	251.1	3.7	−98.5	104.7	+2,729.0
Region 7 (Africa)	36.1	19.4	−46.2	70.5	+263.4
Developed:					
Region 1 (Canada)					
Region 2 (Europe)	49.2	0.0	−100.0	0.0	0
Region 4 (Japan)	1.7	0.0	−100.0	0.0	0
Region 6 (Israel)	90.0	30.0	−66.6	300.0	+900.0
Region 8 (Oceania)	5.0	0.0	−100.0	0.0	0

Source: Computed from figures contained in ***US Overseas Loans and Grants and Assistance from International Organisations, Obligations and Loan Authorizations,*** 1 July 1945 – 30 June 1975 (Washington, US AID, 1976).

Table 11.2: US Arms Sales for Years 1966, 1970, 1975, by Regions (millions of current dollars)

Regions	1966	1970	Per Cent Change	1975	Per Cent Change
Region 2 (Europe*)	24.277	58.719	+ 141.8	322.933	+ 499.9
Region 3 (Latin America)	24.6	25.0	+ 1.6	154.7	+ 518.8
Region 4 (Far East)	5.8	61.3	+ 956.8	439.0	+ 616.1
Region 5 (South Asia)	10.2	51.4	+ 403.9	1,419.2	+ 2,661.0
Region 6 (Middle East)	209.6	143.2	−31.6	2,970.5	+ 1,974.3
Region 7 (Africa)	7.8	7.8	0	330.0	+ 4,130.7
Developed:					
Region 1 (Canada)	70.2	53.1	−24.3	102.1	+ 92.0
Region 2 (Europe)	1,126.423	387.281	−65.5	2,680.767	+ 592.2
Region 4 (Japan)	16.6	21.2	+ 27.7	29.6	+ 39.6
Region 6 (Israel)	72.1	44.9	−37.7	868.7	+ 1,834.7
Region 8 (Oceania)	52.5	59.4	+ 13.1	162.7	+ 173.9

Developed countries: Canada, Japan, Israel, Australia, New Zealand, Belgium, Denmark, France, West Germany, Iceland, Italy, Luxembourg, Netherlands, Norway, United Kingdom, Czechoslovakia, Bulgaria, East Germany, Hungary, Poland, Romania, USSR, Austria, Finland, Ireland, Sweden, Switzerland.

* These European countries are considered 'developing': Greece, Portugal, Turkey, Albania, Malta, Spain, Yugoslavia.

Source: Computed from data in ***Foreign Military Sales and Military Assistance Facts*** (November 1975).

Table 11.3: Dependency of US on Imports of Strategic Raw Materials

Per Cent Imported	Mineral	Major Foreign Sources
100	Manganese	Brazil, Gabon, S. Africa, Zaire
97	Titanium	Australia, India
91	Chromium	USSR, S. Africa, Turkey, Philippines
86	Platinum	USSR, S. Africa, Canada
80	Nickel	Canada, Norway, USSR
88	Aluminium	Jamaica, Surinam, Dominican Republic
88	Tantalum	Australia, Canada, Zaire, Brazil
98	Cobalt	Zaire, Finland, Norway, Canada
86	Tin	Malaysia, Thailand, Bolivia
86	Fluorine	Mexico, Spain, Italy
60	Germanium-Indium	USSR, Canada, Japan
50	Beryllium	Brazil, S. Africa, Uganda
60	Tungsten	Canada, Bolivia, Peru, Mexico
50	Zirconium	Australia, Canada, S. Africa
40	Barite	Ireland, Peru, Mexico
23	Iron ore	Canada, Venezuela, Nigeria, Brazil
21	Lead	Canada, Peru, Australia, Mexico
18	Copper	Canada, Peru, Chile, S. Africa

Source: *United States Military Posture for FY 1977* (Joint Chiefs of Staff, Washington, D.C., 1976).

and resistance ensues. To discipline the polity successfully appears to require reliance on torture and official terror as staple ingredients of rule, at least until the opposition is liquidated or intimidated. An internal security bureaucracy, which includes a network of spies and informers to penetrate all parts of society and often to reach overseas to control exile activity, emerges and grows. As with other aspects of right-wing militarisation, the internal security system is developed in a modern spirit with outside (usually US) support and guidance.[8] Although militarised regimes vary considerably in their tolerance of political and cultural activity, all of them insist upon 'emergency' prerogatives, as needed, to remove undesirables from the scene and to impose policies designed to intimidate the population from any kind of massive protest.[9]

2.9 Geopolitical Links

Often, but not invariably, militarised regimes of the kind I have been describing come into being with the blessing of the United States government. The precise relationship is difficult to demonstrate in most situations, although recent revelations and investigations often disclose a pattern of CIA support for the transition to militarised rule and its subsequent stabilisation.[10] What seems clear is that a militarised rightist polity tends to attract capital and political support both from the market economies in the industrialised world and from international lending institutions dominated by OECD perspectives. Despite severe abuses of human rights, these regimes are rarely victims of diplomatic pressure from the northern liberal democracies, unless their leaders pursue highly erratic and confrontational policies, such as Amin in Uganda and Qaddafi in Libya. More characteristically, the US-led Western global alliance views the principal examples of such regimes – Brazil, Indonesia and, formerly, Iran – as 'junior partners' in the alliance against radicalism. Iran's intervention in Oman to defeat the Dhofar uprising, Indonesia's invasion of East Timor and Brazil's support for counter-insurgency in southern zone countries illustrate these regional 'peace-keeping' roles. In addition, these regimes have also provided the West, especially the United States, with relatively safe havens for military bases, space stations, geopolitical allies and a comparatively secure and profitable setting for overseas capital and market development, including the operations of multinational corporations.

2.10 Statism

Somewhat contrary to section 2.9, the militarised governance pattern, once relatively secure in power, frequently moves strongly to defend its own statist and nationalist directions. Its logic is to establish control, rather than to defer to its outside patron or 'senior partner'. In this repect, some militarised regimes (or some factions within these regimes), despite their internal reactionary policies, have actually joined in the front ranks of the struggle for a new international economic order. Part of this independent posture in international arenas appears to stem from a quest for international legitimacy on the part of governmental leadership. Experience in Brazil, India, Thailand, South Korea and elsewhere suggests that these militarised regimes cannot count upon achieving legitimacy via the popular endorsement of official policies in elections even if they build up a record of economic successes. Unless rigged, the consistent result of 'opening' the system to electoral politics, even of a restricted kind, has been a repudiation of the economic, political and ideological approach of these militarised regimes. More recently, these regimes have refused to forfeit their nuclear options or to accept US leadership in the area of non-proliferation policy. Brazil, for instance, has been steadily diversifying its trade and investment patterns and has refused to define its diplomatic stance in the United Nations by following the US lead (for example, Brazil voted for the anti-Zionist resolution in the General Assembly in 1975). Even on an economic plane the drive for statist internal control has led these regimes to burden foreign investors with an increasing web of regulatory authority. On another level, the growing burden of foreign indebtedness, built up to $160 billion by the end of 1976, reflects not only the extent to which these militarised polities attracted outside capital, but also their degree of dependence and vulnerability: either they accept external interference in their economy to sustain their credit standing or they lose their credit.

By describing the nature of Third World rightist militarisation in a capitalist context, I am not implying uniformity or conspiracy. I only suggest that some underlying circumstances in the Third World have generated a pattern of response in which some shared characteristics are present and are accentuated by the structure of the world economy.

3 Militarism in the Third World

Depicting trends reinforces the argument that militarism is spreading in the Third World. The spread of rightist forms of militarisation in response to internal crises of capital formation and political order is the central focus of this article. To some extent, however, all forms of militarisation, including leftist forms, reveal the apparent inability of moderate forms of governance to survive into the late 1970s in the Third World.

In collaboration with Charlotte Ebel, Ruthann Johansen and Tom Lindenfeld, I am seeking to develop methods of presenting and interpreting data bearing on these trends. Here we attempt to make the basic case for a spread of militarism, and specifically of right-wing militarism, in a series of *world maps* beginning in 1960 (see pp. 221-5). On these maps we indicate those Third World countries subject to militarised rule in each five-year interval since 1960.

We distinguish degrees of militarisation in each of the first four maps. In essence, our view is that militarising pressure is broader than direct control exerted by the military establishment over the governing apparatus or selection of the head of state from the ranks of military officers. Hence, the maps identify those states ruled by military officers, those in which martial law or state of emergency has been declared by the government, and, finally, those in which civilians rule the country but do not allow a political opposition to function normally and depend heavily on the military to keep them in power.

On the fifth map we identify left and right orientations of the militarised governments. We made these judgements on the basis of three criteria: attitudes towards multinationals, pattern of global alignment and socialisation of the economy. Our attempt is to draw these distinctions as reasonably as possible for the most recent year in the eighteen-year period examined.

Even if one objects to a particular decision as to classification, these maps reveal clearly a trend toward rightist forms of militarisation. In Latin America and Africa the shift during the period covered has been specially dramatic. As the preceding discussion of the context of militarisation clarifies, it is the new character of the military outlook that creates occasion for alarm. The ascent to power of the military or of militarised civilians is accompanied by a broadened sense of purpose for the military. The military and their civilian allies now regard their security task as mainly domestic, a matter of protecting the stability of the developmental process against radical social forces. In other words, militarisation is associated, whether wittingly or not, with a new type of politics, that eventuates whatever else in the structures and practices of the rigid state.

In Africa and Asia trends towards militarisation should be associated, in part, with some deferred strains of decolonisation. The post-colonial state has expanded without generally being able to secure a mandate embracing all significant groups encompassed by state boundaries. Hence a crisis of legitimacy has emerged that can be solved in one of two ways: weak governance combined with disorder and economic uncertainty, or strong governance based on imposed authority usually associated with the ascendancy of particular elites. In most Third World countries, because the military has been willing to exercise control, the strong governance option has prevailed.

In sum, the maps support the generalisation about the trends towards militarisation, as well as the sub-trends toward rightist variants. Such trends are vectors of change. Some exceptions exist. India's move towards militarised rule with the Emergency Decrees of 1975 has been repudiated at the polls in an election in March of 1977. The elections suggest the mildness of India's move towards militarisation, although reports suggest that Mrs Gandhi tried unsuccessfully to solicit direct military intervention to offset the adverse election results. It is not clear at all whether the restoration of civilian rule in India will itself enjoy sufficient stability to resist the wider Third World trends; the question is whether the rehabilitation of moderate rule will prove sustainable for long.

4 Implications

There are several significant implications of this trend for the global community. First of all, militarisation encourages the emergence of strong states in many Third World countries. Second, where state power is strong and maintained by military control, a political atmosphere insensitive to international human rights of both an economic and a political character is almost certain to result. Third, a set of militarist Third World governments will be disinclined to push for disarmament initiatives; such an orientation works against a more natural Third World interest in pressing for denuclearisation and disarmament. Fourth, the existence of a large majority of Third World governments that affirm the traditional virtues of sovereignty and statism reinforces the world order *status quo*.

Such a situation creates confusion. On the one hand, militarist governments may push Third World solidarity on a wide variety of issues so as to secure a better relative position for themselves, but, on the other, their framework is traditional statism that includes endorsement of the war system. As such, world order values associated with peace, economic well-being, human rights, ecological balance and positive global identity are not likely to win support from such leadership. Advocacy of a new international economic order is not *necessarily* associated with seeking a just and peaceful world order. And, indeed, an NIEO under militarist auspices is not likely to help the poor strata of national societies satisfy their basic needs in the near future.

In conclusion, alongside the continuing development and spread of the entire spectrum of weaponry is the expansion of militarised governance patterns. The latter augments the former in several damaging respects. While militarism in the Third World is partly a reflection of domestic factors, it is also a consequence of international factors, especially the imperial geopolitics of the United States and the capitalist domination of international economic institutions and procedures.

To reverse the trend of militarised authoritarianism will not be easy. It depends, first of all, on deepening domestic opposition to militarism and authoritarianism, perhaps precipitated by economic failures that extend to deprivations of the poor to the middle classes. Second, prospects for greater global equity, justice and peace will depend on more 'progressive' politics in the leading countries and in the lending practices of the United Nations family of economic assistance agencies like the World Bank and the IMF.

Notes

1. See, for example, Albert Fishlow, 'Some Reflections on Post-1964 Brazilian Economic Policy' and Philippe C. Schmitter, '"The Portugalization" of Brazil', in Alfred Stepan (ed.), *Authoritarian Brazil: Origins, Policies, and Future* (Yale University Press, New Haven, Conn., 1973), pp. 69-118, 179-232.
2. See, especially, the penetrating assessment along these lines in Guillermo A. O'Donnell, 'Corporatism and the Question of the State' in James M. Malloy (ed.), *Authoritarianism and Corporatism in Latin America* (University of Pittsburg Press, Pittsburg, 1977), pp. 47-88.
3. See Alfred Stepan, *The Military in Politics: Changing Patterns in Brazil* (Princeton University Press, Princeton, 1971); for a more general, carefully nuanced assessment see Abraham F. Lowenthal, 'Armies and Politics in Latin America', *World Politics*, vol. XXVII (1974), pp. 107-30.
4. For elaboration see essays in Malloy, *Authoritarianism and Corporatism in Latin America*.
5. Empirical confirmation in Schmitter, 'The "Portugalization" of Brazil'.
6. See Fernando Pedreira, 'Decompression in Brazil?', *Foreign Affairs*, no. 53 (1975), pp. 498-512.
7. See discussion to this effect in Carlos Estevan Martins, 'Brazil and the United States from the 1960's to the 1970's' in Julio Cotter and Richard F. Fagen (eds.) *Latin America and the United States: The Changing Political Realities* (Stanford University Press, Stanford, California, 1974), pp. 269-301, esp. pp. 298-301.
8. For example, 'United States Policies and Programs in Brazil', *Hearings* of Sub-committee on Western Hemisphere Affairs of Senate Foreign Relations Committee, 92nd Cong., 1st Sess., 4, 5 and 11 May 1971; Michael Klare and Nancy Stein, 'Exporting the Tools of Repression', Reprint no. 104, Center for National Security Studies (Dec. 1976), pp. 1-15; Walden Bellow and Severina Rivera (eds.), *The Logistics of Repression* (Friends of the Filipino Peoples, Washington, D.C., 1977).
9. Norman Gall illustrates this characteristic by reference to the callous disregard of human welfare in relation to train safety and service between outlying workers' communities and Rio de Janeiro. See Gall, 'The Rise of Brazil', *Commentary*, no. 63 (1977), pp. 45-55, at p. 50.
10. For example, Robert L. Borosage and John Marks (eds.), *The CIA File* (Grossman Publishers, New York, 1976); 'Covert Action: Intelligence Activities', *Hearings*, Senate Select Committee to Study Governmental Operations, 94th Cong., 1st Sess., 4-5 Dec. 1975.

Notes to Maps

I Indicators used to determine militarisation of a government.

In determining the relative militarisation of a country, we used the following criteria. Although each country had unique arrangements of the succeeding indicators, all indicators seemed to be present to some extent, thereby giving the military a greater relative role in the internal affairs of the country and justifying the classification 'militarised'.

military ruler as head of state;
meaningless or non-existent elections;
power gained through *coup* or other non-electoral process;
increased possibility of arbitrary dissolution or disregard for constitution;
little distributive representation within the government;
high percentage of budget used for military purposes;
arbitrary suspension of civil liberties;
governmental legitimacy based upon military might;
executive power (other than head of state) is held by members of the armed forces in active duty;
military used for internal security in non-emergency situations.

Criteria used to distinguish left-leaning from right-leaning militarised governments (Map 5):

attitudes toward multinationals;
patterns of global alignment;
socialisation of the economy.

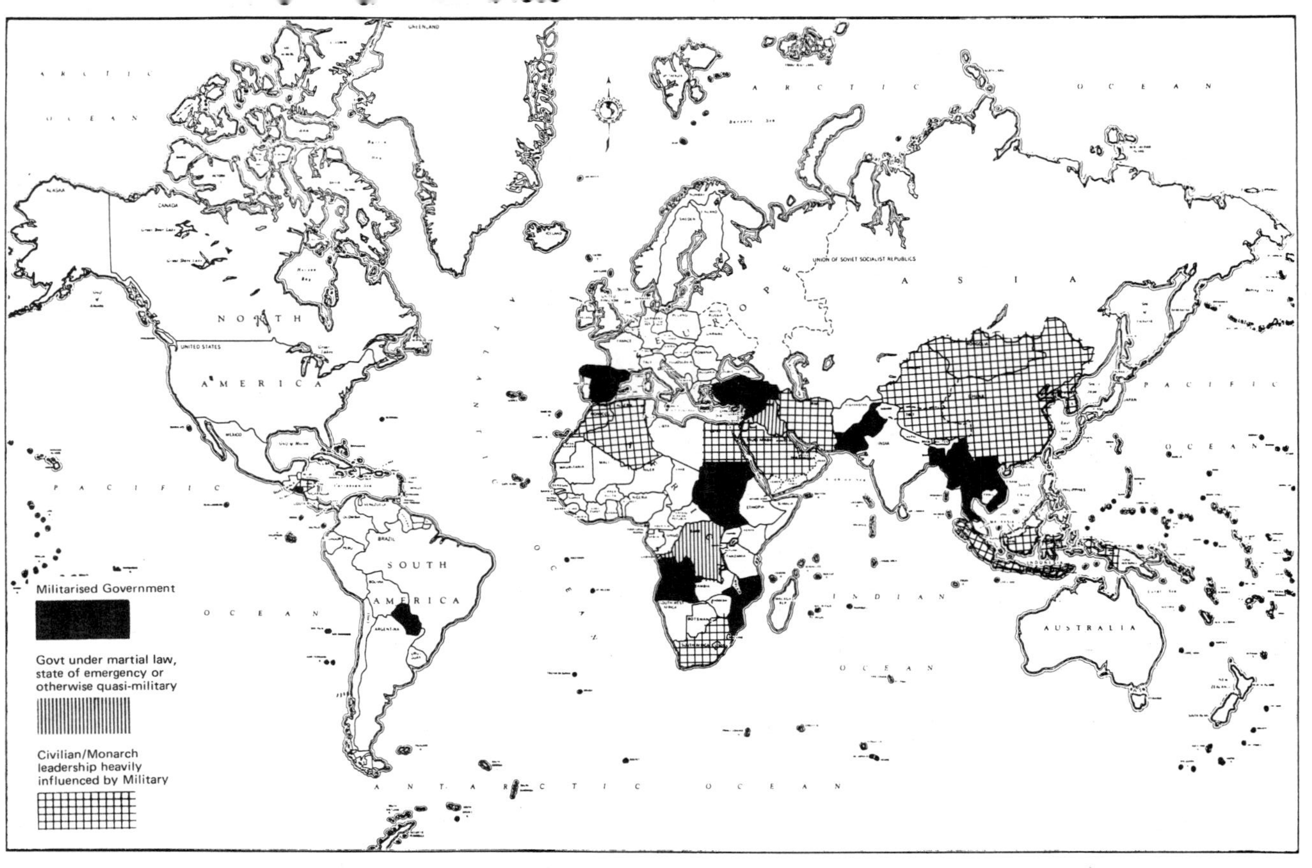
Militarised Government
Govt under martial law, state of emergency or otherwise quasi-military
Civilian/Monarch leadership heavily influenced by Military
ARCTIC OCEAN
NORTH AMERICA
SOUTH AMERICA
EUROPE
ASIA
AFRICA
AUSTRALIA
ATLANTIC OCEAN
PACIFIC OCEAN
INDIAN OCEAN
ANTARCTIC OCEAN
UNION OF SOVIET SOCIALIST REPUBLICS
UNITED STATES
CANADA
GREENLAND
ALASKA
ICELAND
MEXICO
BRAZIL
ARGENTINA
INDIA
CHINA
JAPAN
ETHIOPIA
INDONESIA

Map 2: The Spread of (Right-wing) Militarism, 1965

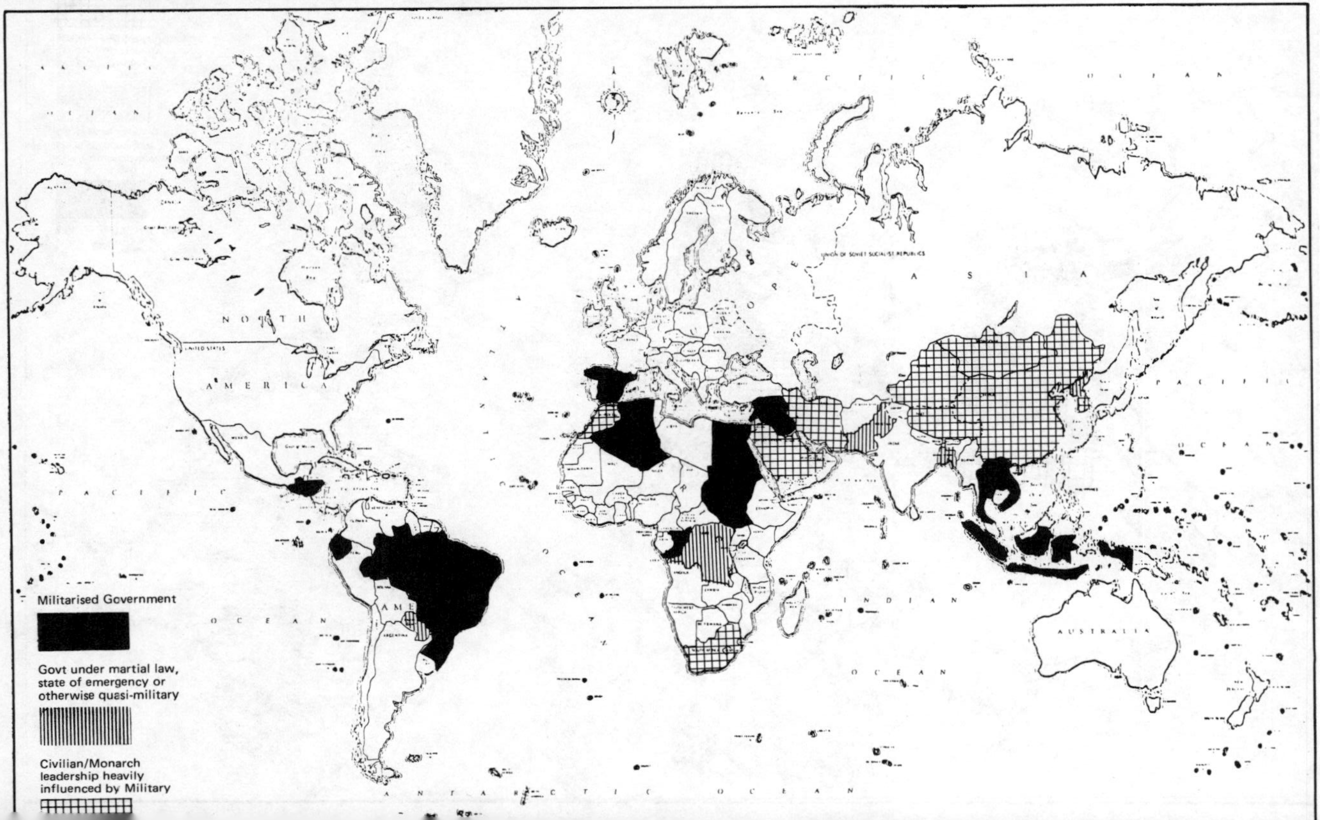

Militarised Government

Govt under martial law, state of emergency or otherwise quasi-military

Civilian/Monarch leadership heavily influenced by Military

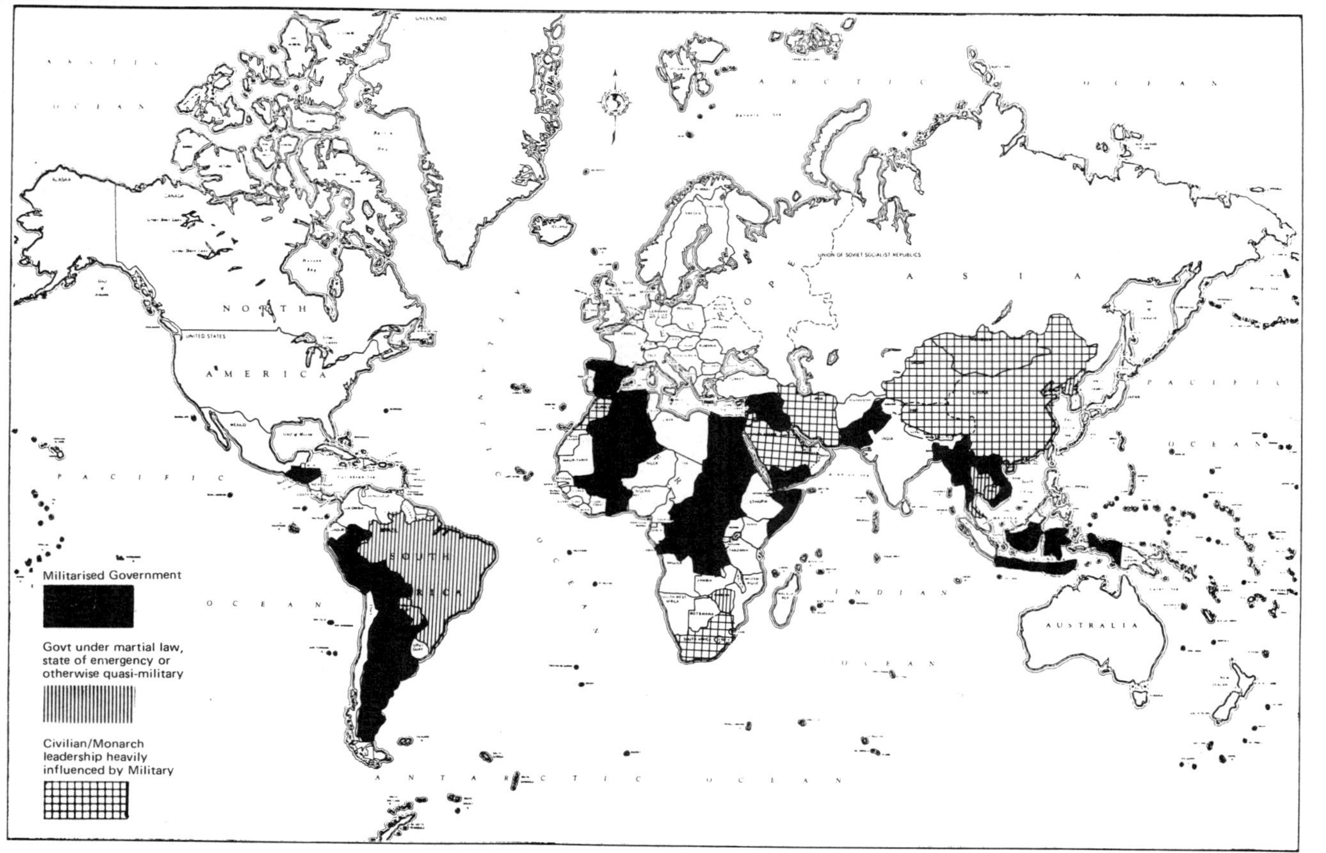

Militarised Government
Govt under martial law, state of emergency or otherwise quasi-military
Civilian/Monarch leadership heavily influenced by Military
NORTH AMERICA
SOUTH AMERICA
EUROPE
ASIA
AFRICA
AUSTRALIA
UNION OF SOVIET SOCIALIST REPUBLICS
UNITED STATES
GREENLAND
ARCTIC OCEAN
PACIFIC OCEAN
ATLANTIC OCEAN
INDIAN OCEAN
ANTARCTIC OCEAN

Map 4: The Spread of (Right-wing) Militarism, 1978

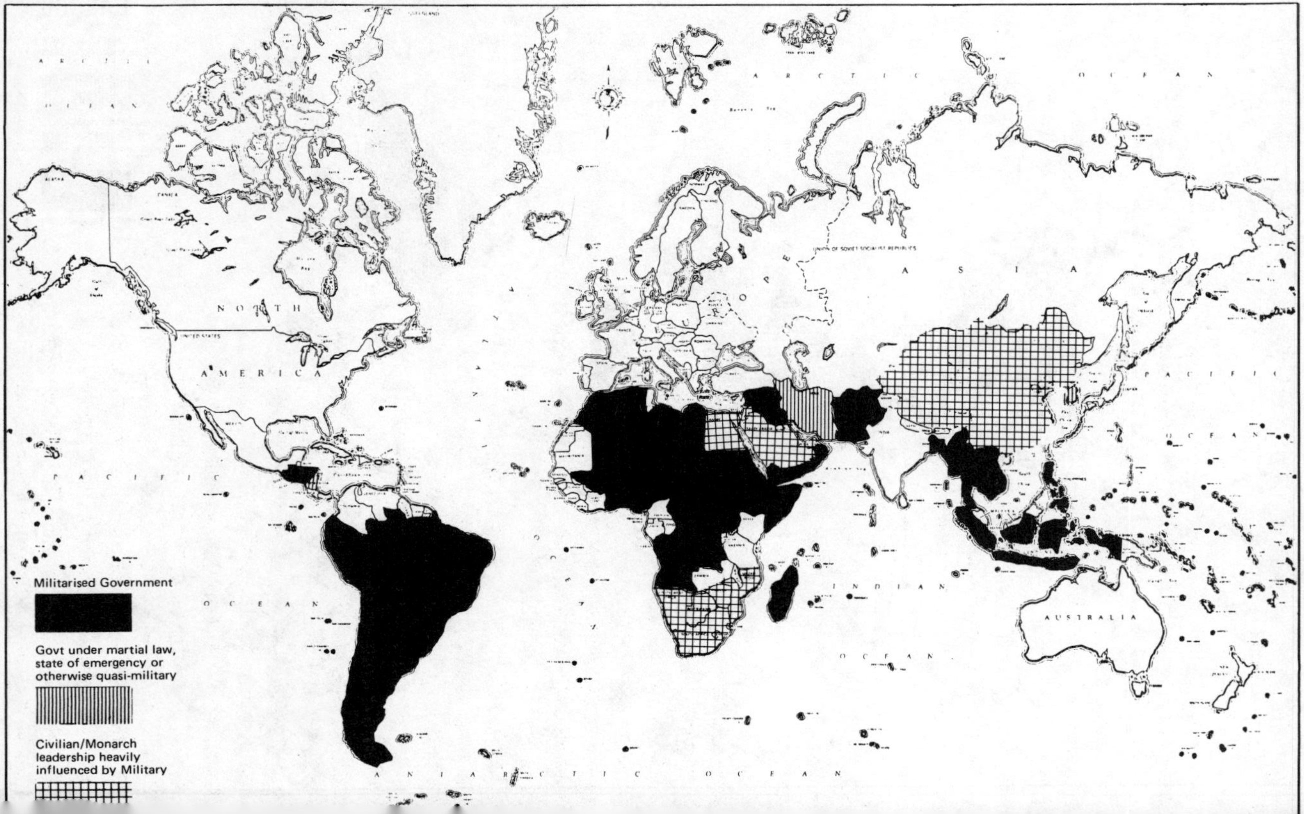

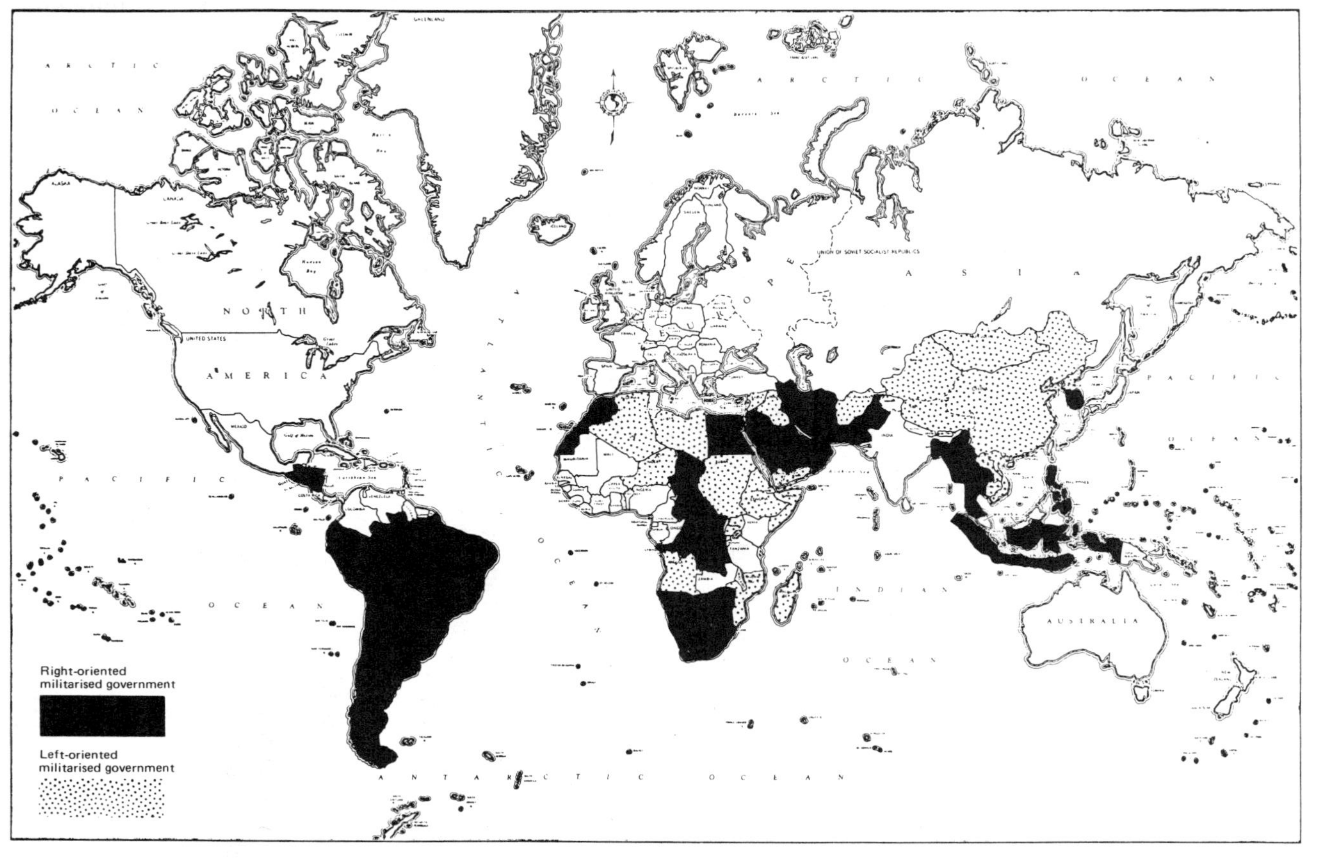
ARCTIC OCEAN
NORTH AMERICA
UNITED STATES
ATLANTIC OCEAN
PACIFIC OCEAN
EUROPE
ASIA
UNION OF SOVIET SOCIALIST REPUBLICS
INDIAN OCEAN
AUSTRALIA
ANTARCTIC OCEAN
Right-oriented militarised government
Left-oriented militarised government

12 THE SIGNIFICANCE OF MILITARY TECHNOLOGY

Mary H. Kaldor

The recent spread of frightful new military technologies to developing countries tends to induce a sense of helplessness among those concerned to encourage development and prevent war. It is not merely the enormity of the problem: it is also the apparent invulnerability of military technology, the idea that technology has a dynamic of its own apparently inpervious to social control.

Yet military techniques, like any others, are the product of men and are used by men. If instead of viewing technology as an abstract body of knowledge applied to a piece of equipment, we were to treat it as a social system, an organisation of men needed for production and use, we might understand more precisely the implications of technology transfer, and this might lead us to practical policy prescriptions.

In any given society, military technology takes a specific form. On the one hand, it is the product of the level of technology in society, itself the consequence of the particular mode of production – i.e. the way in which human relations are organised for the material satisfaction of human needs – that characteristises the society in question. Thus modern military technology pioneered in the United States tends to reflect the US industrial structure. On the other hand, military technology is the appropriate tool for a particular set of military relations: i.e. a particular way of organising men as an instrument of force which generally reflects the prevalent method of organisation in any given society. For example, the feudal army was based on levies, in which serfs owed military service to their lords in much the same way as they owed agricultural service. The army was organised hierarchically around the lords and knights who had for the most part a monopoly of weapons – swords, lances, pikes, etc. It took the introduction of mercenary soldiers, financed by the new bourgeoisie on behalf of the emerging absolute monarchy, before guns, the products of bourgeois technology, could be accepted into the armed forces.

*Paper presented at Pugwash Symposium on Problems of Military-Oriented Technologies in Developing Countries, Feldafing (FRG), 23-26 November 1976. For a related paper, see Mary H. Kaldor, 'The Military in Development', *World Development*, vol. 4, no. 6 (1976), pp. 459-82.

Today, the dominant military technology is the 'weapon system', comprising a weapon platform (e.g. a ship, aircraft or armoured vehicle), a weapon (e.g. gun, missile or torpedo) and a means of command and control. The concept of 'weapons system' can be said to have originated in the first prolonged period of high peacetime military spending, namely the Anglo-German naval arms race before World War I. Socially, the rise of the concept may be likened to the replacement of tools by machines: whereas formerly the weapon was the instrument of man, it now appears that man is the instrument of the weapon system: for a weapon system demands a rigid technical division of labour that admits of little variation in the social organisation of the men operating it. Equally, the weapon system, like the machine, guarantees the existence of certain types of industrial capacity required for its manufacture.

It is not only the structures underlying individual weapon systems that are important. Weapon systems tend to be linked together in a larger *hierarchical* structure. A good example is the aircraft carrier. To be effective and to ensure that at least one aircraft carrier is always in operation, a navy interested in a carrier role must possess at least three carriers. Each carrier carries smaller systems – combat aircraft, missile systems, rescue helicopters, etc. Each carrier must also have a protective screen of destroyers and frigates, at least one hunter-killer submarine, and various supply ships. Each of these is associated with a particular manpower unit of the navy and with a particular type of manufacturing capacity. Thus, the hierarchy of weapon systems is associated with similar military and industrial hierarchies.

Yet it can be argued that the weapons system based force structure is approaching a crisis. It can be deemed an obsolescent technology on two counts. First of all, the weapons system as we know it seems to have reached that stage which all technologies reach sooner or later, in which technical improvement becomes harder to achieve: a stage of diminishing returns where every extra dollar invested yields less technical improvement.

This is reflected in the rapid increase in the cost of new weapon systems and in the decline of the dominant defence-related industries – aerospace, shipbuilding, automobiles, heavy engineering – as evidenced in their declining share of civilian world markets and the frequency of threatened bankruptcy. Second, the force structure based on weapon systems is challenged by new military technologies. In particular, enormous improvements in the accuracy of guidance system have greatly increased the vulnerability of all weapon platforms, calling into question the utility of large, elaborate weapon systems which are difficult to hide and expensive to replace. The new Precision Guided Munitions (PGMs) are extremely cheap – a modern combat aircraft costs a thousand times more than an anti-aircraft missile. Being small and mobile, they can be used by a variety of different military organisations; currently one might anticipate a form of military organisation resembling the assembly line, in rather the same way that the weapon system based force structure reflects the methods of batch production. The new military technologies are also the product of new industries, e.g. electronics, with rapidly growing civilian markets as well.

These considerations suggest two important implications for the transfer of military technology to developing countries. *First*, the transfer of military technology represents the transfer of a social system. In the case of the weapon system, the structure of recipient armed forces is delineated rather precisely; and this, in turn, has important implications for the political orientation of the soldier and the strategy of development. Partly because of the need for an industrial base to service the weapon system based force structure and partly because of the ideology associated with the weapon system – the glorification of industrial technology – the armed forces play an important role in support of governments favouring a development model aimed at imitating metropolis society. This is the significance of the military *coup.*

Second, the growing obsolescence of the concept of the weapon system underpins the need for reproduction. The reproduction of user patterns, i.e. force structure, ensures that the weapon system does not come under military challenge and that perceptions about what constitutes military power are widely shared. The reproduction of producer patterns, i.e. industrial structure, secures, perhaps temporarily, a market and a future for declining industries and endangered companies.

The social relationships which underlie the transfer of military technology are not purely one-sided, however. Just as society in the periphery may be overwhelmed by the impact of their military technology and the social structure for which it stands, so may new social formations in the periphery represent an unexpected challenge to metropolis society. While military technology is invented and produced in rich countries it is mainly applied in developing countries. In rich countries, the weapon system is challenged in terms of reproductive efficiency, i.e. the heavy cost of production as compared with alternatives. In poor countries, it is challenged in terms of military efficiency. Alternative force structures, based on new social groups, have exposed in guerrilla wars the dinosaurial qualities of the weapon system – even without the use of the new PGM technologies. The challenge posed by what appear to be purely military tactics has caused profound crises within armed forces based on weapon systems, and correspondingly in society as a whole. Such was the experience of the US in Vietnam or the Peruvian and Portugese armies.[1] A historical example might be the German response to the Napoleonic wars.

If this analysis is correct, then it follows that social groups in underdeveloped countries committed to alternative development strategies must fully understand the social nature of military technology and build military relationships upon domestic rather than international forms of social organisation. This carries with it the further implication that the rejection of imported military technology inappropriate to such military relationships could provoke changes in the international military system, changes far beyond any local and particular events.

Notes

1. Alfred Stepan has demonstrated the effects of guerrilla warfare on the Brazilian army. Counter-insurgency in the early 1960s necessitated a decentralisation of command and a move away from the weapon system organisation. This upgraded the technical role of sergeants, without corresponding social and economic upgrading, and they began to make common cause with trade unions. On one occasion, sergeants actually prevented an attempted *coup* against President Goulart. The 1964 *coup* can be viewed as an attempt by officers to reassert traditional force structure and hence their political power. See Alfred Stepan, *The Military in Politics: Changing Patterns in Brazil* (Princeton University Press, Princeton, 1971).

13 ARMS TRADE AND TRANSFER OF MILITARY TECHNOLOGY TO THIRD WORLD COUNTRIES*

Signe Landgren-Bäckström

1 Political and Military Significance

> The global arms race after World War II differs in many aspects from what was previously called 'arms race'. While only a few European countries and their allies – like the USA, Japan, and Australia – were involved in the 1930s arms build-up, after 1945 the trend to acquire and produce increasingly sophisticated weaponry has spread, and is still spreading, to more and more countries. In particular, the so-called Third World[1] has in the past decade rapidly increased its share of armaments imports; also, several countries are making the expensive effort to create domestic arms industries.

About 75 per cent of the current world arms trade is now with the Third World. Quantitatively, the volume of military transfers to the Third World has increased more the 15-fold over the past 25 years, or at an average annual increase of some 12 per cent. However, the volume of the arms trade to the Third World started to show a particularly sharp increase in both absolute and relative terms after 1965. The average yearly increase from 1970 to 1976 was 15 per cent, compared with the 1960's, when the corresponding average annual rate of increase was 5 per cent from 1960 to 1966. The boom in the arms trade which characterises the present decade cannot be explained merely by the increase in the number of new nations, which obviously influenced the statistics during the 1950's and early 1960's – when, as a rule, the former Asian and African colonies of the UK and France set up armed forces upon gaining independence.

The underlying theory behind SIPRI's decision to examine the arms trade with the Third World was that this trade is unique in comparison to the trade in any other commodity, because of its political and military consequences, both for the buyers and for the sellers. This has been expressed in many ways by many sources. The following statement by Julius Nyerere, for example, may serve as well as any other to define the political aspect of arms supplies:

*Shortened version from 'The Trends in the Arms Trade with the Third World', *SIPRI Yearbook 1978*, and 'The Transfer of Military Technology to Third World Countries', *Bulletin of Peace Proposals*, vol. 8, no. 2 (1977).

> For the selling of arms is something which a country does only when it wants to support and strengthen the regime or the group to whom the sale is made. Whatever restrictions or limits are placed on that sale, the sale of any arms is a declaration of support – an implied alliance of a kind. You can trade with people you dislike; you can have diplomatic relations with governments you disapprove of; you can sit in conference with those nations whose policies you abhor. But you do not sell arms without saying, in effect: 'In the light of the receiving country's known policies, friends, and enemies, we anticipate that, in the last resort, we will be on their side in the case of any conflict. We shall want them to defeat their enemies.'[2]

In other words, the provision of the means for warfare has an intrinsic political and military significance even where the supplying country states only a commercial interest.

2 The Flow of Arms

The list of main weapon suppliers is identical to that of the leading weapon producers. More specifically, the *governments* of the producing countries control the exports of arms. The non-governmental, so-called illegal, traffic in arms comprises only a small proportion of the total international arms trade, particularly because even a private transaction requires an export licence from the government of the exporting country.

The United States occupies the leading position in the field of military technology and is consequently the leading single exporter of major conventional arms. The US share of total arms exports to the Third World from 1970 to 1976 was 38 per cent (see Table 13.1 for the rank order of arms-exporting nations during this period). The Soviet Union is the second largest supplier, with a total share of 34 per cent. This dual domination of the arms market is not explained by technological capacity alone, but by a quantitative factor as well – both the United States and the Soviet Union possess large armaments industries as regards production capacity and turnover, and are thus able to produce long series of the various types of weapon.

With the increase in the number of countries capable of exporting arms, a noticeable competition for the Third World market broke out, resulting in what might be called a general commercialisation of the arms trade. For the recipient countries this meant that, in cases where the dominant suppliers refused for political reasons to supply certain types of weapon, the emergence of new producers provided the buyers

Table 13.1: Rank Order of Arms Suppliers to the Third World, 1970-6

Supplier	Total Value of Arms Supplies (US $ m[a])	Per Cent of World Total	Largest Recipient Regions	Region's Per Cent of Supplier's Total	Largest Recipient Country in Each Region	Country's Per Cent of Supplier's Total
USA	12,303	38	Middle East	62	Iran	31
			Far East	27	S. Vietnam	12
			South America	7	Brazil	2
USSR	11,057	34	Middle East	57	Syria	23
			North Africa	13	Libya	13
			Far East	13	N. Vietnam	7
UK	3,076	9	Middle East	49	Iran	26
			South America	22	Chile	8
			South Asia	14	India	12
France	2,963	9	North Africa	24	Libya	16
			Middle East	23	Egypt	5
			South America	18	Venezuela	6
Italy	562	2	Middle East	40	Iran	34
			South Africa	27	South Africa	27
			South America	18	Brazil	10
China	537	2	South Asia	46	Pakistan	46
			Far East	29	N. Vietnam	11
			Sub-Saharan Africa	25	Tanzania	16

FR Germany	451	1	South America	74	Argentina	22
			Far East	10	Singapore	6
			Sub-Saharan Africa	6	Nigeria	2
Netherlands	214	0.7	Middle East	40	Iran	28
			Sub-Saharan Africa	25	Nigeria	10
			South America	9	Argentina	6
Canada	178	0.6	South America	60	Peru	23
			Sub-Saharan Africa	28	Zambia	9
			Middle East	4	Lebanon	3
Czechoslavakia	87	0.3	South Asia	59	India	59
			Middle East	30	Egypt	11
			Sub-Saharan Africa	7	Sudan	7
Spain	70	0.2	South America	82	Uruguay	51
			Far East	11	Indonesia	11
			Middle East	7	Jordan	7
Australia	60	0.2	Far East	82	Indonesia	50
			South America	15	Brazil	14
			Middle East	2	Oman	2
Sweden	54	0.2	South Asia	87	Pakistan	87
			South America	9	Chile	9
			Sub-Saharan Africa	4	Sierra Leone	4
Poland	30	0.1	South Asia	99	India	99
			Far East	0.7	Indonesia	0.7
Yugoslavia	24	0.1	Middle East	78	Egypt	70
			Sub-Saharan Africa	22	Tanzania	13

Supplier	Total Value of Arms Supplies (US $ m[a])	Per Cent of World Total	Largest Recipient Regions	Region's Per Cent of Supplier's Total	Largest Recipient Country in Each Region	Country's Per Cent of Supplier's Total
Switzerland	17	0.1	South America	59	Argentina	41
			Far East	18	Thailand	18
			Middle East	12	Oman	12
New Zealand	12	0.04	South Asia	77	India	77
			Far East	23	Thailand	17
Japan	6	0.02	Far East	50	Philippines	50
			Sub-Saharan Africa	50	Zaire	50
Belgium	5	0.02	South Africa	50	South Africa	50
			Sub-Saharan Africa	50	Ethiopia	50
Ireland	2	0.01	Middle East	100	Oman	100
Third World countries[b]	724	2	South Africa	24	South Africa	24
			Sub-Saharan Africa	19	Uganda	15
			South Asia	18	Pakistan	12
World total	32,427	100				

Notes: a. At constant 1975 prices.
b. See Table 13.2 for the rank order of Third World arms suppliers.

with new sellers to turn to. The case of Latin America provides an illustration of this development: during the early post-war period the United States had a virtual monopoly on arms sales in the region, but when the US government refused to sell the supersonic fighters requested, the buyers turned to European producers. South America is now among the three largest recipient regions for weapons from Australia, Canada, France, FR Germany, Italy, the Netherlands, Sweden, Switzerland and the UK. When the Soviet Union, according to Egyptian sources, refused to comply with requests for more sophisticated armaments. Egypt turned to West European producers for the acquisition not only of the weapons but of production know-how.

In regard to the enormous escalation of arms imports in the Middle East, it often goes unnoticed that the USA and the USSR are not the only suppliers to the region – several other countries are involved in securing their share of an apparently unlimited market, for example France and the UK, as well as Italy, the Netherlands, Spain, Switzerland and Yugoslavia.

Among the Third World countries, the major arms exporters are those countries which have concentrated most heavily on the acquisition of military know-how, that is, which have invested in military industries (see table 13.2). Of those Third World countries which have reached an advanced production capability – most notably Argentina, Brazil, India, Israel and South Africa – Israel stands out the most technologically advanced.[3] Moreover, several other Third World countries – in particular North and South Korea and Taiwan – have fairly advanced indigenous arms industries and therefore export capacity, although because they have not yet begun to export, they are not included in the table 13.2.[4]

For the socialist countries, it is also possible to discern a certain spread of export capacity, although on a much smaller scale than in the West. The Soviet Union alone accounts for 94 per cent of the socialist countries' arms exports (and furthermore, Czechoslavakia has on occasion acted as intermediary for Soviet suppliers, for example, to Egypt in 1955). But the past few years have seen an expansion of sales, particularly by Yugoslavia, Poland and Romania.

Iran will probably invest heavily in local arms production, as will Egypt and Saudi Arabia. So far, Iran has re-exported US F-5A fighters, and Jordan's position as third in order of suppliers is likewise explained by the re-export of old equipment to South Africa and Oman.

The inclusion of the Ivory Coat and Gabon in the table is merely due to the export of French-designed patrol boats from French-built

Table 13.2: Rank Order of Third World Arms Suppliers, 1970-6

Supplier	Total Value of Arms Supplies (US $ m[a])	Per Cent of Third World Total	Largest Recipient Regions	Region's Per Cent of Supplier's Total	Largest Recipient Country/ Countries in Each Region	Country's Per Cent of Supplier's Total
Israel[b]	174	24	Central America	35	El Salvador	15
			Far East	30	Singapore	19
			South Africa	20	South Africa	20
Iran	160	22	South Asia	75	Pakistan	75
			Middle East	22	Jordan	21
			Sub-Saharan Africa	2	Ethiopia	2
Jordan	159	22	South Africa	90	South Africa	90
			Middle East	10	Oman	10
			South Asia	0.2	Pakistan	0.2
Libya	77	11	Sub-Saharan Africa	97	Uganda	97
			South Asia	3	Pakistan	3
Brazil[b]	47	6	South America	98	Paraguay	42
			Sub-Saharan Africa	2	Togo	2
South Africa[b]	30	4	Sub-Saharan Africa	100	Rhodesia	98
					Malawi	2
Singapore	17	2	Far East	81	Brunei	51
			Middle East	19	Kuwait	19
Cuba	13	2	South America	100	Peru	100

Ivory Coast	10	1	Sub-Saharan Africa	100	Cameroon	100
India[b]	7	1	South Asia	100	Bangladesh	70
					Nepal	30
Iraq	6	1	Sub-Saharan Africa	100	Uganda	100
Gabon	6	1	Sub-Saharan Africa	100	Cameroon	100
Malaysia	5	1	Far East	100	Indonesia	100
Egypt	4	0.5	Sub-Saharan Africa	67	Nigeria	67
			North Africa	33	Libya	33
Abu Dhabi	4	0.5	Middle East	100	Oman	56
					Yemen	44
Argentina[b]	3.5	0.4	South America	100	Bolivia	55
					Peru	43
					Paraguay	2
Saudi Arabia	1	0.1	Middle East	58	Oman	50
			South Asia	42	Pakistan	42
Chile	0.5	0.1	South America	100	Ecuador	100
Third World total	724	100				

Notes: a. At constant 1975 prices.
b. Most weapons exported are of local production.

Table 13.3: Rank Order of Third World Arms Importers, 1970-6

Importing Region	Total Value of Arms Imports (US $ m[a])	Percentage of Third World Total	Six Largest Recipient Countries	Total Value of Country's Arms Imports (US $ m[a])	Percentage of Region's Total	Largest Supplier to Each Country	Percentage of Country's Total	Four Largest Suppliers per Region	Percentage of Region's Total
Middle East	16,484	51	Iran	4,900	30	USA	45	USA	46
			Egypt	2,864	17	USSR	89	USSR	38
			Israel	2,785	17	USA	97	UK	9
			Syria	2,595	16	USSR	99	France	4
			Iraq	1,122	7	USSR	97		
			Saudi Arabia	962	6	USA	70		
Far East, including Vietnam	5,434	17	S. Vietnam	1,475	27	USA	100	USA	62
			N. Vietnam	881	16	USSR	93	USSR	27
			S. Korea	662	12	USA	99	UK	3
			N. Korea	621	11	USSR	91	China	3
			Taiwan	424	8	USA	95		
			Thailand	262	5	USA	78		
South America	2,818	9	Brazil	612	22	USA	33	USA	29
			Argentina	510	18	UK	28	UK	24
			Venezuela	487	17	France	35	France	19
			Chile	455	16	UK	47	FR Germany	12
			Peru	355	13	USA	25		
			Ecuador	157	6	FR Germany	29		
North Africa	2,474	8	Libya	2,091	85	USSR	69	USSR	59
			Morocco	280	11	France	55	France	28
			Tunisia	54	2	France	94	USA	8
			Algeria	49	2	France	45	UK	2

South Asia	2,461	8	India	1,648	67	USSR	66	USSR	49
			Pakistan	675	27	China	36	UK	17
			Afghanistan	60	2	USSR	100	France	11
			Bangladesh	49	2	USSR	90	China	10
			Sri Lanka	17	1	UK	41		
			Nepal	13	1	UK	38		
Sub-Saharan Africa	1,536	5	Zaire	233	15	France	76	USSR	32
			Uganda	210	14	USSR	48	France	21
			Nigeria	157	10	USA	40	USA	11
			Mozambique	132	9	USSR	100	China	9
			Tanzania	107	7	China	79		
			Zambia	96	6	USSR	31		
South Africa	779	2	–	779	–	–	–	France	51
								Italy	19
								Jordan	18
								Israel	4
Central America	426	1	Cuba	168	39	USSR	100	USSR	39
			Mexico	138	32	UK	81	UK	29
			El Salvador	32	8	Israel	81	USA	16
			Guatemala	23	5	USA	61	Israel	14
			Panama	18	4	USA	22		
			Nicaragua	18	4	Israel	98		
Oceania	3	0.01	Fiji	3	100	USA	100	USA	100
Third World Total	32,427	100							

Note: a. At constant 1975 prices.

shipyards.

3 The Importer-Recipients

Data on the import of major arms by Third World regions and countries (see table 13.3) illustrate the impact of the two big conflicts after World War II, the Arab-Israeli conflict and the war in Vietnam. The Middle East region accounts for a total of 51 per cent of all major arms imports by the Third World during the 1970's. But within the region, the pattern of weapon imports has changed since around 1970. Up to then, those countries which were directly involved in the Arab-Israeli conflict were the leading importers, but by the latter half of the decade Israel and Egypt were overtaken by Iran. Iran is the single country with the largest arms imports in the region, as well as in the Third World, reaching 30 per cent of the total value for the Middle East during 1970-6.

The second-largest arms-importing Third World region is the Far East, where the impact of the Indo-China War is clearly visible in the arms trade data. The political dimension of arms supplies is also well illustrated by the two Korean nations: South Korea relies on the USA for 99 per cent of its major arms imports – a trend which is not likely to be reversed easily, as South Korea is investing more heavily in a local arms production capacity with US aid – and North Korea relies on the Soviet Union for 91 per cent of its major arms imports, the remainder being covered by China. North Korea is also putting much effort into achieving a local production capacity exclusively under Soviet licences.

In Latin America, the US position as the dominant arms supplier has been eroded in favour of the UK and France, and several large orders, particularly for submarines, have been placed with FR Germany. Venezuela, the region's 'oil state', has shown a sharp increase in arms imports during the past decade. Both Brazil and Argentina, the two largest importers in the region, also invest heavily in domestic arms industries.

The position of North Africa as the fourth region according to volume of arms imports is due to military build-up by Libya alone. Libya has turned to the Soviet Union for arms, while the other three countries remain customers of their former colonial power, France.

In South Asia, India stands out as the largest buyer, depending heavily on the Soviet Union. Pakistan has purchased most of its heavy equipment from China, but in future other suppliers will take a bigger share of the market – in particular France, with negotiations under way for a local production of the Mirage F-1.

In Sub-Saharan Africa, the two former colonial powers – the UK and France – dominated the arms trade market until the early 1970's. During the period 1970-6, the Soviet Union supplied 32 per cent of the region's arms imports, but this share is due mainly to large imports of fighter aircraft and tanks by Uganda, and to large supplies to Mozambique during 1976 alone.

For South Africa, the pattern of arms imports illustrates the effects of the 1963 embargo imposed by the United Nations. This meant that the UK, the former dominant supplier, fell back in favour of France and Italy, which have sold production licences for Mirage fighters and counter-insurgency aircraft. In reality the third-largest supplier to South Africa is Israel, which has sold missile-armed patrol boats.

Finally, in Central America, Cuba has since 1960 dominated arms imports, relying exclusively on the Soviet Union for its major arms. During the past three years Cuba has also begun to export arms: to Angola in connection with its military and manpower aid during the civil war, and to Peru in 1977 with the delivery of 12 ex-Cuban Air Force MiG-21s.

4 The Transfer of Technology

The transfer of arms includes also the transfer of know-how. The trend for Third World countries to import not only the weapons but also entire arms industries is rising, although for technical reasons more slowly than the rise shown in the figures of imports of weapons.

These two methods of acquiring arms – by importing, or by producing what is required – are chronologically interrelated: the most common pattern is to begin a military build-up or modernisation of the armed forces by means of importing the arms, the related support equipment, and training. Many underdeveloped countries stop short of trying to import the military technology as well, for obvious economic reasons. But another cluster of Third World nations has concentrated on achieving also a technological capacity, after having been acquainted with such post-World War II types of weaponry as jet combat aircraft, missile systems and fast patrol boats. The number of underdeveloped countries concentrating large economic resources on the build-up of local defence industries is increasing. Moreover, these efforts are continuing without the same type of international attention that recently has been paid to the direct sales of arms – for example, the huge imports by Persian Gulf states.

The acquisition of a local arms production capacity, or the import of technology or technological know-how, is normally a continuation of direct arms imports. But a local production capacity can in practice range from the mere assembly of import sub-systems to the indigenous research and development of a new weapon.

A typical chronological sequence in the build-up of, for example, an aircraft industry by means of licence production is to begin by setting up an overhaul and maintenance plant: then to start importing sub-assemblies of the plane and make the final assembly locally; then to import the components for the plane and make all of the assembly locally; then to manufacture also the components locally from imported raw materials; and finally to produce also the needed raw materials. This scheme theoretically ends with 100 per cent local manufacture of the licensed weapon. In practice, this is not so, as some vital components will always have to be imported – for example, aero engines and electronic and navigation equipment. There are also means of acquiring military technology other than by obtaining licences for local production. An entire production line can be purchased, as was the case when Israel got the production right of the Commodore Jet from the USA. Or the local production capacity may be held exclusively by foreign subsidiary enterprises, such as the Singapore Thorneycraft shipyard. It is also possible, provided that funds exist, for a Third World country to finance the research and development of the desired weapon in a technologically advanced country. This happened with South Africa's air defence system Cactus, which was developed by Dassault in France and up to 85 per cent financed by South Africa. Both Iran and Saudi Arabia finance certain weapons development in the USA.

Finally there is the method of 'copying'. China had acquired production licences for Soviet aircraft well before 1960. After the outbreak of the Sino-Soviet conflict, which meant the withdrawal of all Soviet aid to China, arms production was continued without formal licence agreements. The Chinese proceeded to make their own versions of the Mig-19, developed from the Soviet original, and also produced tank developments. There are other examples: Pakistan still produces the West German Cobra anti-tank missile although FRG formally withdrew the licence in 1965; the Israeli sub machine-gun Uzi has been in production in South Africa since 1961, when it was sub-licensed from Belgium, which was formally revoked after the 1963 UN arms embargo.

In addition to such means of starting arms production of foreign designs, several Third World countries also invest in creating a domestic research and development capability. The financial problems encountered are huge, even for such medium arms producers of Europe as France and the UK; they are multiplied in a developing country with an insufficient technological base and infrastructure. By tradition, both Argentina and Brazil have been engaged in aircraft design since the 1920's. Many projects have remained at the blueprint stage, either because of the unacceptable costs involved or because of unacceptable performance of the weapon, as compared to what is available for import from the leading arms-producing countries. Even if a new producer should succeed in developing a weapons system compatible with those from technologically advanced producers, the problems of marketing it in competition with weapons from well established producers are not easily overcome.

5 The Range of Motivations

The motivations for Third World countries to master military technology in general vary from country to country, but follow a distinct pattern all the same. *National security* is the most commonly evoked reason for the build-up of local arms industries, particularly in those Third World countries which during the last fifteen years have become leaders in this field – India, Israel, South Africa, Argentina, Brazil. They have all at some time experienced an arms embargo, either from their major supplier or from a group of major suppliers, and the decision to safeguard their political independence has followed almost automatically upon the imposition of the embargo.

The concepts of national security and political independence are of course not unique for Third World countries but are shared with smaller arms producers in the industrialised world. Sweden, for example, has emphasised the need for a neutral country to preserve its independence from foreign arms suppliers. The danger of dependence on foreign arms suppliers at a time of crisis can be summarised as implying the possibility of being cut off from suppliers altogether, or being cut off from the supply of spare parts and other related equipment, and thus becoming subject to a foreign political influence or blackmail, deemed unacceptable by a given national government. An illustration is Egypt's recent difficulties in obtaining new spare parts for its large stocks of Soviet weapons.

An indigenous arms industry may therefore help weaken a country's dependence on a foreign arms supplier.

While this combination of a military plus a political motivation is the most common argument at the national level, there are also *economic* arguments in favour of local arms industries. One is linked to the national security concept in so far as it is often claimed, by authorities responsible in this field, that local weapons production means budget savings. Further, it is maintained, through local arms production programme employment for a given number of workers is secured; and through large production runs, individual costs for the weapons are lowered. This is no axiom however – not in the industrialised world either – and the correctness of the argument varies with the type of weapon produced in connection with the export market for that weapon. There are very few Third World illustrations of a local arms project resulting in a net profit: the Israeli Uzi sub machine-gun which became accepted as a standard NATO arm is the exception rather that the rule. On the contrary, there are many instances of projects where costs have kept escalating far beyond quoted import prices for a comparable weapon. The reasons may be technological, but the problem is also due to the changed import structure – it is generally more expensive to purchase certain components rather than a complete weapon.

Other frequently stressed aspects of the economic argument are those related to the development issue in general and to the ongoing debate about development strategies. Advocates of local arms production capacity claim that, through the achievement of military technology, there will be spin-off effects for general economic development in a Third World country. The education and training of the labour force will also benefit the civilian sector, as will the infrastructure – e.g. the building of railroads, roads, or harbours for the needs of military industry. These ideas are open to dispute – which is obvious in connection with the general criticism of the Western approach to the development problems of the Third World and uncritical attempts after World War II to impose 'development models' unsuited to the real needs of developing countries. Technology in general is *not* automatically the most needed type of investment; the thesis that *military* technology in particular should be advantageous to civilian economic development becomes indeed hard to prove. There is a huge field of research concerning the development problems and strategies; and while there is still no consensus on how to tackle these problems, experiences in the Third World have at least shown by now that there is no simplistic solution or clear-cut way to transfer the experiences of Europe and North America to the Third World. 'Present-day technology is mainly a product of economies that have a scarcity of labor and a relative abundance of capital, and therefore tends to be labor-saving and capital-intensive,' says one economic expert on development issues.[5] We may add that present-day *military* technology is also a product of advanced economies, whereas the general poverty pattern of the underdeveloped world includes the lack of capital, the lack of skilled labour, and the existence of large and continually increasing underemployed labour.[6]

In contrast to this general pattern for Third World countries, there are some exceptions: those Third World countries which have important raw material deposits such as oil, uranium, steel or titanium. The economic argument is better applied here, since it is linked to a particular aspect of economic development, the trade pattern: Instead of merely exporting raw materials and importing manufactured goods, the country can develop a manufacturing capability; this applies also to the manufacturing of military hardware as a part of a larger development of the economy. The oil-rich countries in particular have been the focus of attention since 1973 as 'rich and underdeveloped', implying that they possess at least the capital required for whatever investment is wanted. But other countries, like South Africa (which possesses large resources of various minerals) also fit into this group – the past decade has shown a development away from a raw material supplier and towards an export capacity of a range of manufactured goods, including certain types of weapons.

6 Costs of Militarisation

The militarisation of the Third World is enhanced by the import of military technology, as a follow-up of the import of sophisticated arms. This military build-up must be analysed in its proper context and with the right proportions. The resources devoted to military purposes in the Third World in the form of R&D and military expenditures are a fraction of the investments by the leading industrialised countries: in 1975 total world military expenditure was estimated to be $280 billion at current prices. The percentage distribution shows that the USA, USSR and the other NATO and WTO countries answer for 78.1 per cent, while the share of the approximately 100 Third World countries is but 12.3 per cent.[7]

However, the rate of increase is higher for the Third World. While the world total figure is 2.6 per cent, the average annual change for the Third World is 10.3 per cent.[8] Military expenditure measures in percentage of gross national production shows an interesting development. From 1965 to 1974 the developed countries' military expenditure as share of GNP has declined from 7.22 per cent to 5.77 per cent, while the underdeveloped world's share has risen from 4.36 per cent to 5.33 per cent.[9]

Thus, in an analysis of the militarisation of the Third World, the following specific matters have to be taken into account. It remains true that the major powers – the USA and the Soviet Union – are the leading powers in the field of weapons development, followed by the West European producers Britain and France and a group of countries with expanding arms industries, such as Italy, FR Germany, Belgium, Sweden, Switzerland, as well as Israel in the Third World. But the investment in military capacity in the Third World must be connected to the problems of underdevelopment: in which case, it is reasonable to question whether the import of military technology contributes at all to general economic development. Such a 'spin-off' effect is claimed by those with an interest in the military build-up – politicians, industrialists, arms exports, etc. – as a somewhat paradoxical justification for this type of investment, since it surely ought to suffice to claim that a nation's political and military security demands such investment. There is an inherent logical confusion in the argumentation for military technology as an aid to civilian developments: it is true that the rapid technological development of conventional armaments, which began during World War II and continues to date, has meant that the government's R&D resources were directed primarily to the field of military science, from which certain parts have been transferred to the civilian field (for example, within aeronautics and computer technology), in the industrialised world. However, this was the result of combined political and military choices, and not an automatically neccesary development.

There exist rather more substantial arguments *against* the overall economic use for military technology in smaller producing countries: recently the Swedish government has, for economic reasons, recommended the Saab aircraft construction division to abstain from designing any new aircraft after Viggen and instead take up licence production of a foreign design. This will not affect the employment of the work-force as such except for 1,500 highly qualified and specialised designers and technicians. Saab's counter-arguments was that this qualified expertise cannot be used for any other purpose than the construction of combat aircraft: in other words, their technical skills are entirely unusable in the civilian sector.

The resources allocated for military purposes, including investments in local arms industries, the most expensive effort in this field – compared to other efforts such as the import of arms or expansion of armed forces – are necessarily denied other avenues of public and private expenditure. In this way, the distribution of budgetary means is a zero-sum game. For an underdeveloped country, like India, to spend 3 per cent of its GNP on defence literally means depriving the civilian economy of scarce resources.[10]

Notes

1. For the sake of convenience, SIPRI has adopted the originally journalistic concept of the 'Third World' as meaning all countries except Europe, North America, Japan, Australia and the developed Communist countries, including China. In practice, the 'Third World' concept covers the underdeveloped world, but there are some exceptions like South Africa and Israel. This is a different concept from the 'metropolitan periphery' division of countries, since socialist countries outside Europe are also included.

2. J. Nyerere, 'The Devil's Flunkey', *Far Eastern Economic Review*, 30 January 1971.

3. If the production and export of *small arms* were taken into account, both Argentina and India would occupy a higher place in the rank order.

4. With regard to the small suppliers listed in Table 13.1 above, one aspect should be kept in mind – if *small arms* were included in the data, this would mean a change upwards in the position of such leading small arms producers as Sweden, Switzerland and Belgium.

5. Gunnar Myrdal, *Asian Drama* (Pantheon, New York, 1968), vol. 1, p. 693.

6. The problems connected with the transfer of technology in general, quite apart from the even more intricate problem of transferring military technology, are illustrated in the following statements by Everett E. Hagen:

> every Western industry depends for its efficiency on other industries. It assumes the ready availability of materials, components, and tools. It depends also on auxiliary enterprises which can provide technical, financial and managerial services on demand; on a complex network of communication and transportation facilities; and on an intricate system of business practices.
> A Western economy is a technical (and cultural) complex, not a set of isolated pieces of technology. In an underdeveloped society the auxiliary industries are missing and the framework of business practices is different. *One piece cannot be detached from the complex and used efficiently elsewhere without skillful adaptation* (E.E. Hagen, *On the Theory of Social Change, How Economic Growth Begins* (The Dorsey Press, Cambridge, Mass., 1962), p. 31; author's italics).

7. *SIPRI Yearbook 1976*, p. 128.

8. Ibid.

9. US Arms Control and Disarmament Agency, *World Military Expenditures and Arms Transfers 1965–1974* (Washington D.C., 1976), p. 14.

10. International Institute for Strategic Studies, *Military Balance 1976/1977* (London, 1976), p. 79.

14 ARMS TRANSFER AND DEPENDENCY IN THE THIRD WORLD

Miles D. Wolpin

The effects of arms transfer upon dependency relationships are conditioned by the developmental strategy pursued and the origin of the weapons systems. After analysing the socio-economic implications and politico-military sources of dependency, three development strategies are considered: monopoly capitalist; state capitalist; and state socialist. Six hypotheses are then presented. All are premissed upon a fundamental assumption: that in so far as arms transfers are associated with Western training and aid programmes, they operate to impede rather than promote economic and socio-cultural development.

The global rise in arms transfers among nations during the past decade or so has been particularly pronounced for the Third World nations of Africa, Latin America, the Middle East and Asia. In general, it can be said that most such transfers originate in or are licensed by the industrialised nations of the First (open-door capitalist) or Second (state socialist) Worlds of development. Equally apparent has been the association of such transfers with a process of militarisation in the recipient states. Although not true in every case, there has on the average been an increase over the period in governmental resources allocated to military-related purposes, including concomitant external debt service and repayment obligations.[1]

If the foregoing relationships are fairly well established, others evoke considerable disagreement among both academics and attentive publics. In the following paragraphs, I intend to explore linkages between such arms transfers and 'dependency' – a term which over the past fifteen years has come into wide use in depicting North/South relationships that are commonly viewed as inimical to national sovereignty and socio-economic development. First, I shall distinguish the structureal characteristics of economic dependency from its historico-political sources. Then, a number of socio-economic and cultural consequences will be examined. Finally, I shall elaborate a series of propositions relating distinct arms transfer patterns to the efforts by Third World elites to diminish or reinforce such dependency relationships.

1 Dependency as a Structural Relationship of World Capitalism

Although development and international relations theorists who have addressed themselves to the concept of dependency are by no means unanimous as to the scope of relationships to which it refers or, for that matter, to the most appropriate means for transcending them, this is one of the few areas where some measure of agreement can be found between a number of Marxists and non-Marxists. One of the more cogently stated Marxian conceptualisations of dependency within a systemic context has been provided by Theotonio dos Santos, an exiled Brazilian development theorist:

> Dependence is a situation in which a certain group of countries have their economy conditioned by the development and expansion of another economy, to which the former is subject. The relation of interdependence between two or more economies, and between these and world trade, assumes the form of dependence when some countries (the dominant) can expand and give impulse to their own development, while other countries (the dependent) can only develop as a reflection of this expansion. This can have positive and/or negative effects on their immediate development. In all cases, the basic situation of dependence leads to a global situation in dependent countries that situates them in backwardness and under the exploitation of the dominant countries. The dominant countries have a technological, commercial, capital resource, and social-political predominance over the dependent countries (with predominance of some of these aspects in various historical moments). This permits them to impose conditions of exploitation and to extract part of the domestically produced surplus.[2]

While dos Santos and other Marxists such an Andre Gunder Frank and Dale Johnson identify politico-military hegemony as the source of such dependency, they treat the accomplished phenomenon as an integrated and self-reinforcing system in which the consequential economic subordination is reflected in socio-cultural areas that for the most part tend to mirror or reinforce the political subservience of the states in question.[3] Though emphasising such a web of affected internal relationships, Frank, in the following passage, also admits what we call dysfunctional consequences.

> dependence is the result of the historical development and contemporary structure of world capitalism, to which Latin America

> is subordinated, and the economic, political, social, and cultural policies generated by the resulting class structure, especially by the class interests of the dominant bourgeoisie. It is important to understand, therefore, that throughout the historical process, dependence is not simply an 'external' relation between Latin America and its world capitalist metropolis but equally an 'internal' indeed *integral* condition of . . . society itself, which is reflected not only in international and domestic economics and politics but also has the most profound and far-reaching ideological and psychological manifestations of inferiority complexes and assimilation of metropolitan ideology and 'development' theory. At the same time, this dependence generates reactions which are visible through nationalism, the growing class struggle against the capitalist system.[4]

Thus we can summarise the elements of dependency in the modern era as historically conditioned structural or institutional relationships that are hierarchical in terms of both resources and benefits. Further, these extend beyond the economic realm into political, social and cultural areas within the dependent societies. And finally, the exploitative character or content of such economic relationships generates its own antithesis in nationalist and socialist struggles for liberation.

Notwithstanding the tendency of non-Marxists to de-emphasise the unequal character of such relationships which at times are depicted as a natural evolutionary division of labour, some theorists, such as K.J. Holsti, have gone so far as to posit not only dependency's asymmetrical character but also acknowledge its mutually reinforcing attributes as well.

> Dependence characterizes the relations between the developing countries and the industrial West, where dependence is defined as unequal degrees of reliance on markets and sources of supply, and unequal ability of the members of a pair of states to influence, reward, or harm each other. Although there are some notable exceptions, such as the oil-producing countries, the actions or policies developing states undertake have little impact on the political or economic fortunes of industrialized states, even small ones. The policies of an industrialized state, on the other hand, often have significant consequences on a developing country; and any attempt to alter drastically or terminate the relationship is extremely costly to the latter, and less so the former . . . Dependence and interdependence are obviously relative concepts, or different ends of a

> continuum. State A can be dependent on B, but interdependent with C, and virtually irrelevant to D. Likewise, A can be economically dependent upon B, but militarily dependent upon C. Singer argues, however, that the various dimensions of dependence correlate highly with each other: If A is dependent in one dimension, it is likely to be dependent in all dimensions.[5]

Hence it may be hypothesised that once political hegemony is established and used to structure a subordinate economic relationship, other societal areas become similarly dependent. This, however, does not affect the entire institutional panoply but only certain aspects of the economic, socio-cultural and even the political subsystems. Thus, as Sunkel and Fuenzalida have noted, 'a process of *disintegration*' occurs in dependent societies:

> Parts of the bourgeoisie, of the petty bourgeoisie, of the industrial working class, etc., are integrated into the transnational system while other parts are not . . . This is most obvious in its effect on the economy – the setting off of a process of internal polarization, involving the expropriation of local entrepreneurial groups, the disruption of indigenous economic activities, and the concentration of property and income. But disintegration is also discernible in other organized social activities, such as scientific research, architecture, and urban/regional planning, medicine, education, the arts, and at a cultural/personal level . . . The result of these contradictory trends has been an aggravation of internal polarization – increasing poverty and unemployment of the majority and growing affluence of a minority – and foreign dependence – the structural interlocking of the minority into transnational capitalism. The political tensions arising out of these phenomena may well be among the most important causes of the growing number of repressive and authoritarian regimes that nowadays characterize the Third World, and of their strong nationalist reactions towards the industrialized countries.[6]

This notwithstanding the 'unprecedented process of economic growth, industrialization and modernization' catalysed by external economic penetration and investment.

In sum, then, dependency is not limited to external relationship but involves consequential domestic restructuring and antagonistic patterns of reactive nationalism. The appeal of such nationalism is enhanced by downturns in economic growth in a context of rising external debt burdens. And if contemporary national liberation struggles signify one important response to neo-colonialism, then as Joseph Kahl has argued, dependency theory itself can be viewed as 'the weak man's answer to imperialism. It was imperialism as seen from the bottom looking up and suggested that if the process could be better understood it might be mastered'.[7]

2 Politico-Military Sources of Dependency

Notwithstanding the systemic reinforcing character of dependency, analytical clarity may be enhanced by distinguishing its historical politico-military sources from consequential structural relationships. The causal significance of such hegemony has been pointed up by the Marxists dos Santos, Johnson and Gunder Frank, as it has in a more indirect manner by the non-Marxist Fernando Henrique Cardoso, who stresses the primacy of the political in both its causal and reactive dimensions:

> to explain economic processes in terms of social processes requires us to find a theoretical point of intersection *where economic power is expressed as social domination, that is in politics. Through the political process, one class or economic group tries to* establish a system of social relations that will permit it to impose its view on the whole society, or at least it tries to establish alliances to ensure economic policies compatible with its own interests and objectives. Thus, we will emphasize the following: the economic conditions of the world market, including the internal equilibrium of power; the structure of the national productive system and its links with the external market; the forms of distribution and maintenance of national power; and *above all the sociopolitical movements and processes pushing toward change, with their various orientations and objectives.*[8]

Hence, in the remainder of this chapter I shall discuss separately its military or neo-colonial sources, arms transfer patterns, and the relevance of the latter to national struggles for self-determination and development.

It seems clear that the historical origins of socio-economic dependency are traceable to imperial conquest by Britain, France, Spain and several other powers that carved out smaller empires between the fifteenth and twentieth centuries. Although the forms of empire varied somewhat, as did the circumstances and initial goals of conquest, the socio-economic outcomes were quite similar, with the exception of a handful of settler colonies. Thus dual patterns of raw materials production and export dependence were imposed, while manufacturing was stifled so that narrow markets for such products could be monopolised by the colonial power. In the process indigenous paramilitary forces were organised to stabilise such a social order while minuscule local elites were tied to it by being accorded positions and limited socio-economic privileges. Although the administrative centre and a small number of economic enclaves were modernised, the remainder of the colonial territories were only marginally and occasionally affected. Consequently, social stagnation characterised a large domain within these societies, as did what Pablo Gonzalez Casanova has depicted in the Mexican setting as 'internal colonialism', wherein politically hegemonic elements in the modernised 'centre' extracted surplus labour from hinterland areas.[9]

Such patterns persisted in Latin America when Spain's weakness during the Napoleonic era enabled independence movements backed by indigenous land-owning and comprador classes to establish formally sovereign states. Benefits flowing to these classes from the prevailing free trade system integrated them to such a degree that external military reinforcement was readily solicited or acquiesced in when domestic nationalist or lower-class movements threatened the social order's stability. Such 'free trade imperialism', or neo-colonialism, involved the use of force, loans, military training missions, informal cultural exchange and of course crass bribery at one time or another. While Britain played the dominant role during most of the nineteenth century, France, Germany and the United States (especially in the Caribbean region) were also quite active in furthering investor interests.

It can be said without excessive licence that analogous patterns appeared in the twentieth century as 'new nations' emerged in Asia, Africa and the Middle East. Traditional colonial powers were defeated or weakened by war while emergent socialist and trade union movements infused a new element into the politics of many new states. The United States and other neo-colonial powers responded to the challenge directed against what was now euphemistically called the 'open door' by *institutionalising* a broad range of inputs either to destabilise, influence or strengthen Third World regimes. The primary focus of these programmes was Latin America, but gradually increasing emphasis was placed upon other underdeveloped regions. They include not only military and economic aid injections but systematised cultural exchange, propaganda diffusion, covert activities, etc.[10]

Worth some emphasis is that these inputs are anything but neutral with respect to recipient developmental strategies. The United States, and less uniformly other Western programmes, mobilise bias in favour of regimes willing to follow an 'open door' approach at the minimum, and optimally a corporate subsidisation or privilege conferral role by the state. While some specific projects may not appear to carry such ideological baggage, the context and associated programme customarily reveal such a framework of assumptions, beliefs and attitudes.

This obviously also holds for various sorts of injections which have been associated with aid and cultural exchange programmes of Communist or state socialist systems. Their minimum objectives are an end to pro-Western foreign policy alignment and pursuit of an economic development strategy which may be characterised as at least a 'partly closed door'. This may be depicted as a state capitalist developmental strategy in which the state directs the economy and exercises control or dominates the major means of production. While at this historical juncture it is problematic that such a development strategy can fully end structural dependency upon major capitalist powers, the mere existence of major Eastern aid donors and trade possibilities tends to broaden options and thereby diminish the degree of dependency.

State socialist systems appear to be the only regime type that has been able to eradicate such dependency and grow rapidly enough to begin even slowly to close the *per capita* GDP gap with the advanced capitalist societies.[11] With the possible exception of revolutionary Cuba, however, no state capitalist regime has as a consequence of intra-elite conflict been transformed into a state socialist system.[12] While the latter have usually been consequential to Communist-led revolutionary struggles involving guerrilla and/or internal war, the most common fate of the state capitalist system is to experience a rightist 'open door' *coup*. Although the new elite usually retains some of the socially owned sector, it nevertheless curtails or reverses many of the leftist policies that characterised the deposed regime. Cuba is the exception which may or may not prove the rule. For less than two decades of experience lie behind us and it is quite conceivable that, if others follow Fidel's leadership strategy, additional socialist 'revolutions from above' may be effectuated. This is not to minimize the difficulties – rather to stress the fact that alternative futures do in fact exist. As the aid programmes of existing state socialist systems grow along with their cultural and other infusions, a reinforcing external environment for such transformations will gradually develop in the eighties and nineties. Hence the maximal objectives of state socialist donors may be attained in some cases.

One of the newer developments associated with neo-colonial objectives is what has been called the 'low profile' or 'sub-imperialism'. In so far as our interests are concerned, this refers to arms transfers by proxy countries. While in some instances they or their components may be of indigenous manufacture, the exports are customarily assembled or previously imported weapons systems. Egypt, India, Israel and Brazil are four Western countries that have upon occasion engaged in such activities, while Czechoslavakia and the German Democratic Republic have done so for the USSR.

Although some arms transfers – particularly commercial ones that have been in use for some time – involve little political significance aside from their reinforcement of a particular regime's coercive resources, those which include training and advisory support have ideological and intelligence effects.[13] It is not simpy the training in how to handle specific weapons, but the hospitality programme, guided tours and less subtle ideological exposure that accompanies US and other training of foreign officers. In the former case at least, follow-up is handled by military intelligence which in turn co-operates with the CIA. The efficacy of such indoctrination is greatest among those who have done repeated training tours, and for armed forces with the highest proportion of officers who have been exposed to such external socialisation.[14]

3 Patterns of Arms Transfers

Before elaborating a series of propositions that conclude this chapter, it might be useful to distinguish several patterns of arms transfers. The following list indicates the range of possibilities:

one dominant Western supplier;
multiple Western suppliers;
ideologically diversified suppliers;
one dominant Eastern supplier;
multiple Eastern suppliers;
marginal/occasional suppliers.

One factor of considerable importance is of course the technological and organisational capabilities of Third World nations. Politico-military hegemony is accentuated by low recipient capability levels as they tend to increase reliance upon external training and advisory programmes.

4 Propositions on Arms Transfers and Dependency

The following propositions are offered primarily for heuristic purposes. Whilse precise measurement may be quite difficult in some instances, in others the associational patterns can more readily be tested.

(1) *The progression of arms transfer patterns ((a)-(f)) listed in the preceding section is directly associated with the minimisation of dependency*. As noted in an earlier section, the intervening variables are the ancillary training and advisory programmes. These in turn are related to the second proposition.

(2) *The extent of dependency is a function of the degree of politico-military domination*. If, as I and others have argued, the source of socio-economic and cultural dependency is politico-military hegemony, then it follows that political independence is the key to transforming such structural relationships. In the West this implies struggles by radical nationalist and socialist liberation movements – both objects of destabilisation programmes by US military training and covert action agencies.

(3) *The sources of dependency may vary in different epochs*. Direct military conquest played a central role *in the establishment* of colonial empires, while intermittent force in conjunction with economic and cultural intrusions have assumed primary importance in the contemporary neo-colonial era. During the past decade or so similar resources have been employed through third party proxies and what has been called the 'low profile'. Direct intrusions continue to be utilised occasionally.

(4) *The rapidly growing sophistication of modern weapons is an obstacle to the minimisation of dependency*. It is obvious that the inability of many Third World countries to master modern technological and organisational skills has forced weapons recipients to solicit external training and advisory groups. Even the 'transitional', less underdeveloped Third World societies fail to escape this situation because of an escalation of aspirations for the most complex weapons systems.

(5) *Militarisation in the Third World over recent decades has made it more difficult for monopoly capitalist and state capitalist systems to decrease their dependency upon Western neo-colinial powers*. The sharp rise in military expenditure has led not only to increased imports and concomitant training programmes, but also to skyrocketing external debt burdens and to the destabilisation of many state capitalist oriented radical regimes. The latter have included Brazil, Indonesia, Ghana, Mali, Cambodia, Bolivia, Uganda, Egypt, China and Peru.[15]

(6) *State socialism has enabled countries to reduce their dependency and indirectly to have such effects by furthering the diffusion of state capitalism as well as socialism*. The mobilisational capabilities of most new state socialist systems and their Eastern orientation enable them to alter and redirect economic relationships with traditional Western powers and associated economic institutions. This is not to say that some existing links are not maintained and new ones developed. Cuba, because of the state capitalist top-down origins of her socialism, has encountered considerable difficulties in efficiently utilising volunteer labour. Nevertheless, she is following other new Communist-governed countries in developing a spirit of self-reliance, planned economic development and a broad diversification of trading partners. The existence, performance and diffusion of socialist systems in the present century has not only radicalised the consciousness of elite sectors elsewhere in the Third World, but has given them sufficient international room for manoeuvre to allow a real chance for survival during the initial period of radical regime establishment.[16] If most such systems are socialist in name only, they nevertheless represent a marked departure from the monopoly capitalist variant.[17]

Because of our range of historical vision is often circumscribed by the exigencies of the present it can be difficult to see the movement towards the left that has been occurring during this century.[18] Despite the reversals and obvious shortcomings of both state capitalist and socialist systems, these regime variants contribute to the slow weakening of world capitalism and its exploitative structural relationships. Capitalism as a world system may be far from dead, but there is little basis for doubting that with the consolidation of the Bolshevik Revolution it began a long period of secular decline.

Notes

1. The increase in Third World military expenditures from less than 25 billion to more than 50 billion (1965-74) in constant dollars represents a *potential* loss of developmental resources. So does the rise in largely unproductive armed forces from 11.2 million men to 15.6 million during the same period. *Per capita* military expenditures have increased from $10.25 (constant) to $16.84, while the countries have become more heavily militarised as armed forces manpower ratios have risen from 4.7 to 5.3 per thousand. Third World arms imports between 1965 and 1974 rose from $2,139,000,000 to $6,629,000,000 (current dollars) while their exports increased from only $235,000,000 to $463,000,000. Little over a third of the increased imports were accounted for by OPEC members. As used here, 'arms imports' include, but are not limited to, equipment for arms production. See US Arms Control and Disarmament Agency, *World Military Expenditures*

and Arms Transfers: 1965-1974 (Government Printing Office, Washington, D.C., 1976).

2. 'La crisis de la teoria del desarrollo y las relaciones de dependencia en America Latina' (Santiago: *Boletin del Centro de Estudios Socio-Economicos*, no. 3 (1968), University de Chile, pp. 26-7), as quoted by Dale L. Johnson, 'Dependence and the International System' in James D. Cockcroft, Andre Gunder Frank and Dale L. Johnson (eds.), *Dependence and Underdevelopment* (Doubleday-Anchor, Garden City, N.Y., 1972), pp. 71-2.

With respect to dos Santos' references to 'exploitation' and surplus extraction, the following is instructive:

> Between 1950 and 1966 . . . corporations and private citizens brought into the country $59.0 billion in excess of all private dollar outflows . . . direct investments have returned substantial income to their companies in the United States, far greater than the direct investment outflows; . . . from 1950 to 1966 these investments returned in dividends and royalties and fees alone $20 billion in excess of all outflows . . . Recently Professor Behrman argued before the Joint Economic Committee that the payback period for outflows of U.S. dollars for manufacturing investment abroad is about 2½ years on the average. If this is right – and I must say, this estimate comes close to my own experience – this is a very short term indeed (from a speech by John J. Powers, Jr., President of Charles Pfizer and Co., delivered at an American Management Association special briefing on 'New Foreign Investment Controls', in New York City on 10 April 1968, reprinted in the *NACLA Newsletter*, no. 2 (November 1968), pp. 8-10).

Cf. Wendell C. Gordon, 'Has Foreign Aid Been Overstated? International Aid and Development', *Inter-American Economic Affairs*, no. 21 (Spring 1968), pp. 3-18.

3. Thus Johnson acknowledges that 'the combined economic and military power of the imperial countries became instrumental in keeping Latin America nations as *de facto* colonies.' And he goes on to argue:

> Dependence relations also shape the social structure of underdevelopment. A principal factor in the development and perpetuation of underdevelopment was (and is) the coincidence of interest between national oligarchies and the economic structure of underdeverlopment. National businessmen grew up with and benefited from their nations' position as *de facto* colonies . . . (in Cockcroft, Frank, and Johnson, *Dependence and Underdevelopment*, p. 73).

4. 'Economic Dependence, Class Structure and Underdevelopment Policy' in Cockcroft, Frank and Johnson, *Dependence and Underdevelopment* pp. 19-20.

5. *International Politics: A Framework for Analysis* (Prentice-Hall, Englewood Cliffs, N.J., 1977), pp. 89, 91.

6. Osvaldo Sunkel and Edmundo Fuenzalida, 'An Interdisciplinary Research Programme on the Transnationalization of Capitalism and National Development', *Institute for Developing Studies*, November 1976, pp. 3-8.

7. *Modernization, Exploitation and Dependency in Latin America* (Transaction Books, New Brunswick, N.J., 1976), p. 187.

8. Ibid., pp. 156-7.

9. *Democracy in Mexico* (Oxford University Press, New York, 1970).

10. These processes are examined in my *Cuban Foreign Policy and Chilean Politics* (Heath, Lexington, Mass., 1972), pp. 61-96, and *Military Aid and Counterrevolution in the Third World* (Heath, Lexington, Mass., 1973).

11. According to the source cited in note 1 above, the average *per capita* GNP

gap between the advanced capitalist countries and the Third World widened from $2,676 to $3,670 between 1965 and 1974. Similarly, a UN source covering a somewhat larger span acknowledge an 'increasing economic "gap" between the advanced capitalist societies and most of those in the Third World. Between 1960 and 1973, the average annual rate of *per capita* GNP increased by 4 per cent in developed countries, and 3.3 per cent in underdeveloped areas. Even 'at a rate of growth of 3.5 percent, average income per person in the developng world would rise from the 1970 level of $200 to the level of only around $280 (in 1970 prices) by 1980'. The average *per capita* GNP growth rate for the 1960s in the state socialist category (excluding the GDR, USSR and SCR) was 5.3 per cent. See UN Department of Economic and Social Affairs, *Disarmament and Development: Report of the Group of Experts on the Economic and Social Consequences of Disarmament* (UN, New York, 1972), p. 13; UN, Department of Economic and Social Affairs, *World Economic Survey, 1974* (UN, New York, 1974).

12. Three regime types are referred to in this chapter. Under the 'open door' or monopoly capitalist variant, the primary socio-economic role of political elites is to promote the profitability of the private corporate sector. Because the latter tends to be dominated by transnational corporations in most Third World countries, so long as indigenous officials acquiesce in such relations their domestic and even foreign policy choices tend to depend upon favourable reactions by such corporations and associated international financial institutions. Hence, 'dependency' may be viewed as the reciprocal of monoply capitalist in the Third World. State capitalist or 'radical' regimes often attempt to radically reduce dependency by transferring major economic resources to national, usually state, control, promoting industrialisation and by diversifying economic relations toward the East. In state socialist systems the residual private sector is being reduced rather than tolerated as legitimate. It is considerably more restricted and customarily limited to small-scale undertakings. Ruled by a Marxist-Leninist political class, their developmental strategy is distinguished by a collectivist accumulation process, a cadre party system which effectively mobilises mass participation and initiative, a democratic and egalitarian ideology, and a pattern of institutional military subordination. Many societies are obviously on a continuum, and neither linearity of movement nor stability of position are ubiquitous. In short, state socialist systems (Yugoslavia) may move in the direction of state capitalism, while revolutionary elites which take over monopoly capitalist systems (China) can virtually telescope the state capitalist phase by moving quickly towards state socialism.

13. A recent State Department policy release notes that

> U.S. arms are transferred in several ways, including grant aid under the Military Assistance Progam (MAP), now a small part of total transfer; commercial sales – about 10% of the total; and government-to-government Foreign Military Sales (FMS), on a cash or credit basis, which account for most transfers . . . The LDCs . . . are buying foreign arms at a rate faster than any other group of nations, and about two-thirds of global exports go to them.

The United States account for approximately half of world arms exports and the Soviet Union for another 25 per cent. US Department of State, Bureau of Public Affairs, *GIST* (November 1977), quoted in *New York Times*, 5 December 1977.

14. See my *Military Aid and Counterrevolution in the Third World* (Heath, Lexington, Mass., 1973).

15. See my 'Contemporary Radical Third World Regimes: Prospects for Their Survival', a paper presented before the 1977 annual meeting of the American Political Science Association, Washington, D.C. Cf. Richard J. Barnet, *Intervention and Revolution* (World, New York, 1968).

16. In her *Revolution from Above: Military Bureaucrats and Development in Japan, Turkey, Egypt and Peru* (Transaction Books, New Brunswick, N.J., 1977), Ellen Kay Trimberger places considerable stress upon the existence of the following four pre-conditions: (a) social isolation of the officers from a formerly hegemonic but declining property-owning (landed) upper class; (b) a centralised state bureaucratic apparatus isolated in some measure from close social interaction with such a class; (c) propaganda by an indigenous nationalist movement; and (d) international room for manoeuvre.

17. Not only in the extension of public ownership or control over the means of production, but also in the area of egalitarian social reforms. For a summation of such measures by the radical regimes of Mossadegh, Arbenz, Bosch, Goulart, Sukarno, Nkrumah, Keita, Sihanouk, Torres and Allende, see: Miles D. Wolpin, 'Civilian Reformers vs the Military: A Profile of Failure', *Journal of Peace Research*, no. 3 (1978).

18. In the 1960-74 period alone, a UN report on nationalisations and takeovers recorded 875 cases in 62 countries of the world – predominantly in the underdeveloped areas. Africa accounted for 340 of them and 'led in all categories of industry except petroleum – that is, in instances of nationalization of mining, agriculture, manufacturing, trade, public utilities, banking and insurance'. Thus a contemporary analyst of this trend in Africa concludes with the following prediction:

> The pattern of takeovers during the last decade in black Africa, as well as that in the rest of the world, suggests very strongly that they will continue to nationalize and indigenise enterprises whenever they believe it will serve their own interests. The only limitations will be practical ones . . . [as] the growing strength of the natural resources blocs such as O.P.E.C., the spread of socialism, and the increased acceptance of nationalization vastly improve the bargaining position of the nationalizing countries (Leslie L. Rood, 'Nationalization and Indigenisation in Africa', *Journal of Modern African Studies*, no. 14. (September 1976), pp. 427-47).

Data on nationalisation are cited from UN Secretary-General, *Permanent Sovereignty Over Natural Resources*, A/9716, Supplement to E/5425, Annex (UN, New York, 1974), p. 1.

15 LOCAL WARS 1945-76*

Istvan Kende

1 War in Our Time

We define war as any armed conflict in which all of the following criteria obtain:

(1) activities of regular armed forces (military, police forces, etc.) at least on one side – that is, the presence and engagement of the armed forces of the government in power;
(2) a certain degree of organisation and organised fighting on both opposing sides, even if this organisation extends to organised defence only;
(3) a certain continuity between the armed clashes, however sporadic. Centrally organised guerrilla forces are also regarded as making war, in so far as their activities extend over a considerable part of the country concerned.

In the 32 years concerned, a total of 120 armed conflicts qualified by this definition as wars. (The full list is given in the Appendix.) The 120 wars were waged on the territories of 71 countries. If we include all countries which have taken active part through their armed forces in these wars, we find that 84 countries were involved.

During the past ten years, the disperson of wars was greater than before. While the 120 wars were fought on the territory of only 71 countries, in the last 10 years the number of countries was almost the same as the number of wars (49 wars on the territories of 46 countries). Eighty-four countries were involved in the 120 wars – a ratio of 84/120 = 0.70. For the last ten years, this ratio was much higher: 60/49 = 1.22. This indicates that relatively more countries have become involved in the wars of the past ten years than in the previous period. On the other hand, fewer countries were the theatres of several successive wars. In addition, it is an essential feature that missing from the list of seats of war are such important countries as China, both parts of Korea, Indonesia, the Dominican Republic, Cuba and Algeria, which formerly were the seats of considerable wars. The last two, however, were

*Reprinted from *Journal of Peace Research*, vol. XV, no. 3 (1978); this paper followed the article 'Twenty-five Years of Local Wars', *Journal of Peace Research*, vol. VIII, no. 1 (1971).

involved in these ten years in wars fought on the territories of other countries.

In this present paper we examine the situation up to the end of 1976. However, 1977 was not a particularly warless year either. Of the wars stated earlier, eight continued in 1977 and spread into 1978. In the order given in the list in the Appendix, these are as follows: the Burmese war which according to certain sources continued to spread in 1977,[1] the Ethiopian war which spread from the Eritrean arena – and grew into a parallel war – to the arena of Ogaden, involving the Somalian ethnic group and also armed forces of Somalia. The war in Oman (Dhofar) continued: though the considerable number of Iranian troops fighting in support of the Oman government were withdrawn, the Iranian air force continued to reconnoitre above the war theatres.[2] The guerrilla war in Thailand and the war of independence in Zimbabwe/Rhodesia continued to intensify. The guerrilla war in Northern Ireland continues in more or less the same way. Despite contradictory reports, fighting went on in East Timor, where the number of deaths are variously estimated at 10,000 to 100,000, an unprecedently high number, considering that the total population of the area is about 670,000. Geographically the theatre of war grew in the Western Sahara, from where operations spread to the territory of Mauritania.

The picture we have of the Philippines is full of contradictions. Although armistice was signed at the end of 1976, that agreement was short-lived and that in 1977 armed conflict broke out again. There was a short war, though accompanied by considerable tension, in Zaire in 1977.[3] This was the only war to end in 1977; all the others continued in 1978. In addition, reports have arrived from a number of places on sporadic or repeated armed conflicts, on renewed guerrilla (and anti-guerrilla) actions, frontier incidents, often a succession of them. It seems, however, that none of the armed actions grew into such a regular nature as to comply with the above criteria to be declared wars, though the possibility cannot be excluded that the incidents on one or another territory might spread and develop into a true war. (Since the author completed his study in 1978, a number of additional wars have taken place which are not included in his figures and, hence, not in his analysis. These include, in particular, wars between Communist countries: Vietnam/Kampuchea, Vietnam/China, and the Soviet Union's intervention in Afghanistan.)

The total duration of the wars fought since 1945 adds up to somewhat *more than 369 years*. Of these 153 war-years occurred

Table 15.1: The General Trend in Wars 1945-76

Total Time in Wars	Years	Months	Days	Average no. of wars[a]
1945-8	25	1	6	6.3
1949-52	26	4	13	6.6
1953-6	32	11	28	8.3
1957-60	38	6	2	9.6
1961-4	53	0	6	13.3
1965-8	80	4	0	20.1
1969-72	68	5	3	17.1
1973-6	44	5	4	11.1
1945-76	369	2	2	11.5
in which:				
1967	20	11	4	20.9
1968	19	2	20	19.2
1969	18	10	4	18.8
1970	16	7	20	16.6
1971	17	11	11	18.0
1972	14	11	28	15.0
1973	12	10	1	12.8
1974	12	0	16	12.0
1975	9	6	5	9.5
1976	10	0	12	10.0
1967-76	153	0	1	15.3

Note: a. The total duration of all wars in the period divided by the length of the period. This number shows how many wars were fought on an average day in that period.

during the last 10 years. This means that 41 per cent of the total was spent in the last 10 years (that is, during 31 per cent of the 32 years). The average length of wars also increased, from 2 years 8 months for the first 25 years to 3 years 1 month for the whole of the 32 years. To phrase it differently: on every single day of the 32 years, 11.5 wars were being fought. But *on every single day of the last 10 years, 15.3 wars were being waged* (see Table 15.1).

Nevertheless, if we consider the general trend, we find a *consistent decrease* since the late 1960's (Figure 15.1). Compared with the whole

Figure 15.1: Average Number of Wars[a]

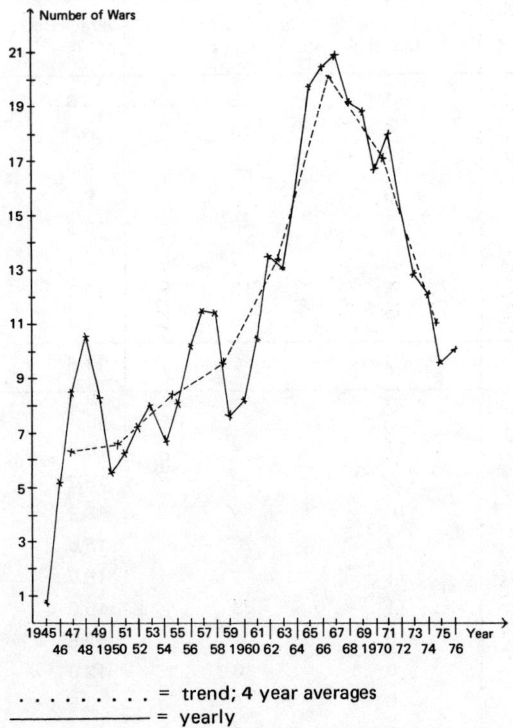

. . . . = trend; 4 year averages
———————— = yearly

Note: a. See note to Table 15.1.

post-war period, the last decade comes out badly. When we break it into shorter intervals, we see that the tide has turned; we find a regular and lasting decrease for the first time in 32 years.

Table 15.2 shows similar data according to regions.[4] These data prove also with reference to 32 years that Europe has remained outside the continents experiencing war. True, in Europe there is one war which entered its ninth year in 1978: the war in Northern Ireland. The intensity of this war is low, and its arena is outside the European Continent as such.

Our rate intensity parameter is more sophisticated. It is based on eight factors, of which two are of decisive importance: the ratio of deadly casualties and of armed participants to the total population of the country on whose territory the war is being fought.

We found that calculations based on the time-parameter and on the

Table 15.2: Regional Distribution of Wars

	Number of Wars		Years Spent at War		Percentage Distribution (years)	
	1946-76	1967-76	1945-76	1967-76	1945-76	1967-76
Europe	5	1	14.0	7.2	3.8	4.7
Asia	35	12	150.3	51.8	40.7	33.9
Middle East	36	17	71.5	26.7	19.4	17.4
Africa	21	14	94.1	53.5	25.5	35.0
Latin America	23	5	39.3	13.8	10.7	9.0
Total	120	49	369.2	153.0	100.1	100.0

intensity-parameter led to roughly similar results. In most cases there is no significant difference between the time-trend and the intensity-trend curves. We therefore consider it justified to refer to the time-curve in general. However, there is sometimes a characteristic different between the two sets of data. With reference to the war in Northern Ireland, we must point out that though, as far as time is concerned, this war amounted to 51.8 per cent of the total time of wars in Europe, in intensity it meant substantially less: only 10.9 of the intensity of wars 'consumed' in Europe. Though the Northern Irish war has been protracted in time, its intensity is much below that of the wars fought earlier in Europe.

2 Regional Trends

Table 15.3 shows the changes in regional data: for every four-year period the yearly average of time spent at war in every region. Thus we see the distribution according to regions of the yearly 11.5 years spent at war during 32 years. The second part of the table gives the same yearly data for the last 10 years.

Figure 15.2 demonstrates clearly the decrease of the war curve of the Third World in the last ten years. It appears, however, that the pattern of decrease differs between regions.

In Latin America the peak was reached in 1965, earlier than anywhere else. From this time onward it dropped gradually, first slowly, then more rapidly to zero. The upward trend of the revolutionary wave and its consequence, the outbreak of guerrilla wars, ended in a low tide. We wish to stress, however, that the present sporadic though often serious and repeated guerrilla (and anti-guerrilla) actions in countries such as Colombia, Nicaragua or the Argentine may not amount to war by our definition, but they do indicate a high level of tension that may erupt in war.

The curve of African wars rose rapidly and without interruption up to 1969. This was followed by a steady downward trend. This does not alter the fact that in the period 1967-70 Africa temporarily became the most war-stricken region in the world.

Asia is a region where the level of violence is permanently high. Here too the maximum of 1971 was followed by a decrease; but the overall level stayed above that of all other regions from 1971 onwards.

With respect to the Middle East, a decrease set in after the maximum in 1966, but in the last period, from 1973 onwards, the curve began to rise again. It is the Lebanese war and the intensively pursued war in Western Sahara which have altered the shape of the Middle Eastern curve.

Table 15.3: Regional Trends 1945-76[a]

(i) 1945-76

Region	45-48	49-52	53-56	57-60	61-64	65-68	69-72	73-76	Average
Europe	1.5	0.2	0.0	0.0	0.0	0.0	0.8	1.0	0.4
Asia	4.0	5.0	3.5	4.5	4.5	5.7	5.7	4.7	4.7
Middle East	0.2	0.4	2.7	3.2	2.6	4.4	2.5	2.0	2.2
Africa	0.2	0.1	1.3	1.1	4.5	6.6	6.4	3.4	2.9
Latin America	0.3	1.0	0.8	0.8	1.7	3.4	1.8	0.0	1.2
Total	6.3	6.6	8.3	9.6	13.3	20.1	17.1	11.1	11.5

(ii) 1967-76

Region	1967	1968	1969	1970	1971	1972	1973	1974	1975	1976	Average
Europe	0.0	0.0	0.2	1.0	1.0	1.0	1.0	1.0	1.0	1.0	0.7
Asia	5.5	4.8	4.0	5.1	6.9	6.7	5.8	5.0	4.0	4.0	5.2
Middle East	4.9	4.0	4.1	2.5	2.0	1.3	1.1	1.9	2.1	2.8	2.7
Africa	6.9	7.3	7.5	6.1	6.0	5.9	5.0	4.1	2.4	2.2	5.4
Latin America	3.6	3.0	3.1	2.0	2.0	0.1	0.0	0.0	0.0	0.0	1.4
Total	20.9	19.2	18.8	16.6	18.0	15.0	12.8	12.0	9.5	10.0	15.3

Note: a. In this and the following table some sums do not add up exactly. This is due to rounding off.

Figure 15.2: Average Number of Wars; Regional Composition[a]

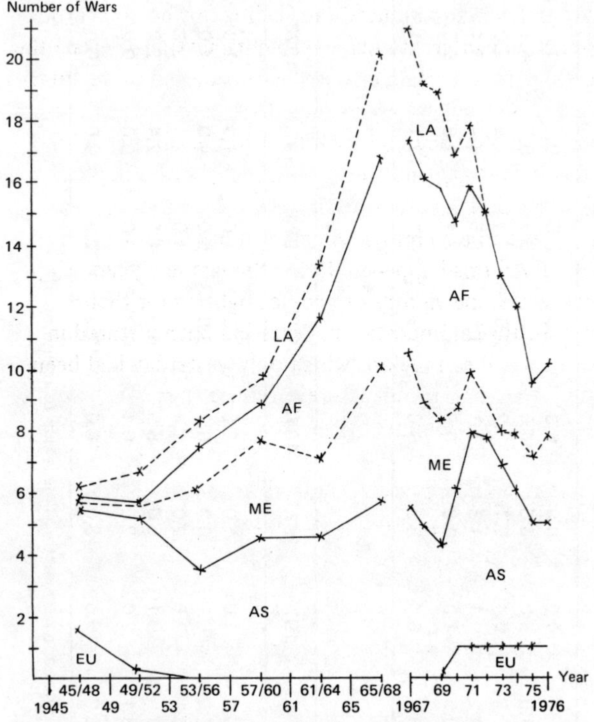

Four-year averages 1945-68, and yearly 1967-76.

LA = Latin America
AF = Africa
ME = Middle East
AS = Asia
EU = Europe

Note: a. Data from Table 15.3.

None the less, the main characteristic of the period investigated – i.e. the past ten years – is a general *downward trend* of wars, primarily due to the end of the major wars in Indo-China and in Portuguese Africa.

Considering the significant decrease manifest in the last ten years we find that this phase – *the phase of regression of wars – coincides more or less with general acceptance of the principle of peaceful coexistence and the realisation of certain elements of* détente. Does this mean that *detente* itself is reflected in the downward curve, that *détente* has directly influenced the theatres of war and caused the retreat of certain belligerent forces? Without wishing to demonstrate a casual relationship between *détente* and the trends of war. I believe, nevertheless, that there is a certain relationship between the two phenomena. The same forces which led to *détente* and induced the leading powers to accept a number of important new international agreements have also caused the retreat of belligerent forces. Certain changes have occurred in the international balance of power which have led equally to the elements of *détente* in the field of diplomacy, in Indo-China to the victories of peoples, to changes in Portugal and to the withdrawal of Portuguese forces from African battlefields. As a result, new independent states came into being or were able to return to peaceful life after many years' heavy fighting. All this happened during the last few years.

The end of these wars, the victory of peoples fighting for their freedom, is of great historical importance. Peace has been restored in precisely those regions and sub-regions which only yesterday had been the most smitten by war. This proves that even those wars which are called by some investigators 'asymmetric' conflicts may end in favour of the 'weaker' party.

We find that some significant new traits have appeared in the course of the last ten years also when investigating the problem of wars from the aspect of their *content or character.*

3 Types of Wars

In our earlier article we gave a typology dividing the wars into the following categories:

	With Foreign Participation	Without Foreign Participation
Internal anti-regime wars [A]	A/1	A/2
Internal tribal etc. wars [B]	B/1	B/2
Border wars [C]	C/1	C/2

In this classification those wars are qualified as anti-regime (A) type wars which are fought within the territories of a country against the government in power – that is, with the aim to overthrow this government, whether this is a national or foreign power, a progressive or reactionary government.

Internal wars in which the objective of the belligerent party is more limited, and where the war is being fought between tribes, ethnic or religious groups, for the separation of certain territories, or for a certain degree of autonomy, count as 'tribal wars' (B). In the present paper we wish to avoid excessive division and have included in this group some wars in which a power wished to regain (or to gain) lost territory (for instance the wars fought for the Quemoy and Matsu Islands for Western Irian).

Those wars are counted as 'border wars' (C) in which two or more countries fight against one another across the borders between their countries for territorial or other objectives.

Finally, we have considered as foreign participation (1) when the armed forces of a country – including the 'Green Berets' – participate actively with actions in the war of another country or region outside of its own state borders. Delivery of armaments, assistance and consultant participation and transfer of technology have not been counted as 'foreign participation'.

The current main type of wars is the anti-regime (A) type war, mainly with foreign participation (Category A/1). This fundamental conclusion was emphasised in our 1971 article. We have stressed the importance of the change which made this kind into the main type of war instead of the border wars which dominated in the past.

The fact that type A but mainly type A/1 wars are in such a majority is an unequivocal consequence of the current political situation. The simultaneous existence of countries belonging to two different social systems; the fact that they represent more or less a balance of power; that antagonistic social and political groups, classes and tendencies are often present within a country; and that the contrast between the national and colonial (or neo-colonial) forces has intensified in the process of disintegration of the colonial system – have all led to conflicts in which *power itself* is at stake. Such anti-regime wars have in the majority of cases led to the overthrow of the force in power, to the realisation of the objectives of the anti-government forces, to the establishment of national independence and of new national states. In more than one case, new social systems have been developed (for instance, as a result of the revolutionary wars fought in China, Cuba, South Vietnam, Laos and Angola).

The importance and pre-eminence of anti-regime wars have been preserved up to the present. The ratio of time spent in type A wars has, however, decreased somewhat in the last ten years; but this decrease is due exclusively to the relative decrease of A/2 type wars. The overall ratio of A/1 wars has risen slightly.

In connection with anti-regime wars fought with foreign participation (type A/1) two important changes must be pointed out. Over the last ten years *an uninterrupted decrease has occurred with respect to the participation of the (former) coloniser*. In earlier periods, the coloniser was the foreign force in 91 per cent of all war-years fought with foreign intervention (that is in all A/1 wars). The foreign participant was almost always the 'initial' coloniser.

In the last years this ratio has decreased considerably, to about half of the time spent by foreign forces in these wars. (And this included – though perhaps not everybody would agree – the military force of the 'white' settlers as colonisers in the Zimbabwe-Rhodesia war.)

The other noteworthy change is *the increasing presence of the forces of Third World countries as foreigners in the wars.* We shall come back to this question later.

The trend of the wars of type B is different. As we stated earlier:

> as soon as a country gains independence, the inner conflicts, mainly of a territorial character, turn into centrifugal conflicts arising from various internal efforts to seize power or to break away from the sphere of influence of the central power. So it is not a mere coincidence that these wars are characteristic of the period of independence and as such have their beginnings from 1956 onwards. In these wars, open foreign participation is not frequent . . . Both the proportions and the absolute duration of B-type wars *with* foreign participation are rapidly falling and are always being outstripped by B-type wars fought *without* foreign participation.[5]

These findings have been supported by recent experience. The bulk of B/2 type wars – with respect to both number and duration – have been waged in the past ten years. Sixty-two per cent of the time spent in wars of type B/2 since 1945 was spent in the last ten years. This means that the proportion of B/2 wars increased considerably in the same period. During the entire 32 years the proportion of B/2-type wars was – with respect to duration – hardly more than 14 per cent. In the last 10 years this proportion rose to 21.5 per cent. This is the only type of war whose relative importance underwent a considerable rise.

As far as the classsical type of wars, the border wars (C), is concerned, they have been waged almost exclusively *with* the participation of a foreign – third – party *up to 1961*. The only exception was the border war between Honduras and Nicaragua in 1951. *Since 1962* they have taken place almost exclusively *without* the participation of a

Table 15.4: Time Spent in Different Types of War[a]

Type	Number of Wars		Years Spent at War		Percent of Total Time at War	
	1945-76	1967-76	1945-76	1967-76	1945-76	1967-76
A/1	56	23	236.1	100.0	64.0	65.4
A/2	17	4	57.5	13.3	15.6	8.7
A	73	27	293.7	113.3	79.6	74.1
B/1	12	5	12.2	5.9	3.3	3.9
B/2	17	10	53.0	32.9	14.4	21.5
B	29	15	65.2	38.8	17.7	25.4
C/1	6	1	5.2	0.1	1.4	0.0
C/2	12	6	5.1	0.9	1.4	0.6
C	18	7	10.3	1.0	2.8	0.6
/1	74	29	253.5	106.0	68.7	69.2
/2	46	20	115.6	47.1	31.3	30.8
Total	120	49	369.2	153.0	100.1	100.1

Notes: a. A = internal anti-regime war
B = internal tribal, etc. war
C = border war

b. 1 = with foreign participation
2 = without foreign participation

Table 15.5: Foreign Military Involvement in Wars

	Number of Wars Intervened in		Years Spent in Wars as Foreign Participants	
	1945 -76	1967 -76	1945 -76	1967 -76
Developed capitalist countries	64	20	233.7	87.8
Socialist countries	6	3	21.3	12.4
Third World countries	17	14	79.6	51.5
of which:				
Coloniser of theatre country	38	10	159.6	53.7
USA	27	11	96.6	46.3
Great Britain	20	3	67.3	14.1
France	12	1	38.8	4.1
Portugal	5	4	35.3	23.2

third party, again with a single exception: the 1973 Israeli-Egyptian-Syrian war, in which the participation of troops from Iraq and Jordan qualifies as foreign participation. In the last years of the 10-year period under investigation type C wars simply ceased to occur.

Thus, in the middle of the post-war period a significant change took place in the nature of the border wars: from presence to absence of foreign forces. We stated in 1971 that certain powers inclined to intervention obviously have realised that 'the independent nations have come of age: they can fight out their wars between themselves'. This does not mean that these powers were absent, but their participation took other forms: arms delivery, economic, financial and political support, military aid, consultants.

Nevertheless, we cannot conclude that this type of war has ceased for good. We believe that it might appear again (see for example the fights between Vietnam and Cambodia), if for no other reason than that, in some newly formed state, nationalist tendencies will necessarily intensify; and since the boundaries of a considerable part of the developing countries (mainly in Africa) have been drawn by forces foreign to them in an artificial manner, taking into consideration their own – foreign – balance of forces or interests and not actual local conditions.

Figure 15.3: Average Number of Wars 1945-76. Composition by Type of War[a]

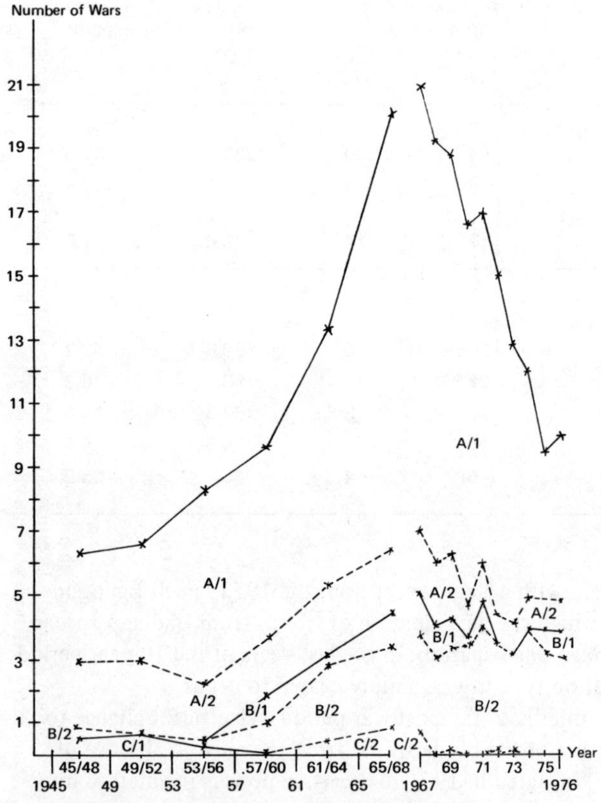

Four-year averages, 1945-68, and yearly 1967-76.

A = internal anti-regime war
B = internal tribal, etc. war
C = border war
1 = with foreign participation
2 = without foreign participation

Table 15.4 proves further that *foreign participation*, very characteristic of the wars of our days, *remains one of the main characteristics of modern wars*. As far as the foreign military forces are concerned, we note *that the main participating forces are the same*. Table 15.5 shows that the main participant, the United States, has participated in proportionally more wars than before. Almost half of the time spent in these wars by US forces – 47.9 per cent of the time – falls into these

Figure 15.4: US Participation by Year in the Presidential Term

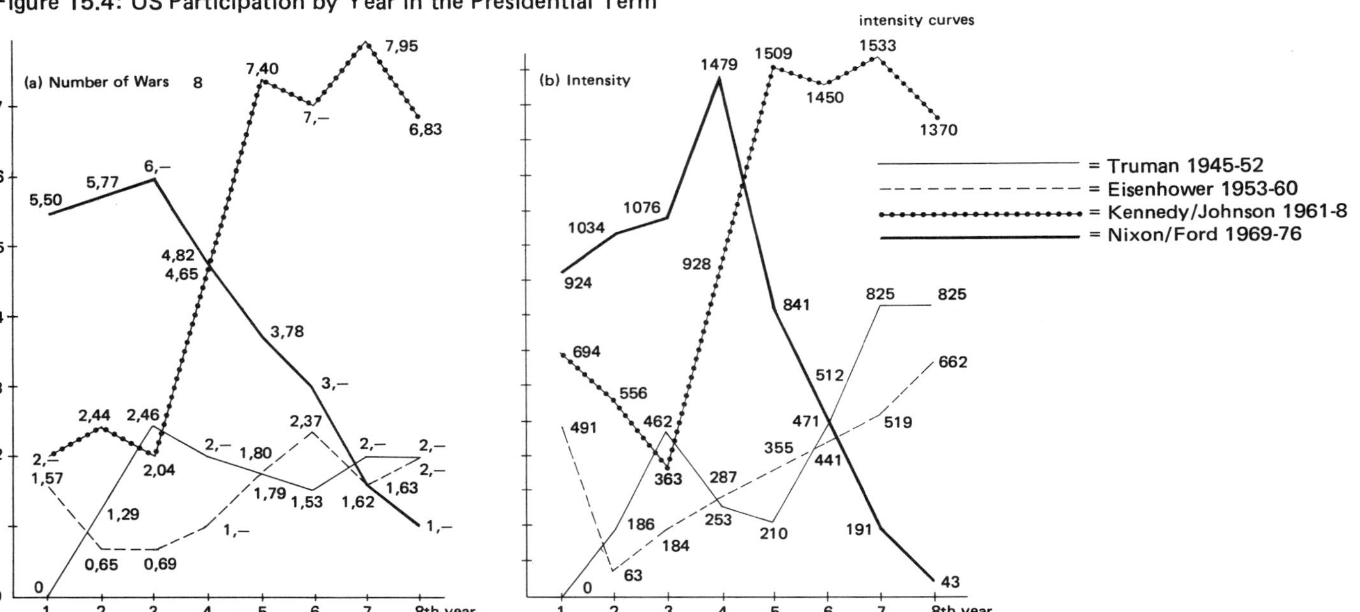

Notes: (a) shows how many wars were fought with US participation on an average in that period.
(b) shows the intensity of war participation based on additional information on the ratio of deadly casualties and of armed participants to the total population of the country on whose territory the wars are being fought.

10 years. In the same period, British and French participation decreased greatly. In 1972 French forces ceased to participate in military actions, when the war in Chad gradually (though perhaps not totally) ceased and the French army stopped its military activities. But in the last days of 1977 new French interventional activities were carried out in Western Sahara.[6] As far as the Portugese forces are concerned, it is obvious that their participation was particularly high in the last ten years.

Since the USA remained the main foreign force, it seems justified to examine the trend of US participation somewhat more closely. In our 1971 article we analysed the causes for relatively decreased US participation in the peak period of the Cold War. The strategy of massive retaliation did not call for systematic intervention into 'local' wars. In this period the United Kingdom and France were trying to keep their colonies by armed force (mainly France), and to promote the coming to power of domestic forces ready to maintain good relations with the colonial power after independence (such as Great Britain).

The new strategy of flexible response (which Kissinger and Osgood liked to call the 'policy of successful limited wars') led to increasingly active participation of US troops and Green Berets in 'local' wars. To show this more clearly, we plot in Figure 15.4 the trend of US participation within presidential terms.

Figure 15.4 (a) shows the time spent at wars waged with US participation and 15.4 (b) the intensity of these wars. The shape of the curves reflects clearly how the strategy of flexible response, the readiness to fight 'successful limited wars' influenced US participation (which of course, influenced in general also the trend of wars, as it can be proved). The curves show further the decrease in the period following the Kennedy and Johnson eras.[7]

To have a broader survey and a more thorough approach to the problem of international, foreign participation, we have examined all types of foreign participations. We have therefore classified the participating countries into the three usual categories: 'Western' (developed capitalist), the 'Eastern' (socialist), and the 'Third World' countries. This last category does not include the Asiatic and Latin American socialist countries Cuba, Vietnam (in the period under examination, the Vietnamese Democratic Republic), the Korean People's Democratic Republic and the Chinese People's Republic included in the second category.

We are fully aware that this classification is not free from problems.

Figure 15.5: Foreign Military Involvement in Wars

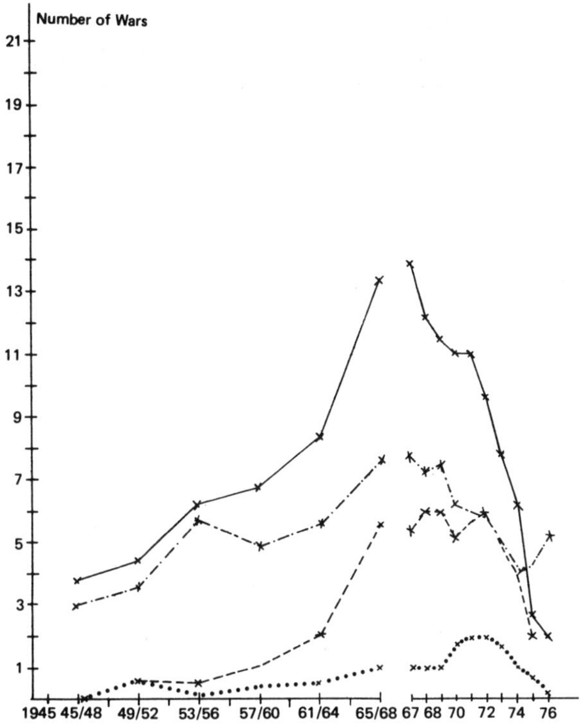

Four-year averages 1945-68, and yearly 1967-76.

——— = developed capitalist countries
—·—·— = of which: former coloniser
-------- = Third World countries
········· = socialist countries

Thus the role of China was very different in the given period from – or just opposite to – the aspirations of the other socialist countries. None the less, China as a foreign participant was present only in the Korean War, that is much before the outbreak of the conflicts within the camp of the socialist countries. The group of Third World countries is even more full of contradictions. A country like South Africa, with its military forces participating in the war in Zimbabwe or Angola, and certain Arab countries which have given military support to other Arab countries in the fights against Israel are unaviodably dumped together. It is obvious that the participation of certain Third World military forces might very much have opposite aims; they have fought in some cases as foreign forces in the internal wars of other countries against each other. As our objective is only to outline the general picture, to disclose the *main trends*, we prefer to shoulder the accusation of oversimplification, in order to present a clear and surveyable picture of the main phenomena[8] (Figure 15.5). In the figure, the phenomenon of the participation of the (former) colonising power in its 'own' colonial territory was plotted separately too, but considered without fail as foreign participation.[9]

It appears from the data of Table 15.5 and the trend of the curve how the proportion of Western participation – and within this to an even higher degree the ratio of the participation of the colonisers – decreased in the period for the reasons already discussed. The proportion of socialist participation rose temporarily in the course of the last period, mainly as a consequence of the wars in Indo-China, in which respect I have considered the presence of Vietnamese forces in Laos and Cambodia as 'foreign' forces, without going into the details as to the causes and circumstances of this participation. Neither need we discuss the kinds of forces responsible for this 'foreign' participation. The curve shows an obvious temporary rise in socialist and a constant decrease in Western participation, though the figure shows clearly the substantial difference in the order of magnitude – in the proportion of the two types of 'foreign participations'. Moreover, in the last 10 years a decrease has been evident in the participation of both Western and socialist camps, though a new war took place with socialist participation on 'foreign territories': the second war in Angola, with South African against Cuban forces.

Figure 15.5 and the data have also shed light on another important phenomenon: the fluctuating, but *rapidly rising participation of the mixed group of the developing countries as 'foreigners' in wars fought on the territory of other countries*. Their participation – after a rapid rise – reached almost the same high level as the participation of the (ex)-colonisers in wars fought on the territory of their 'own' (ex)-colonies in the same 10 years! (True enough, the latter had come to the given level after a lasting decrease.) In any case, the curves intersect; in the last two years the time-curve of Third World 'foreign' participation rose to a level higher than the time-curve, not only of the colonists, but of all the Western countries together. This again indicates that the newly independent developing countries have acquired a new role in international politics. Not only has their solidarity increased – which may motivate their participation as foreigners in each other's wars – but some 'sub-imperialist aspirations' have become also more intensive, finding military expression in interventional activities – for instance, of Saudi Arabia, Indonesia or Iran. This new situation has also given rise to events such as the agreement concerning the division of Western Sahara between Mauritania and Morocco, which led to a war also involving Algeria, and which later caused the intervention of France in this war, the last on our list.

4 Some Conclusions

A general examination of the wars of the last ten years partly confirms our earlier findings, partly discloses and proves new phenomena.

The *overall pattern* has not altered. The picture is still characterised by the fact that the wars are parts of the great international processes and are far from having ceased. Their arena is still the Third World. They are, as before, primarily internal wars which gain their international character from the activity, often coupled with military participation, of the armed forces of countries far away. They obtain an international character due also to a phenomenon not mentioned here: the increasing import of arms of the developing countries from the industrially developed countries and this, as demonstrated in other analyses, primarily from the Western capitalist countries.[10]

However, another change has also taken place: the *decreasing* war trend, a fundamental characteristic of the last 10 years. We do not wish to conclude from this that mankind is soon to reach the age of no wars, we do not dare to hope that the decrease of the curve in Figure 15.1 will continue in the direction and proportion of the trend of the last 10 years. In that case, a world without wars ought to be reached within a decade. No, we are not so optimistic: but we do believe that this observable decrease had its well founded reasons, and on the other hand we believe that this might be considered the foretoken of certain coming changes. We think that one such change is a decrease in the open intervention of the hitherto main intervening forces: after Vietnam it would be, to say the least, more difficult to transport the armies of the leading capitalist powers to the arena of internal wars of other countries. This need not mean a change or decrease in the sphere of attention or interest of these powers; only that they will try to find other ways of exerting influence. This has led to the well documented rising armament trade and arms deliveries. It has also led partly to the intensification and multiplication of sub-imperialist aspirations and might be a cause of the increasing participation of the developing countries in some wars.[11]

A further change is the fact that one of the fundamental motives of the wars of the 32 years – the determination of the colonial people to attain independence – has largely ceased. The world atlas is today covered almost exclusively with the colours of independent national states. As a practical consequence, the cause of internal conflicts within the frontiers of the country will increasingly be rooted in social, class etc. conflicts and anti-regime fights. The achievement of national independence and the transformation of certain regions into national states lead necessarily to the intensification of internal power conflicts, which may result not only in the outbreak of anti-regime wars of a social character; it also leads to the intensification of other internal – tribal, minority, religious – conflicts which again can easily lead to war. Data for the past ten years have shown the growing importance of this type of war, and it seems probable that this trend will continue and accelerate with the increase of type B wars.

Though our data indicate a decrease in the proportion of type C wars, we believe that in a new situation it does not seem probable that this decrease will be a lasting one. The increasing number of national states and their peculiar properties (national and tribal articulation, the inclination to construct outside conflicts to work off certain internal contradications or to mask difficulties, etc.) may easily lead to the outbreak of new type C wars.

I have been careful not to exaggerate the main characteristic of the ten years under investigation, namely the decrease of the war trend. Although considering it an important and significant process, I dare not hope that this process will be consistent and lasting, bringing us down to the zero-point within a short period of time. It is none the less obvious that the continuation of this process of a decreasing war trend *can* be encouraged and promoted. It would be necessary to reach, for instance, international agreements which would effectively exclude active military participation in internal conflicts of foreign territories. Indeed, armed force ought to be banned from the settlement of international problems. These and other similar measures would mean the *transfer of* détente *to the military field*, which I consider a major task of our days. This would be promoted by the limitation not only of the armament race, but also of the race in arms supply, which ought to be accompanied by other limitations. All this would necessitate the elaboration of appropriate new measures concerning the transfer of military technology, the problem of spreading of fissile material, of nuclear reactors, etc. These measures alone would, of course, not prevent the outbreak of conflicts, but they would reduce the risk which these might mean in every case: the spread of wars to other territories.

Our age is an age of contradications, of social transformation, of the fight between social systems, the age of transitions. This unavoidably brings with it conflicts and the intensification of contradication. We should however, question whether the solution of these conflicts must call for such grave human sacrifices as so often in the past. Wars are fought by *people*, and not by arms alone, so the limitation and prevention of wars also depend to a great extent on people.

Appendix: List of Wars 1945-76

Wars being waged or still lasting in 1967-76 are in italics.

Code No.	Site	Period	Type	Foreign Participation[a]
1	Greece	1944-5	A/1	DC
	Algeria	1945	A/1	DC
	Indonesia	1945-9	A/1	DC
	Spain	1945-8	A/2	
5	Indo-China	1946-54	A/1	DC
	Greece	1946-9	A/1	DC
	India (religious)	1946-7	B/2	
	Philippines	1946-54	A/1	DC
	China	1946-9	A/2	
10	Iran	1946	B/2	
	Paraguay	1947	A/1	DC
	Madagascar	1947-8	A/1	DC
	India (Hyderabad, Telganana)	1947-8	A/2	
	India – Pakistan (Kashmir)	1947-8	C/1	DC
15	Yemen	1948	B/2	
	Costa Rica	1948	A/2	
	Burma	1948-	A/2	
	Colombia	1948-53	A/2	
	Israel-Arab countries	1948-9	C/1	DC
20	Malaysia	1948-59	A/1	DC
	Bolivia	1949	A/2	
	Korea	1950-3	C/1	DC, S, TW
	Puerto Rico	1950	A/1	DC
	Egypt	1951-2	A/1	DC
25	Tunisia	1952-4	A/1	DC
	Bolivia	1952	A/2	
	Kenya	1952-6	A/1	DC
	Morocco	1952-6	A/1	DC
	Guatemala	1954	A/1	DC
30	Colombia	1954-7	A/2	
	Algeria	1954-62	A/1	DC
	China (Islands)	1955	B/1	DC
	Costa Rica – Nicaragua	1955	C/1	DC
	Cyprus	1955-9	A/1	DC
35	Cameroon	1955-63	A/1	DC
	South Vietnam	1955-75	A/1	DC, TW

Code No.	Site	Period	Type	Foreign Participation[a]
	Oman	1955-63	A/1	DC
	India (Nagas)	1956-64	B/2	
	Hungary	1956	A/1	S
40	Israel – Egypt (Suez)	1956	C/1	DC
	Cuba	1956-9	A/2	
	Aden, Yemen	1956-8	B/1	DC
	Indonesia	1957-8	B-1	DC
	Honduras – Nicaragua	1957	C/2	
45	Spanish Morocco	1957-8	A/1	DC, TW
	Lebanon	1958	A/1	DC
	Jordan	1958	A/1	DC
	China (Quemoy)	1958	B/1	DC
	Nyasaland	1959	A/1	DC
50	China (Tibet)	1959	B/2	
	Laos	1959-62	A/1	DC, S
	Dominican Republic	1959	A/2	
	Paraguay	1959-60	A/2	
	Zaire (Congo K)	1960-4	A/1	DC
55	*Angola*	1961-74	A/1	DC
	Nepal	1961-2	A/2	
	Cuba	1961	A/1	DC
	Tunisia	1961	A/1	DC
	Ethiopia (Eritrea)	1961-	B/2	
60	Iraq (Kurds)	1961-4	B/2	
	Venezuela	1961-70	A/2	
	India (Goa)	1961	B/1	DC
	Indonesia (W. Irian)	1962	B/1	DC
	Guatemala	1962-72	A/1	DC
65	Colombia	1962	A/1	DC
	Yemen	1962-70	A/1	DC, TW
	India – China	1962	C/2	
	Brunei	1962	A/1	DC
	Guinea (Bissau)	1963-74	A/1	DC
70	Malaysia ('Confrontation')	1963-6	A/1	DC, TW
	Algeria – Morocco	1963	C/2	
	South Yemen	1963-7	A/1	DC
	Dominican Republic	1963	A/2	
	Somalia – Ethiopia	1963-4	C/2	
75	*Zaire*	1963-9	A/1	DC
	Cyprus	1963-4	B/1	DC
	Rwanda	1963-4	B/2	
	Kenya – Somalia	1963-7	C/2	
	Laos	1964-73	A/1	DC, S, TW
80	*Colombia*	1964-72	A/1	DC
	North Vietnam	1964-8	A/1	DC
	Mozambique	1964-74	A/1	DC
	Iraq (Kurds)	1965-70	B/1	TW
	India – Pakistan	1965	C/2	
85	Dominican Republic	1965	A/1	DC
	Peru	1965	A/1	DC

Code No.	Site	Period	Type	Foreign Participation[a]
	Oman (Dhofar)	1965-	A/1	DC, TW
	Sudan	1965-72	B/2	
	India — Pakistan	1965	C/2	
90	Thailand	1965-	A/1	DC
	India (Mizos)	1966-7	B/2	
	Bolivia	1967	A/1	DC
	Israel — Arab countries	1967	C/2	
	Zaire	1967	B/1	DC
95	Nigeria (Biafra)	1967-70	B/2	
	Zimbabwe (Rhodesia)	1967-	A/1	TW
	South Yemen	1968	A/1	TW
	Chad	1968-72	A/1	DC
	El Salvador — Honduras	1969	C/2	
100	South Yemen — Saudi Arabia	1969	C/2	
	Gt. Britain (N. Ireland)	1969-	B/2	
	Cambodia	1970-5	A/1	DC, S, TW
	Sudan	1970	A/2	
	Philippines	1970-6	B/2	
105	Jordan	1970	B/2	
	Guinea	1970	A/1	DC
	Pakistan (Bangla Desh)	1971	B/1	TW
	Sri Lanka	1971	A/2	
	Jordan	1971	B/2	
110	North Vietnam	1972-3	A/1	DC
	Burundi	1972	B/2	
	Uganda — Tanzania	1972	C/2	
	Yemen — South Yemen	1972	C/2	
	Israel — Arab countries	1973	C/1	TW
115	Iraq (Kurds)	1974-5	B/2	
	Cyprus	1974	B/1	DC
	Lebanon	1975-6	B/1	TW
	East Timor	1975-	A/1	TW
	Angola	1975-6	A/1	S, TW
120	West Sahara	1975-	A/1	TW

Note: a. DC = Developed capitalist country/countries
S = socialist country/countries
TW = Third World country/countries

Notes

1. See, for example, *International Herald Tribune*, 7 Oct. 1977.
2. *Keesing's Contemporary Archives* (1977), p. 28353.
3. A new war broke out in Zaire in 1978.
4. As in our 1971 article, we considered every Arab country a Middle East country, both in Asia and Africa, including the Sudan and Mauritania, as well as Cyprus, Iran and Israel. Hence the region 'Asia' refers only to countries east of the boundaries of Iran, and 'Africa' to so-called Black Africa to the region south

of the Sahara.

5. *Journal of Peace Research*, vol. VIII. no. 1 (1971).

6. In 1978, French troops again intervened in Zaire (Shaba province).

7. Northing has been further from us than the intention to attribute some kind of merit to any of the US Presidents for the decrease of US participation. All we wanted to do was to demonstrate unambiguously in this way as well that the period of acceptance of the principle of peaceful coexistence is the period in which the retreat from the main theatres of war has been 'accepted'. We do not believe that either of these two important political phenomena – assertion of peaceful coexistence or the decrease of wars – was the consequence of some kind of suddenly arising personal goodwill, or of essential changes in any system. We are more inclined to the view that significant changes in the international balance of power have led to these results, have compellingly brought about these new phenomena. This again proves the existence of a real and detectable relationship between the trend of wars, on the one hand, and the trend of the general international situation, the main line of development of international politics, on the other.

8. However, certain cases, such as the Suez War, figure twice, because of both French and British participation. But in Table 15.5 all wars in which several powers of the same category participated – such as that in Suez – are taken only as a *single* war. However, if in a war forces belonging to two or three different categories have participated, this war was separately included in *each of the categories*. It should also be mentioned that the time of participation of the foreign force was always calculated for the full duration of the war, as we were not always able to take into consideration the date of belated entry into or earlier retreat from the war. The *industrially developed capitalist countries* participated in the following 64 wars: 1, 2, 3, 5, 6, 8, 11, 12, 14, 19, 20, 22, 23, 24, 25, 27, 28, 29, 31, 32, 33, 34, 35, 36, 37, 40, 42, 43, 45, 46, 47, 48, 49, 51, 54, 55, 57, 58, 62, 63, 64, 65, 66, 68, 69, 70, 72, 75, 76, 79, 80, 81, 82, 85, 86, 87, 90, 92, 94, 98, 102, 106, 110, 116. The participation of the *socialist countries* was calculated for the following six wars: 22, 39, 51, 79, 102, 119. The countries of the *Third World* participated in the following 17 wars: 22, 36, 45, 66, 70, 79, 83, 87, 96, 97, 102, 107, 114, 117, 118, 119, 120.

9. We are aware that not everybody will agree with this classification and will refer to 'legal' arguments or 'acquired rights' and therefore count as 'domestic' forces, for instance, the French army in Algeria. We consider it unnecessary to bring up arguments in support of our classification which considers such a 'presence' a foreign military force participating in the given war, that is differently from certain official historical concepts.

We considered the following 38 wars as such fought with the participation of the (former) colonising power: 2, 3, 5, 8, 12, 14, 19, 20, 23, 24, 25, 27, 28, 31, 34, 35, 37, 40, 42, 45, 47, 49, 54, 55, 58, 62, 63, 66, 68, 69, 70, 72, 75, 82, 87, 94, 96, 98.

10. For details, see Istvan Kende: 'Dynamics of wars, of arms trade and of military expenditure in the Third World, 1945-1976', *Instant Research on Peace and Violence*, no. 2 (1977), pp. 59-67.

11. We do not believe in the 'wars by proxy' theory. The participating countries truly represent – thus defend – interests, systems, principles in the wars fought on foreign territories. That the system for which they fight is at the same time the system of some major power – a capitalist or socialist system – follows necessarily from the nature of our present world. This, however, is not inevitably the same as some kind of 'commission' or 'proxy'. On the other hand, *arms* for such wars or for participation in these wars will generally not be delivered by countries with systems which disagree with them. Admittedly, in certain cases a

given power might consider it more expedient – and cheaper – to promote the participation of others in a war whose outcome is vital for the 'promoter'. This was in fact openly acknowledged in a dramatic speech which was written, but never delivered, for the speaker, President Kennedy, was killed before the planned meeting.

His undelivered Dallas speech declared, among other things:

> Our assistance makes possible the stationing of 3.5 million allied troops along the Communist frontier *at one-tenth the cost of maintaining a comparable number of American soldiers*. A successful Communist breakthrough in these areas, necessitating direct United States intervention, *would cost us several times as much as our entire foreign aid program* – and *might cost us heavily in American lives* as well. (Louis Filler (ed.), *The President Speaks* (Putnam, New York, 1964), p. 405.)

This argument is still valid.

16 THE MILITARY EXPENDITURES OF LESS DEVELOPED NATIONS AS A PROPORTION OF THEIR STATE BUDGETS:* A RESEARCH NOTE

Milton Leitenberg and Nicole Ball

Researchers in political and social sciences often use in their publications various indices of a nation's military burden or expenditure, as part of their evidence or argumentation on a particular point. General indicators often used are as follows:

(1) the nation's military expenditure as a percentage of its gross national product;
(2) *per capita* military expenditure – military expenditure divided by the nation's population;
(3) the number of personnel in the nation's armed forces, *per se*;
(4) the number of military personnel divided by the nation's population;
(5) the military expenditure divided by the number of military personnel;
(6) military expenditure, *per se*;
(7) military expenditure as a percentage of the nation's federal budget.

Of these, the most often and most widely used one is the first – military expenditure as a percentage of GNP. However, one of the authors has long considered this perhaps the least satisfactory of all the indicators. Frequently, the largest proportion of GNP is available for direct allocation by national leaders and policy-makers, and thus the particular 'per cent-GNP' measure cannot demonstrate the priorities of such national policy-makers. In addition, for nations with sizeable GNP's, it takes large changes in military expenditure to appear as anything more than a change of a few tenths of one per cent in such an index. At best, except in case of wartime, time-series data on a country's military expenditure as a percentage of GNP will show only relatively small changes. These can perhaps be examined for year-to-year changes,

*Revised paper presented to the symposium *Armaments, Tension and War*, organised by the Nordic Cooperation Committee for International Politics, Conflict and Peace Research, Hanaholmen (Finland), 26-29 September 1977.

but they can just as easily be obscured by any sizeable change in GNP.

We would suggest that the final indicator on the above list – military expenditure as a percentage of the nation's federal budget – is the one to be considered most useful. It focuses precisely on the priorities of a nation's policy-makers. Oddly enough, this is the indicator that has perhaps been the least used, and it is referred to very rarely in the literature. In addition, we were particuarly interested in knowing the distribution of military expenditure as a percentage of federal budget for *less developed nations*. We found that such data were not already available, and it was necessary to derive the data.[1 2]

World military expenditure is now running at roughly $350 billion per year. Nearly two-thirds of this total – about 60 per cent – is made up of the military expenditure of two nations, the US and the USSR. The purpose of this note is not to obscure this. However, it is also of inerest, in the context of development goals, to see where the priorities of particular LDCs lie.[3]

The data aggregated here in Table 16.1 are for 1974, the most recent year for which the two necessary component figures of national budget and military expenditure could be obtained for most of the countries of interest. The table contains data on 93 developing countries. It shows that of these:

18 (19.4 per cent) spent between 0 and 5 per cent of their budget on military expenditure;
22 (23.7 per cent) spent between 5 and 10 per cent of their budget on military expenditure;
16 (17.3 per cent) spent between 10 and 15 per cent of their budget on military expenditure;
9 (9.7 per cent) spent between 15 and 20 per cent of their budget on military expenditure;
6 (6.5 per cent) spent between 20 and 25 per cent of their budget on military expenditure;
22 (23.7 per cent) spent over 25 per cent of their budget on military expenditure.

Taking the same figures in another way, they indicate that:

nearly 25 per cent spent over 25 per cent of their budget on military expenditure;
nearly 30 per cent spent over 20 per cent of their budget on military

Table 16.1: Military Expenditure as a Percentage of National Budgets[a]

Country	National Budget[b] (in US $ m)	Military Expenditure[c] (in US $ m)	Percentage of National Budget for Military Expenditure	Percentage of GNP
Afghanistan	189.3[d]	28.0	14.8	1.61
Algeria	3,545.9[c]	260.0	7.3	2.28
Argentina (1972)	4,699.2[e]	358.0	7.6	1.34
Bahrain (1975)	339.6[e]	14.0	4.1	2.47
Bangladesh	1,025.5[d] (RE)[f]	53.0	5.2	0.67
Barbados	84.3[d]	1.0	1.2	0.38
Benin	61.1[e]	6.0	9.8	1.70
Bolivia	261.2[d]	41.0	15.7	2.24
Botswana	201.7[d]	0.0	0.0	0.0
Brazil	7,875.5[d]	2,000.0	25.4	2.05
Burma (1972)	394.4[d] (DE)	157.0	39.8	5.60
Burundi	33.4[e]	8.0	24.0	2.57
Cameroon	335.3[e]	30.0	8.9	1.75
Central African Republic	77.5[d] (E)	7.0	9.0	2.30
Chad	90.0[e]	20.0	22.2	5.63
Chile (1973)	848.2[d]	222.0	26.2	3.11
China, Republic of (Taiwan)	2,269.7[e]	971.0	42.8	7.03
Colombia	1,155.2[d]	118.0	10.2	0.99
Congo	118.0[d]	24.0	20.3	4.27
Costa Rica	270.6[e]	0.0	0.0	0.0
Cyprus	107.1[d]	18.0	10.6	2.16
Dominican Republic	494.5[d]	48.0	9.7	1.70
Ecuador	473.8	72.0	15.2	2.09
Egypt	2,350.0[d]	1,550.0	65.9	15.40
El Salvador	197.2[d]	19.0	9.6	1.25

Ethiopia	372.4[d]	67.0	18.0	2.33
Fiji	111.0[d]	1.0	0.9	0.20
Gabon	79.7[d]	11.0	13.8	1.04
Gambia	1.9[d]	0.0	0.0	0.0
Ghana	642.2[d]	51.0	8.0	1.27
Guatemala	322.9[d]	27.0	8.4	0.88
Guyana	150.6[d] (RE)	7.0	4.1	1.73
Haiti	33.3[d]	9.0	27.0	1.31
Honduras	147.6[d] (E)	13.0	8.8	1.37
India	10,273.3[d]	2,600.0	25.3	3.03
Indonesia	2,805.5[d]	709.0	25.3	3.15
Iran	10,819.9[d] (E)	5,970.0	55.2	13.60
Iraq (1975)	12,303.2[e] (Est)	1,850.0	15.0	14.80
Israel	6,166.3[d]	3,070.0	49.8	30.50
Ivory Coast (1973)	539.1[e] (Est)	31.0	5.8	1.16
Jamaica	449.1[d]	15.0	3.3	0.64
Jordan	515.2[e]	139.0[g]	27.0	11.90
Kenya	639.2[e]	40.0	6.3	1.44
Korea, North (1973)	8,321.4[e] (Est)	625.0	7.5	11.00
Korea, South	2,547.4[d]	757.0	29.7	4.53
Kuwait	1,135.7[e]	143.0	12.6	1.31
Laos	47.4[d]	18.0[h]	38.0	7.56
Lebanon	532.6[e]	124.0[g]	23.0	3.43
Lesotho	23.1[d]	0.0	0.0	0.0
Liberia	124.5[d]	4.0	3.2	0.78
Libya	3,545.8[i]	387.0	10.9	3.51
Madagascar	420.3[e]	22.0	5.2	1.46
Malawi	109.5[d]	4.0	3.7	0.66
Malaysia	2,322.2[d] (RE)	397.0	17.1	4.85
Mali	62.2[e]	11.0	17.7	2.48

Country	National Budget[b] (in US $ m)	Military Expenditure[c] (in US $ m)	Percentage of National Budget for Military Expenditure	Percentage of GNP
Mauritania	70.3[e] (Est)	8.0	11.4	2.38
Mauritius	94.2[e]	1.0	1.1	0.13
Mexico (1975)	27,732.7[e]	528.0	2.0	0.88
Morocco	1,966.0[e]	196.0	10.0	2.74
Nepal	124.9[d] (RE)	8.0	6.4	0.61
Nicaragua	285.9[d]	22.0	7.7	1.56
Niger (1973)	70.5[e]	3.0	4.3	0.77
Nigeria (1973)	2,156.0[j] (Est)	702.0	32.6	5.02
Oman (1975)	1,466.1[e]	655.0	44.7	36.60
Pakistan	1,709.0[d]	572.0	33.5	6.68
Panama	392.6[d]	13.0	3.3	0.79
Paraguay	115.5[d]	17.0	14.7	1.27
Peru	4,503.9[e] (RE)	403.0	8.9	3.53
Philippines	1,842.2[d]	262.0	14.2	1.77
Rwanda	40.5[d]	7.0	17.3	2.19
Saudi Arabia	6,425.4[d]	1,150.0	17.9	4.64
Senegal	256.7[d]	25.0	9.7	1.61
Sierra Leone	86.0[e] (Est)	5.0	5.8	0.86
Singapore	912.3[d]	252.0	27.6	4.99
Somalia (1973)	62.9[k] (Est)	17.0	27.0	6.26
Sri Lanka	817.6[d]	26.0	3.2	0.80
Sudan	639.6[d] (PR)	113.0	17.7	3.18
Syria	1,300.0[d] (PR)	452.0	34.8	11.10
Tanzania	626.1[d] (E)	69.0	11.0	3.15
Thailand	1,700.4[d]	354.0	20.8	2.67
Togo	73.2[d] (E)	10.0	13.7	1.83

Trinidad and Tobago (1973)	281.1[d]	4.0	1.4	0.29
Tunisia	923.2[m]	47.0	5.1	1.35
Uganda (1973)	318.0[d]	79.0	24.8	2.97
United Arab Emirates	424.9[d] (DE)	41.0	9.7	0.55
Upper Volta	52.8[e] (Est)	6.0	11.4	1.35
Venezuela	9,228.3[d]	504.0	5.5	1.99
Vietnam, North (1975)	2,583.1[e,n]	310.0	12.0	22.60
Vietnam, South (1973)	791.2[e]	586.0	74.1	18.90
Yemen	73.5[d]	35.0	47.6	5.26
Yemen, Democratic	65.9[d] (RE)	38.0	57.8	10.50
Zaire (1973)	729.2[e]	85.0	11.7	2.94
Zambia	677.5[p]	90.0	13.3	3.31

Notes for Table 16.1 are on p. 292.

Notes to Table 16.1:

a. All budget and military expenditure figures are for 1974 unless otherwise indicated. All non-1974 military expenditure figures are for current, not constant, expenditure. For all 1974 military expenditure figures, 1974 = 100.

b. All National Budget figures originally expressed in local currency. The exchange rates for Bahrain, the Republic of China (Taiwan), Iraq, North Korea, Mexico, Oman, North Vietnam and South Vietnam are derived from *Europa Year Book, 1976*, Vol. II: *Africa, The Americas, Asia, Australasia* (Europa Publications, London, 1976). All other exchange rates are from *UN Statistical Yearbook, 1975*, Table 194, Exchange Rates, pp. 703-4.

c. All military expenditure figures from US Arms Control and Disarmament Agency, *World Military Expenditure and Arms Transfers, 1966-1975* (Washington DC, 1976), Table II, Military Expenditures, GNP, Population and Armed Forces by Country by Year, pp. 19-54.

d. National Budget figures derived from *UN Statistical Yearbook, 1975*, Table 201, Budget Accounts and Public Debt, pp. 728-821.

e. National Budget figures derived from *The Europa Year Book, 1976*, Vol. II: *Africa, The Americas, Asia, Australasia* (Europa Publications, London, 1976).

f. (RE) = Revised Estimates; (PR) = Provisional Remittances; (E) = Voted Estimates; (DE) = Draft Estimates, submitted to Parliament. The above breakdown is valid only for budget figures from the *UN Statistical Yearbook, 1975* (Est) is used to denote estimates from all other sources of budgetary data. *All other figures are for closed accounts.*

g. This figure is unreliable.

h. Figures for the Force Armée Royale.

i. National Budget figures for Nigeria from UN, Economic Commission for Africa, *African Statistical Yearbook, 1975*, Part I; *North Africa*, pp. 3-18.

j. National Budget figures for Nigeria from UN, Economic Commission for Africa, *African Statistical Yearbook, 1974.* Part II: *West Africa*, pp. 16-19.

k. National Budget figures for Somalia from UN, Economic Commission for Africa, *African Statistical Yearbook, 1975*, Part III: *East Africa*, pp. 28-40.

m. National Budget figures for Tunisia from UN, Economic Commission for Africa, *African Statistical Yearbook, 1975*, Part 1: *North Africa*, pp. 6-20.

n. National Budget figure for North Vietnam is unofficial.

p. National Budget figures for Zambia from UN, Economic Commission for Africa, *African Statistical Yearbook, 1974*, Part IV: *Central Africa*. Others in Africa.

expenditure;
57 per cent spent over 10 per cent of their budget on military expenditure.

There are several reasons for assuming that the figures in the table should be taken only as close approximations and not as precise for present percentages of national budget for several of the countries. (For the majority of the nations they may be more or less exact.) A serious and growing qualification is that, for an important group of countries – particularly those involved in conflict – though the figures may respresent their outlays from their *own* resources, it may *not* represent all the funds they expend on miliary expenditure. This is because of additional monies donated to such countries, for military expenditure, from *another* nation. These are grant and transfer payments; they are not paid out of the budget of the nation in question. However, anyone concerned with the *total* expenditure for military purposes by developing nations, or by a particular developing nation, would require data on such transferred sums.

The various factors that qualify the data in the table are set out below.

(1) Several of these countries have raised their military expenditure substantially in the years since 1974. Military expenditure in several of the Middle East countries has risen substantially since 1974. Military expenditure in Mauritania has risen sharply in 1976-7[4] (reaching 60 per cent of expenditure, by one estimate).

(2) There is always the question of whether the publicly stated figure for military expenditure reflected real outlay – from a nation's *own* monies – for this function. This consideration again seems to apply most to several Middle East countries for which there is strong evidence of secret or unstated outlays for military expenditure. In addition, military aid from the US or the USSR, either free grant aid or on credit, to various Middle East states (and perhaps to others as well) is usually not accounted for in the national budget of the recipient state.[5] More recently, Saudi Arabia and Libya have been new suppliers of unstated grant military expenditure to numerous countries, some in the Middle East, but some elsewhere.[6] Saudi Arabia is now paying for US arms purchases by Egypt, Syria, Jordan, Pakistan, Mauritania, North Yemen, Morocco and, perhaps, Tunisia. (Several other nations may soon be added to this list.) The transfer of military assistance of one sort or another *between* LDC, is becoming a reasonably widespread activity. In addition, donation or extension of military

aid may take other forms besides cash grants, such as the loan or extended assignment of jet aircraft pilots, tank operators, or other specially trained military personnel.[7]

One might also raise the question of whether such grants or transfers are really 'a free good', or whether there may not be a national cost attached to them, particularly in subsequent years. Most particularly, this would refer to the subsequent burden of supporting the weapon systems acquired. But there are also two political considerations that may incur subsequent costs. The first is the effect on the nation's own military. The second is the question of whether such transfers and grants may not involve the nation in political relationships and conflicts that it may later regret.

(3) A constant underlying consideration is whether the category of *national* expenditure has a consistent definition, whether federal expenditure is larger or smaller in countries with a primarily socialist economy. Even in any LDC, irrespective of type of economic system, there is likely to be a relatively larger part of the economy *not* in the private sector.

In summary, these figures would indicate that military expenditure is a very sizeable fraction of the government expenditure of many developing nations. SIPRI data have also indicated the relatively sharper rise – from very much lower absolute levels – of the *rate* of increase of military expenditure in the developing nations. The basic trend over the past 20 years has been the relatively rapid rate at which military expenditure has increased in the Third World, compared with military spending on the European and North American continents. In 1957, the two major alliances of industrialised countries – NATO and the WTO – accounted for 85 per cent of total military expenditure. In 1976, this figure had fallen to 70 per cent. The Third World share over ths period rose from about 5 per cent in 1957 to 15 per cent in 1976. Over these two decades, military spending in the Third World increased at an average annual rate of nearly 10 per cent, compared with a world increase of about 3 per cent.

Notes

1. Annual data on military expenditure can be found in several sources: (a) *World Armaments and Disarmament, SIPRI Yearbook*, series of annual Yearbooks, from 1968/69 through the present; (b) *World Military Expenditures and Arms Trade*, US Arms Control and Disarmament Agency; again a series publication, with issues for 1963-73, 1965-74, and 1966-75; (c) *World Military and*

Social Expenditures (R.L. Sivard, Institute for World Order, New York), issues for 1974 and 1976; (d) *The Military Balance*, annual publication of the International Institute for Strategic Studies, London. Starting in the 1975-6 issue, there is a column showing 'per cent of Government Expenditure'. No sources are indicated. The figures differ from ours and relate to 28 developing nations only; (e) *World Tables, 1976*, published for World Bank by Johns Hopkins University Press, 1976. Latest figures are for 1973.

2. In addition, several recent publications have treated the question of military expenditure in general, its definition, or its possible reduction: (a) R. Huisken, 'The Meaning and Measurements of Military Expenditure', SIPRI Research Report, no. 10 (August 1973), (Stockholm International Peace Research Institute, 34 pages). See also *World Armaments and Disarmament, SIPRI Yearbook 1975*, pp. 103-18, and 1974, pp. 172-204; (b) 'Reduction of the Military Budgets of States Permanent Members of the Security Council by 10 percent and Utilization of the Funds thus Saved ro Provide Assistance to Developing Countries', Report of the Secretary General (United Nations, 1975), 40 pp; (c) A.S. Becker, B-C. Ysander, 'International Limitation of Military Expenditures; Issues and Problems', RAND Report, R-1911-ACDA (April 1976), 77 pp; (d) 'Reduction of Military Budgets, Measurement and International Reporting of Military Expenditures', Report prepared by the Group of Exports on the Reduction of Military Budgets. Report of the Secretary-General, 20 October 1976, mimeographed, 62 pp.

3. A single table of 'Defense Budget as a Percent of Government Expenditure, 1967', for 32 African nations appears in D.G. Morrison *et al, Black Africa, A Comparative Handbook* (The Free Press, New York, 1972). It indicates that the data for the table are derived from R.C. Sellers (ed.)., *Armed Forces of the World, A Reference Handbook* (2nd ed., 1968). However the latter book, a third volume of which was published by Praeger in 1971, contains only figures for national defence budgets and for defence expenditure as a per cent of GNP.

Another version of this table will appear in print in the 1978 SIPRI Yearbook, *World Armaments and Disarmament*, In the table in this paper, national military expenditure is derived from US Arms Control and Disarmament Agency (ACDA) figures, whereas in the SIPRI Yearbook, they are derived from SIPRI values. Since these two sources of national military expenditure figures do not produce identical values, the tables will differ and the summary percentages indicated here will differ as well from those appearing in the SIPRI Yearbook.

4. 'Mauritania, Not Our War', *The Economist*, 16 April 1977, p. 71.

5. W. Mallman, 'The Arab-Israeli Arms Build-up Since the June War 1967', outline of a research project and of a forthcoming book, private communication, 1 Oct. 1976.

6. 'Saudi Arabia's Schizophrenia', *Business Week*, 1 September 1977; M. Howe, 'Quaddafi's Prophetic Vision goes well beyond Libya', *New York Times* (Sec. 4), 7 September 1977.

7. It is useful to remember that 'Military Assistance' may take a wide range of forms:

arms trade;
arms aid;
supplying money with which to purchase weapons;
building logistical infrastructure; air bases, naval bases, etc;
paramilitary construction, aid or training – harbours, rolling stock, roads, border police, internal security forces; the categorisation will depend on the usage;
training officers and troops in the recipient country;
training officers and troops in the donor country;

supplying active duty military personnel for operations in recipient countries; advisers, 'special forces', pilots, radar operators, air-defence system operators etc;

supplying mercenaries.

PART V

LEGAL, SOCIAL AND CULTURAL SPHERES

17 MILITARISATION WITH A GLOBAL REACH: A CHALLENGE TO SOVEREIGNTY, SECURITY AND THE INTERNATIONAL LEGAL ORDER*

Asbjørn Eide

1 Introduction

This study challenges the prevailing opinion that military forces in the contemporary world serve only to protect the sovereignty of the states to which they belong, and the security of the individual living therein.

The thesis here is that, on the contrary, the dynamics of global militarisation and its manifestation in the various countries are *the most serious obstacles to the realisation of an international legal order based on sovereign equality of states and security for the human being.*

The *international legal order* is here used as a normative concept. The norms on which it is based are mainly those found in the Charter of the United Nations, as elaborated by subsequent conventions and declarations.[1]

The total impact of the aspirations contained in these norms is to create an international system where states coexist in equality and where the security of the individual is safeguarded.

In practically all countries of the world, however, there exists a *military apparatus*, which often carries with it a threat to sovereignty and security. Many argue that these establishments are there to defend the country against attack from the outside. The claim of this study is that to a large extent this is misleading. To substantiate this, I will in the following carry out a comparison between the evolving international legal order, on the one hand, and the structure of the global military order as well as its national manifestations, on the other.

*I am indebted to my colleagues in the Study Group on Militarization versus Human Rights and Peace, of the International Peace Research Association (IPRA), for discussions on the issues contained in this paper. I would also express my thanks to Marek Thee for concrete comments which have eliminated some of the weaknesses. Literature referred to here is found in the Select Bibliography at the end of the book. The paper is identifiable as PRIO-publication No. S/1979.

2 Sovereignty, Security and International Law

2.1 *Sovereignty is the Basis of the Present International Legal Order*

There have been times in the past when 'sovereignty' has been understood as the range of authority of the *person* in control of a political unit. This person could be the prince, king, czar, shah, emperor, or whatever name was given to him (or, more rarely, her). The range of his power regarding territory and subjects was determined mainly by his capacity for coercion. He did not pretend to derive his legitimacy from the people. In many cultures it was claimed that his authority came from God. Whatever justification was given, the *actual* basis of his 'legitimacy' and hence authority was his capacity to maintain, control and command the institutions for coercion, foremost among which were the armed forces.

It has taken a long time in history to move away from this conception of sovereignty and authority, and there are still places in which the struggle is being fought now. Political thinkers have provided the rational analysis, and peoples' movements have borne the pain of conflict, in transforming states into institutions which are there not to serve the sovereign or an oligarchy, but to serve the people – through their representatives. The struggle has at times been directed against alien occupation and other external dominance, sometimes against domestic repression by autocratic rulers or dominant minority groups. The resulting change in the structure of authority has given rise to changes in the normative basis of the international legal order and has in turn been influenced by those changes. There still remains a substantial legacy of traditional thinking in international law, however. This will only gradually be replaced by a mature understanding of the evolving new international legal order.[2]

This chapter is an effort to assess the impact which the world military structure has on this new legal order.

2.2 *The Security of the Individual and the Sovereignty of States*

To some authors critical of present patterns of dominance and militarism in world society, for example, federalists and world order adherents, the preferred world of the future is one with greater central, global structures of authority. To these authors, the inherent danger in the present system is claimed to be the existence of a great number of independent states. Nationalism is perceived to be a dangerous ideology which has given rise to or has been exploited by the military. The latter are claimed to utilise xenophobia, chauvinism and ethnocentrism as a way of obtaining acceptance inside the nation.[3]

Historically, this description is unfortunately in many cases true. But the reason for this is that nationalism has been perverted and manipulated, i.e. to serve as part of an ideology which equates the *nation* with the persons or groups who happen to be in control, whether or not they reflect the interests of the people (in the past, they mostly did not).

Such nationalism corresponds to the old, but now antiquated, notion of sovereignty. Since in present time sovereignty resides with the people, not the incumbent authorities unless and in so far as they are representative of the people,[4] *nationalism* should be understood as the web of ties binding together a people in solidarity, in its organisation of political institutions, in its co-ordination of cultural life and its utilisation of the natural resources of the country concerned.

The increased attention to human rights in our time has given further importance to sovereignty. The principles of human rights can only be realised through the existence of sovereign units. One of the most important components of human rights is the political one, i.e. the right to participate freely and critically in the conduct of public affairs of the country concerned.

The exercise of this right requires that there exist political entities within which public participation by all can be a meaningful reality. Such entities cannot be too large, otherwise there will be no real participation for most people. Even some existing great powers, like China, India, the United States and the Soviet Union, have *political* institutions whose scale is such that participation is problematic. The utilisation of federal structures with some local autonomy helps, but does not remove totally, the barriers to public participation. It may be assumed that the operation of a *global* world order would extend the distance between the governors and the governed to such an extent that participation would lose all reality.

Political participation by all individuals, the acceptance of the obligation to secure economic and social rights for all members of the society (which can only be achieved through a responsible and shared utilisation of the natural resources of the country), and the maintenance of respect for fundamental freedoms for all to the extent compatible with the realisation of other human rights – this is what creates human security. It is thus through the operation of an all-embracing human rights system that sovereignty can mature and security for the individual can be created.

3 Developments in International Law: Foundations of Sovereign Equality

Parallel developments have taken place within several branches of international law which all go in the direction of strengthening the principle of sovereign equality, as understood in this study.

*3.1 The Prohibition of Force (*jus contra bellum*)*

International law initially grew out of European political developments. When the unity under the Holy Roman Empire and the Catholic Church had been shattered towards the end of medieval times, and the full-fledged European nation-states with their autocratic rulers came to characterise the European political map from the seventeenth century onwards, a *law between nations* became a possibility for the first time. This, however, was a law within which sovereignty was understood to be absolute, having no external or internal limits. The sovereign was assumed to have unlimited rights of coercion against external or internal enemies. No prohibition of the use of force existed, except that which each sovereign was able to enforce on his own, through his coercive institutions.[5]

In reality, this made sovereignty very precarious. It rested on superiority in military power. The princes or kings best able to organise and utilise armed groups annexed new territories through naked aggression and established their jurisdiction over the territories they conquered after having broken the resistance of other sovereigns. The international law of the time did not outlaw such actions, nor did it deny title to land obtained by conquest.

The technical developments in some European states, spurred on by the Industrial Revolution, made it possible to design and produce weapons by which the industrialising European states brought most of Asia, Africa and the Americas under their control, directly or through settlers.[6] Conquest, even carried out by barbarous means, was not considered illegal. Sovereignty over territory was not linked to the *people* living there, but to the *person* wielding authority – and only so long as he was able to continue to do so.

In the twentieth century, all of this has changed *in law*, though not *in fact*. As previously noted, it is the purpose of this study to demonstrate that one of the main barriers to the realisation of this order in fact is the global military structure.

The normative process of change has gone through several steps. The Hague Peace Conferences in 1899 and 1907 were significant, not so much because of the results achieved,[7] but because of the utilisation of an inter-governmental, multilateral negotiating machinery on issues of war and peace. A giant step forward was made through the establishment of the League of Nations,[8] and the development obtained a further impetus by the adoption of the Briand-Kellogg pact (Act of Paris) in 1928.[9] Of the greatest significance, however, was the adoption in San Francisco in 1945 of the Charter of the United Nations, where the principle of sovereign equality of states was made the cornerstone of the new legal system, and given substance by the prohibition of the use of force contained in Article 2 (4) of the Charter.

Further improvements have been made through the adoption, by the General Assembly of the United Nations, of the Declaration on Decolonization in 1960,[10] the Declaration on Principles of International Law Concerning Friendly Relations and Cooperation among States in 1970,[11] and the Declaration on the Prohibition of Aggression in 1974.[12]

This legal development has established a dividing line between unlawful use of force (aggression in all its manifestations) and lawful *defence* (Art. 51 of the United Nations Charter).

It is this part of international law which is now called *jus contra bellum*. (It was formerly called *jus ad bellum*, but this was at a time when the legal scope for use of armed force was wider than it is today.) The changes which have taken place in this branch of international law have transformed the notion of sovereignty. Today, the notion of sovereignty includes the recognition of an obligation to let other sovereign units coexist. Through international law, the scope of action for the most powerful and militarised states has been limited and the reality of sovereignty has increased for the majority of the states of the world.

Another fundamental principle evolving during the same period is the *principle of self-determination*. This principle relates to the *jus contra bellum* in two ways, as can be seen from the following formulation in the fifth paragraph of the principle:

> Every state has the duty to refrain from any forcible action which deprives peoples referred to above in the elaboration of the present principle of their right to selfdetermination and independence. In their actions against, and resistance to, such forcible action in pursuit of their right to selfdetermination, such peoples are entitled to seek and to receive support in accordance with the purposes and the principles of the Charter.[13]

On the one hand, this principle prohibits use of force against peoples which are seeking to obtain self-determination. On the other, when national liberation movements are faced with armed repression, they are legally entitled to use armed force against the repressive side. To be sure, the conditions and scope of this right are a controversial aspect of the principle of self-determination.[14]

There are some who see a conflict between this right to use armed force and the expanding prohibition of force described above. This, however, is a misinterpretation. There is no disharmony between the principle of self-determination and the principle of sovereignty. Sovereignty is not complete unless full satisfaction is given to the principle of self-determination. Liberation movements which resort to arms when they are faced with coercive repression do not act differently from countries which resort to armed defence in case of aggression. Nevertheless, when liberation is carried out through the use of arms it can give rise to some of the negative developments typical of militarisation, developments which will be further discussed below.

3.2 Jus in bello

Significant changes have also taken place in another branch of international law, the *jus in bello*. This is sometimes also called the 'laws of war'. Reference is then mainly to the rules adopted in the Hague in 1899 and 1907.[15] Increasingly, however, it is called the 'humanitarian law applicable in armed conflict'. The initial reference for this designation was the so-called 'Geneva Law', the conventions adopted under the auspices of the International Committee of the Red Cross, in 1864, 1906, 1929 and 1977. With the latest developments, in particular through the adoption in 1977 of two new protocols additional to the Geneva conventions, the scope of this law has been widened in such a way that there is no meaningful difference between the 'Hague law' and the 'Geneva law'. Both will in the future most likely be termed 'humanitarian law applicable in armed conflict'.

It would take us too far here to go into the reorientation taking place within this law, particularly through the adoption of the two new protocols which contribute to a change in the structure of the international legal order. Only some brief indications can be given:

(i) the definition of *international conflict* has been increasingly widened, so that it now also includes wars of national liberation;[16]

(ii) the definition of what constitutes *armed forces* no longer requires that they are 'regular' and belong to a 'sovereign' in the traditional sense of the word;

(iii) the *limitation of means and methods* has been extended so that there are more substantial constraints on the utilisation of superior technology, to give reality to the general prohibition of indiscriminate and unnecessarily injurious means and methods of warfare. In particular, those who hold superiority in the air can no longer engage in unconstrained action typical of the technologically superior, like area bombardment.[17] The claim of military necessity is no longer a blank cheque for any and all actions, even when directed against military targets: if there are goals which cannot be reached by permissible means, then the goal has to be forgone.

3.3 The International Law of Human Rights

Probably no other area of legal developments has greater impact on the structure of the international legal order than that of the protection and promotion of human rights.

The skeleton of this new area of international law can be quickly given. Some antecedents existed before World War II, but almost all of it is the product of post-war developments. In terms of the substantive law, the most important legal instruments are the following:

(1) the Universal Declaration of Human Rights, adopted in 1948;
(2) the Genocide Convention, also adopted in 1948;
(3) the Convention on the Prevention and Eradication of All Forms of Racism and Racial Intolerance, adopted in 1965;
(4) the international Covenants of Human Rights, both adopted in 1966:
  (a) the Covenant on Civil and Political Rights;
  (b) the Covenant on Economic, Social and Cultural Rights.

In terms of institutions, there are the Human Rights Commission of the United Nations, the Human Rights Committee, and various subcommittees.

There has also been a normative development on the regional level, both within the Council of Europe and the Organization of American States.

The normative impact of this development is substantial. To put it briefly, it requires that government is organised in such a way that it is conducted *for* the people (the realisation of economic, social and cultural rights) and *by* the people (the right of everyone to take part in the conduct of public affairs, to have a responsible government, to have the freedom of opinion and expression and thereby critically and creatively to take part in the discussion of and the formation of national politics). Additionally, the system of human rights requires that each people obtains its right of self-determination – otherwise it does not have an institution through which it can control its own affairs and promote its own human rights.

In the language of this study, this means that sovereignty resides with the people, not with whatever authorities happen to be in control.

4 The Global Military Structure

4.1 *Military Demands and Threats: a Survey*

In the following discussion the purpose is to explore the barrier to sovereign equality and individual security caused by militarisation.

This barrier manifests itself in two major ways: one is the *demands* based on military requirements, directed towards the civilian society. These are demands for economic and natural resources and for man-power, demands for organisation of the civilian infrastructure to serve military needs, and a variety of other requirements caused by excessive military preparations. These demands are not directed only to their own civilian society, as some of the most militarised countries also make strong demands on resources, infrastructure and bases in other countries.

The other dimension is the *threat* emerging from the military – the threat of the use of arms. This threat has increased steeply over time. It can be measured by the range and capacity of destruction. The greatest threat is found in the existence and evolution of nuclear weapons, but 'conventional' weapons have also increased in their capacity for destruction. The range of weapons has also increased. (For further details on this, see Robinson, 1979, and Lumsden, 1978.)

The threat is sometimes directed against the authorities of other states, at other times (in collaboration with more or less non-respon-sible authorities) against movements seeking political and economic change in other states. Sometimes the threat is also directed against their own domestic population or parts of it.

4.2 *The Mythology of Military Functions and the Intellectual Process of Liberation from the Myths*

The demands and threats which have been referred to above can easily be detected by even the most superficial of investigations. Therefore, to sustain the acceptance of inflated military establishments, there are a number of myths diffused in society.[18] These myths are more or less consciously spread, through mass media and in particular through the use of the educational system, and they are unconsciously accepted, since there are few alternative conceptions available. Two of these myths will be briefly discussed here as a background for the following analysis. One (presently the most common one) is that the military forces always serve the function of defence, and defence *only*. The other is that the military forces are inherently capable of creating internal security. On the surface, these claims – if they were true – would make the presence and functions of military forces compatible with the international legal order. Defence is a legitimate concern, permissible under international law as provided for in the UN Charter, art. 51. 'Internal security' is a more ambiguous function, but if it was to mean the security of each individual to develop freely, with only the restraints flowing from the need to respect the right of others, then 'internal security' would be compatible with the system of human rights and thereby with the present international legal order.

Beyond the two myths mentioned, there is an assumption which is almost universally shared and almost as universally wrong: the assumption that the military always serves the interests of their own nation and peoples. This assumption is based on the fact that there are separate military establishments in practically all independent countries. From that fact it is taken for granted that the armed forces form an attribute of the sovereignty of the country and that they are there to protect that sovereignty. Since sovereignty in the present international legal order is based on the principle that authority is to be exercised on behalf of and through delegation from the people, the precise assumption must therefore be that the military establishment acts on behalf of the people in order to protect the exercise of authority which is based on delegation from the people.

Not surprisingly, there has in recent years been a stronger effort to increase acceptability, due to the enormous growth in military expenditure and in the capacity for destruction and annihilation. It has been claimed that in non- or low-industrial countries (the category in which most Third World countries find themselves), the armed forces contribute to the economic development of the country concerned. Since economic development is a widely accepted goal, this myth has significantly helped obtain acceptance of the quickly accelerating armaments in the Third World. (For social science contributions which have advanced the theory of modernisation, see Johnson, 1962, and Kennedy, 1974).

Over the last years, however, a process of intellectual liberation from these myths has slowly evolved. Peace research has been instrumental in the process of demystification, through hard empirical work and through further theoretical analysis. The claim is not that the myths are entirely wrong – in most cases, they have a core of truth – but in their general and vague contents they result in highly distorted perceptions which make disarmament difficult.

Several of the authors represented in this reader have contributed significantly to the demystification, partly by the works here included and partly by other works. In the following, some of the steps of demystification will be outlined, and further steps suggested.

4.3 The National Level. How Much is Enough? The Lack of Control

The first challenge to the prevailing myths is that military *preparations*, even when carried out for defence purposes *only*, have unintended consequences which gradually have come to overshadow and pervert the original purpose. A number of research contributions have demonstrated this (Richardson, 1960; Senghaas, 1974; Ahfeldt, 1972; and several others). The main findings can be summed up as follows.

The arms *race* became, from the middle of the nineteenth century, a systemic feature of international society, resulting from the military policies pursued by the states which initiated the Industrial Revolution. Industrial capacity has to a significant extent been turned to the production of weapons, and a continuous process of 'modernisation' of weaponry takes place through heavy investment in military research and development. Military competition between industrial states has led to phenomenal increases in the place allotted to the military in production and research. While at the earlier stages, militarising states competed in the size and quantity of weapons, in recent years the race among the most industrialised states has been mainly in the 'quality', i.e. the range, destruction capacity, precision and other attributes cherished highly by strategists and military leaders (Thee, Ch. 1 of this book). The question of what is *enough* (see Vagts, 1937; and Skjelsbæk, Ch. 4 of this book) has lost practically all meaning, since it can be argued that 'the other side' might come up with some surprising new weapons and that hence the 'own side' has to be continuously abreast of the technological possibilities by inventing and developing new weapons.

A consequence of the arms race has been a continuous increase in the military demands on the civilian society. Not only the armed forces themselves, but also the arms manufacturers, the research establishments, the new security bureaucracy – all of these have developed their vested interests in a continued expansion of military preparations. The military-industrial complex is a prominent feature of some contemporary industrial societies. The demands made by this complex of interest groups on the society at large has very little relevance to what is enough for defence. But defence and national security are still the most common justification.

The arms race, which has made the requirements of defence increasingly irrelevant as a guide for military planning, started as an action/reaction process. A pair of states involved in a deadly quarrel reacted to perceived threats from other states to their security by increasing their military capacity, which in turn gave rise to fears by the other side for its security. But when the militarisation of society reached certain advanced levels, the threat from the outside became increasingly irrelevant: the continuation of militarisation was carried forward by those very forces which had been created by the arms race. Since there are at least some people within the society who react negatively to the high allocation of resources to the military and to the dangers caused by the weapons, justifications had to be given. If no plausible threat could be demonstrated on the immediate horizon, the argument could be used that there was a *potential* threat, which could materialise into an actual threat under different future scenarios. Strategists delivered the speculations required for this. For a long time this has been sufficient to subdue opponents of the growth and sophistication of the military.

The notion of potential rather than actual threat reduced the need to give plausible justifications for military build-ups, since there could always be found some hypothetical 'worst case' in the future which could justify practically any military preparation which the country was economically and industrially able to carry. Added to this was the notion of deterrence, by which it was claimed that the purpose was neither to attack nor to defend the territory, but to deter the other side from attacking by such military preparations which would make the costs of an attack unbearable. This *ideology of deterrence* further reduced the need for plausible justifications of the level of armaments: it was argued that the stronger the deterrence capacity, the greater the cost of attack. Hence, rational preparation for defence *properly speaking*, in the meaning of organising enough resources to defend the territory against an invasion, no longer became a real issue.

Decision-making on questions of military preparations has become a field in which very few are involved. This is not to say that the public at large does not *support* the military preparations. On the contrary, there is in many cases wide acceptance. 'Security' and 'defence' are concepts which relate to highly emotional problems of the insecurity of the individual (Lumsden, Ch. 19 of this book). There is, however, a very low level of knowledge and analysis in the debate among the public on such questions as what are the *real* requirements of defence? in what does the *actual* threat from the enemy consist? what are the *usefulness* and the *functions* of the military installations? what possibility is there to utilise *alternative defence* measures which might have less negative impact on the society concerned?

Even in the parliamentary democracies there is very little public *control*, but only public *acquiescence*. It is much less critical and much less informed in this field than in relation to other state functions such as education and health.

4.4 The Military as Instrument of Domestic Centralisation and Socialisation

In historical terms, it is a myth that the military has developed in order to serve the function of national *defence* or protection of the citizens. The military emerged as an instrument of power by which totalitarian power was sought. The traditional notion of 'sovereignty', as used in the early writings on the theory of state (Bodin, 1576; Hobbes, 1651) reflected the fact that the 'sovereign' was seeking to obtain absolute, internal control. His main instrument was military force. How much has this changed in our time?

This differs in various parts of the world, but the difference is more apparent than real. For a closer examination, the following distinction should be made:

(i) direct, coercive internal control by the military as an organisation, either directed by the military leadership itself, or directed by a single civilian (or an oligarchy of civilians) using the military for the maintenance of authoritarian rule;

(ii) indirect control, by which the needs of the military are given primacy over civilian needs (allocation over the state budget, infrastructural developments, screening of personnel to the civilian administration on the basis of their reliability for military interests, higher priority given to military research than to civilian purposes, utilisation of skilled manpower for military versus civilian purposes, and so on).

It is mainly in the Third World that direct military control can be observed today. In many of those countries in which the military has intervened directly in politics, the level of militarisation (in absolute terms of expenses, equipment, manpower) is rather low, compared with the high level in the industrialised world. This apparent paradox can be explained by two factors. One is that in most of the industrialised countries, the growth of military machinery has gone on for a much longer period. It has gone through wars and crises, and the civilian population has become accustomed to its demands in such a way that these no longer meet serious political resistance. Direct military control is therefore not necessary in order to have those demands met. Second, in *relative* terms, the costs of the escalating militarisation now going on in the Third World are much higher than in the industrialised countries. In particular, there is a much higher share of the state budget allotted to *military* demands than to civilian needs, compared to the situation prevailing in the industrialised countries (see the data presented by Leitenberg and Ball in Ch. 16 of this book). This is one of the reasons why allocations for military purposes in the Third World are so much more immediately detrimental to the civilian population and are therefore pushed through by coercion, and often also by direct intervention by the military.

4.5 Militarised Countries: the Leaders and their Technological Basis

There is in existence an international military structure with hierarchy, dominance and dependence. This structure is the most profound barrier to the realisation of sovereign equality. In the following sections, we will discuss the role of the various units in this structure: the leaders, the followers and the peripheral actors. (See also the contributions by Thee and Øberg, Chs. 1 and 3 of this book.)

Significant for our understanding of the leadership in this hierarchy are the processes which were set in motion by World War II. There had been hierarchy before, influenced not least by the superiority obtained by those states which initiated the Industrial Revolution, but during World War II the patterns were substantially changed.

The war was a major confrontation between the industrial centres of the world. Imperial metropoles harnessed their resources for this massive trial of strength. At no time in previous history had the significance of weapons and capacity for arms production been so important. Some of the major industrial powers exhausted themselves in this giant struggle and were temporarily reduced to inferior positions in the international system. The United States emerged as the militarily most powerful actor, followed by the Soviet Union. The harnessing of vast resources for military purposes left its profound impact on the societies concerned. Dynamics of further militarisation had been set in motion. The process was not substantially reversed when peace was restored in 1945. While there was a substantial reduction of manpower in the armed forces in order to provide labour for industry, arms *production* ran its own course and was fuelled by a massive investment in military research and development.

Half the research and development in the United States and the Soviet Union today is related to military requirements, mainly the development of weapons and supporting technology. The huge funds spent for this has also had considerable impact on the orientation of civilian research. The main justification used for this was the Cold War. Overwhelmingly, military research and development has been concentrated in the United States and the Soviet Union.

In these centres the process of modernisation of weapons takes place. Most important additions in the military arsenal are presently made in the nuclear field, but tremendous changes in so-called 'conventional' weapons have also taken place (SIPRI/Lumsden, 1978). This has significantly reduced the security of peoples throughout the world.

4.6 *Military Alliances and the Decline of Sovereignty*

Research and development contribute substantially to an unequal integration of the economies of state members of military alliances. It serves to create and advance an unequal division of labour between the different members. While the research is spearheaded by the dominant powers of the military alliances, there is an increasing integration of arms production (see Kaldor, 1972).

This is one of the factors which changes the role of the military. The traditional justification of military alliances is that of collective self-defence. This term was originally conceived to mean co-operation in *national* self-defence. States obliged themselves to come to the assistance of other states subject to aggression from the outside. But as a consequence of integration into the military alliances, the *national* element faded progressively into the background, and the defence of the integrated alliance became the prominent concern. Serious research has still not yet been carried out, however, which would have made it possible to demonstrate how far military preparations have gone in the direction of serving the maintenance of the military alliance as such, rather than protecting the national sovereignty against outside threats, from whatever source they come.

Alliances, in fact, have come to have a dual function. There is the stated aim of collective self-defence. On the other hand, there is dominance and covert coercion within the alliance, in some cases even open coercion. This has in particular been demonstrated by the Warsaw treaty alliance, most dramatically by the invasion of Czechoslovakia in 1968. The Warsaw treaty organisation also demonstrates, better than any other, the serious undermining of national sovereignty which can be caused by military integration. The scope for civilian politics, for democratic responses to the demands by the people (again as demonstrated by the 'Prague Spring' of 1968) is profoundly subverted by such integration. Far from protecting the national independence of the respective countries, there is collective coercion led by the hegemonial power.

This is reinforced by the fact that the military has certain characteristics which are different from the civilian – the strong reliance on hierarchy, discipline and secrecy. When military integration also embraces arms production, scientific co-operation and other crucial aspects of society, this means that a military/industrial/scientific/bureaucratic complex evolves on a transnational level.

The ominous aspect of this process is that 'national security' has increasingly come to mean the security of this integrated military alliance.

The greater the inequalities between the different members of the alliance, the more likely it is that the interests and perceptions of the dominant partner determine the orientation to 'national security'. Thereby, the armed forces and their civilian counterparts in the security bureaucracy become bridgeheads which endanger national sovereignty.

4.7 The Integration of Third World Military Establishments into the World Military Structure

One of the most conspicuous features of the dynamics of contemporary global military development is the increasing integration of Third World military forces into the global military structure.

The causes of this are multiple. Some are to be found in the political dynamics inside Third World states. The colonial legacy tells part of the story. In colonial times, the metropolitan power established armed forces into which were integrated, but mainly on the lower levels, personnel from the colonial territory. This personnel was utilised to help maintain control over the local population. The function of internal policing was the task to which these colonial forces became accustomed from an early stage. These forces came to be considered as enemies by the people, and from their side they viewed nationalist movements as subversive elements. The metropolitan power also created a local *bureaucracy* to serve its administrative needs, for which local personnel was used in the lower ranks. An identification based on common interests tied the colonial army and the colonial bureaucracy together, in more or less open hostility to the politically conscious parts of the civilian population.

Where independence was obtained through nationalist mobilisation, latent conflict was bound to exist between the civilian, nationalist leaders and the local components of the colonial army and bureaucracy. This conflict provides much of the explanation for the later military *coups* in many Third World countries (Huq, 1977).

But this is only part of the explanation. The other is the pressure and encouragement coming from the highly militarised industrial countries. In the period of the Cold War, the major world military powers sought also to harness Third World resources in the geopolitical interests of the superpowers, and military 'aid' was used for this purpose. Thus geopolitical interests of dominant centre states coincided with the interests of the military establishments of Third World states, some of whom had considered themselves subdued by civilian politicians. The meeting of geopolitical interests of the most militarised industrial states with the domestic political interests of Third World military leaders resulted in the formation of the Bagdad Pact, SEATO and other military alliances. On the other hand, struggle for independence (when it was not voluntarily conceded by the metropolitan power but went through a stage of armed conflict) in several cases led liberation movements to seek military support from the Soviet Union, which in turn created dependence on that power – a power which increasingly has demonstrated hegemonial ambitions and has used the dependency of weaker states for its own purposes.

This geopolitical competition by the superpowers has given a substantial boost to the strength of the military in Third World countries, a strength which they have used to gain superiority over their civilian counterparts.

Part of the explanation for Third World militarisation is also to be found in the perception of threat from the outside. There is a chain effect of threat policies operating on the global level. The superpower confrontation between the United States and the Soviet Union leads, on a second level, *China* to perceive a threat from the Soviet Union, and on the next level it has brought *India* to perceive a threat from China (which has armed itself), as well as from Pakistan (which has been armed by the United States for purposes of geopolitical interests).

Vietnam, presently one of the most militarised countries in Asia, developed its armed forces during the protracted conflict with the United States and the former South Vietnamese (Saigon) forces. Subsequently, Vietnam has become an ally of the Soviet Union and has been further armed by it. This very alliance has made China perceive Vietnam as a part of a wider threat to China, and has been one of the causes of the Chinese military action against Vietnam in February 1979.

In a world of inequality there is a ladder of threats emanating from the most powerful, reverberating down to the weakest entity in the international military structure. Part of the Third World armament today – but only a part of it – can be ascribed to this system of threat. Thus the heavy militarisation of the industrialised countries bears a significant share of the responsibility for Third World arms increases.

For a long period after World War II, major industrialised countries intervened openly and directly in conflicts within the Third World. In the last few years, direct intervention has become more rare. But interventionist *capacity* is maintained, and represents a continued source of threat to smaller states.

The exercise of sovereignty by Third World states is made precarious through the existence of this interventionist capacity. When Third World states seek to pursue policies of self-reliance, asserting their permanent sovereignty over natural resources in accordance with General Assembly resolution 1803 (1961) and the Declaration of the Economic Rights and Duties of States (Assembly resolution 3281 (1971)) and therefore seek to use their own natural resources for domestic needs, the possibility of direct military intervention from the dominant industrial countries cannot be entirely discounted.[19] This remains, therefore, a justification for continued military build-up in the Third World, but the actual consequence of this is increased dependence, not further independence, as will be shown below.

Though interventionist activities from the North have declined, the military link between dominant industrialised countries and Third World military forces continues in many cases.

One aspect of this is the formation of what has been termed sub-empires, states which serve as intermediate links between the industrial centres and the weaker Third World states. Regional, hegemonial powers, supplied with armaments by industrialised countries, intervene in neighbouring states, mainly to prevent or slow down nationalist political change. *Iran* was for several years one of the most dramatic illustrations of this, having pursued an intense militarisation and equipped itself to intervene in various neighbouring territories. *South Africa* is another case in point. A continuation of the occupation of Namibia, with weapons either delivered from the Western world or locally produced through assistance from Western countries, must in part be explained by the fact that Namibia contains some of the richest uranium deposits in the non-socialist world. The South African intervention in Angola in 1976 was claimed by South African leaders to have been carried out in understanding with the United States.[20] On the other end of the political spectrum, *Vietnam* has developed a sub-imperial role through encouragement by the Soviet Union, which, for example, manifested itself in the invasion of Cambodia in December 1978.

4.8 The Internal Effect of Militarisation in the Third World

Militarisation leads to maldevelopment everywhere, but more openly so in the Third World than elsewhere. The origin of militarisation has been discussed above; what needs to be further underlined here is the impact this has had for the economic, political and social life of the countries concerned.

The military alliance between highly industrialised states of the West or East, and the Third World state in question, became a channel by which the former could influence domestic politics of the latter. This was done more or less deliberately – through military training, which included ideological indoctrination, and through the provision of means of coercion, which gave the military a superior 'argument' in their conflicts with the civilians: the capacity to coerce, even kill, the civilian opponents.

This has had many negative consequences. Among others, it makes policies of self-reliance very difficult to pursue. The exchange between high-cost, technologically advanced weaponry from the industrialised countries, with agricultural products and other raw materials from the Third World, reinforces the unequal division of labour initiated during the colonial period.[21]

Maldevelopment is also the *indirect* consequence of malallocation of scarce domestic resources for unproductive purposes – i.e. for militarisation – in place of allocation for purposes which would advance a civilian economy to satisfy basic needs for all. In social terms, militarisation intensifies inequality, hierarchy and bureaucratisation. The notion of the 'modernising function of the armed forces', so popular in social science in the 1960s, in fact covers a severe maldevelopment which it will take a long time to heal.[22]

Many states of the Third World are increasingly controlled by a small, but powerful and privileged, group of people, military and bureaucratic. In many Third World countries there is hardly any national, civilian bourgeoisie of any significance. There is too often only a highly paid, coercive bureaucracy with military underpinnings, operating as the local cogwheel of an international conveyor belt by which rich, industrialised countries are increasing the profits from the Third World.

The political consequences of this are severe. The process in many cases starts even while civilian governments are still in power, since the integration into a global economic market creates domestic conflict which makes some of these governments rely increasingly on military and police coercion to maintain control. When this has continued for some time, it normally results in direct military take-over, which further leads to an even more severe perversion of the political system, including massive violations of human rights.

4.9 Technological Asymmetry in the Global Military Structure

The military forces of weaker states, it has been shown above, are to a large extent integrated in a global hierarchy and thereby in some ways servants of external interests by hegemonial powers. But this is not the only way in which sovereignty is undermined by the global military order.

In spite of the fact that an increasing number of Third World countries are presently obtaining highly sophisticated weapons, there remains a very obvious armament hierarchy in the world. The most sophisticated weapons are controlled by very few states. This applies not only to nuclear armaments, but also to a wide range of other major weapons. Most of them are *produced* in the industrialised countries. The development of new arms requires heavy investments and a solid scientific and technological base. The heavy concentration on military research and development in the United States and the USSR has been demonstrated by Forsberg (1972), Thee (1978) and Väyrynen (1978). Superiority in military technology brought some military leaders of the industrialised world to advance the concept of 'automated battlefield techniques', by which rich and technologically advanced powers should be able to maintain coercive control over hostile masses in distant parts of the world.[23] The Vietnamese experience, however, proved this to be possible only during shorter periods of time. This is due to the strong counter-forces generated by such warfare. Resistance of a nature which is adapted to the problems posed by 'automated warfare', mainly in the form of guerrilla forces, develops in the target territory. Within the industrialised country carrying out the war, anti-war movements arise due to the indiscriminate and brutal nature of asymmetrical warfare.

Since direct interventionism therefore has become less attractive, greater reliance has been placed on alliances with the armes of the Third World, training, transfer of weapons (including the most sophisticated and modern) and transfer of arms-producing capacity in Third World countries.[24]

The outcome has been to create a technological asymmetry on a second level, *within* the Third World. This has arisen between regimes whose aspirations are to maintain regional and national control mainly through coercion, and on the other hand popular movements which seek autonomy for their peoples or states.

The outcome is a confrontation between heavily armed centres and technologically weak popular movements. In the long run, reliance on means of coercion is probably going to be as self-defeating for the militarised regimes in the Third World as it was for the United States in Indo-China or Portugal in its colonies. The fate of the Shah of Iran can be used to demonstrate the limited 'stability' obtained by military coercion. In the short run, however, transfers of weapons may make governments believe that they can pursue whatever policies they like, even when these do not respond to the interests of the people.

5 Conclusions: From the Present World Military Structure to National Sovereignty and Individual Security

There is today in existence a global military structure with the two superpowers at the top, actively competing with each other and at the same time having a dominant influence on the militarisation of the rest of the world.

The various national military establishments which presently can be found spread around the world occupy various positions in the global structure. They have different functions depending on the positions they hold. At the highest level, i.e. at the level of the superpowers, the military serves the primary function of international control of established dominance. A powerful element in this is the leadership in research and development of new systems, and a continuous technological transformation of the armed forces, thereby maintaining a permanent inferiority and insecurity for other states. Through the mythology of 'national security', they also serve the general purpose of internal control and cohesion.

Moving from the superpowers to more peripheral actors, the role of the local military becomes increasingly subordinate to and dependent on the dominant states. This dependency exists not only in the field of armament technology, dependence on military training and advice, but also dependency concerning the functions served by armed forces. In periphery countries, both in the Third World and in some parts of Europe, the internal function of repression has in many cases the function of adapting the country to an inferior position in the international economic system. This is not always the case: some armed forces have been organised to resist foreign *economic* dominance. Even in such cases, however, links with hegemonial powers reduce the scope of national sovereignty.

Facing these structural conditions, realisation of the aspirations contained in the international legal order (as described in the first part of this paper) is bound to face severe difficulties.

The most important task will be to bring about, through education and consciousness-raising, a new approach to security. In the same way as national sovereignty is based on the support and consent of the people rather than on the will of the 'sovereign', so also will national security have to be based on the security of the individual and the collectivity of individuals rather than on the protection of the military establishments.

Beyond this, we have to recognise what may seem a paradox. The restoration of national sovereignty cannot be achieved by national efforts alone. Efforts carried out unilaterally, by separate states seeking to obtain full self-determination, will stumble on the barriers inherent in the global military structure.

If they seek to secure their own protection by militarisation along traditional lines, they will become *more*, not *less*, dependent. If, on the other hand, they seek to abstain from militarisation, they may remain highly vulnerable to incursions and blackmail.[25]

Part of the answer to these problems lies in the utilisation of low-technology military preparation in a purely defensive posture, where only a small number of persons form the standing nucleus of armed forces, but where there is a preparedness for a nation-wide call-up for guerrilla-like resistance in case of aggression. Part of the equipment could possibly be certain precision-guided munitions which cannot be used in an indiscriminate way nor inflict unnecessary suffering, and certain kinds of missiles which can be carried manually and which can be used to stop or slow down an aggressor, without being utilisable for aggression.

But this can be only part of the answer. No military preparation, of whatever kind, can ever guarantee against aggression. In the military field, the only achievement can be to eliminate all offensive and threat-provoking equipment. The main problem, however, is political – not military.

It lies in the restoration of sovereignty and full-fledged self-determination, guaranteeing the security of the individual. This can only be achieved through international co-operation and through the instrumentality of international organisations.

International organisations can be used in order to make states co-exist peacefully, to adapt to each other, to protect each other from interference, let each one control their own resources, and solve disputes by peaceful means. The historical evolution of a system of dominance and dependence, within which military coercion has played a prominent role, needs an international organisation to help disentangle the various units from each other in a peaceful way.

The evolution of *jus contra bellum* has been possible only in the context of the evolution of international organisations. The *jus contra bellum* has already given greater reality to sovereignty, by stigmatising those who intervene through armed force on foreign territory.

The task which now faces civilisation is to dismantle the global military structure. A process of disarmament, starting from the top (i.e. in those countries which are most heavily militarised) is required. This is not a new observation. What is somewhat new, however, is that the achievement of *sovereignty* and individual *security* demands disarmament. In the past, the very opposite conclusion has been drawn. But by now, armament dynamics have abundantly demonstrated the complete failure of militarisation as a way of obtaining sovereignty or security.

In the process of disarmament, peace-making and peace-keeping by the United Nations will be a necessary part. But it can only work as a part of disarmament. The failure of United Nations peace-keeping in the past has been due to a complete lack of will to reduce the level of armaments, be it in the industrialised countries (who by their military weight bear down heavily on the weaker states) or the new nations of the Third World. The road they have all taken is that of militarisation – and the results are there for all to see. The need is to reverse the trends: disarmament is a precondition for the realisation of national sovereignty and individual security.

Notes

1. For details, see below.

2. The main controversy in the future will be between those who favour a high legal significance for United Nations declarations and other resolutions as a source of international law, and those who do not.

3. There is a comprehensive discussion in recent international literature on the preferred values around which international society *ought* to be organised. Of special interest are the studies prepared within the project 'World Order Models 1990' under the auspices of the Institute of World Order. Among relevant publications in this series are Richard Falk, *A Study of Future Worlds* (Free Press, New York, 1975); Rajni Kothari, *Footsteps into the Future. Diagnosis of the Present World and a Design for an Alternative* (Free Press, New York, 1974); Saul Mendlovitz (ed.), *On the Creation of a Just World Order* (Free Press, New York, 1975); Ali A. Mazrui, *A World Federation of Cultures: An African Perspective* (Free Press, New York, 1977); Johan Galtung, *The True Worlds: A Transnational Perspective* (North Holland Publishing Co., Amsterdam, forthcoming). Even such a profound contributor to the debate on the future world order as Richard Falk tends to see sovereignty as obsolete and dangerous. See his *Status of Law in the International Society* (Princeton University Press, Princeton, 1970), particularly at pp. 554 ff., and in his contribution to the World Order Studies mentioned in the preceding note. But see his notion 'volitional decentralization' which to some extent coincides with my notion of sovereign equality (Status of Law, p. 556).

4. This understanding of sovereignty flows from the formulation of the principle of self-determination as contained in the Declaration on Principles of International Law Concerning Friendly Relations and Cooperation among States (see below, note 11).

5. The legal history of the regulation of the use of force is described by Brownlie (1963) and Ferencz (1972).

6. For details, see SIPRI/Lumsden 1978, Chapters I and II.

7. The outcome, which was very limited in terms of prohibition of force, consisted mainly in a number of conventions on the conduct of war, seeking to restrain its brutality. The original intentions to bring about arms reductions came to nothing.

8. The Covenant of the League of Nations contained no prohibition of the use of force, even for aggression, but contained procedural rules aimed at a 'cooling down' period.

9. The Kellogg-Briand Pact of 1928 (General Treaty for the Renunciation of War as an Instrument of National Policy) was the first to contain an express renunciation of the use of force.

10. Resolution 1514 (XV) of the UN General Assembly, adopted in 1960, denounced the use of force to deprive peoples of their right to self-determination.

11. Resolution 2625 (XXV) of the UN General Assembly, adopted in 1970, containing this declaration, gives further details to the prohibition of the use of force and makes it clearer than before that armed struggle for self-determination is legitimate. The exact scope of this right remains unclear in several directions.

12. Adopted by the UN General Assembly in Res. 3314 (XXIX). It contains a detailed prohibition of aggression and in Art. 7 an express acceptance of the right to struggle for self-determination and to obtain support to that end.

13. From the Declaration on Friendly Relations (see note 11).

14. An illustration can be quoted in the resolution on Namibia, adopted by the General Assembly on 21 December 1976, in which it is stated in paragraph 24: '*Declares* that the continued illegal occupation of Namibia by South Africa constitutes an act of aggression against the Namibian people and against the United Nations as the legal authority to administer the territory until independence . . .'

15. The most important among these was the IVth Convention of 1907 respecting the Laws and Customs of Warfare on Land.

16. Art. 1, paragraph 4 of the new protocol I, adopted in 1977.

17. Articles 48-56 of the new Protocol I.

18. See note 15.

19. There are, even in our days, statements made by authoritative spokesmen of major industrialised countries to the effect that they do not exclude armed intervention to secure their energy supplies from other countries. A recent statement to this effect has been made by the US Secretary of Defense, Mr Brown, on 25 February 1979.

20. South African leaders made several statements during the invasion of Angola, claiming that this had been made with the secret agreement of the United States. No evidence of this has been made available, however.

21. See IPRA Study Group 1978.

22. See Adekson, 1978 (i), Kaldor, 1976 (with extensive references), Eide, 1976, IPRA Study Group, 1978, and the contribution by Ulrich Albrecht to this book.

23. The notion of the 'automated battlefield' has been associated, in particular, with the then Chief of the Staff of the US Army, General Westmoreland, who expressed his views on the nature of future warfare by a highly industrialised county at a lunch in Sheraton Park Hotel in Washington on 14 October 1969. See Congressional Records, US Senate, 16 October 1969.

24. For details, see SIPRI, 1974; Kaldor, Eide and Merrit, 1979, and the contribution by Signe Landgren-Bäckström to this book.

25. The difficulties of Zambia and Mozambique in preventing Rhodesian incursions and bombardments in recent years can be quoted as an illustration.

18 THE CAUSES AND CORRELATES OF WESTERN MILITARISM

William Eckhardt

1 Attitudes, Behaviours and Institutions

Militarism may be studied as an attitude or set of attitudes in the minds of people, as a behaviour or set of behaviours in which people engage, or as an institution or set of institutions which people establish to facilitate or to organise such behaviour. In this chapter we shall not be primarily concerned with military behaviours or events, such as wars or preparations for war, nor shall we be primarily concerned with military institutions, such as armies or military colleges. We shall focus primarily upon military attitudes which presumably make people *ready* to go to a military college, to join an army, to go to war, or to support such activities and institutions financially and morally.

We define an attitude as a readiness or willingness to engage in certain behaviours under certain circumstances. However, this definition begs the question of whether attitudes, as such, are necessarily related to relevant behaviours. More precisely, then, an attitude is simply an expression of liking or approving or agreeing with something, or of disliking, disapproving or disagreeing with something. In the study of attitudes, the burden of proof rests with the student to show that *liking* something leads to *doing* something. It is clear that we might very much like to do something, but not have the ability to do it, in which case we won't do it. However, we may still support either financially or morally those who can do it, in which case our attitude may contribute to the behaviour even though we may not be able to participate directly.

Our attitude or readiness or willingness to pursue certain goals is a complicated process which involves many, if not all, aspects of the human mind. We shall be satisfied to categorise these aspects as affective, cognitive, ideological and moral. 'Affective' refers to our more personal feelings about ourselves, other people and life in general. 'Cognitive' refers to our preferred way of thinking about ourselves, other people, or life in general. 'Ideological' refers to the way we prefer to relate to society or people in general. 'Moral' refers to our basic criteria for determining what is good or bad, right or wrong, just or unjust, in human relations.

Militarism as an attitude, then, is the readiness or willingness to engage in behaviours which have been authorised and institutionalised by a government for the purpose of using or threatening to use destructive weapons against the people and property of another nation, or even against the people (but seldom the property) of one's own nation. This definition is hardly final, but would seem to be sufficient as a point of departure. We shall be looking for affective, cognitive, ideological, and moral aspects of this attitude to militarism in the course of this paper.

2 Questionnaire Method of Study

If we want to know how people feel or think about anything, the most straightforward way of finding out is simply by asking them. This procedure is known as the questionnaire method of study, which is the primary method used in the studies reported in this paper.

There are at least three questions which may be raised about the accuracy and adequacy of the questionnaire method: how honest are people's responses likely to be? how reliable are they likely to be? and how valid are they likely to be?

The honesty of responses seems to depend almost entirely on how much the respondents believe that their responses will not be used against them. Consequently, one might not expect responses to be too honest if the respondent is answering a questionnaire as part of a procedure in applying for a job, especially when the unemployment rate is high. Likewise, if the respondent does not trust the administrator of the questionnaire, responses might not be very honest. In academic and clinical situations, responses are usually fairly honest, especially where anonymity is assured. Even in such situations, poor people and people who live in poorer countries tend to agree with questionnaire items regardless of the direction of their wording (Eckhardt, 1971a, p. 213). This tendency is known as an agreement response set, which is controlled by reversing the direction of item wording. Some people may also tend to give what they believe to be a socially desirable response, rather than to express their own thoughts and feelings. Social desirability scales (sets of items) may be included in any questionnaire in order to control for this response set. Finally, some people may not be familiar with the content of a questionnaire, in which case they may give many uncertain responses, so that their scores do not measure their attitude towards the content so much as they measure their uncertainty about the content. Uncertainty scores are easily obtainable in order to control for this response set.

The reliability of a person's responses to a set of items may be determined in at least two ways. Firstly, we may divide the set of items into two halves, and find out if the scores obtained from these two halves are correlated with each other. This is known as the split-half method of determining reliability. Second, we may administer the same set of items at two different times, in order to find out if responses were affected by transient influences operating at these different times. This procedure is known as the test-retest method of determining reliability. In both cases, if there is a fairly high correlation between the scores obtained from two halves of the same set of items and between the scores obtained from the same set at two different times, we accept the scale (or set of items) as being reliable.

The final question of validity is concerned with whether we are measuring what we claim to be measuring. It is all very well to label the responses to a set of items 'militarism', 'neuroticism', 'intelligence', etc., but how do we know we are really measuring what these labels connote? One way is to find out whether reserve officers obtain higher scores than conscientious objectors on a militarism scale, whether patients in mental hospitals get higher scores than those outside on a neuroticism scale, and whether people in higher school grades get higher scores than those in lower grades on an intelligence test. This procedure is called the 'known groups' method of establishing the validity of any questionnaire. This method has been used in most of the studies reported in this paper. It might be noted that this method, in establishing the validity of a questionnaire, simultaneously establishes some relationship between the attitudes and behaviours, showing the extent to which people's attitudes correspond with their behaviours outside the questionnaire situation.

3 Militarism Scales

Militarism scales have been around for at least fifty years in the social science literature. Porter (1926) developed a militarism scale and validated it by the 'known groups' method. One hundred reserve officers and ROTC students made high scores, while conscientious objectors and pacifist students made low scores. Droba also prepared a militarism scale (Thurstone, 1928). There was nothing in the reviewed literature on any further uses of these scales.

Many other militarism scales have been developed in the meantime, some of which have been reviewed by Eckhardt and Lentz (1967). In the rest of this chapter, I shall confine myself for the most part to those scales which I have had occasion to use during the last 15 years, since I am most familiar with them and with the results obtained from their use.

The Peace Research Group of Des Moines developed a 69-item militarism scale in 1962. This scale was reduced to 29 items by a consensual process, and finally to those 14 items which were most highly correlated with the total score of the 29-item scale. This 14-item scale was then validated by its ability to distinguish between reserve officers and ROTC students on the one hand, and members of peace churches and peace groups on the other (Eckhardt, Manning, Morgan, Subotnik and Tinker, 1967). It was further validated by distinguishing between those students who advocated more aggressive and more conciliatory responses to the Cuban crisis of 1962 (Chesler and Schmuck, 1964). Militarism, as measured by this scale, was analysed into four factors: (1) belief in military deterrence; (2) anti-Communism; (3) trust in the federal government's desire to disarm; and (4) distrust of one person's ability to do anything about world peace. Each one of these factors was validated by distinguishing between reserve officers and conscientious objectors.

The belief in military deterrence was indicated by agreement with such items as: the US should continue developing and testing nuclear weapons; military expenditures should not be spent on health, education and welfare instead; preparations for war do not provoke war; there are no serious alternatives to our policy of deterrence; children should not be educated in the philosophy and techniques of non-violence, such as Gandhi used in India; children should be educated in military and civil defences against war.

Anti-Communism was indicated by agreement with such items as: we should not trust Russia's peaceful intentions; the Communist Party should not have access to the ballot in the US; Red China should not be admitted to the United Nations.

Trust in national leaders was indicated by agreement with items such as: the President (Congress, Pentagon) really wants to disarm.

Distrust in peace action was indicated by agreement with the following item: one person can do nothing to bring about world peace.

This is a fair sample of the kind of items which have generally been used in militarism scales developed in the West during the last fifty years. The factors of belief in military deterrence and distrust of peace action might have at least somewhat similar meanings across the world. But clearly, the factors of anti-Communism and trust in capitalist leaders would presumably be aspects of militarism only in the Western world and some of its allied nations in the Third World. Consequently, this scale is culture-bound, which is not surprising since even tests of intelligence are culture-bound. Consequently, we must admit the cultural limitations of most of the studies reviewed in this paper. We cannot, without further research (some of which will be briefly touched upon later), generalise the meanings of militarism obtained from these studies beyond the Western world. Even within the Western world, the meanings of militarism are not quite the same for children as they are for adolescents and adults, so that our generalisations about militarism will have to be restricted to adolescents and adults in the Western world.

4 Exploratory Studies

The 14-item militarism scale was administered to more than 2,000 people in North America during the 1960's to try to answer three questions suggested by a statement in the preamble of the UNESCO Charter: since wars are made in the minds of people, it is in the minds of people that the foundations of peace must be constructed. These three questions were: (1) what is associated with war in the minds of people? (2) how did it get there? and (3) how can it be changed in the direction of peace?

It was felt that answers to the first two questions concerning the associates and origins of militarism would help to answer the third question. The procedure was to administer the militarism scale, along with a variety of other scales, to a large number of people, and then to correlate the militarism scale scores with the other scale scores. The correlates of militarism, as measured by this scale, included nationalism, authoritarianism, Goldwaterism, anti-welfarism, anti-democracy, conservatism, capitalism, anti-Communism, religious orthodoxy, anti-intellectualism and patriotism. These results suggest that

> Militarism in our culture today would seem to be in defense of *laissez-faire* capitalism, religious orthodoxy, and nationalism, but it would not seem to be in defense of either democracy or idealism. On the contrary, it would seem to be on the side of authoritarianism of the right and materialism. The results of this study are strikingly similar to those of a study conducted by the Canadian Peace Research Institute, which found that foreign policy attitudes in Canada were primarily related to religious dogmatism and fear of socialism (Eckhardt, Manning, Morgan, Subotnik and Tinker, 1967, p. 536).

A review of the social science literature (largely Western) on war/peace attitudes suggested that affective variables (such as extraversion and neuroticism) and cognitive variables (such as dogmatism and rigidity) were also associated with militarism, as well as ideological variables (such as conservatism and nationalism) and moral variables (such as authoritarianism and orthodox religiosity) (Eckhardt and Lentz, 1967).

The Des Moines militarism scale and some other scales were administered to some Canadian subjects in the summer of 1967. Militarism was significantly correlated with dogmatism, intolerance of ambiguity and rigidity (cognitive variables) as well as the ideological and moral variables of authoritarianism, conservatism and orthodox religiosity (Eckhardt and Newcombe, 1969). This complex of variables seemed to be characterised by self-contradiction or inner conflict, projection of denied or disliked aspects of self or nation upon others, and justification of the denied values (such as aggression or authoritarianism) as necessary means to counter these values as perceived (because projected) in others. Consequently, this pattern of attitudes seemed to be more ego-defensive than reality-testing in nature, so that the pattern of militarism (as measured by questionnaire studies) was similar to that of war propaganda (as measured by value-analyses of political documents):

> Warfare values were generally characterized by the following pattern of attitudes and beliefs: one's own nation was believed to be on the side of moral values, especially those of peace and freedom; opposing nations were denounced as enemies of these values; and the end of achieving those values was believed to justify the means of aggression (Eckhardt, 1965, p. 357).

Finally, the 1967 questionnaire study provided a clue towards answering the second question: how did war and its associates get into the minds of people in the first place?

> We conclude that militarism is at least partly a function of hypocritically restrictive childhood training which produces a 'love affair' between anal personality traits and authoritarian military ideologies. So far as childhood training is only one part of a total culture, this hypothesis would be generalized as follows: *Militarism is at least partly a function of a hypocritically restrictive culture* (Eckhardt and Newcombe, 1969, p. 217).

This hypothesis was tested in further studies beginning in the fall of 1967 and continuing to the present time, by incorporating childhood discipline scales in a series of CPRI questionnaires. The most general finding over these last 10 years has been a tendency for frustrating childhood disciplines (as recalled) to be associated with militarism and its correlates (Eckhardt, 1969a, 1969b; Eckhardt and Alcock, 1970; Eckhardt, 1971b, 1971c; Eckhardt and Sloan, 1971; Eckhardt, 1972a; Eckhardt, Sloan and Azar, 1973; Eckhardt, 1974a; Eckhardt, Young, Azar and Sloan, 1974; Eckhardt and Young, 1976; Eckhardt, 1976a, 1976b). The results of these studies will be discussed in the following four sections of this paper, dividing the results into the four aspects of the human mind (affective, cognitive, ideological and moral) which were found to be associated with militarism. Since all of the references for these correlational studies have been given in this paragraph, they will not be repeated in the rest of this paper. A section on the behavioural correlates of militarism will be included to provide a sample of some relations between attitudes and behaviours.

First, a brief description of the method of factor analysis used in these studies would seem to be in order. A correlation coefficient provides a measure of the similarity in the distribution of any pair of scale scores. Factor analysis does the same thing for any number of scale scores, enabling us to group together those scales whose distributions of scores are more similar to one another than they are to the distributions of other scale scores. When scales have been grouped together into primary factors, primary factor scores can then be correlated so that primary factors can be grouped together into secondary factors, etc. Thus, factor analysis is simply a statistical method of generalisation. The method of factor analysis used in the studies reported in this paper was generally that of principal components with normal varimax rotation. The number of eigen values exceeding unity determined the number of factors. The significance of factor loadings was determined by Harman's (1967, p. 435) table of standard errors of factor coefficients. Factor scores were generated by summing standardised scale scores weighted by their factor loadings.

It should be especially emphasised that these statistical methods help us to establish which variables tend to go together, but they never establish the cause-effect direction of these relationships. These have to be established outside the statistical results by common sense, experimentation, logic or theory. Even if we time-lag our variables, so that one variable precedes another, this does not establish beyond any question that the first variable causes the second variable. It may be an argument for a causal relation, but not its final determination. One thing following another, even with a great deal of consistency, does not mean that the second event was necessarily caused by the first. We might like to argue that since frustrating childhood disciplines precede militarism in time, and since the two are correlated with each other, therefore the frustrating disciplines cause the development of militarism. If this argument is convincing, fine. If not, the statistical relations require no one to accept it. The statistical relations merely help to make the argument, they do not prove it.

Since we shall want to make some causal inferences from our statistically established relations, it may be well to mention briefly the four kinds of causal relations originally suggested by Aristotle, so that we may be clear about the possibilities of causal inference that are open to us and not get locked into thinking that causal relations can only occur with time sequences. (1) Efficient causes, where one thing hits another thing, causing it to move, or to accelerate its motion, or to change its direction of motion. This might be called the billiard ball model of causation, which is a favourite model (and sometimes the only model) for a positivist philosopher of science. (2) Material causes, where behaviour is caused by the material make-up of the behaving object, such as a rubber ball bouncing because it is made of rubber, or people behaving in certain ways because of their personality make-up. (3) Formal causes, where the appearance or behaviour of something is caused by its relations to other things or to its environment in general. This kind of causation was introduced to science by Einstein's theory of relativity. Gestalt psychologists brought it into the field of psychology in the form of relational determinism. Sociologists often refer to this kind of causation as structural determinism. In general, it is the basis of any field theory. (4) Finally, final causes, where behaviour is directed by the end to be achieved. Such behaviour is often called purposive behaviour, which presupposes some level of conscious development.

5 Affective Correlates of Militarism

Affectively, people who obtained higher scores on militarism tended to be more extraversive, misanthropic, subject to more frustrating childhood disciplines in the past (as they recalled them), socially irresponsible, neurotic, lacking empathy, impulsive, experiencing more family discord in the present, more egoistic, and more conformist in their personal relations.

For these and other correlates of militarism, see the Appendix to this paper for some illustrative items. Here, we shall simply give a general impression of what these variables seem to mean, considering all of the items in the various scales.

Extraversion was characteristic of people who depended upon their social environment for the guidance and motivation of their behaviour. Left on their own, they seem to lose their bearings.

Misanthropy implied a basic and pervasive distrust of other people.

Frustrating childhood discipline (as recalled) included anxious, directive, inconsistent, punitive and restrictive training practices.

Social irresponsibility was expressed by behaviour problems in school and in society generally.

Neuroticism implied a basic and pervasive distrust of oneself. Misanthropy and neuroticism, taken together, suggested a lack of faith in people generally.

Lack of empathy suggested an inability or unwillingness to consider the needs of others as well as oneself.

Impulsivity implied a lack of self-control.

Family discord involved frustrating relations within one's present family, so that there was frustration not only in past childhood disciplines but also in present family relations.

Egoism clearly implied putting oneself first and foremost in personal relations.

Conformity implied the desire for a well structured social situation in which the rules and regulations were clearly spelled out by authorities or majorities.

It should be emphasised here that these labels are not meant to indicate dichotomies, but rather continuous dimensions along which those with higher scores on militarism tended to obtain higher scores in the direction of these affective labels. It should be further emphasised that the relations between these affective variables and militarism were statistical rules at best and never universal laws. Although these relations were generally present, they were not always strong relations, nor were they always found. There were many individual exceptions and some group exceptions to these general rules. It should also be emphasised that most of our samples were civilians and not people in the military services. Some civilian groups obtained higher scores on militarism and its correlates than some military groups. Consequently, we should remind ourselves that militarism implies the encouragement and support of military behaviour as well as direct participation. Some supporters were far more militaristic than some military people.

With these caveats and qualifications in mind, we may describe the militarist (who may not be in the military services) as a person who has been subject to relatively frustrating childhood disciplines which have caused (note that we are arguing for a causal relation here without proving it) that person to develop a lack of trust in both self and others, making that person apparently more selfish in relation to others at the same time that he/she (there were no sexual differences in militarism nor in most of its correlates found in these studies) is quite dependent upon others for guidance and satisfaction. Guidance may be forthcoming, but satisfaction would generally seem to be doomed to frustration. Full of self-contradictions, inner conflicts and social conflicts, this person's development has laid the foundation for mental illness or emotional problems.

However, by way of conformity, this person may find an outlet for this affective pattern in socially acceptable cognitive styles, political ideologies and moral philosophies, without ever becoming a psychiatric case. This depends, of course, on the nature of the society to which the person is conforming. In a society where mental health and rationality are defined in terms of self-interest, without consideration for others, this person might feel quite comfortable and never become mentally ill or emotionally disturbed.

6 Cognitive Correlates of Militarism

Cognitive processes generally have to do with the way we see things and think about them. Cognitively, the militarist is likely to be anti-intellectual, lacking creativity, dogmatic, intolerant of ambiguity, rigid, ego-defensive, less intelligent (including knowledge of foreign affairs) and positivist (*v.* humanist) in one's philosophy of human consciousness, knowledge, science, truth, etc.

Anti-intellectualism emphasised a preference for doing something without thinking about it. This would seem to be the cognitive parallel of affective extraversion.

Lack of creativity seemed to imply a lack of interest in aesthetic relations. Like anti-intellectualism, lack of creativity seemed to involve a sensory process concentrated upon practical results without much interest in the process of getting there.

Dogmatism suggested a need for certainty and a lack of curiosity.

Intolerance of ambiguity reflected this same need for certainty in an unwillingness to find oneself in a doubtful position.

Rigidity implied persistence in method with a tendency to disregard the end to be served by one's persistence. Taken together with the previous cognitive variables, rigidity seemed to parallel affective conformity in the sense of concentrating upon mechanical methods to reach given ends, which are not to be questioned.

Ego-defensive thinking, as opposed to reality testing, seemed to follow from affective egoism, so that thinking had to defend the self and its position rather than to open the mind to wider horizons, which might threaten the self's position in the centre of its world (egocentricity).

Positivism defined the human mind as a passive reflector of external reality. Given this definition or philosophy of consciousness, knowledge, science, etc., the positivist truth was simply a statement of what is out there, uncontaminated by human thoughts and feelings about reality. Facts, and nothing but facts, were the only legitimate object of knowledge. Humanism, on the other hand, defined the human mind as a creative agent which virtually created reality in the process of perceiving it, perception itself being loaded with theories and values. Since reality, as perceived, was loaded with values, the abstraction of these values from any statement about reality was bound to be a false or distorted statement. The humanist truth was that reality was full of values as well as facts.

This list of correlates would suggest that militaristic thinking tended to be egocentric and ego-defensive rather than testing reality to the limits of knowledge. The concentration upon facts seemed to involve some fear of human thoughts and feelings, which followed from the affective distrust of onself and others. Dogmatic, rigid thinking, intolerant of ambiguity and creativity, effectively narrowed one's perception down to the facts, leaving the values to be determined by the powers that be. This kind of thinking would be highly valued by those who want to maintain any *status quo*, for there was nothing about this kind of thinking which could question any *status quo*. Whatever is, would seem to be all right. Any attempt to change the *status quo* would more likely seem to be wrong. At this point, cognitive processes begin to merge with moral judgements, reminding us that dividing the personality into four parts is a somewhat arbitrary process of classification, which serves the purpose of convenience but which need not be taken too seriously.

The self-contradiction between egocentricity and factuality in this kind of thinking paralleled the affective conflict between egoism and conformity. This isomorphism (similarity of structure) between feeling and thinking made the two fit together like a hand in a glove, simultaneously causing each other. Affective conflicts were controlled by rigid thinking, serving personal purposes. The total pattern also suits the powers that be, leaving their power to establish values and to make unilateral decisions unquestioned. People who question no values and obey all rules make good soldiers, whether in or out of the military services. Factuality and conformity pay off the individual by throwing up smokescreens to conceal egocentricity. But how is egocentricity concealed at the leadership level? The ideological and moral correlates of militarism may provide some clues towards answering this question.

7 Ideological Correlates of Militarism

Ideologically, militarism was associated with punitiveness in childhood training and criminal treatment, nationalism, patriotism, racialism, anti-Communism, conservatism, capitalism, political cynicism, anti-welfarism, imperialism and valuing freedom more than equality.

Punitiveness in childhood training or criminal treatment was preferred by people who were punished themselves whenever they did anything wrong, so that we are once again referred back to frustrating childhood disciplines as one source of militarism and its associates in the human mind. It should be noted that frustrating childhood disciplines at home might be less effective unless they were reinforced all the way down the line by frustrating disciplines in church, at school, at work, in the university in the form of a positivist philosophy of science, etc. Conversely, satisfying disciplines in the home might be cancelled out by frustrating disciplines in some of these later life situations, including the military services themselves.

Nationalism and patriotism seemed to be extended forms of egoism, putting one's own nation before others, etc.

Racialism implied white supremacy, another form of egoism, putting one's own race before others. Nationalism and racialism could have quite different meanings in poor black countries than in rich white countries, of course.

Conservatism and capitalism against Communism and welfarism constituted other forms of egoism in our culture today which valued freedom much more than equality, implying that we cared much more for our own freedom than that of others. Freedom itself, in our culture, clearly implied the freedom of some to exploit others. In its extreme form, the capitalism that we want to defend by militarism was *laissez-faire* capitalism, not welfare capitalism, since the latter contradicted our notion of freedom. Welfarism may be necessary and tolerable, but hardly desirable.

Political cynicism implied personal powerlessness to do anything other than the wishes of the powers that be. A strange contradiction of freedom, indeed, clearly implying that freedom was not for everyone.

Imperialism involved the notion that empires were good for the peace and prosperity of all. It seemed natural indeed that those who lived in or who were allied with the imperial centre, and who consequently benefited from the imperial spoils, should look kindly upon imperialism. We should hardly expect imperialism to be associated with militarism in many of the world's poor countries, nor in the Communist countries, so that this correlate clearly identified the militarism discussed in this paper primarily as Western militarism, or as any other militarism in the service of imperialism.

The ideological contradictions associated with militarism seem to be overwhelming. The freedom extended to the *laissez-faire* capitalist was not so freely extended to others, whose freedom was restricted by perceived powerlessness, imperialism, nationalism, racialism and punitive disciplines. Western freedom was clearly for some, but not for all. It was not generally or generously extended to workers, people lower on the social totem pole, average citizens, imperialised nations, social change agents, other nations (some of whom might be allies, but treated as subordinates), non-white races, children and criminals. We might also add women to this list of the unfree.

8 Moral Correlates of Militarism

Higher scores on militarism were correlated with higher scores on law and order, authoritarianism, orthodox religiosity, conventional morality, double standard of value, myth of superiority, hypocrisy, defining justice in terms of inequality, and defining peace in terms of law and order.

Law and order emphasised *status quo* maintenance and behavioural non-violence, regardless of how violently a society might be structured and need to be changed.

Authoritarianism implied the need for a hierarchy of unequals in order to fulfil the divine or natural order of things (social Darwinism). Some were meant to rule by virtue of their superiority, and others to be ruled by virtue of their inferiority.

Orthodox religiosity involved conventional beliefs about God and the after-life.

Conventional morality implied putting law and order before justice in human affairs.

The double standard of value involved more freedom for self than for others, for business than for labour, for whites than for blacks, for men than for women, etc.

The myth of superiority was opposed to the myth of equality in human relations.

Hypocrisy implied the lack of a critical attitude towards prevailing values, not questioning their authenticity.

Justice was defined in terms of maintaining the *status quo* of inequality, instead of changing it towards more equality.

Peace was defined in terms of maintaining law and order rather than achieving justice. Military and police violence were justified as necessary means to maintain law and order. However, behavioural violence as such did not distinguish between the militarist and the non-militarist, since the latter was also ready to justify revolutionary violence in order to achieve social justice (structural non-violence).

Morally, the militarist was clearly following the authoritarian values established by the powers that be, and those values included defining values such as peace and justice in such a way as to further the interests of a capitalist structure within nations and an imperialist structure between nations. It is this field or structure of relations between and within nations that would be suggested as the basic and pervasive cause of militarism and its correlates in our culture today. This may tell us little or nothing about militarism in other cultures which are either victims of imperialism or fighters against imperialism. Militarism in these cultures would presumably reflect their antagonistic or dependent position in relation to Western imperialism, a hypothesis in need of further research.

In his developmental model of military man, Krieger (1971) suggested that frustrating childhood disciplines led to misanthropy and neuroticism (distrust of self and others), which in turn led to authoritarianism, which led to conservatism and nationalism, which led to militarism. Some evidence to support this model, especially in Western nations, was provided by Eckhardt (1971b). This model clearly linked the affective, ideological and moral correlates of militarism discussed in this chapter. The present review would suggest that these developmental or temporal causal relations need to be supplemented by the cognitive correlates as well. Furthermore, it would now be suggested that this developmental or temporal model might gain greater clarity and richness if it were thrown into a field-theoretical framework, so that both the earlier childhood disciplines and effects and the later ideologies and moralities could be seen to be joint effects of the same cultural field. From this point of view, the temporal cause-effect relations would be simultaneously caused by the cultural field of which they are all part-effects. The question is not whether the whole-part causal hypothesis is the 'truth' and the time-sequence causal hypothesis is an artefact. Rather, the question is, which ordering of these hypotheses helps us to make the most sense out of this study of the correlates of militarism and, especially, which ordering of these hypotheses helps us to make the most sense out of this study of the correlates of militarism and, especially, which ordering of these hypotheses helps us to develop the most effective strategies for changing from war to peace in the minds of people?

9 Behavioural Correlates of Militarism

Although this paper has concentrated on militarism as an attitude, it seemed desirable to list here some of those groups who obtained higher than average scores on militarism and related scales, in order to provide some indication of the kind of behaviours and institutions which were associated with militarism:

Punitive teachers in a learning experiment. (329)
Mormons in the US Air Force. (309)
Jesus People. (293)
Military-dependent high-school students in Turkey and West Germany. (292)
Military and police personnel. (291)
Religious people and orthodox church members. (290)
Military intelligence interrogators. (284)
People living in or around Washington, D.C. (283)
Infantry captains and lieutenants. (282)
US Air Force Academy cadets.
Reserve officers and ROTC students.
Fascist leaders.
Business leaders.
Capitalist voters
Electronics engineers.
Guided missile scientists.
Engineering faculty and students.
Independent inventors.
Right activist students and non-activist students.
Business administration students.
Supervisory industrial personnel.

The first nine groups in this list were ordered according to scores obtained from a 96-item questionnaire, which included militarism and some of its affective, ideological and moral correlates. The rest of the groups were not placed in any particular order, since their scores were obtained from different questionnaires of militarism and/or some of its correlates, which were not strictly comparable to the 96-item questionnaire, nor to one another. The order of the first nine groups shows that religious people obtained somewhat higher mean scores than military and police personnel on militarism and its affective, ideological and moral correlates. The affective differences among these groups were not great, except for the punitive teachers who were extremely high on the affective correlates of militarism. The Air Force Mormons were especially high on the ideological and moral correlates of militarism. Otherwise, the differences among military and religious people were not very great, although no significance tests have been conducted on the differences among these total mean scores (shown in parentheses following the group names). It is of some interest to note that people living in or around Washington, D.C., also obtained scores higher than the average score of 269 for 40 groups tested, mean scores ranging from 211 to 329. The lowest mean scores on this questionnaire were obtained by students in two different peace studies courses (253, 239), non-religious people (245), Indian students (244), German youth and students (240, 236), University of Guelph faculty (232), women's liberation (226), war resisters (214) and Grindstone School for Peace participants (211).

The list of high scorers on militarism and its correlates can clearly be described, for the most part, as either potential or actual members of the military-industrial complex, including the political and religious establishments which determine the ideological and moral values institutionalised by this complex. More detailed listings of high and low stcorers on militarism and its correlates will be found in Eckhardt (1971c; 1972a, pp. 212-18; 1974a, p. 2; 1976a, pp. 15, 29-30, 49-50; 1976b, pp. 113-14).

10 Summary and Conclusions

The results reviewed in this paper will be summarised in relation to the three questions raised by the statement in the preamble to the UNESCO Charter: since wars are made in the minds of people, it is in the minds of people that the foundations of peace must be constructed. The three questions were: (1) what is associated with war in the minds of people? (2) how did it get there? and (3) how can it be changed in the direction of peace?

War in the minds of people was operationalised by responses to militarism scales, which were validated by their ability to distinguish significantly between groups known to be preparing themselves for war and groups known to be preparing themselves for peace. Responses to these militarism scales were then correlated with responses to a wide variety of other scales which measured affective, cognitive, ideological and moral aspects of the human mind. Some of these scales were original, but most of them were adapted from the social science literature, where their reliability and validity had already been established. Most of our own work and that of others reported in this paper was done with adolescents and adults living in 10 or 12 developed nations of the Western world. The results were not the same for children, nor for young people in the Communist and Third worlds. Consequently, these results cannot be generalised without qualification beyond the Western world.

10.1 The Correlates of Militarism

Militarism was more highly correlated with the cognitive, ideological and moral aspects of the human mind than with the affective aspect, as a general rule, conformity being an exception to this general rule. Militarism was also correlated with military behaviour and military institutions, but it was not limited to the military services. Some civilians could be just as militaristic in their attitudes as some soldiers and sailors (many of whom may be conscripted, and not unduly militaristic in their attitudes at all). *Some* civilians, especially conventionally religious people and politically conservative people, may be more militaristic than *some* military people. In these cases, military attitudes play a very important role in their support of military behaviours and military institutions, even though they may not lead a person to join the army or to go to war.

A glance at the illustrative items in the Appendix to this paper shows a striking isomorphism (structural similarity) between the correlates of militarism in the different 'parts' of the personality. Each part seems to be characterised by some apparent contradictions: affective egoism *v.* conformity, ego-defensive thinking *v.* positivism, ideological racialism *v.* freedom, and moral superiority *v.* orthodox religiosity. This apparent contradiction is resolved if we notice that the second term serves to conceal, deny, project and justify the first term in every case. This is a psychological process which has been commonly noted by Western philosophers throughout the centuries and by Western psychologists at least since the time of Freud. Concealed and denied selfishness is projected on to others, intensifying their apparent selfishness, which completely justifies our being selfish in relation to them. This process has been called 'false consciousness' by Marx, 'unconscious self-deception' by Freud and 'bad faith' by Sartre.

Another outstanding common feature of the different 'parts' of the military-industrial personality is the association of egoism with frustration in a positive feedback relationship. Frustrating disciplines in the home, church, school and society in general contribute to affective egoism which, expecting too much of others, tends to be frustrated, generating a vicious cycle spiralling downward. Ego-defensive thinking needs absolute, certain and objective knowledge for the sake of personal security, but this need is frustrated by the relativity, subjectivity and uncertainty of human knowledge. Ideologically, the will to power (in the forms of capitalism, imperialism, nationalism, racialism) is constantly frustrated by people's tendency to believe that they are created equal. Authoritarian, conventional and orthodox morality is constantly frustrated by the perpetual resurrection of this myth of equality in human minds.

In brief summary, the correlates of militarism are affective conformity, cognitive positivism, ideological conservatism and moral authoritarianism, shot through with egoism, frustration and inner conflicts of self-contradictions, which are often projected in the form of interpersonal conflicts, class conflicts, family conflicts, national conflicts, racial conflicts and sexual conflicts. The military mind is a mind in conflict with itself and others, a mind determined (consciously or otherwise) to contribute to a wide variety of social conflicts in a relatively destructive manner. The military mind is part of a society in conflict with itself and other societies, so that there is isomorphism between personality and society which is mutually reinforcing and rewarding, which compensates for some of the frustrations. The most basic and devastating contradiction of the military mind is its conflict with the essence of being human which seems to mean being equal to other human beings. This summary of the nature (or definition) of militarism is culture-bound, and cannot be generalised to other cultures without further analysis and research.

10.2 The Causes of Militarism

In trying to answer the second question: how did militarism and its correlates get into the minds of people? It may be useful to order our responses in terms of Aristotle's four causes: efficient, material, final and formal.

Efficient Causes. Efficient causes in human relations take the form of developmental theories, which state that earlier life experiences determine the attitudes and behaviours of later life. Freud especially emphasised frustrating childhood disciplines as the cause of neurotic, psychotic and sociopathic personalities. The results of our studies fully supported this relationship, with the qualification that, although such personalities might always be a function of frustrating childhood disciplines, these disciplines did not always lead to such personalities, but could lead instead to socially acceptable attitudes and behaviours such as extraversion, positivism, racialism and religiosity. Early frustrating disciplines could also be overcome by later satisfying disciplines, such as occur in psychoanalysis, for example.

Studies of the authoritarian personality (Adorno, Frenkel-Brunswik, Levinson and Sanford, 1950) linked authoritarianism of the right to frustrating childhood discplines in a developmental theory which was also supported by the results of our studies. Krieger's (1971) developmental model of military man traced militarism back to frustrating childhood disciplines through a chain of affective misanthropy and neuroticism, moral authoritarianism and ideological conservatism and nationalism. This model was also supported by the results of our studies, so far as the Western world was concerned.

On the basis of our results, we can add to Krieger's model that the positivist discipline of traditional schools, the bureaucratic discipline of traditional workplaces, and the religious discipline of orthodox churches and Sunday schools also contribute to militarism through the frustration of cognitive, ideological and moral development, even as anxious, directive, inconsistent, punitive and restrictive disciplines at home frustrate affective development.

Material Causes. Material causes in human relations take the form of personality structures. That is, given a certain personality, regardless of its antecedent causes, that personality is likely to engage in certain behaviours and join certain institutions because these fit the personality like a glove. The person feels comfortable and at home doing certain things with certain like-minded people. Consequently, given a personality structured by the affective, cognitive, ideological and moral correlates of militarism, then militarism simply and simultaneously follows from the structure of that personality.

Although Freud never abandoned his early theory of frustration, he did supplement it with a later theory of the death instinct as an explanation (or cause) of human aggression. Other instinct theories have been proposed before and since Freud in order to explain the phenomenon of war. These theories have found no support in the results of our studies, including anthropological studies of primitive militarism (Eckhardt, 1975). What has been empirically established, however, is that people who *believe* in hereditary or instinct theories of war and aggression are more likely to be capitalist, militarist and racialist in their attitudes in the Western world, and that mean scores on such theories are higher in the West than they are in Communist and Third World countries (Eckhardt, 1972b). Consequently, although we accept the personality itself as a material cause of militarism, we reject any hereditary or instinct theories of the personality as explanations of militarism and its correlates, on the basis that there is no reliable evidence to support such theories.

Final Causes. Final causes in human relations are human goals, purposes, reasons and values for behaving in one way rather than another, or for joining some groups or institutions rather than others. Final causes seem to imply conscious choices, making them different from material causes where the personality simply expresses itself without having to think or evaluate anything consciously. Militarism may serve any of the values involved in any of its correlates. People may adopt military attitudes and engage in military activities, or support such activities, simply in order to conform or to do their duty (Eckhardt, 1974c). They might be militaristic to defend their material values, or to express their patriotism. They might be fighting for freedom, without knowing that they are fighting against equality in the case of imperialistic wars. Final causes, like material causes, may have their origin in past or current disciplines. However, regardless of their own causes, they may nevertheless act as causes in their own right here and now. They may become functionally autonomous of their origins (Allport, 1937).

Formal Causes. Formal causes in human relations are immediate impacts of culture on personality, of the society upon the individual, of the environment on the mind, of the whole upon the part. Militarism may be caused by past disciplines, present personalities, or future goals, as already discussed. On the other hand, militarism, disciplines, personalities and values may all be caused simultaneously (even though they don't occur at the same time for any individual) by the total culture of which they are all part-effects. Militarism and all of its correlates, past or present, may be partially caused by one another (with or without time sequences). But, so far as they are all functions of the same culture, that culture may be the prime mover, the prime cause of them all at the same time.

So far as the culture causes militarism and all of its correlates (including frustrating disciplines in childhood and later life) to be correlated and causally interacting with one another in the first place, it is necessary to raise the further question: what causes the culture to do this? What kind of culture has this kind of effect? This question might lead us into an infinite regression of causes, leading nowhere, unless we can save ourselves from this predicament by applying the concept of material or natural causation at this point.

What is the nature of militaristic cultures, as militarism has been defined in this chapter? Throughout human history, we might argue (without proving a thing) that imperialistic cultues have fostered militarism and its correlates, including frustrating childhood discipline, all the way down the line. There is some anthropological evidence to support this argument (Eckhardt, 1975), as well as some historical evidence to be found in the most elementary history books.

Imperialistic cultures are the most compulsive of cultures, in the worst sense of the term compulsion. They are apparently compelled to do the absurd, the irrational, the superfluous, the unnecessary. To be compelled to do what is necessary in order to survive, or to achieve one's rights, seems to be a natural sort of compulsion. It may involve undesirable behaviour, and even violent behaviour, but at least it is necessary in the sense of defending authentic values. A carnivorous animal has to kill other animals, and vegetarians have to kill plants, in order to live. So much seems to be natural and unavoidable. A smaller nation has to defend itself against a larger nation, or else submit to being massacred, enslaved or exploited, all of which are absurd, violating the principle of equality which defines humanity.

Of course, if social Darwinism provides a sound foundation for looking at the world, then even imperialistic violence can be justified. But if social Darwinism is not sound, and we assume it is not, then violence against imperialistic aggression may be a justified violence against unjustified violence. The militarism of imperialism, as described in this chapter, is unwarranted aggression because it creates, expands and reinforces unequal relations between and within nations, adding structural violence to its behavioural violence. The militarism of nations dependent upon imperialism is somewhat more justified, since it is compelled by the dependent position of these nations in the imperialistic structure of the world today. Dependent nations have fewer options than dominant nations. The militarism of those nations or groups within nations which are fighting against imperialism is not militarism at all, as defined in this chapter, but a rational response of self-respecting defence against a self-assertive aggressor who believes that he or she is entitled to more than their fair share of the earth's resources. Anti-imperialistic militarism differs from imperialistic militarism in at least two basic ways: qualitatively and quantitatively. Qualitatively, the directions, goals, purposes and values are quite different in that imperialistic militarism aims its behavioural violence towards the creation or maintenance of structural violence, while anti-imperialistic militarism aims its behavioural violence towards the creation or maintenance of structural non-violence (social justice, defined in terms of equality). Quantitatively, this results in more violence being caused by imperialistic militarism than by anti-imperialistic militarism, even at the behavioural level alone – if only because imperialistic militarism has so much more power to inflict damage and injury at its disposal. However, beyond the capability (and even causing the capability in the first place) imperialistic militarism has the *will* to use the power created for the purpose of achieving and maintaining its power, while anti-imperialistic militarism is trying to share the power rather than to monopolise it.

We conclude that the prime mover of militarism and all of its correlates in our culture today is the imperialistic structure of the world created by Western imperialism during the last five centuries. According to this analysis, Western militarism primarily serves the purpose of securing an empire more than it is concerned with any particular nation's security or economy. It is that imperialism which has structured our present world into dominant nations (Western world), dependent nations (Third World) and antagonistic nations (Communist world). Each kind of culture fosters its own kind of discipline, which develops its own kind of modal personality (Eckhardt and Young, 1974a), which is compatible with its own kind of militarism, which is designed to play its dominant, dependent or antagonistic role in relation to the imperialistic structure of the world today, either to maintain it or to destroy it. Bronfenbrenner (1970) has provided some evidence to show some disciplinary differences between capitalist and Communist countries.

10.3 Changing from War to Peace

So much for the causes and correlates of militarism in our culture and our minds today. Their primary utility lies in the clues they may provide for changing from war to peace in the minds of people. So far as militarism is a function of imperialism, the abolition of militarism ultimately depends upon nothing less than the abolition of imperialism. This is a formidable task, no doubt, but a necessary one if the present analysis is correct. Fortunately, the task can be divided into a number of parts paralleling the parts of the personality correlated with militarism. It can also be divided into the three worlds of militarism. This chapter hardly provides the scope for going into much detail about the changing of minds and worlds, so that only the briefest sketch of general guidelines can be provided here. In any event, most of the details will have to be worked out in the process of change by different people working in different cultures with different opportunities under different circumstances.

To begin with, social change agents may take some encouragement, but not too much, from the self-contradictory nature of imperialism itself. Imperialism is one of those processes which tends to obstruct its own progress. To some extent, it contains the seeds of its own destruction in its own self-contradictions, which go against the grain of being human, which means to be equal to other human beings. Consequently, any movements towards equality should be welcomed as movements against imperialism: class equality, national equality, racial equality, sexual equality, etc. Equality between and within nations is the antithesis of imperialism. The promotion of the myth of equality on philosophical, religious and scientific grounds can go far towards undercutting the myth of superiority which helps to rationalise and support imperialism.

Materially, imperialism also contradicts itself, which has led many prophets (including Marx and Lenin) to predict its doom prematurely. They underestimated its flexibility in shifting costs and benefits in such a way as to prolong its existence long after it should have extinguished itself by its logical and material contradictions. It is important to realise that contradictions discovered in one part of a system can be resolved by shifting them to another part of the system where they may be less noticeable or more tolerable. For example, Cecil Rhodes noticed about the turn of this century that English unemployment and overproduction was causing civil unrest. For the sake of peace and prosperity in England, he claimed that imperial expansion was a necessity in order to establish more colonies to absorb the surplus working population and more foreign markets to absorb the surplus production which could not be bought locally by unemployed people (Eckhardt, 1977). Such displacements reduce the poverty and strife in a dominant part of the imperial system by shifting them to dependent parts (colonies and neo-colonies) where they are less noticeable and made more tolerable by the doctrine of social Darwinism.

The cost of such displacements has been high in Third World countries, both behaviourally in terms of imperialistic wars (Alcock and Young, 1974; Köhler, 1975a, 1975b), and structurally in terms of lower life expectancies and higher infant mortality rates (Eckhardt and Young, 1974b, 1977; Köhler and Alcock, 1976; Høivik, 1977; Russett, 1977). The cost in structural violence alone has been at least 15 million lives per year, on the average, throughout the twentieth century in the Third World (Eckhardt and Köhler, 1977), where most of the behavioural violence has occurred as well since the end of World War II (Köhler and Alcock, 1976; Eckhardt and Azar, 1977). In addition, some of these imperial displacements have run into conflicts with other imperial nations in the two world wars of this century, not to mention the many imperial conflicts of previous centuries. However, the structural violence in the Third World in the twentieth century has been at least 25 times greater than the behavioural violence of both world wars taken together.

Consequently, the devastating structural effects of imperialism have been far greater and less noticeable than its behavioural effects. Throwing more light on these structural effects should contribute towards the abolition of imperialism, whose existence today depends partly, if not largely, upon our ignorance of its lethal and unjust structure. We cannot concentrate on the behavioural violence of militarism with any significant effect without simultaneously concentrating on the structural violence of imperialism. This structural violence, institutionalised by militarism in the first place, now causes militarism to continue for the sake of its maintenance or destruction. We cannot talk about abolishing militarism, including its military behaviour and arms expenditures, without talking about the abolition of imperialism at the same time. It is at least difficult, and sometimes impossible, to change an effect without first changing its cause. Operating on symptoms may shift the symptoms without curing the disease.

Many divisions of labour will be required to accomplish this task, including research, education and action against the various aspects of imperialism and its militarism. All of these methods need to be applied inside and outside prevailing institutions. Efforts to change existing institutions should go hand in hand with the development of alternative institutions built on egalitarian principles.

Discipline would seem to be a vital focus for change. Although traditional disciplines are associated with imperialism and its militarism, it does not mean that *no* discipline is the solution to these problems. Far from it. Discipline simply means learning, and learning in itself is essential no matter what kind of a system we are trying to maintain, change or create. The question is not whether we are going to have discipline or not, but rather what kind of discipline will promote peace rather than war in the minds of people? Without going into any details, we can only mention briefly the kinds of discipline associated with the four parts of the personality.

Instead of anxious, directive, inconsistent, punitive and restrictive childhood disciplines in the home, which contribute to militarism, our findings would suggest the need for more calm, non-directive, consistent, rewarding and permissive disciplines. The latter would also be more conducive towards happier childhoods and better mental and emotional health in later life.

A humanistic philosophy of research and education would contribute towards more creative disciplines in schools and colleges, which would develop more curiosity, instead of the prevailing positivist philosophy which tends to deaden creativity and curiosity, and to foster conformity and law and order approaches to conflict resolution.

A radical or socialist philosophy of human nature would contribute towards more faith in people, instead of the conservative philosophy which tends to pit people against one another in a competitive struggle for existence, placing faith in power instead of people.

An egalitarian philosophy of morality would help to promote the practice, as well as the preaching, of the Golden Rule, instead of the authoritarian philosophy which leads us not to practise what we preach, making our conventional morality and religion hypocritical. Egalitarianism in the workplace would replace bureaucratic disciplines with more democratic disciplines, giving workers more power in deciding what to make, how to make it, and how to distribute it, making work more satisfying and less alienating in the process. Finally, egalitarianism would define justice in terms of equality, providing a sound foundation for the resolution of conflicts in human relations.

These various disciplines would all promote further development in the affective, cognitive, ideological and moral aspects of the personality. At the same time that these disciplines are opening the personality to further development, they would also be opening to further development the institutions and societies in which they are practised. Their thrust would be to undercut dominance in the imperial centres, to undercut dependence in the imperial peripheries, and to operate against the dominance-dependence structure of imperialism in general.

It might be noted here that any theory of imperialism is at once a field theory and a dialectical theory. It is a field theory in so far as it emphasises formal or structural causes, as well as material, mechanical and final causes in the explanation of behaviour. As a field theory, it would also suggest that changes in the whole field have more pervasive effects than changes in the parts, and that changes in central and dominant parts of the field have more pervasive effects than changes in peripheral and dependent parts. For example, radical changes in the United States (the centre of Western imperialism today) are more likely to influence the whole system than changes in some peripheral countries of the Third World. However, if changes in the United States simply shift the imperial centre on to Japan or back to the European Economic Community, then Western imperialism will remain intact, even as changing the centre from England to the United States earlier in this century changed nothing essential to Western imperialism. Likewise, if the abolition of Western imperialism results in its replacement by Soviet imperialism, nothing may be gained. The challenge is to abolish imperialism, not merely to shift its centre or to change its form.

An imperialism theory is a dialectical theory in so far as it emphasises confrontation as a way of resolving conflicts. However, it is not limited to dialectical materialism in this paper, which gives equal weight to the dialectics of ideas and values as well as practices. Theories, as well as practices, are essential to the creation, maintenance or change of any social field. So far as both practices and theories express and promote human values (Eckhardt, 1972c), all three should be confronted with one another and worked together as coherently as possible. If Marx turned Hegel on his head by replacing dialectical idealism with dialectical materialism, then we are now turning both Marx and Hegel on their sides and placing them at the two ends of a horizontal line, which forms the base of a triangle whose apex is neither practice nor theory, but value.

Where the facts may be equally well satisfied by conflicting theories, then that theory should be adopted which promotes the values of peace and justice, defined in terms of the key value of equality. For example, given the choice between hereditary and environmental theories of any human behaviour to be changed, choose environmental theories, because we can easily change social environments created by us, but we cannot so easily change genetic structures not of our own making. Furthermore, environmental theories encourage us to spend more time and energy on social change, while hereditary theories inhibit and restrict such expenditures.

In choosing to work on social environments rather than genetic structures, we need not fall into the deterministic trap of either nature or nurture. As important as the social environment may be in determining human behaviour, being human means being free as well as being equal to other human beings (Eckhardt, 1971d). Unequal social structures make some people freer than others, so that they have more options and better opportunities. Consequently, people are not equally free, which is part (and one of the most basic parts) of the structural violence in the world today which needs to be changed. The purpose of an egalitarian society is not to determine human behaviour against human freedom, but rather to equalise freedom so that everyone can have a more or less equal say in what they are going to do in relation to other people and their natural environment. Although we are determined by our environment, we can structure our environment to make us equally free instead of unequally free, which seems more fair.

Consequently, in a nutshell, the best cure (and prevention) of imperialism is to encourage people to exercise their freedom as equally as possible, and to use their equal opportunities as freely as possible.

11 Further Research

This chapter has provided a fairly detailed, if somewhat sketchy, description and explanation of Western militarism. Further research would be most desirable to do the same for militarism in the Communist and Third worlds. This should be done by researchers living in these worlds, using their own methods and procedures in order to obtain the most meaningful results for their cultures.

The general pattern of Western militarism presented in this chapter undoubtedly has its variants and even some sports, which are lost in the general picture, and deserve further research. Militarism in the Communist and Third worlds undoubtedly has its variants and sports as well. Further research into these variations and deviations from the general patterns may be only of academic interest, but it may also have some practical implications which cannot be known unless and until the research is done.

What is of immediate practical importance in all three worlds is research into the relations between research, education and action, so that these three methods of social change may be confronted with one another and worked together to the greatest possible advantage. Likewise, various areas and topics of research, education and action need to be co-ordinated for maximum effectiveness. 'Areas' refer to the various scholarly and scientific disciplines, various kinds and levels of education, and various types of parliamentary and extra-parliamentary activities. The 'topics' in all of these method areas might range from family structures to global structures. All of these methods, areas and topics require the utmost co-operation and co-ordination in order for them to be most effective. Divided, our efforts are weak and their effects may be negligible. Divided, we may simply be shifting symptoms from one to another. Divided, we are more likely to take two backward steps for every step forward. Divided, we hardly need to be conquered.

Together, the methods, disciplines, areas, topics, etc. may so fertilise one another as to provide a more complete picture of the problem and a more coherent way towards its solution. This research on togetherness will probably have to be done in action rather than in words.

Appendix: Items from Scales Correlated with Militarism

Affective Scales

Extraversion: I have a right to enjoy life even if it means neglecting other things.

Misanthropy: If you don't watch out for yourself, people will take advantage of you.

Frustrating childhood discipline: My mother and father often made me obey even when I thought it was unreasonable.

Social irresponsibility: It is all right to get around the law if you don't actually break it.

Neuroticism: I certainly feel useless at times.

Lack of empathy: When I know someone is suffering it doesn't bother me.

Impulsivity: I enjoy the excitement of a crowd.

Family discord: There is very little love and companionship in my family as compared to other homes.

Egoism: I like to excel in whatever I do.

Conformity: I like to follow rules and regulations closely.

Cognitive Scales

Anti-intellectualism: Ideas are all right but it's getting the job done that counts.
Lack of creativity: I am not at all interested in drama or music or poetry.
Dogmatism: Most people just don't know what's good for them.
Intolerance of ambiguity: Most people are either good or bad.
Rigidity: I am a methodical person in whatever I do.
Ego-defensiveness: I am not like other people.
Positivism: That theory is true which best fits the facts and nothing but the facts.

Ideological Scales

Punitiveness: Crimes of violence should be punished by flogging.
Nationalism: We need more leaders who have the morals and the strength to put our national honour above appeasement.
Patriotism: My country, right or wrong.
Racialism: Negroes have their rights, but it is best to keep them in their own districts and schools and to prevent too much contact with whites.
Conservatism: In general, full economic security is bad: most men wouldn't work if they didn't need the money for eating and living.
Capitalism: A greater degree of government control over business would result in a weakening of this country's economy.
Cynicism: There are some powerful men in the government who are running the whole thing and they don't care about us ordinary people.
Imperialism: Empires are generally useful arrangements which work to the mutual advantage of all of their parts.
Freedom *v.* equality: Independence, free choice *v.* brotherhood, equal opportunity for all.

Moral Scales

Law and order: Peace is primarily a matter of maintaining law and order.
Authoritarianism: Some equality in marriage may be a good thing, but by and large the husband should be the final authority in family matters.
Orthodox religiosity: The revelation of God's word is the final authority for human beings.
Conventional morality: When Negroes were slaves, it was wrong to help

slaves to escape.

Myth of superiority: Superior people are best able to make decisions for the benefit of everyone.

Hypocrisy: Whatever is, is right, because reality is determined by forces outside human control, such as God or Nature.

Other illustrative items used in these studies may be found in Eckhardt (1969a, pp. 87-105, which includes all 466 items used in the 1967 CPRI questionnaire; 1969b, pp. 131-2; 1972a, pp. 272-7), Eckhardt, Sloan and Azar (1973, pp. 183-4); Eckhardt (1974b, pp. 295-7, which includes all 14 items in the 1962 Des Moines militarism scale); Eckhardt (1976a, pp. 38-66, which includes all items in the CPRI questionnaires of 1971, 1974 and 1975, with answer sheets, scoring instructions, references and norms for the scales included in these questionnaires).

For some illustrations of the behavioural and institutional correlates of militarism, see Section 9 of this paper. The list of high and low scorers on militarism and its correlates in this section provides a small sample of the hundreds of groups of subjects used in the attitude studies reviewed in this paper. More details on these subjects will be found in the references.

See Section 3 of this paper for illustrations of items in a militarism scale.

References

Adorno, T.W., Frenkel-Brunswik, E., Levinson, D.J. and Sanford, R.N. 1950. *The Authoritarian Personality*. New York: Harper

Alcock, N.Z. and Young, C. 1974. Imperialism. *Peace Research,* **6**, 75-83

Allport, G.W. 1937. *Personality: A Psychological Interpretation.* New York: Holt

Bronfenbrenner, U. 1970. *Two Worlds of Childhood: U.S. and U.S.S.R.* New York: Russell Sage

Chesler, M. and Schmuck, R. 1964. Student reactions to the Cuban crisis and public dissent. *Public Opinion Quarterly,* **28**, 467-82

Eckhardt, W. 1965. War propaganda, welfare values, and political ideologies. *Journal of Conflict Resolution,* **9**, 345-58

Eckhardt, W. 1969a. Ideology and personality in social attitudes. *Peace Research Reviews,* **3**, 2, 1-106

Eckhardt, W. 1969b. The factor of militarism. *Journal of Peace Research,* **6**, 123-32

Eckhardt, W. 1971a. Cross-cultural patterns of ideological, national and personal values. *International Journal of Group Tensions,* **1**, 203-29

Eckhardt, W. 1971b. Cross-cultural militarism: A test of Krieger's developmental model of military man. *Journal of Contemporary Revolutions,* **3**, 2, 113-19

Eckhardt, W. 1971c. The military-industrial personality. *Journal of Contemporary Revolutions,* **3**, 4, 74-87

Eckhardt, W. 1971d. An existential philosophy for the social sciences. *ABRAXAS,* **1**, 135-45

Eckhardt, W. 1972a. *Compassion: Toward a Science of Value.* Oakville, Ontario: Canadian Peace Research Institute Press

Eckhardt, W. 1972b. Cross-cultural theories of war and aggression. *International Journal of Group Tensions,* **2**, 3, 36-51

Eckhardt, W. 1972c. Practice, theory, and value. *Journal of Contemporary Revolutions,* **4**, 2, 100-9

Eckhardt, W. 1974a. A progress report on the measurement of compassion-compulsion. *Peace Research,* **6**, 1-8

Eckhardt, W. 1974b. Cross-cultural militarism: A test of Krieger's developmental model of military man. Revised in S.W. Schmidt and G.A. Dorfman (eds.), *Soldiers in Politics*, pp. 275-300. Los Altos: Geron-X

Eckhardt, W. 1974c. A conformity theory of aggression. *Journal of Peace Research,* **11**, 31-9

Eckhardt, W. 1975. Primitive militarism. *Journal of Peace Research,* **12**, 55-62

Eckhardt, W. 1976a. *A Manual on the Development of the Concept of Compassion and its Measurement, 1962-1975*. Oakville, Ontario: Canadian Peace Research Institute Press

Eckhardt, W. (ed.) 1976b. Cross-national measures of compassion. *Peace Research,* **8**, 109-49

Eckhardt, W. 1977. Global imperialism and global inequality. Paper presented at the University of Denver Conference on Global Inequality, Estes Park, Colorado (June)

Eckhardt, W. and Alcock, N.Z. 1970. Ideology and personality in war/peace attitudes. *Journal of Social Psychology,* **81**, 105-16

Eckhardt, W. and Azar, E. 1977. Major world conflicts and interventions, 1945 to 1975. Paper presented at the annual meeting of the Peace Science Society (International), Southern Section, Chapel Hill (April), and at the annual meeting of the Canadian Peace

Research and Education Association, Fredericton, New Brunswick (June)

Eckhardt, W. and G. Köhler. 1977. Behavioral and structural violence in the 20th century. Paper presented at the Grindstone School for Peace Research, Education, and Action, Portland, Ontario (August)

Eckhardt, W., and Lentz, T.F. 1967. Factors of war/peace attitudes. *Peace Research Reviews,* **1**, 5, 1-114 (page numbers in the 1971 revised edition are 1-102)

Eckhardt, W., Manning, M., Morgan, C., Subotnik, L. and Tinker, L.J. 1967. Militarism in our culture today. *Journal of Human Relations,* **15**, 532-7

Eckhardt, W. and Newcombe, A.G. 1969. Militarism, personality, and other social attitudes. *Journal of Conflict Resolution,* **13**, 210-19

Eckhardt, W. and Sloan, T. 1971. Attitudes and values at a peace research summer school. *Peace Research,* **3**, 10

Eckhardt, W., Sloan, T. and Azar, E. 1973. The measurement of compassion. *Review of Peace Science,* **1**, 183-94

Eckhardt, W. and Young, C. 1974a. Psychology of imperialism. *Journal of Contemporary Revolutions,* **6**, 3, 90-102

Eckhardt, W. and Young, C. 1974b. Civil conflict, imperialism, and inequality. *Journal of Contemporary Revolutions,* **6**, 2, 76-95

Eckhardt, W. and Young, C. 1976. The value of compassion and definitions of peace. *Peace Research,* **8**, 7-18

Eckhardt, W. and Young, C. 1977. *Governments under Fire: Civil Conflict and Imperialism.* New Haven: Human Relations Area Files Press

Eckhardt, W., Young, C., Azar, E. and Sloan, T. 1974. Grindstone attitudes and values. *Peace Research,* **6**, 99-115

Harman, H.H. 1967. *Modern Factor Analysis.* Chicago: University of Chicago Press

Høivik, T. 1977. The demography of structural violence. *Journal of Peace Research,* **14**, 59-73

Köhler, G. 1975a. War, the nation-state paradigm, and the imperialism paradigm: British war involvements, *Peace Research,* **7**, 31-41

Köhler, G. 1975b. Imperialism as a level of analysis in correlates-of-war research. *Journal of Conflict Resolution,* **19**, 48-62

Köhler, G. and Alcock, N. 1976. An empirical table of structural violence, *Journal of Peace Research,* **13**, 343-56

Krieger, D. 1971. A developmental model of military man. *Journal of Contemporary Revolutions,* **3**, 1, 68-74

Porter, G. 1926. Student opinions on war. Doctoral dissertation,

University of Chicago

Russett, B. 1977. The marginal utility of global income transfers: A first attempt at welfare comparisons. Paper presented at the University of Denver Conference on Global Inequality, Estes Park, Colorado (June)

Thurstone, L.L. 1928. Attitudes can be measured. *American Journal of Sociology,* **33**, 529-54

19 MILITARISM: CULTURAL DIMENSIONS OF MILITARISATION*

Malvern Lumsden

1 Structure and Superstructure

Although the terms 'militarism' and 'militarisation' are often used interchangeably, a case is made in this paper for distinguishing them. It is argued that the term 'militarisation' can best be applied at the level of social and economic structures, while militarism can best be interpreted at the level of cultural superstructures. There are complex relationships between these levels of analysis.

Within social sciences a number of traditions have emphasised the importance of social structures in determining, or at least influencing, other social phenomena. The notion of social structure has also proved fruitful in peace research.

'Structuralism' within social sciences, however, has come to mean many things to many people. While hitherto peace researchers have mainly focused their attention on social structures – conceived as a set of objective and material social relations – much less attention has been paid to the structure and dynamics of 'superstructures'. 'Superstructure' is a Marxist theoretical term which closely approximates to the Western anthropological term 'culture', particularly non-material or subjective culture. That is to say, while structure refers to patterns of economic, social and political relations, superstructure (or culture, which will be used here synonymously) refers to patterns of values, beliefs, ideologies, norms, symbols and so on, and the institutions which bear them.[1]

In the materialist conception of history, the superstructure of subjective ideas (which may be shared by a collectivity) is seen as largely determined by the underlying social structure or base.[2] This view continues to be disputed by others who argue for the primacy of culture over material conditions.[3] In this debate it would appear

*This is a revised version of a paper presented at the 28th Pugwash Symposium, held at Oslo, Norway, 21-5 November 1977, and at the 7th General Conference of the International Peace Research Association, held at Oaxtepec, Mexico, 11-16 December 1977. The author is grateful to the International Peace Research Institute, Oslo, for providing financial support during the time this paper was written.

that the deterministic nature of the materialistic conception of history has sometimes been exaggerated. It may be recalled that Engels wrote:

> Political, juridical, religious, literary, artistic, etc. development is based upon economic development. But all these react upon one another and also upon the economic basis. It is not that the economic situation is *cause, solely active*, while everything else is only passive effect. There is, rather, interaction on the basis of economic necessity, which *ultimately* always asserts itself.[4]

For his part, Marx wrote that 'what distinguishes the worst architect from the best of bees is this, that the best architect raises his structure in imagination before he erects it in reality'.[5] To this, George Thomson adds:

> This preconceived image has two aspects. On the one hand, it embodies the knowledge, acquired from previous practice in production, which enables the producer to conduct the process in such a way as to achieve his purpose. This is its objective or cognitive aspect. On the other, it embodies the desire, derived from previous practice in consumption, which provides the will to produce. This is its subjective or affective aspect. In these two aspects of the labour process – the purpose and the will – we may recognise the germ of the distinction between science and art.[6]

Clearly, the distinction between idealism and materialism is not as clear-cut as is sometimes asserted. Both within Marxist and non-Marxist traditions there is increasing emphasis on the complex relationships between nature and society on the one hand, and man's notions of nature and society on the other. Within the basic constraints of ecological adaptation, man's culture can evolve a rich variety of allegories, myths of scientific theories, all seeking to explain the same reality and guide Man's actions in the real world.[7] We may assume that notions of reality are not only influenced by the development of society but that they also play a role in the development of society.

In the present chapter it is assumed (a) that a useful distinction can be made between society/structure/base on the one hand and culture/superstructure on the other; and (b) that there is a dynamic relationship between the two aspects.

The further assumption is made that *militarisation* is primarily a problem at the level of social structure and the economy, whereas *militarism* is a problem at the level of superstructure or culture. Militarisation is part of, and must be seen in relation to, other aspects of socio-economic and political structures, whereas militarism is part of, and must be seen in relation to, other aspects of culture. Just as there is a dynamic relationship between social structure and culture, so there is between militarisation and militarism.

On the basis of a given set of environmental and material conditions, a social structure is developed in order to exploit and adapt to these conditions. Military forces may play an important role in imposing or maintaining a particular social structure, and a part of the economic product extracted by the society may go to maintaining military forces. In this way the society and economy may be more or less militarised, or show an increasing or decreasing degree of militarisation.

Just as social structures are to a large degree maintained and justified by cultural values and beliefs, so are the various roles of military forces within a society maintained and justified. Culture, like society, can be more or less militarised. However, in this chapter, we shall go a step further in defining militarism as a particular aspect of militarised culture.

2 Militarisation and Social Structure

A considerable amount of work has been done on the study of militarisation and it is only necessary to refer to it briefly here.[8] Most studies have analysed the role of the military in particular societies[9] or, for example, the impact of military expenditures (or conversely, disarmament) on the economy.[10] More recently, a number of studies have examined the global role of the military in the world economic order.[11]

In a previous paper it was argued that a primary role of the military is to maintain the present world economic order (structure), an order which is characterised, on the one hand, by a global competition between rival industrial systems, and on the other by vast discrepancies in the utilisation of resources, both within individual countries and between the centre and peripheral elements of the global systems of nations. It was concluded that militarisation (measured in terms of increasing military budgets in the Third World as well as in industrialised countries, the arms trade, military *coups*, and so on) was due to several related aspects of the present world order: the competition between great powers; attempts by great powers to maintain control of their subsystems by means of direct or covert intervention or by recruiting and training local military elites; conflicts within and between local military elites as they gain in power; and attempts to overthrow oppressive regimes and, conversely, efforts by these regimes to keep in power.

In brief, militarisation is an important element in the dynamic development of social structures at the national and international levels and can be measured by objective indicators.

3 The Role of the Military in Society

Before discussing the relationship between militarism and culture it is necessary to examine the role of the military in society. This role has both *legitimate* and *illegitimate* aspects. The legitimate aspect is to defend society from external military attack, and in so doing provide the security necessary for normal social life.

The fundamental paradox with this legitimate aspect is that strong defence forces in one country may be perceived as a threat by another country which is thereby motivated to increase its forces – in turn provoking increases in the forces in the first country.

The danger is that this paradox will be exploited for illegitimate reasons.

Military forces belong to the category of social groups which *do not themselves produce* for their own material requirements (food, etc.). Like rulers, administrators, priests, artists and scientists, they are dependent upon expropriating the surplus produce of others. This expropriation may either take place by force – which military forces are well equipped to do – or by 'legitimising' the expropriation either by providing security in the event of a real attack *or by inventing an appropriate mythology*.

All too often in history, rulers, administrators and the military form a coalition with groups of priests, artists and scientists in order to 'legitimise' the expropriation of surplus produce by a combination of force and mythology, becoming 'macroparasites' rather than protectors of the people. All too often too, this pernicious coalition has been able to mobilise support for attempts to expropriate the surplus (or means of production, whether land or labour) of other societies – the phenomenon known as imperialism. Because of the legitimacy paradox referred to above, imperialism generates external hostility which 'legitimises' the further build-up of 'defensive' forces which are in fact essentially parasitical.

4 Militarism and Culture

History abounds with examples of relatively small armies controlling large populations and enabling their surplus produce to be expropriated with surprisingly little opposition. In effect, as tribal societies gave way to settled, agrarian societies, a dual society, with two cultures ('high' and 'low' or folk culture) emerged, the former parasitic upon the latter.[12] Folk culture includes beliefs and values appropriate to a peasant economy, with a world-view largely bounded by the range between the peasant's plot of land and the market. High culture is shared by an elite which may be widely dispersed geographically throughout an empire but is usually focused on a central point, the court of the emperor. The emperor is often seen as an earthly incarnation of god and this religious myth serves as a moral justification for the exploitation of the peasants.

Of the original main high cultures (Incan, Mayan, Aztec, Mesopotamian, Egyptian, Harappan and Chinese), only that of China survived until the twentieth century.[13] However, many contemporary states base themselves upon older cultures and show many of the characteristics of the dual society. Several living feudal or semi-feudal monarchs, for example, claim a line of descent to an original prophet or god.

In the ancient civilisations, religious beliefs played important roles in maintaining the socio-economic system. For example, the Aztecs believed that human sacrifice was necessary to bring back the sun each day – a vital factor in a maize-based economy. This is turn meant that the Aztecs were continually at war with their neighbours, as they sought to maintain a constant supply of sacrificial victims. As a result, military men gained in status and prestige as measured by the number of victims captured.

Religious myths were important in justifying the spread by armed force of Christianity and Islam and the emergence of new civilisations in which trade played an important role. Explicit attempts were made to penetrate folk cultures with new religious myths, particularly after the emergence of bourgeois capitalist states with colonial dependencies acquired by a combination of military force, economic penetration and ideological transformation, with missionaries in many cases taking care of the latter. Christianity was particularly successful in this respect, perhaps because its original ideology was essentially that of the oppressed in an occupied colony. However, under the edict 'Render to Caesar that which is Caesar's' it could be readily adapted to serve the aims of imperial exploitation.

An example of the role of religious myths in colonial conquest is the brown-skinned Virgin of Guadalupe in Mexico. Shortly after the

Spanish conquest a native Indian supposedly saw a vision of the Virgin Mary with brown skin. The Indian was able to produce a cloak with an image of the Virgin inside. Four hundred years later an imposing cathedral has been opened (the latest in a line) to house the image and every year many thousands of Indians travel to Mexico City to worship before this image. Similar myths arose in Peru and elsewhere.

In such ways during the colonial period elements of high culture penetrated folk cultures, though almost always blending with older cultural elements. The transformation of culture parallels the transformation of the relationship between man and land from one economic/ecological relationship to another.

In the present epoch we see the emergence of 'mass culture' which consists of degenerate elements of both high culture and folk cultures and which is diffused on an industrial scale to the far corners of the world.

Each of these periods is faced with internal contradictions. In the classical and colonial periods there was a basic contradiction between the producer/consumers and the non-producer/consumers which could be overcome as long as the producers were able to produce sufficient for the needs of both classes. As long as the producers received the minimum for survival it appears that the non-producers were able to expropriate the surplus with only relatively limited inputs of military force and mythology. The development of the high culture depended upon keeping the productive classes at a minimum standard of living. Such societies often existed for hundreds and even thousands of years, depending, perhaps, upon whether they maintained a measure of ecological balance. Where this balance was upset, as a result of natural catastrophes, disease, war or inbuilt factors in the system (such as the salting up of irrigated lands), the society collapsed.

The contemporary period is qualitatively different in that the wealth of the ruling classes depends not simply on extracting surplus produce from the primary producers, but also on selling more industrial products to an ever-increasing market of consumers. *The role of mass culture is intended to increase mass consumption, not to decrease it, or maintain at at a minimum level as in the classical civilisations.*

There are obviously contradictions in offering the masses a vision of conspicuous consumption and at the same time controlling their demands for better living standards. For in practice, what often happens is that increased consumption is only possible for a portion of the masses and a middle class emerges, jealous of aristocratic privileges *and* frightened of the impoverished underclass – emotions which create a fertile climate for militarism.

This contradiction is heightened by the problem of *ecological imbalance*. The drive towards excessive consumption in the global economy leads to local imbalances and serious social disturbances which can easily threaten the more visible holders of power. Whereas the classical civilisations could maintain themselves in ecological balance for long periods with only limited use of force, it seems possible that, in the present period, ecological imbalances and other contradictions require much greater inputs of mythology and military force in order to maintain social control.

Although military force appears to play an increasing role in many countries, it may be that 'mythological force' is more effective:

> A considerable amount of thought control is achieved not by frightening the masses but rather by inviting them to identify with the governing elite and to enjoy vicariously the pomp of state occasions. Public spectacles such as religious processions, coronations, and victory parades work against the alienating effects of poverty and exploitation . . . [D] uring Roman times, the hostility of the masses was kept under control by letting them watch gladiatorial contests and other circus spectaculars . . . '[E] ntertainment' delivered through the air directly into the shantytown house or tenement apartment is perhaps the most effective form of 'Roman circus' yet devised.[14]

The tenacity of mythological remnants from bygone periods testifies to the force of mythology in human history and there is much evidence that cultural revolution may be much more problematic than social revolution. If reactionary armed forces can be overthrown by revolutionary armed forces (which is a difficult enough task), there is still the problem of overthrowing or displacing reactionary mythologies with the true consciousness of social structure which is needed to generate activity to transform the pattern of social relations into one which prevents further oppression.

Conversely, if mythologies can be disposed of, reactionary armed forces may no longer be strong enough to go on expropriating surplus produce, and the task of revolutionary forces will be much easier.

We are now in a position to define more clearly what we mean by militarism:

> *Militarism is the military exploitation of 'mythology' in order to 'legitimise' the expropriation of surplus produce for illegitimate macroparasitic purposes.*

In the rest of this paper some examples of what is meant by the military exploitation of mythology are given.

5 The Social Functions of Mythology

Before examining more specifically military applications of mythology it is as well to point out some of the general social functions of mythology.

Man is more than an adaptive creature, passively responding to environmental stimuli. He is able to produce a surplus of energy which can either be used for *transformation* of the environment or maladaptively for destruction. Man's ability to go beyond mere adaptation is due to several features, in particular the ability to use tools, to communicate by means of language and thereby to form complex social organisations and to transmit culture from one generation to another.

In order to act upon the environment it is necessary to have some understanding of the way the environment works. Observation of regularities in the environment provides empirical data which form the basis of understanding, but this raw data must be organised into causal explanations. One function of mythology is to provide causal explanations of natural phenomena.

But human beings do not only act upon the environment as individuals. Myths perform important functions in developing group solidarity and in 'explaining' why certain group activities are done the way they are.

More theoretically, in order to act, human beings must cognitively reduce the uncertainty due to their natural and social environment. Myths, like science, are a means of reducing uncertainty, thereby enabling human beings to act in circumstances in which they would otherwise be passive and helpless.

However, human beings do not only act on the basis of what they believe is probable (cognitive aspect) but also on the basis of what is believed to be desirable (affective aspect). This is of particular importance where the source of uncertainty is other, autonomous human beings, because other human beings or groups are not bound to act according to 'observed regularities'.[15]

As a result, in strategic interactions, the affective component (e.g.

X is bad, therefore he will attack me) is dominating. In social interactions, therefore, the main function of mythology is not so much to explain why things are as they are but rather to reinforce in-group identification (group solidarity) and out-group rejection. The same applies to public manifestations such as military parades and organised sport.

Let me give an example of a modern myth, for which I am grateful to the late Professor Svale Solheim of Oslo University.[16] Shortly after the German occupation of Norway on 9 April 1940, it was reported that a bus driver who had been ordered to drive German troops had deliberately driven his bus over a cliff so that he and the enemy soldiers perished. The story aroused a great deal of attention and money was collected for his family. Subsequently, it appeared that the incident had never occurred.

In Soviet Union, a short story appeared during World War II in which an old man, forced to act as a guide to German troops, deliberately led them into an ambush, in which he himself was killed. In this case, the story was based on fact.

These stories from recent history have the same structure as many tales in Scandinavian and Russian folklore. They may or may not be based on fact – but they have the important social function of boosting the morale of an occupied people and mobilising activity to drive out the enemy.

In these examples it will be noted that the myths were generated by the weaker party in a situation of aggression, domination and oppression, with the positive social function of mobilising resistance. But mythology can also be used as a vital tool in the maintenance of oppression, as in the case of the brown-skinned Madonna of Mexico. It is this problem that we are more concerned with in the study of militarism.

To summarise, two social functions of mythology are particularly important in the study of militarism: (1) the manipulation of uncertainty and associated anxiety; and (2) the reinforcement of group solidarity.

6 The Manipulation of Uncertainty and the Reinforcement of Group Solidarity

A consequence of the necessity of reducing uncertainty and associated anxiety in order to act is that human beings are willing to 'pay' those who can reduce uncertainty for them. Those who are in a position to increase uncertainty – and then offer to reduce it – are in a good position to create for themselves an expanding market.

This is a basic principle of part of the press. The headlines which glare at you from the news-stand create uncertainty which you are invited to reduce by buying the newspaper. This, I believe, is the main explanation of the well known emphasis on 'negative' news.

This principle is also a fundamental one in psychological warfare: on the one hand, it aims to create anxiety, and on the other to offer the victim a means of reducing that anxiety. This applies just as much to psychological warfare on the home front and in peacetime as to operations directed against an enemy in war.

Thus, in order to legitimise the maintenance of vast military establishments in peacetime, great efforts are made to exploit news items which create public anxiety about the intentions of a possible enemy. The public are then invited to contribute more tax money to buy more military equipment as a means of reducing their anxiety. The creation of the myth of the 'missile gap' is a classic example, but we are continually subjected to massive efforts of the same kind.

Control of information has, of course, long been used as a basic tool of domination: 'For at least 400 years control of the presses was one of the most powerful instruments in the hands of authority, molding the fate of nations . . .'[17]

Conversely, conscientisation campaigns which seek to explode dominant mythologies are a powerful force for social change.

Myths and the manipulation of information can be skilfully used to reinforce in-group solidarity and out-group rejection. The World War II and folklore myths referred to earlier are examples.

A drastic example of a different kind is related by Fletcher Prouty in his book on the CIA.[18] He relates the manner in which support for local military commanders in a developing country could be artificially built up. In the course of a counter-insurgency exercise, one group of soldiers is dressed up as 'guerrillas'. *The local people are not told that it is an 'exercise'.* In the course of time, the local commander may have sufficient local support to be able to launch a bid for power at the national level . . .

The use of *agents provocateurs* in this way serves both for manipulation of uncertainty and to reinforce in-group and out-group identifications.

7 The Functions and Dysfunctions of Militarism in Mass Culture

The purpose of militarism in mass culture is, of course, to promote the militarisation of society and thereby to maintain the power of the elite to expropriate the surplus value of mass society and use it for consumption or investment in overseas military or commercial adventures.

The manipulation of uncertainty and out-group rejection may have dangerous and destabilising consequences, particularly in societies subject to rapid change or which for other reasons harbour powerful emotional forces. In some countries, for example, the opportunity for war has been greeted with great popular enthusiasm. The old elite may lose control of events and find itself swept along on a tide which may eventually smash it.

8 The Military Subculture

Myths, symbols, even totems play a considerable role in the military subculture from the time of the new recruit's induction into the 'tribe' and the ensuing *rites de passage*.

Indeed, the military, along with religious sects, are the main bearers of tribal cultural remnants in modern society. The main function of military ritual and symbolism is the strengthening of group solidarity which is often at the expense of solidarity with the civilian population, and should not therefore be underestimated.

9 Combating Militarism and Militarisation

If, as has been persuasively argued, military force is at the very core of the nation-state, then combating militarisation requires fundamental changes in the nation-state system of the world. But leaving side this difficult problem, the conclusion of the present analysis is that combating militarism requires action at the *cultural*, or subjective, level, in addition to action at the political and economic, or objective level, to restrain the militarisation of society.

> To deny the importance of subjectivity in the process of transforming the world and history is naive and simplistic. It is to admit the impossible: a world without men . . . If men produce social reality . . . then transforming that reality is an historical task, a task for men.[19]

More specifically, combating militarism requires a transformation of militaristic culture and an attack on all the forces which promote militaristic culture, in the mass media, in religion, in the arts and in the sciences. It requires an attack not only on 'arms control' (as distinct from disarmament) but an attack on thought control for militaristic ends.

This attack requires an analysis of the cultural dynamics of particular societies, the forces at work in each culture, the role of science, arts, religion, the mass media, and so on, and in particular of the way in which uncertainty is manipulated and out-group rejection artificially reinforced (arms control negotiations being a good case in point). The analysis must then form the basis of action at the cultural level, action which has been very appropriately termed cultural action or *The Pedagogy of the Oppressed*:

> The pedagogy of the oppressed, as a humanist and libertarian pedagogy, has two distinct phases. In the first, the oppressed unveil the world of oppression and through the praxis commit themselves to its transformation . . . In the second stage . . . this pedagogy . . . becomes a pedagogy of all men in the process of permanent liberation. In both stages, it is always through action in depth that the culture of domination is culturally confronted.[20]

Notes

1. Thus E.B. Taylor in his book *Primitive Culture* (1871) describes culture as 'that complex whole which includes knowledge, belief, art, morals, law, custom, and any other capability and habits acquired by man as a member of society' (1958 ed., p. 1). Marx in his Preface to *A Contribution to the Critique of Political Economy* uses the term superstructure to refer to 'the social, political and intellectual life in process in general' and 'the legal, political, religious, aesthetic or philosophic – in short, ideological forms' which should be clearly distinguished from 'the material transformation of the economic conditions of production'. In Western social science a distinction has recently been made between material culture (meaning, in particular, physical artifacts) and 'subjective culture', referring to values, feelings and, most generally, meanings; see C.E. Osgood, 'Probing Subjective Culture', *Journal of Communication* (Winter 1974), pp. 21-34.

2. Marx (loc. cit.) writes: 'The mode of production of material life conditions the social, political and intellectual life process in general. It is not the consciousness of men that determines their being, but, on the contrary, their social being that determines their consciousness.' With regard to social change, he goes on: 'With the change of the economic foundation the entire immense superstructure is more or less rapidly transformed.' There is a strong tendency to interpret these words mechanistically: first change the ownership of the means of production and people's world-views will change accordingly. Paolo Freire, in *The Pedagogy of the Oppressed* (Penguin, Harmondsworth, 1972), however, criticises this mechanistic interpretation.

3. See, for example, M. Sahlins, *Culture and Practical Reason* (University of Chicago Press, Chicago, 1976) for a recent example of this argument.

4. Letter to H. Starkenberg, 25 January 1894.

5. *Capital*, vol. 1, p. 178.

6. G. Thomson, *The Human Essence* (China Policy Study Group, London, 1974), p. 7.

7. L.E. Stover, *The Cultural Ecology of Chinese Civilization* (Mentor, New York, 1974), following the ideas of Professor Julian H. Steward of Columbia University, defines cultural ecology as 'the functional interrelationships between the basic spheres of life as this pattern is worked out in the course of man's cultural adaptation of the environment'. For an introduction to general anthropology based on this approach see M. Harris, *Culture, Man and Nature* (Crowell, New York, 1971).

8. Examples of this literature and some criticisms of it include H. Bienen (ed.), *The Military Intervenes* (The Russell Sage Foundation, New York, 1968); *The Military and Modernization* (Aldine, Chicago, 1971); S.E. Finer, *The Man on Horseback* (Pall Mall, London, 1962); W.F. Gutteridge, *Military Institutions and Power in the New States* (Praeger, New York, 1965); *The Military in African Politics* (London, 1969); S.P. Huntington, *Political Order in Changing Societies* (York University Press, New Haven, Conn., 1969); J.J. Johnson (ed.), *The Role of the Military in Underdeveloped Countries* (Princeton University Press, Princeton, 1962); M. Janowitz, *The Military in the Political Development of New Nations* (University of Chicago Press, Chicago, 1964); J.M. Lee, *African Armies and Civil Order* (Chatto, London, 1969); C.E. Welch, *Soldier and State in Africa* (Northwestern University Press, Evanston, Ill., 1970). Details of actual arms transfers are provided in Stockholm International Peace Research Institute, *Arms Trade Registers: the Arms Trade with the Third World* (Almqvist and Wiksell, Stockholm, 1975) and US Arms Control and Disarmament Agency, *World Military Expenditures and Arms Transfers, 1966-1975* (Washington, D.C., 1976). A special issue of the *Bulletin of Peace Proposals* (1977, no. 2) is devoted to the problem of the arms trade and the transfer of military technology. See also M. Kaldor, 'The Significance of Military Technology', *Bulletin of Peace Proposals*, no. 2 (1977), pp. 121-3; P. Lock and H. Wulf, 'Consequences of the Transfer of Military-Oriented Technology on the Development Process'; M.D. Wolpin, 'Military Dependency versus Development in the Third World', all in the *Bulletin of Peace Proposals*, no. 2 (1977).

9. There are an increasing number of studies of the role of the military in the development of particular countries, among them: R.M. Fields, *The Portuguese Revolution and the Armed Forces Movement* (Praeger, New York, 1975); A.R. Luckham, *The Nigerian Military: a Sociological Analysis of Authority and Revolt, 1960-1967* (Cambridge University Press, Cambridge, 1971); A.A. Mazrui, *Soldiers and Kinsmen in Uganda: The Making of a Military Ethnocracy* (Sage, Beverly Hills, California, 1975); N.J. Miners, *The Nigerian Army, 1956-1966* (Methuen, London, 1971); R. Pinkney, *Ghana Under Military Rule, 1966-1969* (Methuen, London, 1972); A. Stepan, *The Military in Politics: Changing Patterns in Brazil* (Princeton University Press, Princeton, 1971); W.J. Stover, 'The Armed Forces and Nation-Building: Revolutionary Socialist Theory and Praxis in China', *Journal of Contemporary Asia*, vol. 6, no. 3, pp. 323-3; A. Abdel-Malek, *Egypt: Military Society*, trans. C.L. Markmann (Random House-Vintage Books, New York, 1968). See also L. Hamon (ed.), *Le Role Extra-militaire de l'Armée dans le Tiers Monde* (Press Universitaires de France, Paris, 1966); E.A. Nordlinger, 'Soldiers in Mufti: the Impact of Military Rule upon Economic and Social Change in the Non-Western States', *American Journal of Political Science*, vol. LXIV, no. 4 (December 1979), pp. 1131-48; R.M. Price, 'A Theoretical Approach to Military Rule in the New States: Reference Group Theory and the Ghanaian Case', *World Politics*, vol. XXIII, no. 3 (April 1971), pp. 399-430.

10. Studies of the more specifically economic aspects of military investments are E. Benoit, *Defense and Economic Growth in Developing Countries* (Lexington

Books, Lexington, 1973) and G. Kennedy, *The Military in the Third World* (Duckworth, London, 1974). The role of military and economic aid as a 'Trojan Horse' has been pointed out by S. Weissman *et al.*, *The Trojan Horse: A Radical Look at Foreign Aid* (Ramparts Press, San Francisco, 1974). See also N. Stein, 'The Pentagon's Protégées: U.S. training programs for foreign military personnel', *Latin America and Empire Report* (North American Congress on Latin America), vol. X, no. 1 (January 1976), pp. 1-32; W.R. Kintner, 'The Role of Military Assistance', *Proceedings of the US Naval Institute* (March 1961), pp. 76-83.

11. J. Øberg, 'The New Economic and Military Orders as Problems to Peace Research', *Bulletin of Peace Proposals*, no. 2 (1977); M. Lumsden, 'The Role of the Military in the World Economic Order', paper presented at the 7th Nordic Peace Research Conference, 1976, and revised for the use of UNESCO, 1977 (a short version appeared in the *Bulletin of Peace Proposals*, no. 1 (1978)).

12. See Stover, *Cultural Ecology*, for an account of the phenomenon in China.

13. Ibid.

14. Harris, *Culture, Man and Nature*, p. 407.

15. If the interaction between the two groups is one of competition, or contains mixed elements of co-operation and competition, it becomes *strategic*. By strategic interaction is meant one in which what one party does is determined by what he thinks the other party thinks he will do, and vice versa. Reasoning in a strategic interaction is *recursive* so that, formally speaking, it is impossible to assign probabilities to the opponent's (or partner's) expected acts. (See M. Lumsden, 'Perception and Information in Strategic Thinking', *Journal of Peace Research* (1966), pp. 257-77.)

16. S. Solheim, 'Historical Legend – Historical Function', *Acta Ethnographica Academia Scientarum Hungaricae*, Tomus 19 (1970), pp. 341-6.

17. T.K. Derry and T.I. Williams, *A Short History of Technology* (Clarendon Press, Oxford, 1960), p. 707.

18. *The Secret Team* (Prentice-Hall, Englewood Cliffs, N.J., 1973).

19. Paolo Freire, *The Pedagogy of the Oppressed* (Penguin, Harmondsworth, 1972), p. 27.

20. Ibid., p. 31.

PART VI

APPENDICES

APPENDIX 1: WORLD MILITARY EXPENDITURES*

World military expenditure is now running at an annual rate of about $410 thousand million, or nearly $1 million per minute – an increase (in constant prices to take inflation into account) of about 50 per cent over the past two decades. The Third World's share of this total has increased over this period from about 4 per cent to about 14 per cent.

The rate of increase of Third World military spending varies considerably from region to region. During the 1970's, for example, Middle Eastern (including Egyptian) spending increased (in constant prices) about 2.8 times. African (excluding Egyptian) military spending increased about 2.4 times. Asian and Latin American military spending each increased about 1.5 times. For the Third World as a whole, military spending has so far doubled during the 1970s, increasing faster than the GNP. It is noteworthy, however, that Middle Eastern (including Egyptian) military spending since 1976 has actually decreased by about 20 per cent. Nevertheless, about 45 per cent of total Third World military expenditure comes from the Middle East. Asia spends about 27 per cent, while Africa and Latin America each spend about 14 per cent.

Many believe that the Third World can least afford increasing levels of military spending and that most, if not all, available resources should go to development. It is for this reason that Third World military spending provokes comment, even though, compared with that of industrialised countries, it is still quite low in absolute terms.

*Excerpted from *World Armaments and Disarmament. SIPRI Yearbook 1979* (Stockholm International Peace Research Institute) (Taylor and Francis Ltd, London, 1979).

Figure A1.1: The Trend in World Military Expenditure, 1949-78

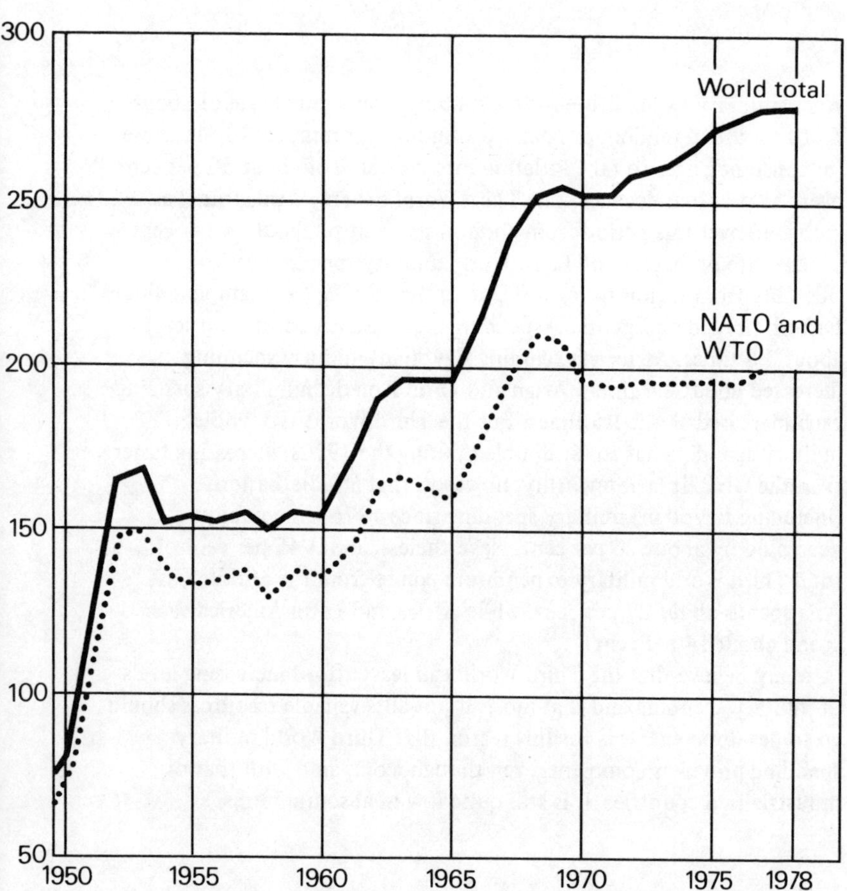

The values are US $ thousand million, at constant (1973) prices and 1973 exchange rates.

Table A1.1: World Military Expenditures: Summary

Figures are in US $ m, at 1973 prices and 1973 exchange rates.

	1953	1963	1968	1973	1978	Percentage of World Total 1978
USA	69,622	75,824	103,077	78,358	71,475	25.5
Other NATO	27,301	36,697	37,795	43,326	47,937	17
Total NATO	96,923	112,521	140,872	121,684	119,412	42.5
USSR	30,500	48,900	58,000	66,000	71,000	25.5
Other WTO	2,780	4,239	5,396	7,025	8,816	3.5
Total WTO	33,280	53,139	63,396	73,025	79,816	29
Other Europe	3,225	3,999	4,560	5,382	6,212	2
Middle East	1,225	1,810	4,425	13,482	17,046	6
South Asia	1,100	2,317	2,176	2,745	3,414	1
Far East (excl. China)	3,100	3,977	6,086	8,181	10,850	4
China	[8,000]	[13,800]	[21,800]	[26,200]	[29,200]	[10.5]
Oceania	976	1,166	2,101	2,102	2,048	1
Africa (excl. Egypt)	275	967	1,828	2,674	5,461	2
Central America	375	548	742	826	1,017	0.5
South America	2,060	1,810	2,549	3,872	4,472	1.5
World Total	150,539	196,054	250,535	260,173	278,948	100.0

Table A1.2: Major Military Spenders and their Rank in Economic-Social Indicators, 1975

	Military Expenditures		Rank among 140 Nations											
				GNP	Education					Health				
	US $	Rank among 140 Nations	Economic Social Standing Average Rank	Per Capita	Public Expenditure per Capita	School-age Population per Teacher	School-age Population in School	Women in Total University Enrolment	Literacy Rate	Public Expenditure per Capita	Population per Physician	Population per Hospital Bed	Infant Mortality Rate	Life Expectancy
USSR	94,000	1	17	27	25	23	46	7	1	27	1	6	34	29
United States	90,948	2	6	6	7	12	4	22	1	13	18	33	13	7
China	18,000	3	79	103	97	55	43	7	26	97	93	117	51	56
West Germany	15,299	4	9	9	15	30	28	45	1	3	9	4	21	18
France	13,093	5	4	11	15	12	23	15	1	6	23	17	8	10
United Kingdom	11,477	6	16	23	18	8	5	61	16	15	26	20	13	10
Iran	7,742	7	65	44	46	71	92	78	85	46	69	105	106	77
Egypt	5,368	8	88	100	82	90	96	70	80	76	52	78	71	84
Italy	4,856	9	24	28	29	23	41	37	30	18	11	14	26	10
Japan	4,640	10	24	21	21	44	20	92	1	16	33	16	2	3
Saudi Arabia	4,260	11	63	20	3	79	117	112	114	31	72	102	113	104
Israel	3,517	12	22	25	24	2	41	22	37	24	2	40	25	10
Canada	3,074	13	4	10	4	8	3	27	26	4	19	21	13	7
India	3,008	14	111	125	121	90	100	78	86	118	83	132	95	88
Netherlands	2,869	15	15	15	5	39	43	74	16	7	22	4	2	1
East Germany	2,644	16	13	24	26	17	32	17	1	23	13	11	13	18
Poland	2,384	17	28	31	35	41	66	12	16	26	17	29	29	29
Sweden	2,344	18	1	4	2	1	10	37	1	1	20	1	1	1
Spain	2,200	19	31	30	48	39	32	53	32	25	25	44	10	10
Turkey	1,971	20	70	59	72	83	85	94	72	79	59	79	83	10

Notes to Table A1.2 are on p. 375.

Notes to Table A1.2:

a. This table includes a single figure for each nation to summarise its rank among all nations in economic-social indicators. Three factors are combined: GNP per capita, education and health. The method of averaging gives equal importance to each of the three elements. For education and health, this means that a summary rank is first obtained for the five indicators shown under each category.

The ranking method makes it possible to combine a variety of indicators. Other combinations are, of course, possible, and will be further explored. In this case, the indicators chosen for education and health represent both input of national effort (e.g. public expenditures, teachers) and output (e.g. literacy, infant mortality). Input factors give credit for effort, which will determine social progress but may not yet show in slower-acting indicators of results.

There are obvious omissions in coverage at present. Housing is one and nutrition is covered only through mortality and life expectancy. Perhaps even more important, only one of the eleven indicators now in the composite (percentage women in total university enrolment) begins to reflect the unequal distribution of resources within countries. One objective for future editions is to incorporate available data on distribution of incomes into the averages.

Large military expenditures and social well-being seldom go well together. The strongest military powers invariably make a relatively poorer showing in economic-social development.

The table above shows how the two goals diverge. Of the ten major military spenders in 1975, only one ranked as high in economic-social standing. Of the next ten in military power, only four ranked as well or better on the economic-social scale.

Source: Ruth Leger Sivard, *World Military and Social Expenditures 1978* (WMSE Publications, Leesburg, Virginia, 1978).

APPENDIX 2: WORLD-WIDE MILITARY COUPS SINCE 1945: A SHORT NOTE ON DATA COLLECTION

Milton Leitenberg

Literally thousands of books and papers have been written about particular post-World War II military conflicts such as the war in Vietnam or the several Israeli-Arab wars in the Middle East. However, another form of the use of military force, military *coups*, the overthrow of governments – either civil governments or ones already ruled by the military – by one or more of the military forces of the state has received hardly any attention at all by comparison. Aside from studies of individual *coups*, there are less than a hundred comparative studies covering the subject of military *coups* since 1945, the end of World War II. The reasons for this relative lack of attention seem arbitrary and superficial. Military *coups* are often brushed aside as less consequential because they may be over in a matter of hours, they are often completed with little or no loss of life, and they are 'domestic' or 'internal' affairs. However, the long-run domestic *and* international political implications of military *coups* are often no less significant than inter-state wars.

This short appendix has a very limited purpose. It grew out of the need to find a data base from which one could do further research on the effects of arms transfers and military assistance of varying kinds[1] on the incidence and frequency of military *coups*. An attempt was made to survey all available comparative studies of post-World War II military *coups*, and it quickly became apparent that no such data base existed. Of the available papers with substantial comparative data on military *coups*, only about half contained actual lists of identified *coups*. Twenty papers were found with lists of successful military *coups*, and 11 papers with lists of unsuccessful, or attempted, ones. The data contained in these studies were then tabulated. As can be seen from Tables A2.1 and A2.2, the numbers of *coups* covered by these studies varied widely. An equal number of other comparative studies, many quite valuable, studied particular variables relevant to military *coups*, but contained no actual lists of the events in question in which individual *coups* could be identified.[2] These other studies are not dealt with further in this appendix.

The rest of this contribution is simply a compendium of the data contained in those papers which contained actual lists of military *coups*, both successful and unsuccessful ones, and an explanation of the methodology used in making the compilation. The data are presented in four tables. Tables A2.1 and A2.2 are lists of the studies from which the data were derived. (Table A2.1 for successful military *coups*, Table A2.2 for unsuccessful ones.) Each table indicates the study (author, publication source, etc.), its year of completion, and the number of military *coups*, their geographical area and time span covered by the study. Tables A2.3 and A2.4 are tabulations of the incidence and frequency of both successful and unsuccessful (attempted) military *coups* since 1945. grouped by five- and ten-year periods, and by five geographical regions: Europe, Africa, Latin America, Middle East and Asia (Table A2.3 for successful, Table A2.4 for unsuccessful).

Something can be said about the composite data derived from this effort, and something should be said of the validity, purpose and utility of such an exercise. The composite data do not seem to show any marked trends, but one can safely draw several general conclusions:

(1) the number of military *coups* since the end of World War II is a very large number;
(2) there seem to have been just as many *un*successful, or attempted, as successful military *coups*;
(3) the 1960-70 period seems to have been somewhat more active in producing military *coups* (unless the unreliability of the data is sufficient to wash out the slight increment).

There are two categories of problems concerning an aggregate data compilation such as this. The first concerns its validity, or accuracy, the second its utility and purpose. Regarding the validity of the compilation, *it is absolutely essential to indicate that the reliability of these data is very uncertain*. The compilation was obtained by summing the inputs from the various studies; we did not set up our own criteria for each event, nor did we ourselves decide which were in fact military *coups* and which were not. The result is that the summary tables can be no better than the input of the original studies, and the quality of these again seems highly variable. There is some indication of this by the variables shown in Tables A2.1 and A2.2, and in the discussion which follows. To begin with, the term 'military *coup*' was used in this appendix to mean only a *coup* by one or more of the military services of a state. It was *not* used in the sense of an armed *coup* by a civilian group, which some authors also term a 'military *coup*'. Hoadley provides a somewhat broader usage of the first kind: 'the definition of a military *coup d'état* was broadened to include all major disturbances of a nation's constitutional and political order caused by or associated with unorthodox behavior of that nation's military officers.'[3] The number and events that Hoadley provided – ostensibly on the basis of these criteria – were used. One or more authors also use 'military intervention' in thise sense.

Several of the lists of both successful and unsuccessful military *coups* did not appear as separate lists in the work of the authors (Richardson, Christensen, Kellogg). They were embedded in larger lists of wars, crises, conflicts, etc. However, the individual events were identified as successful or unsuccessful military *coups* by the authors, which made it possible to extract relevant items. Happily, one or two authors (Kellogg, Richardson) provided short synopses or descriptions for the events they called '*coups*', or military *coups*, and it was possible to winnow out those *not* carried out by the military. These synopses also permitted one to guess that a very substantial number of the '*coups*' in Li and Thompson's paper were *not* made by military groups; in fact, some may not be '*coups*' of *any* kind. However, they were left in the compiled table in most instances, except for cases that were most certainly not military *coups*.

The second concern is the utility and purpose of such aggregate data. What questions do they answer, and what questions don't they answer? Of what use are the numbers aside from questions of their accuracy? It is clear that the numbers do *not* answer many important and basic qualitative questions. Once a military *coup* takes place in a particular country, after a long period of years in which there may not have been any, it may be much easier for subsequent military *coups* to take place. This would affect the distribution of numbers over time. Second, it can easily be argued that a particular *coup* may be far more important in the political history of a nation, and in that of its neighbours, than ten other *coups* elsewhere. For example, the military *coups* in Brazil in 1964, in Peru in 1968, in Chile in 1973, in Uganda in 1971, and others in Egypt, Syria, Iraq, etc. carried far more significance in terms of social and political developments within the country, subsequent regional arms races, international political alignments, regional wars and political role of the military, etc., than the 'average' *coup*, or than many other *coups*. The overthrow of the Battista government in Cuba in 1960 was not a 'military' *coup* at all, but is certainly one of great political importance. In other countries the military leadership is able to hold and to exert substantial and often determining political power without resort to periodic *coups.*[4] In other words, the qualitative analysis of military *coups* may be far more important than their quantitative analysis.

Nevertheless, the aggregate data have two elementary uses. First, they provide some understanding of what is occurring over time regarding a political phenomenon of growing importance. Military juntas rarely turn over their power to civilian leadership once a *coup* has been made. Given this tendency, and a more or less constant rate of military *coups*, a larger and larger proportion of developing countries are now ruled by military elites. More than 60 developing countries have had at least one military *coup* since 1945, many have had several, and many have had quite sizeable numbers of such events. More than half of the developing countries in the world are now ruled by military governments. One should then be concerned to understand the effect of maintenance of political power by the military in developing countries, on the allocation of resources and on the subsequent military development of these states, on their patterns of acquisition of arms, etc.[5]

Second, aggregate data are necessary for anyone who wants to do research and to draw conclusions on the effects of arms transfers and military assistance *on* the *incidence* of military *coups* in developing nations. That is true whether the assistance is of sophisticated weapons, conventional small arms, 'police' weapons or of training. It is impossible to make judgements on the causal relations between arms transfers and military assistance and military *coups* without aggregate data. The data compilation was therefore essentially made as an aid to research and researchers in this area.

[A collated detailed list of successful and unsuccessful military *coups* in the period between 1945 and 1977 is available from the author.]

Table A2.1: List of Studies of Successful Post-World War II Military Coups

	Name of Study	Year of Completion of Study	Years Surveyed of Study	Geographical Area Surveyed	Number of Successful Coup Events Reported
(1)	T.N. Dupuy and W. Blanchard, *The Almanac of World Military Power* (Barker, London, 1974)	1974	1950-74	World-wide	84
(2)	C. Veliz, *The Politics of Conformity in Latin America* (OUP, Oxford, 1967)	1966	1945-66	Latin America only	49
(3)	R. First, *The Barrel of a Gun; Political Power in Africa and the Coup D'Etat* (Allen Lane, London, 1970)	1969	1952-69	Africa only	24
(4)	E. Fossum, 'Factors Influencing the Occurrence of Military Coups d'Etat in Latin America', *Journal of Peace Research*, vol. 4, no. 3 (1967), pp. 228-51 (Appendix I)	1966	1945-66	Latin America only	47
(5)	R.P.Y. Li and W.R. Thompson, 'The Coup Contagion Hypothesis', *Journal of Conflict Resolution*, vol. 19, no. 1 (March 1975), pp. 63-88	1970	1946-70	World-wide	140
(6)	J.S. Hoadley, *Soldiers and Politics in Southeast Asia* (1975)	1975	1945-71	Asia only	27
(7)	J.C. Kellogg, *A Synopsis of Military Conflict, 1945-64* (Bendix Corporation, Michigan, 1965)	1964	1945-64	World-wide	23
(8)	Cheryl Christensen Memorandum (MIT, Cambridge, Mass., 1974)	1974	1945-70	World-wide	49
(9)	E. Luttwak, *Coup D'Etat* (A.A. Knopf, New York, 1969), pp. 204-7	1967	1945-67	World-wide	66
(10)	S. Decalo, *Coups and Army Rule in Africa* (Yale University Press, New Haven, 1976)	1975	1963-75	Sub-Saharan Africa only	32
(11)	S.E. Finer, *The Man on Horseback*, 2nd edition (Penguin, Harmondsworth, 1976)	1976	1958-73	World-wide	91

(12)	D.G. Morrison *et al.*, *Black Africa, A Comparative Handbook* (Free Press, New York, 1972)	1972	1955-72	Africa only	26
(13)	R.P. Richardson, *An Analysis of Recent Conflicts* (Center for Naval Analysis, Washington, DC, 1966)	1966	1946-65	World-wide	55
(14)	F.A. Casadio, 'I Conflitti' (PhD thesis, Rome, 1976-7)	1977	1945-76	World-wide	128
(15)	'The Power Tables', *Defense and Foreign Affairs Handbook, 1976-1977* (Copely Associates, Washington, DC), p. 643	1977	1975-6	World-wide	4
(16)	G. Kennedy, *The Military in the Third World* (Duckworth, London, 1974), pp. 338-44	1974	1945-72	World-wide	148
(17)	M.C. Needler, 'Political Development and Military Intervention in Latin America', *American Political Science Review*, vol. 60, no. 3 (September 1966) pp. 616-26	1966	1945-64	Latin America only	40
(18)	M.D. Wolpin, *Military Aid and Counterrevolution in the Third World* (Lexington Books, Mass., 1972), pp. 123-4, 205-10	1972	1945-70	Omits Latin America	71
(19)	E. Luard, *Conflict and Peace in the Modern International System* (Little, Brown, Boston, 1968), pp. 146-54	1968	1960-6	World-wide	48
(20)	Loftus, J.E. *Latin American Defense Expenditures, 1938-1965* (Rand Corporation, RM-5310-PR/ISA, January 1968)	1968	1945-65	Latin America only	39

Table A2.2: List of Studies of Unsuccessful Post-World War II Military Coups

	Name of Study	Year of Completion of Study	Years Surveyed	Geographical Area Surveyed	Number of Unsuccessful Coups
(1)	J.C. Kellogg, *A Synopsis of Military Conflict, 1945-1964* (Bendix Corporation, Ann Arbor, Michigan, 1965)	1964	1945-64	World-wide	14
(2)	R. First, *The Barrel of a Gun, Political Power in Africa, and the Coup d'Etat* (Allen Lane, London, 1970)	1969	1952-69	Africa only	15
(3)	E. Luttwak, *Coup d'Etat* (A.A. Knopf, New York, 1969), pp. 204-7	1967	1945-67	World-wide	30
(4)	R.P.Y. Li and W.R. Thompson, 'The Coup Contagion Hypothesis', *Journal of Conflict Resolution*, vol. 19, no. 1 (March 1975), pp. 63-88	1970	1946-70	World-wide	134
(5)	T.N. Dupuy and W. Blanchard, *The Almanac of World Military Power*, 2nd edition (Barker, London, 1974)	1974	1950-74	World-wide	25
(6)	S.E. Finer, *The Man on Horseback*, 2nd edition (Penguin, Harmondsworth, 1976)	1976	1958-73	World-wide	39
(7)	Cheryl Christensen, Memorandum (MIT, Cambridge, Mass., 1974)	1974	1945-70	World-wide	18
(8)	D.G. Morrison *et al.*, *Black Africa, A Comparative Handbook* (Free Press, New York, 1972)	1972	1955-72	Africa only	17
(9)	R.P. Richardson, *An Analysis of Recent Conflicts* (Center for Naval Analysis, Washington, DC, 1966)	1966	1946-65	World-wide	35
(10)	'The Power Tables', *Defense and Foreign Affairs Handbook, 1976-1977* (Copely Associates, Washington, DC), p. 643	1977	1975-6	World-wide	1
(11)	G. Kennedy, *The Military in the Third World* (Duckworth, London, 1974), pp. 338-44	1974	1945-72	World-wide	136

Table A2.3: Successful Military Coups

Region	1945-50	1951-5	1956-60	1961-5	1966-70	1971-5	1976-8[a]
Europe	–	–	3	–	1	4	–
Africa	–	–	3	20	32	19	7
Latin America	26	15	13	21	11	12	4
Middle East	4	8	4	10	10	3	2
Asia	3	7	14	20	8	5	5
Total	33	30	37	71	62	43	18

Note: a. Very incomplete.

Table A2.4: Unsuccessful Military Coups

Region	1945-50	1951-5	1956-60	1961-5	1966-70	1971-5	1976-8[a]
Europe	3	–	1	3	1	3	–
Africa	–	2	5	25	41	17	8 +
Latin America	20	14	31	20	7	9	1
Middle East	1	1	5	9	9	4	–
Asia	10	3	7	13	4	1	2
Total	34	20	49	70	62	34	11 +

Note: a. Very incomplete.

Notes

1. It is useful to remember that 'military assistance' takes a wide range of forms:

arms trade;
arms aid;
supplying money with which to purchase weapons;
building logistical infrastructure; air bases, naval bases, etc.;
paramilitary construction, aid or training – harbours, railroads, rolling stock, roads, border police, internal security forces; the categorisation will depend on the usage;
training officers and troops in the recipient country;
training officers and troops in the donor country;
supplying active duty military personnel for operations in recipient countries; advisers, 'special forces', pilots, radar operators, air defense system operators, etc.;
supplying mercenaries.

2. By way of example, McKinlay and Cohan have extensive data on military regimes, without, however, indicating the dates of individual *coups*; Jackman provides the duration of military rule, again without giving dates of *coups*; Thompson also contains relevant data, again without supplying particulars about specific *coups*. Another 15-20 studies of equal value for comparative study are available, although they do not itemise individual military *coups*. The references are not included here.

(a) R.D. McKinlay and A.S. Cohan, 'A Comparative Analysis of the Political and Economic Performance of Military Civilian Regimes', *Comparative Politics*, vol. 8, no. 1 (October 1975); see also McKinlay and Cohan, 'Performance and Instability in Military and Nonmilitary Regime Systems', *American Political Science Review*, vol. 70, no. 3 (September 1976), pp. 850-64.

(b) P. Jackman, 'Politicians in Uniform', *American Political Science Review*, vol. 70, no. 4 (December 1976), pp. 1078-97.

(c) W.R. Thompson, 'Regime Vulnerability and the Military Coup', *Comparative Politics*, vol. 7, no. 4 (July 1975), pp. 459-87.

3. J.S. Hoadley, 'Social Complexity, Economic Development, and Military Coups d'Etat in Latin America and Asia', *Journal of Peace Research*, nos. 1-2 (1973), pp. 119-20.

4. F.A. Falk, 'Militarization and Human Rights in the Third World', *Bulletin of Peace Proposals*, vol. 8, no. 3 (1977), pp. 220-32. It should be noted that according to Falk's third criterion for 'militarization' those countries 'in which civilians rule the country but disallow a political opposition to function normally and depend heavily on the military to keep them in power', his maps should show an even wider spread of 'militarization' than they do, though the additional nations that fit the criterion would not all have been added in the most recent years. For a short survey of studies 'of the extent of military intervention in the domestic order', see L. Sigelman, 'Military Intervention, a Methodological Note', *Journal of Political and Military Sociology*, vol. 2, no. 2 (Fall 1974), pp. 275-81.

5. For a review, see M. Kaldor, 'The Military in Development', *World Development*, vol. 4, no. 6 (June 1976), pp. 459-82; see also M. Kaldor, 'Military Technology and Social Structure', *Bulletin of the Atomic Scientists*, vol. 33, no. 6 (June 1977), pp. 49-53.

See also:

(a) M. Leitenberg and N. Ball, 'The Military Expenditures of Less Developed

Nations as a Proportion of their State Budgets', *Bulletin of Peace Proposals*, vol. 8, no. 4 (1977), pp. 310-15. Also in *World Armaments and Disarmament, SIPRI Yearbook, 1978*, pp. 134-41, and in *Mazingira*, no. 7 (1978), pp. 53-7.

(b) P.C. Schmitter, 'Foreign Military Assistance, National Military Spending, and Military Rule in Latin America', in P.C. Schmitter (ed.), *Military Rule in Latin America, Function, Consequences and Perspectives* (Sage Publications, Beverly Hills, 1973), pp. 117-89.

(c) J.E. Loftus, *Latin American Defense Expenditures, 1938-1965* (RAND, RM-5310-PR/15A, January 1968, 132 pages).

(d) F.C. Doran, 'US Foreign Aid and the Unstable Polity: a Regional Case Study', *Orbis*, vol. 22, no. 2 (Summer 1978), pp. 435-52.

(e) L. Einaudi, *et al., Arms Transfers to Latin America, Toward a Policy of Mutual Respect* (RAND, R-1173-DOS, June 1973, 80 pages).

(f) F. Abolfathi and T.W. Park, 'Military Spending in the Third World, the Interactions of Domestic and International Forces' in C. Liske *et al.* (eds.), *Comparative Public Policy, Issues, Theories and Methods* (Sage-John Wiley, New York, 1975), pp. 109-25; see also three other Abolfathi publications.

(g) M.D. Hayes, 'Policy Consequence of Military Participation in Politics: an Analysis of tradeoffs in Brazilian Federal Expenditures' in Liske *et al., Comparative Public Policy.*

APPENDIX 3: THREATS OF THE USE OF NUCLEAR WEAPONS SINCE WORLD WAR II: AN INTRODUCTORY NOTE

Milton Leitenberg

The last twenty years have seen numerous studies of both strategic and conventional weapon competition between the US and the USSR. For the most part, these studies and analyses all deal with static measures: the strategic balance, other particular force balances, force levels, military expenditure. The studies which concern the *uses* of force have been case studies of individual instances, such as Vietnam, Czechoslovakia or the Dominican Republic, and they have been nearly entirely focused on the use of conventional weapons. Case studies of the Cuban missile crisis would be an exception.

To someone whose primary concern is to identify to what degree and in which instances the use of nuclear weapons has been involved in post-World War II situations, the very few survey studies of the post-World War II use of military force all contain major drawbacks. Of the few studies that exist, most were done for the US government, and have seen only extremely limited circulation, and in addition these deal only with conventional warfare.[1] The recent large study by George and Smoke with the explicit title *Deterrence in American Foreign Policy: Theory and Practice* is very heavy on theory, and extremely thin on what would matter most to its title, a thorough examination of the instances of US crisis deployments of nuclear weapons.[2] Howe's volume *Multicrises* is excellent, but only deals with two events, the Middle East war of 1967 and the Quemoy conflict of 1958.[3] The most recent and extensive study, by Blechman and Kaplan, is constrained by overly restrictive criteria for the events it surveys, which again steers its focus away from consideration of the use of nuclear forces in crises.[4] This is a short introductory note intended to supply a minimum of information. A larger study on this subject which is being undertaken by the author is not yet completed.

Threats to use nuclear weapons can be grouped into four categories of what might be termed 'immanence':

(1) *Routine Deployments*, though these may be of systems on very high readiness, such as the US Minuteman ICBM and Poseidon SLBM systems, or in areas of direct confrontation

of opposing military forces, such as the USSR deployment of theatre nuclear forces along its border with China or US deployment of similar systems close to the NATO border with the Warsaw Treaty Organisation nations.

(2) *Verbal Threats* to use nuclear weapons, such as those by the USSR against France and England at the time of the 1956 Suez crisis, via diplomatic messages delivered to a head of state.

(3) *Increased Alert Levels* of part or all of a nation's nuclear weapon systems, either publicly announced, or without public announcement.

(4) *Specific Deployments* of nuclear weapon systems during a crisis, either aircraft, aircraft carriers or submarines.

The USSR has most often made use of verbal threats, while the US has made more frequent use of specific crisis deployments and of nuclear alerts, both announced and unannounced, and often of the two in conjunction. It is the public US nuclear alerts about which there is the most knowledge, such as those during the Cuban missile crisis in October 1962 and the Middle East crisis in October 1973. However, there have been many more situations of increased alert levels than the public knows about, and there have probably been about 100 specific deployments during one or another crisis since the mid-1950's when nuclear weapons began to be deployed on board US aircraft carriers.

The following tables concerning the deployment of nuclear forces are taken from the study by Blechman and Kaplan. All of the tables concern the deployments of United States nuclear forces. Table A3.1 is a list of incidents in which US *strategic* nuclear forces were involved. It is *not* a complete list. Nineteen incidents are listed. Table A3.2 presents a series of 'most significant' incidents, grouped in five geographical regions (Europe, Middle East, East Asia, South-East Asia, Caribbean). Those in which US *strategic* nuclear forces were involved are indicated, in this case 16. Table A3.3 indicates the criteria that were used in the study to distinguish the level of forces used by the United States in any particular crisis and the number of incidents in the five different geographical regions at different levels of US military effort. It should be pointed out that any involvement of a single US aircraft carrier task group would be equivalent to a specific deployment of nuclear weapons. Table A3.4 indicates the level of US military effort that was applied in various incidents in relation to USSR or Chinese involvement in these same incidents.

Table A3.1: Incidents in which US Strategic Nuclear Forces were Involved

Incident	Date
US aircraft shot down by Yugoslavia	November 1946
Inauguration of President in Uruguay	February 1947
Security of Berlin	January 1948
Security of Berlin	April 1948
Security of Berlin	June 1948
Korean War: security of Europe	July 1950
Security of Japan/South Korea	August 1953
Guatemala accepts Soviet bloc support	May 1954
China-Taiwan conflict: Tachen Islands	August 1954
Suez crisis	October 1956
Political crisis in Lebanon	July 1958
Political crisis in Jordan	July 1958
China-Taiwan crisis: Quemoy and Matsu	July 1958
Security of Berlin	May 1959
Security of Berlin	June 1961
Soviet emplacement of missiles in Cuba	October 1962
Withdrawal of US missiles from Turkey	April 1963
Pueblo seized by North Korea	January 1968
Arab-Israeli War	October 1973

Table A3.2: The Most Significant Incidents[a]

Region	Name	Date Incident Began	Strategic Nuclear Force Units Used
Europe	Security of Berlin	April 1948	Yes
	Security of Berlin	June 1948	Yes
	Security of Europe	July 1950	Yes
	Security of Berlin	February 1959	No
	Security of Berlin	May 1959	Yes
	Security of Berlin	June 1961	Yes
	Cyprus crisis	January 1964	No
	Invasion of Czechoslovakia	September 1968	No
Middle East	Suez crisis	October 1956	Yes
	Political developments in Jordan	April 1957	No
	Political developments in Syria	August 1957	No
	Political developments in Lebanon	May 1958	No
	Political developments in Lebanon	July 1958	Yes
	Political developments in Jordan	July 1958	Yes
	Civil war in Jordan	September 1970	No
	Arab-Israeli War	October 1973	Yes

Region	Name	Date Incident Began	Strategic Nuclear Force Units Used
East Asia	Civil war in China	April 1946	No
	End of Korean War	July 1953	No
	Security of Japan/South Korea	August 1953	Yes
	Tachen Islands crisis	August 1954	Yes
	Quemoy/Matsu crisis	July 1958	Yes
	Seizure of the *Pueblo*	January 1968	Yes
	Shoot-down of the EC-121	April 1969	Yes
South-East Asia	Civil war in Laos	January 1959	No
	Civil war in Laos	April 1962	No
	Tonkin Gulf incident	August 1964	No
	North Vietnam offensive	May 1972	No
	Collapse of South Vietnam	March 1975	No
	Seizure of the *Mayaguez*	May 1975	No
Caribbean	Guatemala accepts Soviet bloc support	May 1954	Yes
	Trujillo assassinated	June 1961	No
	Cuban missile crisis	October 1962	Yes
	Civil war in Dominican Republic	April 1965	No

Note: a. Incidents scoring 1 or 2 on level of force scale; strategic nuclear force units were involved in incidents ranked number 1.

Table A3.3: Level of Force Used by Force Type

(a) Type of Force

Level of Force	Naval Forces	Ground Forces	Land-based Air Forces
Major	Two or more aircraft carrier task groups	More than one battalion	One or more combat wings
Standard	One aircraft carrier task group	No more than one battalion, but larger than one company	One or more combat squadrons, but less than one wing
Minor	No aircraft carriers included	No more than one company	Less than one combat squadron

(b) US Level of Military Effort, by Region and Time Period/Number of Incidents

Region	Military Level of Effort					Total
	1	2	3	4	5	
Western hemisphere	2	2	6	18	32	60
Europe	5	3	12	19	4	43
Middle East	4	4	7	7	16	38
Sub-Saharan Africa and South Asia	0	0	0	6	7	13
South-East Asia	0	6	17	8	10	41
East Asia	4	3	4	6	3	20
TIME PERIOD						
1946-8	2	1	6	11	4	24
1949-56	5	1	10	9	7	32
1957-65	6	10	24	31	41	112
1966-75	2	6	6	13	20	47
Total	15	18	46	64	72	215

Table A3.4: US Level of Military Effort as a Function of Soviet-Chinese Participation Percentage of Incidents at Each Level of Effort Nature of Soviet/Chinese Participation

	US Level of Effort	Used Force	Threatened to Use Force	Participated, but No Use of Force	Did Not Participate
(1)	Nuclear weapons plus 'major' components	53	27	0	20
(2)	Two or three 'major' components	39	6	11	44
(3)	Nuclear weapons or one 'major' component	15	4	22	59
(4)	'Standard' components only	16	9	13	63
(5)	'Minor' components only	11	7	15	67
All Levels		19	8	14	59

This information only supplies the reader with a slight introduction to one of the most crucial topics of post-World War II military political history – the use of nuclear weapons in crises, both between the US and the USSR, and between the US and other nations. It may also be the least studied topic. Soviet verbal nuclear threats are not discussed here. They are known to have been made on something between ten and a dozen occasions. In some cases these occasions also involved simultaneous deployments. In other cases, there were simultaneous deployments of both the US and the USSR – and the number of events in this category is increasing as Soviet military capabilities have increased. In several other cases, the US and the USSR exchanged notes involving nuclear threats during a particular crisis. The cases in this last group also usually involved coincident US nuclear weapon system deployments.

The point of this information is that in addition to the abstract notions of deterrence ostensibly conferred on the US and the USSR by their mutual nuclear weapons capabilities held in readiness against the other, these weapon systems have been utilised in crises far more often than people – including political scientists – are aware of. We have been fortunate that this level of use has not yet led to actual use in wartime, but that has perhaps been due to more complex factors than the restraint with which we ordinarily assume nuclear weapons are handled.

Notes

1. By way of example: *United States Naval Operations in Low Level Warfare*, vols. I and II (December 1968) (Aerospace Systems Division (Bendix), Ann Arbor, Michigan); and *An Analysis of International Crises and Army Involvement* (Historical Appraisal, 1945-1974), Final Report (Strategic Studies Institute, US Army War College, October 1974).

2. A.L. George and R. Smoke, *Deterrence in American Foreign Policy: Theory and Practice* (Columbia University Press, New York, 1974), 666 pages.

3. J.T. Howe, *Multicrises; Sea Power and Global Politics in the Missile Age* (Massachusetts Institute of Technology Press, Cambridge, Mass., 1971), 412 pages.

4. B.M. Blechman and S.S. Kaplan, *The Use of the Armed Forces as a Political Instrument* (The Brookings Institution, Washington, DC, 1976). (Now published as *Force Without War: U.S. Armed Forces as a Political Instrument* (The Brookings Institution, Washington, DC, 1978).)

SELECT BIBLIOGRAPHY

Part 1: The Phenomenon of Militarism

Abrahamsson, B. *Military Professionalisation and Political Power* (Sage Publications, Beverly Hills, 1972)

Afheldt, H. *et al.* (eds.). *Durch Verhütung zum Krieg* (Hanser, Munich, 1972)

Andreski, S. 'Militarism' in J. Gould and W.L. Kolb, *A Dictionary of The Social Sciences* (Free Press, New York, 1964), pp. 429-30

Andrezejewski, Stanislaw. *Military Organization and Society* (Routledge, London; Humanities, New York, 1954)

Aspaturian, V. 'Internal Policies and Foreign Policy in the Soviet System' in B. Farrell (ed.), *Approaches to Comparative and International Politics* (Northwestern University Press, Evanstown, Ill., 1966), pp. 212-87

Auer, J.E. 'Japanese Militarism' in *U.S. Naval Institute Proceedings*, IC (1973), pp. 46-55

Battine, C. 'What is Militarism?', *Fortnightly Review*, vol. CXI (1919), pp. 375-84

Donovan, J.A. *Militarism USA* (Scribner, New York, 1970; Düsseldorf, 1973)

Doorn, Jaques van (ed.). *Armed Forces and Society* (Mouton, The Hague, 1968) (Paris, 1968)

Doorn, Jaques van (ed.). *Military Profession and Military Regimes* (Mouton, The Hague, 1969)

Eckhardt, W. 'The Factor of Militarism', *Journal of Peace Research*, vol. VI (1969), pp. 123-32

Erickson, J. *The Soviet High Command* (Macmillan, London, 1962)

Erickson, John and Mommsen, Hans. 'Militarism' in C.D. Kernig (ed.), *Marxism, Communism and Western Society*, vol. V (McGraw-Hill, New York, 1973), pp. 436-55

Finer, Samuel E. *The Man on Horseback: the Role of the Military in Politics* (Praeger, New York, 1962)

Gallo, José-Antonio Viera. *The Security Trap. Arms Race, Militarism and Disarmament. A Concern for Christians* (IDOC International, Rome; The Commission of the Churches on International Affairs, World Council of Churches, Geneva, 1979)

Giradet, R.D. *La Société Militaire dans la France Contemporaine*

(Plon, Paris, 1953)

Holloway, David. 'Technology and Political Decision in Soviet Armaments Policy', *Journal of Peace Research*, vol. XI, no. 4 (1974), pp. 257-80

Huntington, Samuel P. *The Soldier and the State: the Theory and Politics of Civil-Military Relations* (Harvard University Press, Cambridge, Mass., 1957)

Jahn, Egbert. 'The Role of the Armaments Complex in Soviet Society', *Journal of Peace Research*, vol. XII, no. 3 (1975), pp. 179-94

Joffe, E. *Party and Army. Professionalism and Political Control in the Chinese Officer Corps, 1949-1964* (Harvard University Press, Cambridge, Mass., 1965)

Klaus, G. and Buhr, M. 'Militarismus' in G. Klaus and M. Buhr (eds.), *Marxistisch-Leninistisches Wörterbuch der Philosophie*, vol. II (Leipzig, 1969), pp. 724-7

Kolkowicz, R. *The Soviet Military and the Communist Party* (Princeton University Press, Princeton, 1967)

Kourvetaris, George A. and Dobratz, Betty A. 'The Present State and Development of Sociology of the Military', *Journal of Political and Military Sociology*, vol. 4 (Spring 1976), pp. 67-105

Krippendorff, E. 'Militarismus in den USA', *Neue Politische Literatur*, vol. X (1965), pp. 125-33

Lang, Kurt. 'Military' in David L. Sills (ed.), *International Encyclopedia of Social Science*, vol. IX (Macmillan, London, 1968), pp. 305-11

Lapp, R.E. *The Weapons Culture* (New York, 1968; Bern-München-Wien, 1969)

Lasswell, Harold D. 'The Garrison State and the Specialists on Violence', *American Journal of Sociology*, no. 46 (1941), pp. 455-68

Lasswell, H. 'The Garrison State Hypothesis Today' in S.P. Huntingdon (ed.), *Changing Patterns of Military Politics* (Free Press, New York, 1962), pp. 51-70

Lee, W. 'The Politico-Military-Industrial Complex of the USSR', *Journal of International Affairs*, vol. XXVI (1972), pp. 73-86

Lemarchand, Rene. 'African Armies in Historical and Contemporary Perspectives: the Search for Connections', *Journal of Political Military Sociology*, vol. 4, no. 2 (Fall 1976), pp. 261-75

Little, Roger W. (ed.). *Handbook of Military Institutions* (Sage Publications, Beverly Hills, 1971)

Luxemburg, R. 'Miliz und Militarismus' in R. Luxemburg, *Gesammelte Werke*, vol. I (first half-volume) (Berlin (Ost), 1970), pp. 446-66

Magdoff, H. 'Militarism and Imperialism', *American Economic Review* (Papers and Proceedings), vol. LX, no. 2 (1970), pp. 237-42

Maxon, Yale C. *Control of Japanese Foreign Policy: a Study of Civil-Military Rivalry, 1930-1954* (University of California Press, Berkeley, 1957)

Melman, Seymour. *The Political Economy of Pentagon Capitalism* (McGraw-Hill, New York, 1970)

Melman, Seymour. 'Twelve Propositions on Productivity and War', *Armed Forces and Society*, vol. 1, no. 4 (1975), pp. 490-6

Messerschmidt, M. *Wehrmacht im NS-Staat* (Decker, Hamburg, 1969)

Messerschmidt, M. *Zum Verhältnis von Militär und Politik in der Bismarckzeit und in der Wilhelminischen Ära* (Darmstadt, 1973)

Millis, W. *Arms and Men* (New American Library, New York, 1967)

Millis, Walter, Mansfield, Harvey C. and Stein, Harold. *Arms in the State: Civil-Military Elements in National Policy* (Twentieth Century Fund, New York, 1958)

Mills, C.W. *The Causes of World War Three* (Secker and Warburg, London, 1959)

Milovidov, A.S. and Kozlov, V.G. (eds.). 1972. *The Philosophical Heritage of V.I. Lenin and Contemporary War*, US version published as no. 5 in the series *Soviet Military Thought* by US Government Printing Office (original USSR version by Voyennoye izdatel'stvo, Ministerstvo Oborony, Moscow)

Moore, B., Jr. *Social Origins of Dictatorship and Democracy* (Beacon Press, Boston, 1966; Frankfurt, 1969)

Moskos, Charles C., Jr. (ed.). *Public Opinion and the Military Establishment* (Sage Publications, Beverly Hills, 1971)

Radway, Laurence I. 'Militarism' in David L. Sills (ed.), *International Encyclopedia of Social Sciences*, vol. IX (Macmillan, London, 1968)

Russell, Elbert W. 'Christianity and Militarism', *Peace Research Review*, vol. 4, no. 3 (1971)

Sarkesian, Sam C. (ed.). *The Military-Industrial Complex. A Reassessment* (Sage Publications, Beverly Hills, 1972)

Schelling, Thomas C. *The Strategy of Conflict* (Oxford University Press, New York, 1963)

Seizabuno, S. 'From Party Politics to Military Dictatorship', *The Developing Economies*, vol. V (1967), pp. 666-84

Stevenson, Paul. 'The Military-Industrial Complex. An Examination of the Nature of Corporate Capitalism in America', *Journal of Political and Military Sociology*, vol. 1, no. 2 (Fall 1973), pp. 247-59

Tanin, O. and Yohan, E. *Militarism and Fascism in Japan* (Lawrence,

London, 1934)

Thee, Marek. 'The Dynamics of the Arms Race, Military R&D, and Disarmament', *International Social Science Journal*, vol. XXX, no. 4 (1978), pp. 904-25

Thompson, M. 'Militarism 1969. A Survey of World Trends', *Peace Research News*, vol. V (1968), pp. 1-96

Vagts, Alfred. *A History of Militarism. Romance and Realities of a Profession* (London, 1938; New York, 1959, with new sub-title 'Civilian and Military'; Free Press, New York, 1967)

Yarmolinsky, Adam. *The Military Establishment, its Impact on a Society* (Harper and Row, New York, 1971)

Part 2: the World Military Order

Adler-Karlsson, Gunnar. *Western Economic Warfare 1947-67: a Case Study in Foreign Economic Policy* (Almqvist and Wiksell, Stockholm, 1968)

Albrecht, Ulrich. 'Technology and Militarization of Third World Countries in Theoretical Perspective', *Bulletin of Peace Proposals*, vol. 8, no. 2 (1977), pp. 124-6

Albrecht, Ulrich, Ernst, Dieter, Lock, Peter and Wulf, Herbert. 'Armaments and Underdevelopment', *Bulletin of Peace Proposals*, vol. 5, no. 2 (1974), pp. 173-85

Albrecht, U., Ernst, D., Lock, P. and Wulf, H. 'Militarization, Arms Transfer and Arms Production in Peripheral Countries', *Journal of Peace Research*, vol. XII, no. 3 (1975), pp. 195-212

Albrecht, U., Ernst, D. Lock, P. and Wulf, H. *Rüstung und Unterentwicklung* (Rowohlt, Hamburg, 1976)

Bay Area Group of the Inter-University Committee to Stop Funding War and Militarism. 'After Vietnam: Resurgent U.S. Militarism', *Social Policy* (January-February 1977), pp. 8-15

Blechman, Barry M. and Kaplan, Stephen S. (eds.). *The Use of the Armed Forces as a Political Instrument* (The Brookings Institution, Washington, DC, 1976)

Disarmament Study Group of the International Peace Research Association. 'Between Peace and War: the Quest for Disarmament', *Bulletin of Peace Proposals*, vol. 6, no. 3 (1975), pp. 262-80

Eide, Asbjørn. 'The Transfer of Arms to Third World Countries and their Internal Uses', *International Social Science Journal*, vol. XXVIII, no. 2 (1976), pp. 307-25

Eide, Asbjørn. 'Arms Transfer and Third World Militarization', *Bulletin of Peace Proposals*, vol. 8, no. 3 (1977), pp. 220-32

Galtung, Johan. 'East-West Interaction Patterns', *Journal of Peace Research*, vol. 3, no. 2 (1966), pp. 146-77

Galtung, Johan. 'A Structural Theory of Imperialism', *Journal of Peace Research*, vol. VIII, no. 2 (1971), pp. 81-118

Gantzel, Klaus Jürgen. 'Armament Dynamics in the East-West Conflict, an Arms Race?' *The Papers of the Peace Science Society* (International), vol. XX (1973), pp. 1-24

Gleditsch, Nils Petter. 'Trends in World Airline Patterns', *Journal of Peace Research*, vol. 4, no. 4 (1966), pp. 336-408

Groom, A.J.R. and Taylor, Paul (eds.). *Functionalism: Theory and Practice in International Relations* (University of London Press, London, 1975)

Herrera, Luis. 'The Military as a Link in the Domination Chain of Latin America', *Instant Research on Peace and Violence*, vol. V, no. 4 (1975), pp. 197-206

Hoffmann, Fredrik. 'Arms Debates: a Positional Interpretation', *Journal of Peace Research*, vol. 7, no. 2 (1970), pp. 219-28

IPRA Study Group on Militarization. 'The Impact of Militarization on Development and Human Rights', *Bulletin of Peace Proposals*, vol. IX, no. 2 (1978), pp. 170-82

Joenniemi, Pertti. 'How to Explain Demobilization: Notes on the Economic Effects of Qualitative Armament', paper presented at the 6th Nordic Conference on Peace and Conflict Research in Rättvik, Sweden, 4-8 June 1974

Kaldor, Mary. *European Defence Industries* (Sussex University, Institute for the Study of International Organization, Brighton, UK, 1972)

Kaldor, Mary. 'The Military in Development', *World Development*, vol. 4 (1976), pp. 459-82

Kaldor, Mary. 'The Significance of Military Technology', *Bulletin of Peace Proposals*, vol. 8, no. 2 (1977), pp. 121-3

Klare, Michael T. 'The Political Economy of Arms Sales', *The Bulletin of the Atomic Scientists*, vol. 33, no. 9 (November 1976), pp. 11-18

Klare, Michael T. 'The Proliferating War Industry: America Exports its Know-How', *The Nation*, 12 February 1977, pp. 173-8

Klare, M.T. and Stein, Nancy. 'Exporting the Tools of Repression', *The Nation*, 18 October 1976

Klein, Jean. 'Commerce des Armes et Politique: Le Cas Francais', *Politique Etrangère*, no. 5 (1976), pp. 563-86

Knorr, Klaus. 'On the International Uses of Military Force in the Contemporary World', *Orbis*, vol. 21, no. 1 (1977), pp. 5-27

Landgren-Bäckström, Signe. 'The Transfer of Military Technology to Third World Countries', *Bulletin of Peace Proposals*, vol. 8, no. 2 (1977), pp. 110-20

Lock, Peter and Wulf, Herbert. 'Consequences of Transfer of Military-Oriented Technology on the Development Process', *Bulletin of Peace Proposals*, vol. 8, no. 2 (1977), pp. 127-36

Louscher, David J. 'The Rise of Military Sales as a U.S. Foreign Assistance Instrument', *Orbis*, vol. 20, no. 4 (1977), pp. 933-64

Lumsden, Malvern. 'The Role of the Military in the World Economic Order: Perspectives for Peace and Development Research', opening plenary lecture at the 7th Nordic Peace Research Conference, Silkeborg, Denmark, 26-29 July (mimeo.)

Lumsden, Malvern. 'Global Military Systems and the New International Economic Order', *Bulletin of Peace Proposals*, vol. 9, no. 1 (1978), pp. 30-4

Melman, Seymour. 'Inflation and Unemployment as Products of War Economy: the Trade Union Stake in Economic Conversion and Industrial Reconstruction', *Bulletin of Peace Proposals*, vol. 9, no. 4 (1978), pp. 359-74

Mitrany, David. *A Working Peace System* (Quadrangle Books, Chicago Press, 1966)

Oeberg, Jan. 'Arms Trade with Third World as an Aspect of Imperialism', *Journal of Peace Research*, vol. XII, no. 3 (1975), pp. 213-34

Oeberg, Jan. 'The New International Economic and Military Orders as Problems of Peace Research', *Bulletin of Peace Proposals*, vol. 8, no. 2 (1977), pp. 142-9

Oeberg, Jan. *The New International Military Order – the Real Threat to Human Security*, Paper No. 65 (Chair in Conflict and Peace Research, University of Oslo, Oslo, 1979)

Richardson, Lewis F. *Arms and Insecurity* (Boxwood Press, Pittsburgh, 1960)

Rosen, Steven (ed.). *Testing the Theory of the Military-Industrial Complex* (D.C. Heath, Lexington, Mass., 1973)

Senghaas, Dieter (ed.). *Peripherer Kapitalismus. Analysen über Abhängigheit und der Unterentwicklung* (Edition Suhrkamp, Frankfurt am Main, 1974a)

Senghaas, Dieter. 'Towards an Analysis of Threat Policy in Interna tional Relations', *German Political Studies*, vol. I (Sage Publications, Beverly Hills, 1974b)

Senghaas, Dieter. 'Armaments Dynamics and Disarmament' in W. von

Bredow (ed.), *Economic and Social Aspects of Disarmament* (BPP Publications, Oslo, 1975), pp. 105-34

Senghaas, Dieter. 'Die neue internationale Militärordning' in *Weltwirtschaftsordnung und Entwicklungspolitik. Plädoyer für Dissoziation* (Edition Suhrkamp, Frankfurt am Main, 1977a), pp. 223-60

Senghaas, Dieter. 'Military Dynamics in the Contemporary Context of Periphery Capitalism', *Bulletin of Peace Proposals*, vol. 8, no. 2 (1977b), pp. 103-9

SIPRI Yearbook 1977: World Armament and Disarmament (Stockholm International Peace Research Institute, 1977) (armaments expenditures 1956-76 see pp. 222-3)

SIPRI/Lumsden. *Anti-Personnel Weapons.* Written for Stockholm International Peace Research Institute by Malvern Lumsden (London, 1978)

Sivard, Ruth Leger. *World Military and Social Expenditures 1977* (WMSE Publications, Leesburg, Virg., 1977)

Skjelsbaek, Kjell. 'Shared Memberships in Intergovernmental Organizations and Dyadic War, 1865-1964', in Edwin H. Fedder (ed.), *The United Nations: Problems and Prospects* (University of Missouri, St Louis, 1971)

Skjelsbaek, Kjell. 'Peace and the Structure of the International Organization Network', *Journal of Peace Research*, vol. 9, no. 4 (1972), pp. 315-30

Thee, Marek (ed.) *Armaments and Disarmament in the Nuclear Age, a Handbook* (Stockholm International Peace Research Institute, 1976a) (see chapters on Conventional Weapons and Arms Trade, pp. 148-77, on Armaments Dynamics and Military Research and Development, pp. 179-99, and on Economic and Social Consequences of Armaments, pp. 200-10)

Thee, Marek. 'International Arms Control and Disarmament Agreements: Promise, Fact and Vision', *International Social Science Journal*, vol. XXVIII, no. 2 (1976), pp. 359-74

Thee, Marek. 'The Nuclear Arms Race: Trends, Dynamics Control', *Instant Research on Peace and Violence*, vol. VI, nos. 1-2 (1976c), pp. 18-28

Thee, Marek. 'Arms Control: the Retreat from Disarmament. The Record to Date and the Search for Alternatives', *Journal of Peace Research*, vol. XVI, no. 2 (1977), pp. 95-114

UN Consultant Experts. *Economic and Social Consequences of the Arms Race and of Military Expenditures* (United Nations, New

York, 1977)
Väyrynen, Raimo. 'Military R&D as an Aspect of the Arms Race', *Current Research on Peace and Violence* (Tampere, Finland), vol. I, nos. 3-4 (1978), pp. 177ff.
Väyrynen, Raimo and Herrera, Luis. 'Subimperialism: from Dependence to Subordination', *Instant Research on Peace and Violence*, vol. V, no. 3 (1975), pp. 165-77
Wolpin, Miles D. 'Military Dependency versus Development in the Third World', *Bulletin of Peace Proposals*, vol. 8, no. 2 (1977), pp. 137-41
World Council of Churches, Executive Committee. *Programme on Militarism and Armaments Race*, Document N.13 (February 1977)

Part 3: Third World Militarisation

Adekson, J. 'Bayo. 'Military Organization in Multi-Ethnically Segmented Societies: a Theoretical Study, with reference to Three Sub-Saharan African Cases/Balew's Nigeria 1958-1966/7, Oboto's Uganda 1962-1972, Nkrumah's Ghana 1957-1967' (PhD dissertation, Brandeis University, Waltham, Mass., May 1976)
Adekson, J. 'Bayo. 'On the Theory of Modernising Soldiers: a Critique', *Current Research on Peace and Violence*, vol. I, no. 1 (April 1978a), pp. 28-40
Adekson, J. 'Bayo. 'Towards Explaining Civil-Military Instability in Contemporary Sub-Saharan Africa', *Current Research on Peace and Violence* (Tampere, Finland), vol. I, nos. 3-4 (1978b)
Barber, W.F. and Ronning, C.N. *Internal Security and Military Power. Counter-Insurgency and Civic Action in Latin America* (Ohio State University Press, Columbus, Ohio, 1966)
Decalo, Samuel. *Coups and Army Rule in Africa* (Yale University Press, New Haven, 1975)
Eide, Asbjørn. 'South Africa. Repression and Transfer of Arms and Arms Technology' in Kaldor, Eide and Merrit (eds.), *World Military Order. The Impact of Military Technology in the Third World*
Feit, E. *The Armed Bureaucrats. Military-Administrative Regimes and Political Development* (Houghton Mifflin, Boston, 1973)
First, Ruth. *Power in Africa* (Penguin Books, New York, 1972) (first published under the title of *The Barrel of a Gun* by the Penguin Press of London, 1970)
Gutteridge, William. *Armed Forces in New States* (Oxford University Press, London, 1962)
Gutteridge, William. *Military Institutions and Power in the New States* (Oxford University Press, London, 1964)

Huq, Muzammel. 'Consequences of US Military Policies in South Asia', paper presented to the 28th Pugwash Symposium, Oslo, 21-24 November 1977

Jackman, Robert W. 'Politicians in Uniform: Military Governments and Social Change in the Third World', *American Political Science Review*, vol. 70, no. 4 (1976), pp. 1078-97

Janowitz. Morris. *The Military in the Political Development of New Nations: an Essay in Comparative Analysis* (University of Chicago Press, Chicago, 1964)

Johnson, John D. (ed.). *The Role of the Military in Under-Developed Countries* (Princeton University Press, Princeton, 1962)

Kaldor, M., Eide, A. and Merrit, S. *World Military Order. The Impact of Military Technology in the Third World* (Macmillan, London, 1979)

Kennedy, G. *The Military in the Third World* (Duckworth, London, 1974)

Lefever, E.W. *Spear and Scepter: Army, Police and Politics in Tropical Africa* (Brookings Institution, Washington, DC, 1970)

Luckham, R. *The Nigerian Military* (Cambridge University Press, Cambridge, 1971)

Murray, R. 'Militarism in Africa', *New Left Review*, vol. XXXVII (1966), pp. 35-59

Nordlinger, E.A. 'Soldiers in Mufti. The Impact of Military Rule upon Economic and Social Change in the Non-Western States', *American Political Science Review*, vol. LXIV (December 1970), pp. 1131-48

Perlmutter, A. 'The Praetorian State and the Praetorian Army: Towards a Taxonomy of Civil-Military Relations in Developing Politics', *Comparative Politics*, vol. I (1969), pp. 382-404

Price, R.M. 'A Theoretical Approach to Military Rule in New States. Reference Group Theory and the Ghanaian Case', *World Politics*, vol. XXIII (1971), pp. 83-103

Pye, Lucian W. 'Armies in the Process of Political Modernization' in John J. Johnson (ed.), *The Role of the Military in Underdeveloped Countries* (Princeton University Press, Princeton, 1962)

Salamon, L.M. (1971). 'Comparative History and the Theory of Modernization', *World Politics*, vol. XXIII (1971), pp. 83-103

SIPRI. *The Arms Trade with the Third World* (Stockholm International Peace Research Institute/Penguin, London, 1974)

Tibi, Bassam. *Militär und Sozialismus in der Dritten Welt* (Suhrkamp, Frankfurt am Main, 1973)

Vatikiotis, P. *The Egyptian Army in Politics: Pattern for New Nations?*

(Indiana University Press, Bloomington, Indiana, 1961)
Wood, D. *The Armed Forces of African States*, Adelphi paper no. 27 (Institute for Strategic Studies, London, 1966)

Part 4: Sovereignty and International Law

Abi-Saab. 'Wars of National Liberation and the Laws of War' in *Annales d'Etudes Internationales*, vol. 3 (Geneva, 1972), pp. 93-117
Austin, John. *The Province of Jurisprudence Determined* (1832)
Baxter, R.R. 'The Legal Consequences of the Unlawful Use of Force under the Charter', *Proceedings of the American Society of International Law at its Sixty-Second Annual Meeting*, 25-27 April 1968 (Washington, DC)
Blix, Hans. 'Is there a Need for a Definition of "Aggression"?', *Dag Hammarskjöld Seminar on the Structure, Role and Functions of the UN System, Uppsala, Part I* (Dag Hammarskjöld Foundation, Uppsala, 1969) (Lecture no. 7), pp. 1-14
Bodin, Jean. *Six Books of a Commonweale* (1576)
Boutros Samaan, S. 'Définition de l'agression', *Révue égyptienne de droit international* (Le Caire), no. 24 (1968)
Broms, Bengt. *The Definition of Aggression in the United Nations* (Turku, 1968, 162 pp.) (Turku, Finland. Yliopisto. Julkaisuja. Sarja B: Humaniora, 108)
Brownlie, Ian. *International Law and the Use of Force by States* (Clarendon Press, Oxford, 1963)
Chacko, C.J. 'International Law and the Concept of Aggression', *Indian Journal of International Law* (New Delhi), vol. 3 (October 1963), 396-412, vol. 4 (January 1964), pp. 85-96
Chkhikvadze, V. and Bogdanov, O. 'Definition of Aggression – an Important Instrument in the Struggle for Peace', *International Affairs* (Moscow), no. 7 (July 1969), pp. 27-32
Cockram, B. 'The United Nations and Resistance to Aggression', *South African Law Journal* (Cape Town), 80 (November 1963), pp. 490-504
Delivanis, Jean. 'La légitime défense en droit international public moderne; le droit international face à ces limites' (Paris, Librarie Générale de Droit et de Jurisprudence, XV, 201 pp.) (Bibliothèque de droit international, 59) (Thèse. Caen, France, Université Faculté de Droit et des Sciences Economiques, 1969)
Eagleton, C. *The Attempt to Define Aggression* (Carnegie Endowment for International Peace, New York, 1930) (International

Conciliation, no. 264)

Falk, R.A. 'Quincy Wright: on Legal Tests of Aggressive War', *American Journal of International Law* (Washington, DC), 1, no. 66 (July 1972), pp. 560-71

Ferencz, Benjamin B. *Defining Aggression as a Means to Peace* (B'nai B'rith International Council, Washington, DC, 1972)

Garcia Lupo, Rogelio. *Contra la ocupacion extranjera*, 2nd edition (Editorial Sudestada (Coleccion presente politico), Buenos Aires, 1968)

Herezegh, Géza. 'The Prohibition of the Threat and Use of Force in Contemporary International Law', *Questions of International Law* (Hungarian Branch of the International Law Association, Budapest, 1964), pp. 70-92

Higgins, R. 'Legal Limits to the Use of Force by Sovereign States – United Nations Practice', *British Yearbook of International Law*, vol. 37 (Oxford University Press, London, 1962), pp. 269-319

Hobbes, Thomas. *Leviathan* (1651)

Langer, Robert. *Seizure of Territory, the Stimson Doctrine and Related Principles in Legal Theory and Diplomatic Practice* (Princeton University Press, Princeton, 1947)

Nincic, Djura. *The Problem of Sovereignty in the Charter and the Practice of the United Nations* (Nijhoff, The Hague, 1970), 358 pp.

Rousseau, Jean-Jacques. *The Social Contract* (1762)

Spiropoulos, J. 'La question de la définition de l'agression devant les Nations Unies', *Mélanges en l'honneur de Gilbert Gidel* (Paris, 1961), pp. 543-56

Wright, Q. 'The Concept of Aggression in International Law', *American Journal of International Law* (Washington, DC) no. 29 (1935), pp. 373-95

Zivic, J. 'Definition of Aggression', *Review of International Affairs* (Belgrade) no. 21 (January 1970), pp. 11-41

NOTES ON CONTRIBUTORS

Ulrich Albrecht Free University of Berlin.
William Eckhardt Canadian Peace Research Institute, Oakville, Ontario.
Asbjφrn Eide International Peace Research Institute, Oslo.
Richard Falk Center of International Studies, Princeton University.
Mary H. Kaldor Institute for the Study of International Organisation, University of Sussex.
Istvan Kende Karl Marx University, Budapest.
Michael T. Klare Institute for Policy Studies, Washington, DC.
Ejub Kučuk The Federal Secretariat of National Defence of Yugoslavia
Signe Landgren-Bäckström Stockholm International Peace Research Institute.
Milton Leitenberg and Nicole Ball Center for International Studies Peace Studies Program, Cornell University
Julian Lider The Swedish Institute of International Affairs, Stockholm.
Malvern Lumsden International Peace Research Institute, Stockholm.
Robert D. Matthews Department of Political Economy, University of Toronto
Jan Øberg Department of Peace and Conflict Research, University of Lund, Sweden.
Ernie Regehr Institute for Peace and Conflict Studies, Conrad Grebel College, Waterloo, Ontario.
Dieter Senghaas Department of Social Science, University of Bremen.
Kjell Skjelsbaek Department of Political Science, University of Oslo and International Peace Research Institute, Oslo.
Marek Thee International Peace Research Institute, Oslo.
Miles D. Wolpin Department of Political Science, State University of New York.

INDEX